DONALD G. WETHERELL

IRENE R.A. KMET

TOWN
Life

Main Street and the
Evolution of Small Town
Alberta, 1880-1947

First published by
The University of Alberta Press and
Alberta Community Development

Copyright © Donald Wetherell, Irene Kmet and
the Minister of Alberta Community Development, 1995

ISBN 0-88864-268-7

The University of Alberta Press
Athabasca Hall
Edmonton, Alberta
Canada T6G 2E8

Canadian Cataloguing in Publication Data

Wetherell, Donald Grant, 1949–
Town life

(Alberta reflections)
Includes bibliographical references and index.
ISBN 0-88864-265-2

1. Cities and towns—Alberta—History. 2. Northwest Territories—
History—1870–1905... 3. Alberta—History—1905–*
4. Alberta—Social conditions. I. Kmet, Irene, 1950–
II. Alberta. Alberta Community Development. III. Title. IV. Series.
HT384.C32A43 1995   307.76'2'097123   C95-910518-2

Printed on acid-free paper. ∞
Printed by Best Book Manufacturers, Louisville, Quebec, Canada.

*Frontispiece: A general view of Lacombe's downtown in 1908. Archives Collection,
A11279, PAA.*

COMMITTED TO THE DEVELOPMENT OF CULTURE AND THE ARTS

TOWN LIFE

*Main Street and the Evolution of
Small Town Alberta, 1880-1947*

THE UNIVERSITY OF ALBERTA PRESS

ALBERTA COMMUNITY DEVELOPMENT

CONTENTS

ALBERTA

2005

The year 2005 will mark the centennial of the Province of Alberta. In 1988 a group of Albertans from various backgrounds met in Red Deer to discuss the possibility of producing a multivolume history of the province in time for the hundredth anniversary. The result was the creation in 1991 of the Alberta 2005 Centennial History Society, a nonprofit association devoted to producing a history that is both accurate and accessible. The principal work of the Society since that time, apart from fund-raising, has been to identify the areas of Alberta's past most in need of further research and to sponsor a series of research studies aimed at filling in the blanks. Our intention is to commission about twenty specialized studies in the series that we call Alberta Reflections.

We are very pleased to have Donald Wetherell and Irene Kmet's *Town Life: Main Street and the Evolution of Small Town Alberta, 1880–1947* as the first in the series. Not only have the authors been involved with Alberta 2005 since its inception in 1988 but their study of small town life is an excellent example of the kind of important but neglected topic that needs to be explored before a comprehensive provincial history can be written. Six other projects have been commissioned and are in various stages of preparation on such diverse topics as; the history of art in Alberta, history of religion, literary history, a biography of Ernest C. Manning, a historical and archaeological study of the buffalo robe trade and a regional study of the Crowsnest Pass.

Most of our money so far has come from the Alberta Historical Resources Foundation and we gratefully acknowledge their support.

R.C. MacLeod
PRESIDENT, ALBERTA 2005
CENTENNIAL HISTORY SOCIETY

ACKNOWLEDGMENTS

The nine Alberta towns used as a sample in this study have all been associated with the Alberta Main Street project, a heritage preservation and economic revitalization programme begun by the Heritage Canada Foundation and taken over and expanded by Alberta through the Alberta Historical Resources Foundation. In support of this programme, as well as part of its wider mandate to expand knowledge about the history of Alberta, this study was commissioned by Historic Sites and Archives Service, Alberta Community Development. We appreciate that Historic Sites and Archives Service gave us complete freedom in our research, analysis and writing.

Many people made our work easier. Frits Pannekoek and Carl Betke of Alberta Community Development helped initiate the project. Michael Payne administered the project on behalf of the province and also provided us with thoughtful comments on the text. Tom Thurston of Historic Sites and Archives Service agreed that his section would assist by preparing maps of each town. Eduard Wiens drew, with sensitivity and skill, the nine maps of the towns. Geoffrey Lester, Cartography, Department of Geography at the University of Alberta, prepared the map of Alberta.

While the archives at which we worked were, as always, helpful, we owe special thanks to David Leonard and the staff at the Provincial Archives of Alberta. So too, special thanks is owed to Lorne Buhr and the staff of the Legislature Library, who made the considerable task of researching small town newspapers easier and more convenient. Dun and Bradstreet Canada Ltd. gave us permission to photocopy from the microfilm Dun and Bradstreet Ratings held at the Provincial Archives of Alberta. The co-ordinators of all the main street offices in the nine towns were unfailingly helpful and provided us with many insights into the history of small town Alberta. The knowledgeable and professional manner in which Mary Mahoney-Robson and Alan Brownoff of the

University of Alberta Press shepherded the book through editing and production is greatly appreciated. We also thank the two anonymous reviewers who read the manuscript for the University of Alberta Press and the Aid to Scholarly Publications Programme for their valuable comments.

This book has been published with the help of a grant from the Social Science Federation of Canada, using funds provided by the Social Sciences and Humanities Research Council of Canada.

ABBREVIATIONS

AAA   Amateur Athletic Association

ARMA   Alberta Retail Merchant's Association

BPSC   Bruce Peel Special Collections Library, University of Alberta, Edmonton

C&E   Calgary and Edmonton Railway

CNOR   Canadian Northern Railway

CPR   Canadian Pacific Railway

ED&BC   Edmonton, Dunvegan and British Columbia Railway

GAI   Glenbow Alberta Institute Archives, Calgary

IODE   Imperial Order Daughters of the Empire

LDS   Church of Jesus Christ of Latter Day Saints

GTP   Grand Trunk Pacific Railway

NWMP   Northwest Mounted Police

PAA   Provincial Archives of Alberta, Edmonton

PP   Premiers' Papers

RCMP   Royal Canadian Mounted Police

SABR   Saskatchewan Archives Board, Regina

UAA   University of Alberta Archives, Edmonton

UFA   United Farmers of Alberta

YMCA   Young Men's Christian Association

INTRODUCTION

Conflicting emotions have long character-
ized prairie Canadian attitudes towards the city. The growth of cities has
been celebrated as evidence that the region was attaining the same level
of development as longer established and wealthier parts of the country.
Yet, farms and small towns were also thought to protect and foster a distinctive essence in prairie life. These contrary views have placed towns
in what novelist Aritha van Herk calls "the uneasy limbo between rural
innocence and urban sophistication."[1] One measure of this tension is that
people on the prairies, while lamenting the decline of the small town,
have for over a century resolutely and often happily moved to the city.
Even so, Canadians have rarely swung as erratically as have Americans
between an adoration of the town's social values and a loathing of its
parochialism. Crocus, W.O. Mitchell's mythical prairie town, like Stephen
Leacock's Mariposa, remains central in the Canadian ideal of small town
life.[2]

The historical evolution of small Alberta towns is explored by studying the development of nine very different small centres scattered
throughout the major economic areas of the province and representing
most phases of provincial history. In the south, Cardston, Fort Macleod
and Claresholm represent a cluster of cultural and economic forces. Each
demonstrated particular aspects of provincial development, from policing and ranching at Fort Macleod, to Mormon settlement at Cardston,
and wheat monoculture at Claresholm. The role of coal mining in the
provincial economy and its relationship to social development are
demonstrated through two towns in the Crowsnest Pass, Blairmore and
Coleman. Another mining town, Drumheller, exhibits a marriage of the
mining and agricultural economies. A parkbelt service town, Lacombe,
illustrates the role of agricultural service in a mixed farm economy. Peace
River and Grande Prairie are representative of town growth after World

War I, as part of the expansion of the settlement frontier into northern Alberta.[3]

Our study focuses on the main street that in all small towns, as in Leacock's Mariposa, was the town's "artery, heart and soul."[4] It defined the purpose and culture of the town, it reflected its leaders' preoccupations and ambitions, and it mirrored the growth of the town. Reflecting the history of the region, most towns were relatively new. While their subsequent relative decline as cultural and economic centres was perhaps inherent in their founding, their establishment was central to the Euro-Canadian settlement of the region. As local centres for finance and commerce and as the hubs of local transportation systems, they spearheaded the settlement of the prairies. Although Alberta cities rapidly grew in size, until the late 1940s the rural population in Alberta continued to dominate—split between people living on farms and those in hamlets, villages and towns. After World War II, the population of the largest cities overtook that of the rural areas, a trend that intensified after the 1950s.[5]

The historical study of towns is relatively new. On the prairies, students of rural history have tended to ignore town history in favour of that of farming. As C.A. Dawson and R.W. Murchie rather dismissively remarked in their 1934 study of the Peace River country, "town building, after all, was only incidental to the wave of [farm] land settlement."[6] Since the end of World War II, however, and especially since the 1970s, urban history has emerged as a distinctive field of study. So far, most attention has been given to large cities, which in Alberta means the two major centres of Edmonton and Calgary, with decreasing attention to intermediate points like Red Deer, Medicine Hat and Lethbridge. These places have been successful in terms of growth, and have been highly influential in the broad process of urbanization.[7]

Yet the focus of urban history has begun to widen. Geographers and sociologists have recognized towns as significant in social and economic development as well as in the alteration of the landscape.[8] In part, it has been assumed that urban development is a process; one that expresses a wide spectrum of connections and interactions among a range of urban centres and rural areas. This concept has become increasingly important for historians as well. As urban historian, Gilbert Stelter, notes, "towns and cities are subsystems within larger political, economic and social systems and can only be fully understood from the perspective of those larger systems." Thus, towns and villages should be studied as part of "the complex web of population concentrations within an area or country."[9] One aspect of the town's role in this process has been as a meeting point for urban and farm lives and as an essential unit in binding together urban and rural communities. Moreover, towns evolved in response to both local and external events and factors. As Stelter argues in his support of recognition of the region as an appropriate analytical framework for urban history, cities have been important for high level economic activities, but "the towns, villages and country more clearly represent the region's *distinctive* character, reflecting the particular economic base and mixture of population."[10]

The application of such concepts means that towns are no longer seen as isolated units with little reference beyond their boundaries. Another consequence has been the emergence of a better understanding of what constitutes an urban area. As the geographer Fred Dahms demonstrated in his study of a group of small Ontario towns, the definition of what is "urban" has broadened as technological change has decreased the barriers of time and space between places. In turn, this evolving definition of what is "urban" provides clues in understanding the changing functions and activities of a range of towns.[11] Crucial to this concern is a recognition that "urban" should be defined "quite as much in terms of how contemporaries saw its distinguishing features as how we see them now."[12]

The study of towns represents a breakdown of the common bias in urban history that the only urban places worth studying are those that have grown. As Donald Davis has remarked, urban historians have been "congenitally more interested in growth than in decline."[13] David C. Jones has imaginatively turned this obsession on its head in his history of Alderson and area. Alderson, which has now disappeared completely, was established before World War I in southern Alberta during a frenzy of booster speculation. By placing Alderson and other local centres in the broad history of settlement before World War I, Jones explains the fate of the town and its surrounding farming districts.[14]

Such a perspective studies the town in relation to its local social and economic functions as well as in the wider historical context of the region and the nation.[15] As Peter Ennals has noted in his examination of the small town in the Maritimes, it has traditionally been characterized simply as "the leading edge of the frontier" and as connecting hinterland with metropolitan markets. Indicating a broader approach, Ennals emphasizes that the study of small towns serves to demonstrate their role in integrating "both rural folk and townsmen alike into a larger social and political fabric."[16] At the same time, various theories that purport to explain broad historical changes or the nature of society have rarely succeeded in explaining the details of this process at a local level. As Gilbert Stelter has remarked, "ideally any study of an individual place should deal with both internal and external forces. The mix seems to be different for every place, defying attempts to formulate precise models of development."[17] This too is Paul Voisey's conclusion in his historical study of the Vulcan area of southern Alberta. Voisey asks if several popular theories about the settlement frontier can satisfactorily explain the history of the Vulcan area. Was its society produced by unique forces and conditions on the frontier, or did it express transplanted traditions and cultures from metropolitan centres? Concluding that neither model adequately explains frontier development, Voisey sees a combination of frontier, metropolis and tradition acting to shape the history of the place.[18]

These questions have also been asked about frontier urban development in the United States. There, historians have often seen urban development as reproducing urban patterns already familiar to settlers. Although distinctive character crept in over time, settlers on the United States frontier aimed not "to innovate, to create something new," but "to emulate the character and culture of the great cities of the east coast."[19] The reproduction of urban patterns was not, however, only a product of cultural activity. Economics and corporate actions were also highly significant. As the geographer, John Hudson, argued, towns on the American Great Plains were interdependent components of plans formulated by large corporations (usually railways) to make profit from dependent hinterlands. Thus, as part of a total system designed by railway companies and promoters, they showed little adaptation to local conditions. Yet Hudson sees town development as part of an interconnected historical process, what he terms the "threefold division of variables"— that of people, activities (such as social and economic behaviour), and structures (such as location of a town and its physical form or layout). All these variables operated in their "relevant context of time and place."[20]

A similar process has been identified in a study of Belleville, Ontario and its hinterland in the nineteenth century. Randy William Widdis found that social and economic ties bound town and country together. While he notes that small towns and rural communities were from the start a part of "larger regional, national and international systems of production," the increasing pace and intensity of their integration into wider economic and social systems are important in understanding town development. He suggests that the function as well as the range of relationships between town and country can best be understood through a "contextual view" that recognizes the different levels in which these relationships changed in importance over time.[21]

The use of a contextual approach provides a flexible framework for the study of the history of the small town. By providing sufficient detail to focus analysis, it recognizes the place of urban process in shaping town life. While we employ this approach, a full scale analysis of urban process showing all the interactions between large and small centres through time is beyond our scope. Through the study of nine towns, we analyze the main street, where business and social life was centred, as a means of understanding town history. Our emphasis is on the political, economic, architectural, and social meaning of the main street rather than its spatial evolution over time. Main street in Alberta towns was a primary focus for urban-rural linkages; for the town's perception of itself as urban; as the focus for individual and communal activities; and as expressing some of the town's unique social qualities. It also asserted, as nothing else did, the economic reasons for a town's existence. Barbara Ruth Bailey, whose study of main street development and form in northeastern Oregon was a pioneering effort, has observed that the social and economic role of the main street is a unique aspect of the small town urban experience because it concentrated this function in the town in a way not found in large cities.[22]

Before World War II, Alberta towns experienced two major phases: a period of high growth and expectations, which had generally dissipated by the conclusion of World War I, and the years until the end of the next war, throughout which most towns struggled to hold their population and wealth. Yet, while the end of World War I marked the end of a period of economic growth and exaggerated expectations associated with the expansionary settlement period, there were strong elements of continuity throughout these two periods.[23] In both historical phases, a central concern in Alberta towns was growth of population and trade. Because towns existed for trade, this objective had often been significant in determining their location and it remained a force in knitting together a patchwork of local concerns and policies. Before 1920, and especially before the economic collapse of 1912-13, expectations about growth were extraordinarily high. After the economy collapsed, town leaders lowered their expectations. They were forced to implement fiscal retrenchment to stave off bankruptcy of the towns, but continued to try and hold population and promote programmes to encourage moderate growth. These ambitions were expressed in a variety of ways in town and business life. Town leaders, such as newspaper editors, local politicians and prominent business owners, claimed that a town could influence its future through various interconnected techniques. These included expanding the town's economic hinterland; diversifying the local economy and retaining capital in the town; promoting urban social and political cohesiveness; and making the townscape physically attractive and up-to-date. These objectives ran like a thread through the political and social attitudes found in Alberta towns, although they were pursued in different ways and with different emphasis depending on location and time.

These objectives were also espoused by city spokesmen and some urban historians have argued that these activities significantly contributed to urban growth, especially in the early phase of a centre's existence. Growth, it is argued, was a function of the cohesiveness, daring and energy of the urban elite and its ambition and foresightedness in making its town or city a success.[24] This view presumes, in part, that an urban place is a distinctive and "creative" agency that shapes the economic and social activity within its boundaries. While we found that the town, as a "container," self-evidently focused certain activities and allowed expression of others not possible without a concentrated population, the dynamics of town economic growth were more complex and often beyond local control. Although the role of the individual whose independent action contributes to collective success cannot be discounted entirely, location and external forces seem more significant. Thus, the forces shaping a town's life and future varied. While it is a given that local elites were concerned with personal success, were locally powerful, and recognized that their personal prosperity was linked to that of the community, the causal connection between elite behaviour and town growth was rarely so direct or easy. The relationship between a town and the farm areas upon which it depended for much of its economic life shifted continuously in relation to changes in transportation and in rural culture and politics. So too, corporate decisions, such as those by railways and mining companies, significantly shaped town life, as did the actions of senior governments, especially the province. Often these decisions were made without reference to local demands or sensibilities or were framed within terms of partisan political advantage. Similarly, although in a different way, town life was shaped by more diffuse forces that were operating broadly throughout society. The fashions and standards of the time, especially what was seen as up-to-date and progressive (which usually meant "city-like"), exerted a profound and direct impact on the look of town buildings and streets, on the way leisure and recreation operated in the town, how business was conducted, and how town culture was expressed. This culture was also firmly cast in an Anglo-Canadian mould. People of "British" origin were dominant in most of the towns studied (see Appendix II, Table 3), coming from other parts of Canada, the United States and Britain. Only in the coal mining towns were non-British groups numerically significant, and then only in Blairmore was the percentage of "British" townspeople less than 50 percent. Thus, the reference of most townspeople was to North American and British economic, social and political culture. This further helped ensure the integration of Alberta towns into the rest of the Anglo-American world.

PART

I

Town
Formation

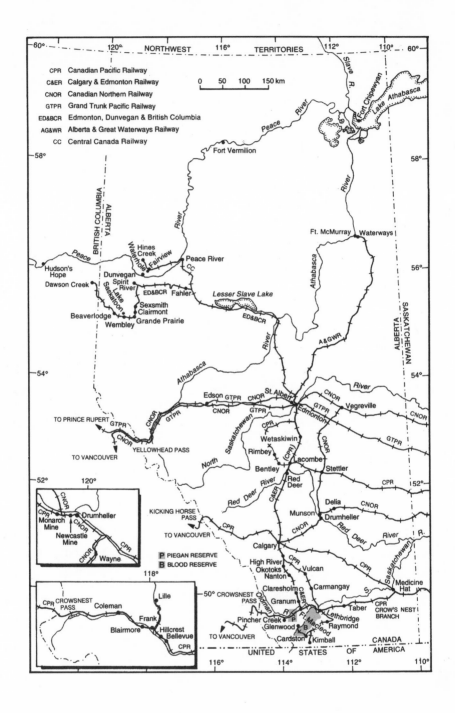

CPR   Canadian Pacific Railway
C&ER   Calgary & Edmonton Railway
CNOR   Canadian Northern Railway
GTPR   Grand Trunk Pacific Railway
ED&BCR   Edmonton, Dunvegan & British Columbia
AG&WR   Alberta & Great Waterways Railway
CC   Central Canada Railway

0   50   100   150 km

NORTHWEST   TERRITORIES

BRITISH COLUMBIA

ALBERTA

SASKATCHEWAN

Slave R.

Fort Chipewyan

Lake Athabasca

Peace River

Fort Vermilion

Ft. McMurray   Waterways

Peace River

Hudson's Hope

Dawson Creek

Hines Creek

Fairview

Peace River

CC

Dunvegan

Spirit River

ED&BCR   Fahler

Lesser Slave Lake

Lake Saskatoon

Sexsmith

Clairmont

Beaverlodge

Wembley   Grande Prairie

ED&BCR

Athabasca

A&GWR

Athabasca

River

Edson   GTPR   CNOR   St. Albert

CNOR

Vegreville

TO PRINCE RUPERT   GTPR

GTPR

GTPR

CNOR

Edmonton

GTPR

CNOR

CNOR

TO VANCOUVER

YELLOWHEAD PASS

North Saskatchewan River

Wetaskiwin

Rimbey

(CPR)

Lacombe

Stettler

CPR

Bentley

Red Deer

C&ER

Red Deer River

Delia

CNOR

KICKING HORSE PASS

Munson

Drumheller

Red Deer

River

R.

TO VANCOUVER

CPR

CNOR

Saskatchewan River

Calgary

P   PIEGAN RESERVE
B   BLOOD RESERVE

High River

Okotoks

Nanton

Vulcan

Carmangay

S.

Medicine Hat

Monarch Mine

Drumheller

CNOR

CPR

Newcastle Mine

CNOR

CPR

Wayne

118°

Claresholm

Granum

CROWSNEST PASS

C&ER

Taber

CPR

CROW'S NEST BRANCH

Lille

CPR   CROWSNEST PASS   Coleman

Frank

Blairmore   Hillcrest

Bellevue

CPR

TO VANCOUVER

Pincher Creek

Glenwood

Oldman R.

Ft. Macleod

Lethbridge

Raymond

Cardston   Kimball

CANADA

UNITED   STATES   OF   AMERICA

1

THE ORIGIN *and* DEVELOPMENT *of* TOWNS *in* ALBERTA

As the last urban places settlers passed through before reaching their farms, towns were a key part of the process of prairie settlement. A few centres existed before the great rush of white settlers began in the 1890s, the earliest being fur trade and mission settlements, police posts, and a few agricultural service settlements. By provincial standards, some had existed for a long time. Fort Chipewyan was probably a settlement community of some sort almost from its beginning as a fur trade post in 1788. In 1861, a Roman Catholic mission was established at St. Albert, and by 1865 a small settlement had grown up around the mission. By 1870 inland settlements (that is, ones without rail service) were scattered through the northern and central portions of what would become Alberta. Some of these tiny centres were little more than a store and a few houses.

The coming of the railway brought increased settlement and shifted the Euro-Canadian population towards the south. In 1883, the Canadian Pacific Railway (CPR) running westward from Regina reached Calgary, then a small settlement established as a North West Mounted Police (NWMP) post in 1875. As the railway moved through an area, many of the tiny pre-railway settlements were abandoned and the buildings moved to a railway townsite. Some survived for a time because a post office was located in one of the stores, but most often, merchants in towns bypassed by a railway moved to one newly created by the railway or to an inland town that had gained rail service.[1]

The urban pattern of Alberta was reshaped by the railway that sited towns in a predetermined pattern. The same process was observed by

John Hudson in his study of North Dakota. Hudson notes that this conclusion runs counter to "most studies of central place systems or individual towns," that assume "that activity begets structure and that economic transactions give rise to commerce between places. Thus, farmers
produce crops that have to be moved to market, so transport routes are
provided." But in North Dakota, as in Alberta, such an explanation does
not apply since it is "demand driven, and ignores the design with which
such transactions take place." The railways supplied transportation facilities as well as "structures, at the regional, local and townsite scale, that
gave the settled landscape its commercial geometry."[2]

THE DYNAMICS of TOWN
LOCATION: THE FRONTIER
and INLAND PHASE

Many Alberta towns were able to bridge the
two phases of development defined by the coming of the railway. One
was Fort Macleod. As the site of the NWMP post established after the
force's great march from Dufferin, Manitoba in 1874, it was intimately
connected with the Canadian settlement of the prairie region. The original settlement grew up around the NWMP post established on an island
in the Oldman River. The site was selected for defensive reasons, and
while businesses there attracted trade from Natives and local ranchers, a
police decree in the early 1880s prohibiting civilian buildings close to
the fort, coupled with speculation that the fort might be closed, limited
growth and the willingness of residents to invest in local improvements.
Further inconvenience arose because goods, brought in by ox teams from
Fort Benton, Montana, and later from Lethbridge, had to be ferried to the
island settlement. Residents wanted to see the town moved, and the
spring of 1882 was like many in previous years with "a bustle of excitement about moving." But that year saw no move and by late summer the
excitement had "gone up in a bubble, and we are here yet."[3]

Business owners resented this uncertainty, and by 1883 a number had
moved off the island and established themselves on the mainland. The
federal government acted the next year when it laid out a large townsite
consisting of 216 blocks on government land on a high riverbank about
three kilometres west of the island. The police fort was moved there, and

| *This 1884 photo shows the town of Fort Macleod after its relocation to the mainland. Ernest Brown Collection, B2427, PAA.*

lots were later sold by auction, with the government keeping title to all unsold lots. By 1885, the old town on the island had "a very deserted and forlorn appearance," its best buildings moved or rebuilt at the new town, leaving behind only a few shacks. Even without rail connections, the new town grew. By 1892, as the centre of the NWMP and the ranching industry in southwestern Alberta, it had about 350 residents and assessed property of about $200,000.[4]

The other major settlements in southwestern Alberta by 1890 were Lethbridge, a mining and transportation centre east of Fort Macleod, and Pincher Creek, a ranching centre to the west. To the south, Cardston had been established in 1887 by American members of the Church of Jesus Christ of Latter Day Saints (LDS), commonly known as Mormons, who were searching for a refuge from persecution and a place where polygamy could be practised. During an exploratory trip in 1886, Charles Ora Card, son-in-law of Brigham Young, the founder of Salt Lake City, selected a site and 41 settlers arrived from Utah the next year. It was a sponsored movement in that the parent community in Salt Lake City gave both financial assistance and direction to the settlement.[5] In dramatic contrast to the buying, selling and speculating that usually governed urban land dealings, land at Cardston was distributed by means of drawing lots, giving each settler "an equal share."[6]

Situated immediately south of the Blood reserve, Card had chosen the site because of its water, good soil and mild climate. Its proximity to the United States border was also important because the settlement was seen as a temporary refuge until conditions had improved in the United States. While hostility to Mormons declined in the United States after 1890 when the church revoked its policy on polygamy, the Canadian colonies were by then showing promise and return to the United States was abandoned. Instead, further Mormon colonization was undertaken and by 1898 the district around Cardston had a population of about 1,000. Cardston was the district's main service centre, and, perhaps more importantly, it was a significant religious centre. Further settlement and increased growth occurred with the development of irrigation and sugar beet farming and the arrival of the railway in 1907.[7]

In the Peace River country in the northern part of the province, early Euro-Canadian settlement was associated with the fur trade and missions. Posts such as Fort Vermilion, Dunvegan, and Peace River had been located in river valleys and small inland settlements had developed at or near these locations. In the southern area of the Peace River country, settlers had begun arriving by trail by the turn of the century. Some of this settlement occurred around the future town of Grande Prairie. While a Hudson's Bay company post had been established nearby in 1881, it was only a seasonal outpost of Dunvegan, and this later settlement represented the beginning of a new phase in the region's history. There was much speculation that either the Grand Trunk Pacific Railway (GTP) or the Canadian Northern Railway (CNoR), both of which ran through Edmonton, would build to the coast through the southern Peace River country. This prospect excited the imaginations of agricultural settlers and land speculators. Many townsite companies were formed to take advantage of this anticipated development. One of these was the Argonauts Company, created in 1909 by a group of Edmonton promoters who had recently bought 80 acres of Métis scrip at the site of a Roman Catholic mission.[8] The company surveyed a townsite, named it Grande Prairie City and began promoting it and lobbying for rail connections. By 1911, a bank, a post office and a dominion lands office were set up in the settlement, which was incorporated as a village in 1914.

With the failure of any transcontinental railway company to build through the area, rail connection from Edmonton was provided by the Edmonton, Dunvegan and British Columbia railway (ED&BC). Construction began in 1912, and the line reached Peace River Crossing in

| *Town growth was often rapid in the settlement period. Between 1913 (top) and 1935 (bottom), Grande Prairie had emerged as a community centre with modern stores and amenities. Public Affairs Bureau Collection, PA3267/1 (top); Archives Collection, A6902, PAA (bottom).*

late 1915. A branch line reached Grande Prairie in 1916.[9] The railway did not build beyond Grande Prairie for 12 years, and as the head of steel in the area, the village became the metropolis for the settlements on the rich lands further west.[10] In both Grande Prairie and Peace River, the arrival of the railway was heralded, as it was said in Peace River, as bringing the settlement "into communication with the rest of the world." It was "the one thing without which all else would pale into insignificance, and without which other progress would be either impossible or valueless."[11]

TOWN DEVELOPMENT *in* *the* RAILWAY PHASE

Neither Grande Prairie and Peace River in the north nor Fort Macleod and Cardston in the south owed their origin to the railway, but all depended on it for economic viability in the new economy that was emerging in the Canadian west. The restructuring of life in western Canada fostered by the railway obligated towns founded within the earlier economic framework to obtain connections with the new system or stagnate or, worse, disappear. Since about three quarters of all towns incorporated in Alberta were established and laid out by railway companies, railways were the most powerful influence on town location in the province.[12]

All railway companies received public lands as well as cash to subsidize construction. Most of the land was sold as farm land, although some was laid out in townsites and was sold by the lot. In either case, the railway received immediate revenue as well as long-term profitability through the creation of traffic along its lines. Ann Holtz, in her study of town formation in Alberta, found that all railway companies followed a similar development pattern. A prospective route was first reconnoitred and potential townsites identified. Then, the detailed route was determined by surveyors who plotted the line in terms of natural features best suited for trains. Sidings were created every six to ten miles, but not all received stations. Rather, stations were "arbitrarily" sited every 10 to 20 miles on the basis of the perceived economic potential of the area and its likely traffic. Finally, the townsite was surveyed and lots were sold.[13]

A hierarchial pattern of towns was created as part of a total system. Hamlets and villages grew around sidings and handled local traffic.

Towns developed as local service centres around stations. As Holtz notes, "townsites only became towns when they obtained stations; remaining as a siding revealed the corporate perception of poor potential viability." Divisional points, at which cars and crews were switched and passengers given a break, were located 125 to 135 miles apart. Becoming a divisional point was beneficial to a town because crews were changed there and so lived in the town, while disembarking passengers also created some trade.[14]

To ensure immediate profitability and the long-term value of a townsite, railway companies employed many land development policies. While these often varied between main and branch towns, and changed over time in response to market effectiveness, by 1912 most companies were utilizing relatively consistent techniques. For example, the CPR encouraged settlement in its townsites by selling lots at reduced rates for hospitals, schools, and sometimes hotels. The CNoR used the same approach, selling land at lower rates for banks and lumber yards. Reflecting a significant degree of corporate integration, some railway companies owned lumber companies which received preferential treatment in the distribution of land. In other cases, railway companies entered into exclusive agreements with business associates. The CNoR, for example, gave its banker, the Bank of Commerce, first choice of lots in CNoR towns.[15]

While most townsites were chosen by railway companies, land was sometimes sold to nonrailway interests for development. At Claresholm, the Calgary and Edmonton Railway (C&E) opened a station in 1891, but the adjacent land was sold in 1901 to an individual who subdivided it and laid out the town. By 1903, the town had a population of about 200.[16] While this theoretically made Claresholm a privately developed rather than a railway town, it would never have developed in that location if the station was not there. Indeed, the needs of the railway were paramount. The station, and hence the town, was located at the bottom of a dip with a slough. Its sloping grade helped prevent box cars from sliding away while the slough provided water for the trains.[17]

In a few cases, railways purchased land on which to lay out a town or place a station. This was either homestead land or land being held by a speculator trying to anticipate the location of a station. Private land holders were vulnerable, however, because if their demands were too high, the railway simply bypassed their land and established elsewhere. Most stood the best chance if they developed the land on a shared basis with the railway company. This approach was commonly used by the GTP for branch line towns of uncertain potential.[18] But, generally, stations were sited in existing settlements, such as Drumheller, only if the railway already owned land there. In the Peace River country, the progress of the railway was marked by the abandonment of existing settlements and the enhancement of those few that the railway touched or in which it had interests. As a result, "towns and hamlets were lifted bodily from their old locations and placed on sites from two to five miles distant. These sites were chosen by the railway officials."[19] In Grande Prairie, the station was sited on two quarters of land that had been "tied up" by the railway company just outside the village boundary. While this was relatively convenient to the infant main street and did not challenge the future of the town, it ensured that the downtown would develop towards the land owned by the railway. Serving the interest of both the town and the railway company, the railway lands were incorporated into the village in 1918.[20] A somewhat similar process took place at Lacombe which was created by the C&E in 1891. It was sited about two kilometres east of Barnett's stopping place, a wayside on the Calgary-Edmonton trail. Barnett owned a substantial portion of the land on which Lacombe developed, and while Lacombe consisted only of a station and combined post office and store, its location on the rail line drew economic activity away from the old transportation route.

For relatively well established small towns like Fort Macleod, being bypassed by the railway created a crisis. By the late 1880s, the leaders of Fort Macleod began lobbying for rail connections to enhance the town's future and the exploitation of the area's natural resources.[21] It was ironic that when the C&E built south towards Fort Macleod in 1892, it applied the tactic commonly used by railway companies on the prairies. It refused to locate in the town and instead created a rival town across the river on its own land.[22] For Fort Macleod, the rival town might have spelled disaster. In response, meetings were organized and government figures were lobbied. Some contended that since the government owned most of the land in the town, it should turn over half of its lots to the C&E to entice it into Fort Macleod. Indeed, the *Macleod Gazette* urged the government to "give" the railway "almost everything they want, but do not let them destroy…the hard-won fruits of deserving pioneers."[23]

The government rejected this advice, and the C&E refused all attempts at a negotiated settlement. It would not sell lots in the new town at a lower rate to those wanting to move, nor would it accept lots in the old settlement as security from purchasers. Thus, the citizens were forced to resist. As an unincorporated town, Fort Macleod was without a town council to spearhead the campaign, and its only community institution, a board of trade, was moribund. The fight was carried out by a voluntary committee of property owners. General opinion vigorously endorsed staying in the old town, and those who wavered were socially coerced into support, or at least silence. Few could afford to move, most having just moved from the island five years before. Resolve was further strengthened by hopes that a CPR line westward to the Crowsnest Pass from Lethbridge would soon be announced, and by passing through Fort Macleod, save the town from the C&E. A formal agreement was drawn up in which the property owners closed ranks and pledged "to stand by each other, not to buy lots in the new town and to fight for our existence."[24]

In the meantime, the C&E built a station and freight sheds in the new town (named Macleod, which was seen as another insult to the old town), a hardware store opened and construction began on other business buildings. But the townspeople sustained their boycott of the new town, and it attracted few businesses or residents. Fort Macleod soon became a symbol of the rapacity of the railways. The Lethbridge newspaper called the C&E "no better than pickpockets," while the *Regina Leader* editorialized that although railways were essential and should be given every incentive, "we will not consent to be walked on as though we were dirt" nor see whole towns moved like chess pieces "at the mere whim of railway magnates, speculators and boomsters." With the slogan "Remember Edmonton," where the C&E had established Strathcona as a rival townsite to Edmonton, one Fort Macleod resident, ominously signing himself "Jericho," suggested that the new town be named Monte Carlo as a symbol of "the spirit of speculation and greed which creates it."[25]

Gloom and uncertainty prevailed in Fort Macleod. The townspeople faced a powerful opponent, unbending in its promotion of its new town. Property values steadily depreciated in the old town, and lenders refused to lend money secured by property located there. Fears were openly voiced that the voluntary alliance of citizens against the railway would fall apart. A minority of townspeople, who for the previous five years had promoted the incorporation of Fort Macleod, took advantage of the situation. Proposals for incorporation had been unpopular because of fears that it would bring extravagant government and high taxes, but the

| *While the new train station at Fort Macleod in 1898 was not located near the main street, train travel created new and important linkages for the town. Archives Collection, A3957, PAA.*

challenge to the town's existence overcame these fears since there was "a company to fight and incorporation is to help us fight it." On the last day of 1892, Fort Macleod was incorporated as a town, and the ratepayers went to the polls, though many with fear of the "ruination" that might come with civic government.[26]

Incorporation effectively ended the struggle with the C&E, even though the station continued to operate in its original location, to the inconvenience of travellers and businesses. A rival town failed to grow around it because of the continued refusal by Fort Macleod townspeople to purchase property there, and by 1899 it was described as a "dreary and desolate monument" to those who had "evil designs upon Macleod." The station's inconvenient location was mitigated by the hope that the CPR would build a station in the town when constructing its line to the Crowsnest Pass, and the town sent a delegation to Ottawa to ensure that its interests were respected. Success seemed guaranteed when a clause was inserted in the charter of the Crowsnest Pass Railway (a CPR subsidiary which ran westward from Lethbridge to the British Columbia interior) that the station would be built within Fort Macleod's town limits.[27]

Given Fort Macleod's earlier experience with railway land developers, it was not surprising that faith in this agreement was misplaced. When the Crowsnest Pass railway reached the town in 1897, instead of locating its station close to the main street, it was placed about three kilometres away. Because of the large size of the town's survey, this was still within the town limits and did not breach the railway's charter, but it was scarcely the result the townspeople had anticipated. Once again the old debate about moving the town arose, but resistance to moving was strong and the residents stuck with the old townsite. Given the building that had taken place since the previous crisis, moving would have represented an even greater loss than it would have in 1892. In response to the ensuing public agitation, the CPR announced that if the townspeople were unsatisfied with the location of the station, it would cancel its plan to create a divisional point in the town. This combined promise and threat led the townspeople to endorse the station's location. Within three years, however, the CPR had effectively closed its divisional point at Fort Macleod and moved it to Cranbrook, leaving Fort Macleod with only the disadvantage of a remote station. In 1901, the town offered the CPR $5,000 to move its station into the town, but this was unsatisfactory to the CPR and the station was only moved closer to the town centre in 1906 after further negotiations.[28]

In the end, the location of Fort Macleod did not change despite the actions of the railway companies. This showed that the power of railways over townsite location was not absolute and could be challenged with sufficient unity and sense of purpose. Although the townspeople had to put up with a station distant from the main street, they had managed to prevent the destruction of the town. Fort Macleod was not a speculative townsite that could be abandoned when better opportunities arose. The prospect of a rival line had given the people a reason to fight, and well established businesses in the town strenuously resisted moving, especially since many had moved once already during the mid 1880s.

While most mining towns in Alberta were not established by railway companies, they nonetheless offered railways special opportunity. Some companies owned mines that supplied coal for use on the railway, and all freighted coal produced by the mines. At Drumheller, a few ranchers had settled in the valley by 1896, and this agricultural base was extended with the establishment of grain and mixed farms after 1907 when the district was surveyed. By about 1912 the valley was served by a railway through Munson (north of Drumheller), which for a time was the major town in the area, while merchants in what was to become Drumheller were "subsisting on hope and scenery."[29] In 1910, learning of coal deposits in the area, Samuel Drumheller, an American entrepreneur who had come to Alberta in the early 1900s, took out mineral leases in the area and purchased the homestead of T.P. Greentree. In his plans for the area, Drumheller involved the CNoR which was looking for a western source of coal for use on its prairie lines. The resources at Drumheller fit into this plan, and Mackenzie, Mann and Co. Ltd, owners of the CNoR, developed coal fields at Drumheller as one of its prairie supply points. In 1912 the rail line reached the settlement. While the quality of Drumheller coal ultimately proved unsuitable for steam engines, its potential had created the indispensable link for the development of the coal resources of the town and area. The settlement, named after its most energetic promoter, was incorporated as a village in 1913.[30]

An even more important mining area was the Crowsnest Pass. The first settlement was called Tenth Siding, then The Springs, and, finally, Blairmore in honour of A.G. Blair, the minister of railways. Although the railway was built through the Pass in 1898, Blairmore was initially a highly speculative venture because mines were not developed there for about five years. H.E. Lyons, station agent and postmaster, and Felix Montalbetti, section foreman, built houses there in 1899, and each subsequently claimed to own the townsite. Litigation followed, and with the involvement of more powerful parties, dragged on for about a decade. The difficulty in obtaining clear title to some town lots stymied development of the town.[31] But coal mining was the obvious future of the Pass, and in 1901 the village of Frank was established by Montana mining interests to serve their mine in the area. The village soon became the leading centre in the Pass. In 1903, however, a portion of nearby Turtle Mountain collapsed, burying part of the town and killing at least 70 people. This ended Frank's promising future, and in the following years urban growth shifted westward to Blairmore. Coleman, which had been the site of small mining operations since 1901, was formally established in 1903 when the International Coal and Coke Co. of Spokane, Washington, bought the area, surveyed the townsite, and sold lots.[32] Thus, the Pass towns owed their origin to the potential for coal mining in the area and to the activities of mining promoters and companies. Both Coleman and Frank were created and owned by mining companies (as were numerous other towns in the vicinity such as Hillcrest and

Bellevue). Only Blairmore did not fit this pattern, but there too, mining companies came to own a portion of the town, and the subsequent evolution of its urban form was shaped by the activities of private mining companies.

Railway land development policies ensured that the abandonment by business of inland towns in favour of railway towns was neither accidental nor merely a by-product of naturally occurring market forces. It was deliberately encouraged, and the network of towns created proved the effectiveness of the policy. By restricting the possibility of growth in towns that they bypassed, the railways both created towns where business could be carried on profitably and doomed other existing centres.

Thus, a town's exact location was less important for its success than was its interconnection to the transportation system, and hence the broader economy. W.L. Morton recognized that prairie geographical isolation and its export based economy meant that "site" was as much a relationship as a physical entity. For him, it was inseparable from what might be termed urban process. As he argued, site was a "position of relative advantage for production, exchange or transfer." It was "not mere position, but a function more or less complex, of position, environment and technology."[33]

In this context, the system created by the railways brought in a new era. The old economy and way of life had been replaced with something new, and, theoretically, more progressive. In Fort Macleod in 1892, when the railway reached the town, the *Macleod Gazette* editorialized that the town until then had existed apart from "the outside world almost as completely as Napoleon on the Island of St. Helena." Now it had become "part and parcel of that vast system which is such a feature of this American continent." However, this exhilaration about the future was tempered by the myth of a happier time before the railway. As the editorial went on to note, "we have had an existence peculiar and original to the district we live in, it had its drawbacks, perhaps, but its charms also." The next year, in the eleventh anniversary editorial of the newspaper, such feelings had intensified. The town had experienced great changes the past decade, it noted, and not necessarily for the good. Now, there was "an iron grasp of depression that was never known before" and the district's cash was "slowly filtering into the maw of some power-ful company or other, and hardly anything coming in return." The future was an enigma, "but true nevertheless is the old Latin proverb that 'everything unknown is magnificent' and sincerely it is to be hoped that the reality will not disappoint the many who are waiting for it."[34]

2

TOWN
CULTURE

In 1928, Cecil Burgess, professor of architecture at the University of Alberta, observed in a radio talk that "towns are, after all, only little spots in the country."[1] For city people, this may have been a popular view, but town people rarely saw themselves in this way. Indeed, most saw themselves as living in urban centres, which served urban economic functions and expressed urban concerns and priorities. While critical of many of the social aspects of city life, their inspiration was most often drawn from city and not farm life.

The siting and creation of a settlement was usually followed by its incorporation as a village or a town. Appendix II, Table 1 shows the distribution of cities, towns and villages for the three prairie provinces and changes in population between 1901 and 1941. Table 2 in Appendix II shows the population of the towns in the study sample, and, for comparative purposes, of Alberta cities from 1891 to 1946. As these tables show, between 1901 and 1921, the map of prairie Canada was filled in with settlements.

In Alberta, the type of urban status obtainable depended on population and initially was gained by petition of the residents to the provincial government. Town status was more attractive than incorporation as a village because it carried greater borrowing and other powers, but both offered increased self-government in local matters. Cities enjoyed the greatest range of powers and were governed by individual charters granted by the province. Of the centres in our study, only Drumheller obtained city status before World War II, gaining it in 1930.

Local urban authorities had power to raise money by taxation and long-term borrowing, spend money on fire protection, sewage systems and garbage disposal, construct sidewalks, bridges and streets, provide social welfare and regulate building and health. They could also license businesses and trades and build, own and operate grist mills, grain elevators, factories and electrical utilities.[2] These powers had, since the mid nineteenth century, permitted the development of what historian John Taylor called "independent centres of local power." They were "part of a widening effort to develop the commercial city of the day into an instrument of expansion for the commercial classes."[3]

Even though local autonomy was seen in most of Canada as a way of enhancing local interests, there was a pervasive feeling in prairie Canada by the late 1880s that incorporation brought only debts, extravagance and ever mounting taxes. The debt of Manitoba towns incorporated in the 1870s and 1880s was popularly cited in Alberta as proof that incorporation was an irreversible and costly mistake.[4] While advocates of incorporation argued that it was essential for economic growth and improvement of local sanitary conditions, they could not overcome the hostility to taxation. In this, townspeople showed an attitude identical to that of farmers, who until at least World War I commonly resisted forming rural municipalities because of a fear of taxes.[5] Essential needs could be met through other forms of local government organization. School districts usually preceded the establishment of municipal organizations in the Northwest Territories, and other forms of local government, such as fire and labour districts, had the power to levy taxes for fire fighting and road construction. Because the territorial government lacked financial resources, it encouraged urban and rural municipalities to administer the developing territory. In an effort to overcome fears that incorporation brought ruinous financial obligations, the territorial government by 1889 had limited urban government borrowing to a fixed percentage of the assessed value of assessable property and required the approval of two-thirds of the ratepayers for any borrowing for a period of longer than one year. The irony that this limiting of local power was designed to enhance its allure seems not to have raised comment, nor did the limitation seem to convince sceptics of the benefits of local government.[6]

Resentment of taxation could not make the need for local services disappear, and in lieu of an incorporated body, voluntary organizations were sometimes used. In 1886, Fort Macleod merchants banded together to hire someone to clear the main street of stones. Because this approach had no continuity, a "board of trade" was organized among local ranchers, farmers and town businesses in 1888. This urban/rural alliance was welcomed by some because until then, "important public questions" had been addressed only in "a straggling way." This was "the first effort which we have made to push forward the interests of the district."[7] The board intended to "act in the place of a council or other corporate body in representing the feeling of the community with regard to questions affecting the general interest, outside of politics." It collected money on a voluntary basis for cleaning the main street, tried to attract settlers to the district, encouraged railway construction, and pushed for public works and local improvements.[8] This substitute for "the more expensive" alternative of an incorporated town started off enthusiastically, although there was some criticism that its claim to represent public opinion was a "piece of unwarranted impudence, no matter how right or just their cause may be."[9] In any event, the board disintegrated sometime around 1890. Despite its claims, it had done little more than save residents of Fort Macleod the cost of proper government, all the while unsuccessfully petitioning the Territorial government to spend its funds on public works in the town.[10] As local government, it had been a marked failure.

Incorporation came about in Fort Macleod only under the duress of the railway crisis in 1892, and did not represent an appreciable change in attitude. One ratepayer argued in 1893 that while he supported incorporation to fight the railway, he did not feel any sense of urban purpose. "He did not believe in spending a cent until the town was firmly established. He didn't want sidewalks, he didn't want the streets cleaned up, he didn't want fire protection. Let matters stand as they have been. They've done us very well so far." Such sentiments remained, and in 1894 many residents were grumbling that incorporation of the town had brought them no benefits, only taxes.[11]

Within a decade, the public expression of such views had largely vanished. In 1896 residents of Lacombe petitioned for an unincorporated village so that "necessary public improvements may be effected and nuisances abated." Similarly, in 1903 the 200 residents of Claresholm petitioned for authority to elect an overseer "to look after the welfare of the village, especially the sanitary condition which at present is very bad" and to issue a debenture to install water works. The view that local urban government provided a way of bettering local conditions and stimulating economic growth was embraced unequivocally. Instead of fears that incorporation brought only spendthrift government and ruinous taxes, it was now an eagerly courted symbol of growth and future prospects, and deemed the only practical way to obtain public services. Indicating this changed attitude, it was proudly noted in 1910 that 50

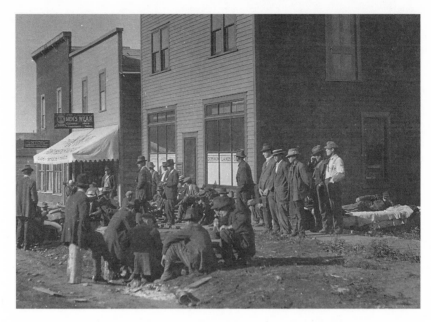

| *Land speculation was an integral part of early town culture. This 1914 photo shows people waiting for the Dominion Land Office to open in Peace River. Note the man on the right who came equipped to sleep over the night in the line. Harry Pollard Collection, P3975, PAA.*

towns and villages had been incorporated in Alberta since 1907. There was "no more tangible evidence of the development of the Province," because "all over Alberta there are now towns and villages where, one, two or three years ago there was prairie."[12]

Aspiring towns no longer wanted to be administered by rural municipal governments which treated them merely as a clustered rural population. Incorporation as a town or village became an expression of an entirely new approach to society. In 1909, eight years after its incorporation as a town, it was commented in Cardston that while incorporation should have meant discarding "rural conditions," it sadly had not happened:

when we were incorporated our ideals should have advanced to the status of urban life and conditions, leaving behind us the mud holes, the barb wire fences, frog ponds, cow pastures and race tracks within the limits. Besides all this, we anticipated the grading of streets, laying of sidewalks, installation of water system, electric lights and sewage and the general rehabilitation of every beauty spot within the limits of the corporation.[13]

Such regret expressed the ambitions of emerging urban social and economic entities. This sense of urbanism was also evident at Grande Prairie, which was incorporated in mid 1914. Until then, the settlement encompassed a handful of residents living on land subdivided into urban lots administered as part of the municipal district of Bear Lake. The residents of the emerging village paid taxes to the municipal district council but complained that it refused to provide an appropriate level of services in return for "the taxes due the town." The phrasing of this grievance suggested both a sense of physical distinctiveness and a sense of urban priorities, which was confirmed by an editorial in the local newspaper the same year. While there was a district board of trade, the "town" needed one of its own since "it is only proper that our affairs should be handled by people more directly interested in the town than the country at large." Once it was incorporated as a village, the Bear Lake municipal council immediately rescinded its planned expenditures on Grande Prairie's streets, and the village was on its own.[14]

The cultivation of these urban sentiments represented a cultural remaking of the countryside and was directly encouraged by local business interests. In general, sufficient growth had taken place that local property owners, especially on main street, now wanted to protect their investments through local government which would give the centre a sense of permanence and lead to lower fire insurance rates because of the installation of water and fire fighting systems. Real estate promoters also exerted pressure on villages and towns to extend their boundaries to increase the number of lots for sale.[15] Bigger was better, and this view often found expression in the desire to rise from village to town status. In 1911, the village council and most local businesses demanded that Blairmore be incorporated as a town. In part, it seems that this desire arose because Blairmore's rival, Coleman, had become a town in 1910, but it was also reasoned that such a move would permit greater borrowing to install services, which would increase property values with only a slight increase in taxes. The local press recorded only one dissenting view which came from the general manager of West Canadian Collieries, the major employer in the town. Noting that he did not believe in the likelihood of lower taxes, he argued that he knew of "several capitalists" who were considering establishing industries in Blairmore if incorporation was delayed for at least a year, since it would be "a great inducement" to firms to establish "where they would be practically exempt from taxes for a while at least." This observation represented only a minor road block to the drive for incorporation. Since incorporation gave local authorities power to encourage economic development, one advocate enthusiastically observed that any "new industries establishing in Blairmore after we are incorporated should be exempt from taxes for several years" anyway.[16]

BOOSTERISM *and* FORMATION

of TOWN CULTURE

While local government was seen as the vehicle by which local communities could gain the power to shape their future, the boosterism that infused almost the whole spectrum of town life formed the intellectual and social framework for such aspirations. Urban historian Alan Artibise has described the basic tenets of boosterism as a single-minded commitment to economic growth and scorn for anyone who did not wholeheartedly support it. Boosterism also demanded a united community spirit in support of booster priorities, and posited "a loose attachment to Social Darwinism and a belief in the special role of local government in fostering urban growth."[17] The ambitions and attitudes of boosters were the same in both cities and smaller centres, and were typified by the "pointers" to stimulate "public spirit" set out in 1913 by Winnipeg's Industrial Bureau. They included advice such as "the success of any city depends upon the progressiveness of its citizens," "the growth of a town depends absolutely upon the cooperative efforts of its citizenship," "citizens who organize for the common good of the city are the greatest factors in social, financial and commercial betterment," and, among others, that "good business men make big cities, for they grasp the great opportunities to be gained through progress and development." In reprinting these aphorisms, the *Cardston Globe* added that if Cardston followed them, this "would redound to the community's well-being."[18]

Like their city counterparts, town boosters saw growth not only as the product of location, urban linkages and history, but of individual self-initiative working in tandem with public support. By granting business owners status as the natural leaders of society, town government was viewed largely as a support for private enterprise and not a public effort with complex and varied goals. If a town provided the infrastructure and subsidies to attract and sustain commerce and industry, the benefits would spread to its population through higher employment, increased real estate values, and the trickle-down of wealth. As various studies of cities have shown, this "privatism" delivered the benefits it promised only to a small elite, and it often created wider social problems.[19]

The booster ethos drew heavily on turn-of-the-century capitalist social and economic theory which reinforced the work ethic and portrayed economic life as an unremitting competitive struggle for survival and mastery. Growth was a central measure of success, and it was easily understood: the larger the town, the more successful. Towns, like private corporations, grew, died, or stagnated in direct ratio to the initiative of their leaders. Thus, the observation in 1908 that Claresholm's growth was due not only to its natural advantages but "to the energy and enterprise of its leading citizens" represented a stock explanation for urban growth. One corollary to this was an obsessive charting and debating of population figures. Thus when the 1911 census showed Claresholm's population as 809 instead of the anticipated 1,200, the figures were denounced as a conspiracy against the west, and town leaders "broke out and joined the chorus of disappointed and disgusted municipalities and almost said d-n."[20]

In towns, like cities, boosterism relied upon simple-minded endorsement of positive thinking. Before 1913, it was commonly said, and more often implied, that the lack of development of a town was the result of negative thinking. This found expression in various terms; "kicking," "knocking," and "croaking" were popular. Sometimes, these terms may have been intended to curb gossips—always a force to be feared in the small town—but generally, croakers were portrayed as malicious and spiteful individuals who hurt a town's reputation and its ability to attract settlers and investment.[21] Critics who unfavourably compared their new home to the east or the United States were commonly advised in newspaper editorials to go back to where they had come from. And sometimes more drastic solutions were proposed. In 1909 the *Lacombe Western*

Globe criticized a "very undesirable person" who made "it his prime object in life to run down the town and district to every new comer who takes time to listen to his fool talk." While this talk was compared to "the ravings" of insanity, the paper believed that his "senseless and malicious libels" should be stopped and suggested that the police "take this matter up."[22]

The emphasis on positive thinking took various forms. In the expansionary years, slights, imagined or real, to a town's reputation or its growth were usually met with a prickly defensiveness. A typical example occurred in 1912 when the *Calgary News Telegram* called Claresholm an "insignificant but aspiring and ambitious one-man town." The comment became front page news in Claresholm, a petition was got up condemning big city arrogance, and an apology was demanded and received from the *News Telegram*. Many of these contests, such as the charge in 1919 that the Edmonton board of trade was trying to "strangle settlement" in the Peace River country to the advantage of Edmonton's immediate hinterland, were economic in nature.[23] While such paranoia was often justified, it was also a cultural style and formed part of the tone of public life. Similarly, the line between truth and deception was often blurred in booster rhetoric, although lying, especially the promotion of worthless land, was said to be the mark of a "boomster" instead of a "booster."[24] But in boosterism too, ethical lines were often cloudy. At its most innocuous, bragging about the present and forecasting the great future of a town led to a reinvention of the past. For example, a promotional sketch of Blairmore in 1913 claimed that the town's population in 1903 had been 50, living in a half dozen shacks, but now stood at 2,000 with hundreds of houses and businesses, an increase of forty times. While Blairmore's growth had indeed been dramatic, the 1901 census showed its population as 231, and the 1911 population as 1,137, or an increase of five times in the decade. But a selective view of the world was inherent in the booster culture and its rhetoric. As people in Cardston were advised, "if necessary, put blinders on the visitor, and let him see only what you want him to see. When he asks you what chance a poor man has in the town, tell him the truth, a poor man is the only man who has a chance." And if all else failed, unpalatable truths could be dismissed as croaking. When in 1912 a geological study showed continued instability in Turtle mountain, public alarm naturally increased. The *Blairmore Enterprise* dismissed anyone with such worries as "croakers." The reports were made by "outsiders," "strangers to the truth" who refused to recognize the great mining potential of the Pass. Society, it went on, was divided into those who worked "patriotically, vigorously and intelligently" for the town's growth; those who were indifferent; and the "croakers" who took "a curious delight in discouraging others." If the Pass towns rid themselves of croakers, "people from a distance will form a good opinion of the place" and might "locate with us and become permanent and substantial citizens."[25]

While such boosterism affected the economic and political life of a community, it also had an obvious impact on the social and intellectual life of a town, especially in the sort of public discourse that was tolerated. While boosters may have been committed to individual economic effort, individual expression was highly problematic. Seemingly, only those who possessed a booster pedigree could criticize anything affecting economic development. Others ran the risk of being labelled disloyal croakers, and there were few forums in which contrary opinions could be formally or rationally expressed. The standard booster response to this limitation of public expression was that if one disagreed with the course of public life, one should become involved and change conditions from within. However, since booster rhetoric governed not only public discourse but public institutions in small centres, even criticism from within was suspect. While the cultural and political ideal of free speech could not be denied, it was still best to avoid negative thinking. On two occasions the Claresholm newspaper tried to explain the difference between legitimate criticism and knocking. In 1907 it noted that "good honest criticism however severe is always welcome, but do it openly and above board." It was thus consistent for the paper the next year to endorse "honest criticism" of the town council to keep it "alive to the duties intrusted to them by the citizens of the town." But there remained a deep suspicion of critical judgement, especially if it affected economic development. As the paper explained, "knocking and criticism are altogether different. The one hinders progress, the other if given in the right time and place helps to push things along in the right direction."[26]

It was not only through shaping the character of public debate that boosterism influenced the social life of towns. Booster arguments about civic pride theoretically encouraged volunteer activity on boards of trade, town councils, and community agencies. Volunteering for public responsibilities was said to be one way of demonstrating a positive attitude, civic co-operation, and progressiveness, all of which would benefit both the town and the individual. In one of its campaigns for members, the Cardston board of trade neatly combined the civic pride arguments of the boosters with an appeal to self-initiative and individualism when it argued that "living upon the corn that others sow" made poor citizens. They, and perhaps like the pathology exhibited by knockers, "suffer in their inner selves and their ultimate personality becomes cramped or warped." The mere making of money was not "the goal upon which the soul most prospers or the personality expands."[27]

By 1912, boosterism was a fully elaborated ethos in Alberta, positing reasons for growth and setting out a compendium of social attitudes and civic obligations. Growth resulted from self-initiative, community cohesiveness, and positive thinking, and success could be measured precisely by population, bank clearings, and buildings. In the first real test they faced in Alberta, boosters suffered a shock from the economic collapse of 1912–13. The collapse proved that boosterism could not deliver what its proponents promised and that growth was not a mere matter of promotion. Nor did its doctrines help its proponents understand the remote forces that were shaping their lives. Thus, it was not unexpected that some claimed that the economic crisis was merely the result of negative thinking and that the economy would turn around if "the false efforts of the pessimist" were discouraged and people pulled together and did "their share in an optimistic campaign" to attract investment.[28]

The old language of boosterism revived briefly at the end of World War I,[29] and continued to find expression in most places during the interwar years. For example, in 1930, the *Cardston News* editorialized that through positive thinking local farmers and real estate interests could increase the value of their holdings. It noted that in one part of Alberta, land of the same quality was selling at double the price as in Cardston because there was not a "kicker" in the place. Even though the district had suffered hail, drought, grasshoppers and crop failure, "they didn't advertise, nor tell anybody about it, but rather presented a united front of contentment and satisfaction with their prospects." The result was higher land values, and the lesson was to be "a booster whether you like or not. Never speak ill of the place you live in. Whenever you do, you are cutting off your own nose to spite your face. You are automatically foreclosing on your own farm. You are preparing yourself for bankruptcy."[30]

Overall, however, such rhetoric was becoming obsolete. By the late 1920s, it was increasingly seen as garish, loud, and, perhaps most dangerous for its social authority, old fashioned. The "hot air" of "the old worn-out booster bunk" was replaced with more sober attention to "the truth, attractively presented and persistently displayed." The old boosterism was being replaced with marketing. The "irresponsible lauding of incidents of little importance" was now seen as an unproductive and "dangerous habit."[31] Even so, some people missed the certitude of booster rhetoric. In 1931, it was remarked in Lacombe that the Depression had sealed the fate of the old style booster. But the "vain prophecies" and the "glib statements of the professional optimists" had "touched our vanity, our pride of country and city, which tickled us because they were the sort of remarks that warmed our too inflammable hearts. Two or three years ago a man who suggested that all was not right with the world was looked upon as a grouch."[32]

Yet, if the style and techniques of boosterism had changed, its essentials retained authority. Its emphasis on community cohesiveness and positive thinking, its defence of business needs and priorities and their linkage with self-initiative and definitions of self-worth continued to be powerful forces in towns. Often this was simply a defence of the work ethic, but hard work was more than a means to success. It also defined self and society. As noted in Peace River in 1926, the remedy for slow business was to "get a wiggle on," and even if this did not produce much money, "you will increase your own self-respect and win that of those around you." Indeed, in 1933 the mayor of Drumheller, in language indistinguishable from that of the boosters before the war, denied the existence of the Depression. He did "not like the word 'depression' so he referred to this business stagnation as 'uncertain times', claiming that if we attain peace and contentment, 'uncertain times' would be of no consequence to us."[33]

These doctrines drew upon the social and economic theory that had been integral to prewar boosterism, and other attributes of boosterism also survived the war. The belief in the necessity for civic pride persisted, but was reworked into a broader social concern often focused around the work of service clubs and community enhancement. Boosterism's emphasis on social cohesiveness as essential for urban growth also remained apparent in the belief that pride in one's town translated into positive thinking and a better and wealthier community. While much of this was now expressed in the language of American theory of community development, its roots lay in older booster sentiments.[34]

Interwar contentions about "civic pride" included a belief that town cohesiveness worked to meet the attractions offered by city life. Cecil

Burgess paid a rather backhanded compliment to this view in 1929 when he remarked that outsiders "might be amused at the boosting and whooping some of us make about our little tin-pot affairs. But in any case it is better to have ambitions and to make efforts than to have none." Even so, he held that "this wonderful motive force of civic pride remains for the most part totally undeveloped and runs mostly to waste." Sport was one popular route to civic pride, but Burgess thought that true civic pride came from adequate social services, good hospitals and schools, opportunities for leisure, recreation, and intellectual development, and a beautiful civic environment.[35]

Boosterism in small town Alberta, like in so many other places in prairie Canada, was not home-grown. While it fit directly with perceptions of local needs, its language and techniques were interchangeable between town and city. Of course, boosters always cited specific local resources as proof of a community's great future, but there is a remarkable sameness in these claims. Their uniformity, universality, and internal consistency suggest that they were more than the expression of local ambition. Their use in explaining a varied range of social and economic phenomena and their service in creating a code of behaviour suggest that they represented the ideology of most business and commercial interests in the province. While some people, even before World War I, disagreed with the style of boosterism, its fundamentals were basic in defining social and political objectives and action. Its philosophy of why growth occurred was part of its attraction, but its tenets were also part of the social and economic ethos of the ruling groups and represented their assumptions about the attributes of success. There was little quarrel in most towns with the belief that the growth, decline or stagnation of a town was in the hands of its citizens, led by business owners. Generally, what was good for business was good for the town, and town policies and programmes were directed to this end. Thus, civic concern and expenditure on social institutions, medical and educational facilities, roads and transportation, types of buildings on the main street, and the condition of streets and sidewalks were all justified, at least in part, by their contribution to the success of town businesses.

Defining Community

The town's role as an intermediate point between the farm and the city was pivotal in defining the nature and quality of the small town community. Did it belong to a farm-centred community or a city-centred one? Or did it fall somewhere in between, a hybrid that took reference from both environments? These issues were never separate from broader economic concerns in towns, especially after 1912–13. Failure to sustain population growth or an actual loss of population created worries about the future, and changes in transportation brought by the automobile represented a new challenge.

It was obvious that the city set the tone for the towns, forcing them to counter its draw and meet its standard of living. Thus, any discussion about the town and its future was framed, often obsessively, by the social role of the city. As the *Coleman Journal* remarked in 1928, increased travel and the images seen in movies made small town people discontented with "things as they used to be." They wanted "to be on par with their brethren of the cities," and this stimulated "improvement and progress." These changes were both social and material. As the paper further noted in 1933, the lure of the city with its "bright lights" and fast pace invigorated town visitors where they stepped "a little faster and where competition is more keen than you are accustomed to." The next year, these arguments were extended in an editorial which claimed that the city's better buildings, art, music and educational opportunities made it "more progressive than small towns." And its faster pace marked an advance over town conditions where the slower pace of life made people "less sprightly in their habits and attitude. Environment has great influence." These views demonstrated that towns essentially wanted, as the province's town planner, Horace Seymour, noted in 1931, to have "many 'city' conveniences and amenities while having but a 'village' population."[36]

This did not mean, however, that towns denied their own importance. Generally, town commentators noted, as did the *Macleod Gazette* in 1941, that small communities were the "backbone" of the province's trade and commerce. It was further pointed out that cities like Calgary and Lethbridge relied on the farm and town trade for most of their economic activity.[37] This was a traditional argument: the city could not exist without the town and the farm. But the town and its relationship with the farm was equally central for the smooth working of the economy. While the economic functions of the city were begrudgingly recognized by an article in the Grande Prairie newspaper in 1926, it urged farmers not to patronize mail order businesses which drew trade from local businesses. "While some larger centres are necessary, it is the country towns, not the big cities, which are the backbone of Western Canada." Merchants sustained the town, and without them "there could be no town. Without the towns, it would hardly be possible to maintain existence on the farms."[38]

Such arguments were popular, as was the view that the town played a valuable role in preserving the morality and vigour of society in general. Much of this rhetoric echoed that of the country life movement, which asserted the social significance of the farm in society. Town advocates argued that great men came from small towns which created reflective individuals imbued with the work ethic, enthusiasm and optimism.[39] Also borrowing from the country life movement, the town was said to be an upright and decent place to live. Its small size and slower pace created a personable and moral environment. It was the perfect urban environment, possessing the advantages and none of the drawbacks of the city. One article, originally published in the *Christian Science Monitor*, was copied in small town papers so often over almost a decade and a half (often as an editorial and without credit) that it clearly touched small town sensibilities and represented a core set of beliefs about town life. It asserted that turning from a city newspaper to a town one was like "stepping from the slums full of vile odors into an old fashioned garden with honeysuckle and the scent of perennial flowers." While reports of murder, infidelity and selfishness in city papers were depressing, reports in town papers renewed "faith in life. Here are set forth only that which uplifts the community—the activities of the businessmen, the church news, the civic good accomplished by the women, school gatherings" and the like. They were "the simple annals of the great common people who are really the foundation of this broad country of ours." And when scandals were reported in small town papers, they were reported with a "kindly touch" since the offenders might be a neighbour or well known in the community.[40]

Such views of the city seem to have been widely accepted, but an equally strong, although contradictory, impulse also existed. Running like a fault line through town attitudes was a love/hate relationship with cities. At the same time that the city was described as a vile environment, the highest accolade townspeople gave their town was that its conveniences, buildings and services were "city-like." These tendencies penetrated most levels of town society, as was evident in an essay contest about Claresholm sponsored by the local Elks Club in 1926. The prize winning essay trumpeted that "we have the conveniences of water, light, and power that belong to the big cities." The town was reportedly in good financial shape, and it "has already grown to a good size and is far enough away from any city to become itself a large centre." The second prize winner was also committed to town growth and pride, and made the usual comparison with city facilities: Claresholm had hotels that provided accommodation equal to many in the city.[41]

If views of the city in smaller centres were somewhat contradictory, the relationship between town and country was clearer. The town needed the farm trade to survive. This inevitably forced the town into an accommodating relationship with area farmers. Nonetheless, there was at times an uneasiness in the relationship. Of particular concern to town business owners was farmers' patronage of mail order businesses. This was characterized as a rejection of the town and its function. In one of the most extreme statements of this view, the *Cardston Globe* wrote in 1916 that "it is quite evident that the Cardston town and farming communities are not working as harmoniously together as they should. Community interests have been overlooked. It has been every man for himself, and in our eagerness to save a five cent piece our common interests have been sacrificed." Lest this be interpreted as criticism of town businesses, the editorial placed the blame squarely on district farmers, only one-third of whom showed "co-operation" with local business through regular patronage. In an unequivocal assertion of town priorities, the *Globe* recommended that such people:

> should keep out of town, or he should tie his horse or leave his car outside the town limits, and walk on the grass. He has contributed nothing for the building of the sidewalks and the making of the roads, and he has no right to walk on them or use them. The council would be perfectly justified in charging him every time he made use of any of the conveniences of the town.[42]

By the 1920s public expression of such sentiments had lessened. Farmers continued to be urged to patronize the home town, but there was a new sensitivity. It was readily apparent that the choice created by motor vehicles now made threats inappropriate. Instead, towns had to rely on service, entertainment, civic improvements and their urban advantages to attract the farm trade. One popular expression of this view was that the town should build a "community centre" to lessen the distinctions between "town" and "farm." In 1918, as part of its suggestions for postwar reform, the Claresholm newspaper editorialized that a community centre including a reading room, sports facility and committee rooms was necessary. A broader definition of community was intended since "it should belong not to the town alone but the entire community, the district tributary to Claresholm." Further, new political institutions would be needed to accommodate the new conditions:

> if our municipalities had been organized with one town as the center, conditions for organizing social centers would have been much better. Instead of having a municipal council and a town council, we should have a council representing the town and the community around it. The town exists for the country, and the farmer whose wealth and trade build up the town should have something to say regarding the kind of town that he will create. The automobile has drawn the town and country closer together. The question of good roads to the town, good sidewalks and a public building where all can meet for social or intellectual pleasure, are matters of equal concern, alike to farmer or townsman.[43]

Such facilities were rarely built, although demands for more modest facilities such as community stables, town weigh scales or rest rooms for women, that would link town and country, continued to be voiced.

Before World War I, the aims of political life in small towns were focused around local promotion. Partisanship was important for local patronage and as a periodic entertainment, but it was never expected to interfere with the economic development of the constituency. In other words, the MLA should be a local booster. This did not, however, affect the relationship between town and country. Before World War I, farmers did not quarrel with the booster pledge of economic growth, and as Paul Voisey notes, in the Vulcan area at least, cross linkages between town and farm economies led town boosters and farmers alike to hope to profit from town growth.[44]

While such factors continued to characterize the relationship between town and country, the politicization of farmers immediately before World

War I created an added dimension. Because it threatened to split town and country, the farmers movement was sometimes viewed with alarm. In 1910 the first farmer candidate was nominated in the constituency of Fort Macleod, causing some concern in the town about a potential rift between the two communities. Yet the clear expression of farmers' needs also created opportunities for community co-operation and a realization of interdependence. As J.M. Lamont of the Peace River district United Farmers of Alberta (UFA) wrote in 1916, society had reached an "era of inter-class organization." He believed that "in the very best of all possible worlds we cannot do without one another. There can be no city worthy of the name without a happy, contended rural population adjacent to it, and there can be no progressive and comfortable satisfying farm life without the social humanizing influences of a clean and healthy town. So let us get together."[45]

Such sentiments were not always realized. J.Y. Card of the Cardston board of trade argued in 1930 that, "especially since the advent of the UFA government in Alberta," there had developed "a sort of barrier between the towns of Alberta and the rural districts." Clearly, some in the UFA also recognized this development. In 1928 A.M. Scholefield, the Vice President of the UFA, told the Drumheller board of trade that "it was impossible to build up a good social system unless all components were working harmoniously together." Yet, UFA doctrines about group government remained important. Thus, while it stressed the need for co-operation, it unapologetically asserted that "the UFA admitted that every group, class and industry had a right to organize, consequently they felt that they were following a true principle in building up their own organization."[46] In any event, while the UFA preached occupational and class organization, it did little to implement these policies in a practical manner. Any barriers it created between town and country were largely of appearance and not substance. But greater challenges arose with the election of Social Credit in 1935. Social Credit's attacks on what it called the money system produced a more complicated response, and by the late 1930s, town merchants generally were opposed to the government, its attacks on banking and, as business perceived it, its anti-business attitudes.

A desire for permanency, and a fear of instability, helped shape the nature of town life. The years between 1900 and 1914 were formative in establishing the ethos of town business and political life. Many town promoters endorsed incorporation as the means to unlimited growth, but the benefits they claimed would follow were rarely realized. Many factors were at play, including circumstance, the evolution of government, and a misunderstanding of the nature of the economy within which the towns operated. In general, towns had neither the legal authority nor the wealth to influence the dominant provincial economic and political trends to their own advantage. Boosterism was part of the legacy of this settlement period, and once cast in this mould, from which escape was both unwanted and impossible, the booster ethos was tempered only after World War I. Its dreams of self-help and initiative, its promise to allow the individual to cast his own fate, its pledge of social acceptance for those who supported its tenets, its belief in the importance of community cohesiveness and positive thinking to promote individual success, and its habitual blurring of the lines between private interests and those of the community created the intellectual and political framework of town life and shaped and justified its business and social life until at least 1947.

Town culture also developed within a general belief that the differences between towns and cities were not only distinctions of power and future prospects but of culture. In comparison to the city, the town was friendly, sociable and safe. Its familiarity and supposed homogeneity created an orderly environment which expressed a social ideal for its proponents. Yet, the challenge of the city could not be dismissed or ignored. While towns continued to see themselves as representing a moral and ideal culture, they recognized that they had to meet city living standards and civic amenities in order to retain their population and their economic relationship with farmers. This contradictory impulse shaped the ongoing discussion about the policies that towns should pursue and how town culture could be fostered and enhanced.

POLITICAL *and*
ECONOMIC
LIFE *of* TOWNS

3

TOWN
GOVERNMENT

Local governments were the creatures of the province that created them and granted them their power.[1] As Alberta's Deputy Attorney General noted in 1912, local governments could not spend money or pass bylaws unless specifically allowed by provincial statute.[2] Even this limited autonomy declined throughout Canada before 1920, but its erosion quickened after World War I as the provinces assumed a greater supervisory role. In Alberta, this occurred somewhat earlier because of the crisis that the economic collapse of 1912-13 created for local governments. This frustrated the hope that incorporation would allow towns to use their civic powers to promote local economic growth. Town efforts to promote economic development and growth fit poorly with the realities and limitations of local government.

CIVIC GOVERNMENT

The ideal of town government was limited democracy through elected representation. After 1893 the franchise in civic elections in the Northwest Territories was exercised by ratepayers (including women ratepayers after 1888) through secret ballot. In Alberta it was broadened in 1917 to include a ratepayer's spouse and children over 21 if resident in the town.[3] This retained the connection between owning property and voting, embodying an attitude that those without property were transient and irresponsible. Some objections were voiced, but only in 1927 was Fred White, a Calgary labour MLA, able to push through amendments to the *Town Act* to extend the franchise to male tenants and their wives and daughters over 21 years of age if they had rented an assessed parcel of land for a year preceding enumeration day.[4] In addition to the franchise, democratic principles were enshrined in the requirement that debentures be approved by ratepayers. Further, an annual meeting of the electors had to be held at which the mayor and council presented the financial statements, reported on the past year, and responded to questions about town affairs. As well, these meetings were often the occasion for nominating candidates for upcoming civic elections.

Town government was centred on the mayor and council. Council members met both collectively and in committees such as finance, public works and utilities. Sometimes called the "departmental system," this approach organized the town's affairs in lieu of an extensive town bureaucracy. While the provincial government in later years provided advice on organizing local administration, principles in use elsewhere initially were copied and applied as local conditions required. Fort Macleod's town council, for example, adopted the procedural rules and regulations in use in Lethbridge in 1893.[5] Systems of organization used in cities, such as commission government, were rarely considered appropriate for towns.[6] Town bureaucracies were small, and positions like solicitor, medical health officer, assessor or auditor were usually filled by local professionals for a fixed annual fee. Some permanent officials were nonetheless required. All towns had a secretary-treasurer, often a policeman, sometimes a poundkeeper and a work crew. Often, one person performed several of these tasks; in Blairmore in 1915, for example, one individual was policeman, fire chief and sanitary inspector. At times, this proved inefficient. In 1929 the Peace River town council fired the town secretary because he was not completing his tasks. As the *Peace River Record* editorialized, however, given his responsibilities it was a puzzle how he could "make even a show of keeping up with the duties of his office." He looked after the town's day-to-day operations, bookkeeping and accounts, managed the electricity plant, and when the town installed a municipal shower bath, "again the secretary was asked to keep another account." Town employees were also often politically vulnerable. As noted in Blairmore in 1921, civic elections were "responsible for much inefficiency" because town employees became "the victims of the caprices of the ever changing personnel" of the council.[7]

Qualifications for town councils and mayors were set by the *Town Act*. In 1912, candidates had to be British subjects literate in English, at least

21 years old, and had to reside and own property free of liens and tax arrears in the town. Besides these legal requirements, it was widely accepted that business owners made the best mayors and councillors. The Drumheller newspaper approved of those elected in 1919 because they had the supposed business characteristics of being "cool, levelheaded and conservative." Local prominence was also beneficial for those aspiring to the mayoralty or the town council. Moreover, they were almost always male. W.A. Beebe, who came to Blairmore in 1902 and was village overseer until about 1909, was one of the most prominent figures in the town. He was a realtor and insurance agent and later sat on the town council and served as mayor. H.C. McConkley, mayor of Drumheller from 1924 to 1927 and again in 1930, was a mine operator and owned the Drumheller Flour Mill.[8] Middle level businessmen were also active in local government, but all were drawn from the main street business and professional groups which formed the effective elite of the town.

Before 1934 the province prohibited any form of payment to mayors and councillors. Their work was expected to be motivated by a commitment to community. While the dominance of town government by business owners generally meant that business interests were promoted and that volunteerism was not selfless, many contributed generously of their time and talents to town affairs. Yet some did receive payment indirectly—in 1923 the Department of Municipal Affairs ordered the Blairmore council to stop awarding its members free light and water.[9] In 1934 the province allowed a per diem payment for councillors. While it was commented in Grande Prairie that "in these depressed times" it was unlikely that the new provisions would be implemented, within a year the town council was discussing the matter. Although it was tabled because of its cost, its allure nagged at the councillors, and a month after the 1936 election they decided on a referendum to approve a bylaw allowing payment of councillors. Perhaps sensing hostile public opinion, the bylaw was not presented to the voters until 1937 when it was defeated. Similar bylaws in Blairmore and Drumheller met the same fate.[10]

Ideally, those citizens who did not run for civic office expressed their commitment to the town by exercising their franchise, participating at the annual meetings, and by taking an ongoing interest in civic matters. By positing a uniformity of interest among all citizens, such views about "public spirit" assumed that the town gained purpose and direction through an informed and active citizenry. Yet, civic politics were often marked by public apathy, occasionally punctuated by bitter personality conflicts. As early as 1894, the *Macleod Gazette* found the "considerable wrangling" at town council meetings over "trivial and silly measures" disgraceful.[11] Similarly, while elections were occasionally spirited, mayors and councillors were most often returned by acclamation. This pattern emerged at an early stage—elections after the incorporation of Fort Macleod were vigorous affairs, but by 1899 most civic elections in the town, as in the rest of the Northwest Territories, created little public interest.[12] Given this environment, a small group often dominated civic life. In Drumheller, for example, while eight individuals acted as mayor between 1916 and 1947, three dominated, together holding the chair for two-thirds of the total period.

A lack of interest also often characterized annual meetings; it was not uncommon for only town officials to be present. Yet there were times when attendance was high and debate was serious. Fort Macleod's annual meeting in 1913, when the town was clearly facing a financial crisis, was well attended and "very stormy." Yet crisis did not always draw out the public. The same year, people in Claresholm were called on to attend the annual meeting because debts were high and "the dilatory tactics of the past cannot longer continue. The financial situation must be handled without gloves." But the meeting was a "listless" affair; the financial audit of the town and reports by the town council were not ready, and the public was indifferent. Similarly, despite allegations of scandal involving the Blairmore town council, its annual meeting in 1925 was poorly attended.[13]

While some argued that elections by acclamation and poor attendance at annual meetings showed public satisfaction with civic affairs, this view was neither universal nor wholly convincing. Enthusiasm about civic issues through annual meetings was difficult to sustain, and the honest airing of opinions in public could not always be expected in small towns where everyone knew everyone else. Yet while people wanted the right to choose their leaders, they rarely demanded a hand in actual decision making. They reserved the right to blame those they elected for errors, but the general attitude was, as it was phrased in Grande Prairie in 1947, "whatever you do, don't raise the taxes." The limited jurisdiction of local government, the perceived identity of interest among townspeople, and a belief that the town's social structure was relatively open led to an emphasis on informality. But the system was not as fluid as it appeared. The hegemony of main street business and professional groups prevailed—their interests were paramount and concerns other than theirs were rarely relevant. This too contributed to public lassitude. In Grande Prairie in 1947, "the usual procedure" on nomination day was "for some businessman to rush around with nomination papers about fifteen minutes before nominations close and get a friend to agree to stand for office."[14]

Such attitudes had been the norm throughout the province for the previous 50 years. They helped to confirm public acceptance of the booster doctrine that government was a "business" and that argument and debate threatened the cohesiveness and economic objectives of the town. If government was a business, who better to run it than business owners or professionals like lawyers? This in turn prompted a view that democracy was at times cumbersome and expensive. In 1909 it was hoped that a mid term vacancy on the Claresholm town council would be filled by acclamation and save the cost of an election. When another by-election was required the next year, the *Claresholm Review* again hoped that the seat would be filled by acclamation, but three candidates stepped into the ring. The only saving grace for the *Review's* editor was that all were businessmen, and once the bothersome election was over, he hoped "we will now have a quiet spell and allow our new council to work unrestricted."[15]

Within these overall trends in local politics, partisanship was rarely seen as a legitimate structure for debate, even though everyone would have known a candidate's provincial or federal party affiliation. The extension of the franchise to tenants in 1927, however, created a changed political attitude in some places. In Drumheller and the Crowsnest Pass towns, the widening of the franchise and a growing polarization of political life stimulated the formation of citizen's committees that ran slates or backed particular candidates. The citizen's committees, while having the appearance of a political party, claimed to be nonpartisan and interested only in local affairs. The committee in Drumheller, calling itself the Civic Government Association, was formed to run candidates for all positions on the town council and school board in 1928. Its slate was elected except for its candidate for mayor. The Association endorsed "responsible and capable candidates" and promised to assist "all lawfully constituted authorities in...upholding and maintaining the best traditions of British institutions." It looked "forward to the day when the small town politician and petty schemes will be a thing of the past, and to the era when all classes of Drumheller's citizens will co-operate in good clean municipal government." It promised "increased prosperity for all classes"

| *Police frequently helped to break strikes in the coal fields. This photo shows an armoured car used by the Alberta Provincial Police in the Drumheller Valley in 1923/24. Archives Collection, A4815, PAA.*

through "businesslike economy," "a clean town in all senses of the word," and, among other things, "adequate fire protection."[16]

The Association's concerns were at two levels. There had been charges in 1927 that the Drumheller town council was irresponsible for not curbing gambling and bootlegging in the town. It was also blamed for inefficiency because the town's fire protection system was poor and because tax arrears were very high, standing at about $73,000. These problems, it was said, could be corrected by councillors working in a businesslike and nonpartisan manner. It was the familiar rhetoric that the town was inherently united and cohesive through its identity of interest. At another level, however, the Association was highly political. Fears about communists were high in coal towns in the late 1920s; the Drumheller valley had been the location of a bitter strike in 1925 which had partly contributed to the formation of the radical Mine Workers Union of Canada, a communist dominated union. Although the more conservative United Mine Workers of America remained dominant in the valley, it was apparent that radicalism had not been defeated, and shortly after Drumheller's civic election, these fears were confirmed by a bitter strike at Wayne. Thus, the Association's appeal to class co-operation and its pledge to defend "British institutions"—a typical anti-communist phrase in use by the late 1920s in Alberta—defined loyalty and had direct political implications.

If class and radicalism were among many concerns about local government in Drumheller, it was the major issue in Blairmore and Coleman in the early 1930s. While their civic politics had largely been indistinguishable from other Alberta towns, the 1927 amendments to the *Town Act* created a new dynamic by giving nonproperty holders the vote at a time when an ongoing crisis in the coal fields was politicizing many workers. In the first election after the amendment of the Act, an unparalleled 500 people voted in Blairmore, then a town of about 1,600 people. The next year two "union" candidates ran for town council, but both were defeated. In the following year all seemed back to normal—all councillors were returned by acclamation, although two ran as a miners' slate for the school board. Both were defeated.[17] The early 1930s, however, brought dramatic change. In Coleman the miners captured the town council in 1932, although not the mayor's seat. The owning classes and anti-communists in the town organized a Citizen's League which drew members from throughout the Crowsnest Pass. The league, headed by A.S. Partington, an Anglican minister from Coleman, and Alex Morrison, a Coleman businessman and local politician, pledged to "uphold the laws of the country against the propaganda of those who openly preached sedition and revolution."[18] While the unionists in Coleman were subsequently defeated, the mayoralty and all seats on Blairmore's town council and school board were won by communists in 1933.

The Communist victory in the 1933 Blairmore election was inseparable from the labour troubles and the political culture of the Pass in the early 1930s. The issue was complicated by almost a decade's struggle between moderates and communists in the Alberta coal fields. For seven months in 1932, most of the Pass miners were on strike over attempts by the mine companies to rid the mines of radicals. The coal companies refused to negotiate with the communist Mine Workers Union of Canada at Coleman, and the strike was broken when the more conservative United Mine Workers gained the upper hand. In Coleman, Anglo Canadians were the majority and tended to be more conservative than miners of European descent.[19] In Blairmore, however, the communists held their power base despite divisions between moderates and radicals.[20] Blairmore's striking miners had their light and water supply cut off by the town and the strike ended only after intervention by Premier

| During the political turbulence leading to the election of a Communist town council, the Blairmore town bandstand was a popular site for demonstrations and speeches. Watched by a mounted policeman, these demonstrators on May 2, 1932 carried a banner calling for "Abolition of Vagrancy Laws." NC-54-2018, GAI.

Brownlee. Before the 1930s, all towns had a handful of people receiving welfare, but it was much higher in mining towns such as Blairmore and Coleman where uneven coal production and labour unrest periodically created high unemployment and destitution. The strikes of the early 1930s intensified the inequities arising from local control of welfare, making it another rallying point for the radicals. By the fall of 1932 when the Citizen's League was formed, the Pass was bitterly divided. In Blairmore, the league denied backing anyone for mayor—it did not "as a body, take any part in local municipal or school elections," but aimed only to give "moral assistance to those who are charged with the enforcement of law and order."[21] The reality was quite different. At one point, the local RCMP officer reported that the league's leaders were "going around dragging their coats behind them, hoping someone will step on them." The next day he noted that it was "very difficult" to make some members of the citizen's league "realize that their opponents cannot be prosecuted without cause."[22]

The radicals viewed the Citizen's League as a powerful political force, backed by equally strong commercial interests. In December 1932, the *Blairmore Enterprise*, for example, saw the League's legitimacy as part of a tradition of paternalism:

"And what can you do when you have the Citizen's League working against you?" This remark came from an individual in the Crow's Nest Pass who had been or has turned Red. And, if the truth were known, possibilities are that man's family has been largely dependent upon certain members of the Citizen's League for food and clothing for a considerable time past.[23]

A month later, the communists had gained enough support and had toppled the traditional powers of the town council. While their claim that "we made the merchants and will break them" was characterized by the *Blairmore Enterprise* as "the line of guff contained in the silly mottoes of the local communists," a new political language had come to the fore in Blairmore's civic life. So too had a wholly new disrespect for members of the business group as town leaders. The newly elected town council immediately reduced the cost of a peddlar's license (which was designed to protect local merchants from travelling salesmen) and imposed a 5 percent business tax. And showing a world turned on its head, business owners appearing before the town council asking for reduced property assessment were treated, said the *Blairmore Enterprise*, like they were "asking for relief."[24]

The political radicalism of the communists in Blairmore, in comparison to other local governments in Alberta, was significant. As historian Allen Seager has rightly cautioned, the radicalism in the Pass was not merely a response to misery but also expressed political ideals and culture.[25] Yet, although they were hampered by the confines of civic jurisdiction, the communists did not overturn the established elites of Blairmore. Local businesses had little to fear from a town council whose greatest concern was with social welfare, or "relief." This was the overwhelming civic issue in Blairmore and an important plank for the communists who promised to clean up the relief system and give the unemployed dignity. The council imposed a four mill social service tax and asked for a 5 percent voluntary contribution from those employed to assist the unemployed. Many responded, including ordinary workers, the school staff, the F.M. Thompson Co. (merchants), and even some officials at West Canadian Collieries. The Mine Workers Union of Canada also contributed $2,000. In language unsuited to someone the Citizen's League had called a traitor, Mayor Knight remarked that the success of the appeal proved "that the Christian feeling is not yet dead in some places." Equally remarkable was his belief that "we have come to the conclusion, after a great deal of deliberation, that redness is the state of the stomach. It is time that people's opinions regarding this color business were changed and that we get together as we were previous."[26] Nonetheless, the language and attitudes of the Blairmore town council and the communist school board galled, often frightened, and always embarrassed the Blairmore elite. In 1933 the town council endorsed a petition calling for the abolition of the RCMP, and in 1935 it declared a public holiday for the visit of Tim Buck, the leader of Canada's communists. The school board had similar policies. In 1934, unlike all other schools in Alberta, it declared a holiday for November 7, the anniversary of the Russian revolution, but not for the marriage of a British prince. This was not, stormed the *Blairmore Enterprise*, "civilized."[27]

The Citizen's League and other anti-communists tried to dislodge the duly elected town council and challenge its policies. They asked the Department of Municipal Affairs to replace it with a provincially appointed administrator, which the department refused to do.[28] The business tax was hated by business owners, as in every other town in Alberta, and a number of Blairmore businesses challenged its legality in early 1933. This was more a gesture of defiance than a reasoned legal challenge. The *Enterprise* contended that Mayor Knight was trying to convince the unemployed of Blairmore "that the businessmen of the town are determined to starve them," even though they were only objecting to an "unjust, illegal and unnecessary business tax."[29] This view failed to note that many other towns already had a business tax, or had one at some time in the past, including Blairmore during World War I.

Such selective memory was typical of the reporting in Blairmore's newspaper. It made little real contribution to the debate about the political issues involved, and only sniped constantly about "little Moscow" and the humiliation of living under a communist town council. And the council greatly incensed the local newspaper in other ways. Rather than paying to publish town notices and the annual financial statements in the newspaper as was customary, the town mimeographed and left copies for the public to pick up at the post office.[30]

The radicals at Blairmore continued to retain their popularity, and in 1935, an all "red" slate was returned, some by acclamation.[31] While Bill Knight did not run for mayor in 1937, a full slate of "progressives" again defeated the "independents." Ten years later, Knight's successor as mayor, Enoch Williams, was elected for his sixth term. By then, the cumulation of wartime changes and prosperity had lessened the radicals' fire, and the reaction to a miners' government had softened to the point where the *Enterprise* advised against an election in order to save money. Blairmore was now like any other town in Alberta, and poor attendance at the annual meeting was said to signal public satisfaction with the council and mayor. By this point as well, Blairmore was free of debt. Indeed, past struggles had become so muted that the *Enterprise* remarked that Blairmore should imitate some other towns that had pictures of former mayors and councillors hung in the town hall, "to help to build up local history to some extent."[32]

FINANCING *and* CONTROL
of TOWN GOVERNMENT

While local governments provided services like social welfare and infrastructure like sewage systems, sidewalks, fire protection, and utilities, they received no capital or operating grants from senior governments to assist in these projects. They were financed through debenture debt serviced by local taxes. Everywhere in Alberta, borrowing was high: between 1906 and 1913, the debt of towns in Alberta increased from $100,000 to $2.9 million.[33] Usually, one of the first acts of a village or town council was to request public approval to borrow money. Blairmore's first two bylaws after its incorporation as a town were for debentures totaling $45,000 for waterworks and a fire hall.[34]

Such expenditures accounted for most of the debt incurred in the towns studied. In some cases, this debt was taken on with an optimism approaching negligence. In 1912, for example, Fort Macleod planned a $165,000 town hall as part of an effort to show the world its splendid prospects.[35] In early 1913, the town borrowed money for the project, increasing its total bond indebtedness to $517,000, plus a $216,000 bank overdraft. It also continued to borrow from the "town lots account"—a complicated and highly unorthodox practice unique to Fort Macleod. This enabled the town to borrow cash against raw town land, while holding the combined mill rate at 13 mills—lower than it had been in 1897. Those critical of what they called a "ridiculous scheme" were countered by the mayor and his supporters "with the 'knocker' accusation," which they invariably used "in lieu of argument."[36] While Fort Macleod's case was an extreme example of the state of municipal finance by 1912, municipal borrowing in general was out of hand because of booster predictions about the future and dreams of unlimited growth. Such expectations were not realized, but the debt had to be serviced, which became increasingly difficult because of depressed times. And, at the same time that tax arrears were growing, new methods of taxation were brought in that lowered town revenues.

Before 1912 urban governments raised most of their revenue through taxes on land and buildings. Some revenue also came from license fees and other taxes. Among the latter was the poll tax levied on renters, who, it was said, received the benefits of community services paid for by property owners. Although none of the towns studied adopted it before 1912, towns were also permitted to implement a single tax system—a tax on land values exclusive of improvements like buildings. As well, they were allowed to levy business taxes and taxes on personal property and incomes.[37]

In all the towns surveyed, arrears on property taxes were high before 1912.[38] Boom times seem to have mitigated official concern, and village and town councils were often reluctant to enforce payment. Fort Macleod passed a bylaw in 1898 denying the franchise to those with tax or utility arrears, and the Blairmore town council discussed a similar policy in 1912. But there was little will to face the consequences of enforcing such bylaws. In Blairmore, it was found that Malcolm McKenzie, the provincial treasurer of Alberta and one of the town's largest landowners, had not paid his taxes for two years. As the council concluded, unless people like McKenzie could "be made to dig up, it is not reasonable to expect that a poor individual holding a little square of land should be made to toe the line."[39]

Poll taxes were also often in arrears. Although never an important source of revenue for agricultural service towns like Cardston, Claresholm, and Lacombe, a poll tax was nonetheless assessed.[40] It was a more profitable tax in mining towns, and both Coleman and Blairmore implemented it in 1908, with Coleman collecting $1,100 in the first year.

It was an unpopular tax, and when collected for the first time in Blairmore in 1908, "quite a lot of explanations" were necessary.[41] Business taxes were equally unpopular, but with a more influential group, and none were imposed before 1912 in the towns studied. Licensing of trades and transient traders also provided some revenue, usually amounting to between 5 and 10 percent of a town's total receipts.[42] As well, all towns required dog licenses, more to control the dog population than for revenue. The debate they occasioned was out of all proportion to the minuscule revenue they produced, and their main consequence was the death of many dogs and much unpleasant work for town policemen.[43]

While these taxes represented considerable taxing power, towns could tax only as permitted by the province. As part of the rationalization of the administrative system inherited from the Territorial years, Alberta established the Department of Municipal Affairs in 1912 to oversee certain aspects of local government. It also enacted the *Town Act* and the *Village Act* which required that the financial records of towns and villages be audited, leading one scholar to conclude that the new legislation "limited the autonomy of local authorities only in so far as their bookkeeping and records were involved."[44] In fact, local autonomy was profoundly affected because the legislation radically changed the tax system. The single tax system was made mandatory, and all other taxes, including poll and business taxes, were abolished.[45] This was designed to stimulate building and reduce the amount of raw land held for speculation. Since all land was now taxed on the same basis, landowners would, in theory, eagerly improve raw land by putting up buildings that could be sold or rented, without triggering a tax increase. At the same time, the legislation placed a ceiling on the mill rate. These changes reduced taxation on property with the most valuable buildings, namely the main street. And even though this property was still assessed at a higher rate because of its greater land value, the ceiling on the mill rate limited the taxes. Given the well-known and sizeable tax arrears of most towns, and the even greater debenture debt, support for any decrease in taxation should have been cautious indeed. Yet many urban governments in Alberta were enthusiastic proponents of this system, as was Premier Sifton.

The single tax, while possessing a certain logic, was in practice disastrous. Its proponents refused to believe that speculation in raw land was often an end in itself, that land values were inflated by speculation, and that levels of debt carried by most towns were extremely high. These problems were compounded by a collapse of real estate values in 1912. By 1913, tax arrears were even higher, and towns began to object to the single tax system that they had so recently welcomed. Some began ignoring the ceiling on the mill rate, others began levying taxes on improvements, and yet others increased the assessed value of land in efforts to increase revenue.[46]

Towns had few options since the market for their debentures was very weak—nor could they sell the huge amounts of raw land continually being forfeited for nonpayment of taxes. As a result, cutting costs became a major concern. Expensive capital projects like Fort Macleod's town hall were dropped, and while most towns added piece-meal to their sewage and water systems, major expansions were cancelled or postponed. Operating costs were cut as well. Because 40 percent of the 1913 taxes and "a considerable portion" of the 1912 taxes were owing, Blairmore fired its policeman. Reflecting the quandary of local government finance, this measure brought only minor immediate savings which had to be weighed against its cost. Since fines levied by the mounted police were paid to the provincial treasury while those levied by town police went to the town, Blairmore was "naturally anxious" to collect what revenue it could, and by mid 1915 it rehired a police officer to enforce town bylaws.[47]

A particular concern was collecting accounts in arrears. Utility arrears represented one challenge, and in 1913, Claresholm had over $1,100 in unpaid water and light accounts. These were mostly small amounts, but the town was in such difficult straits that it could not honour its payroll until the accounts were paid.[48] Property tax arrears were a thornier problem. In Fort Macleod, only between 35 and 40 percent of property taxes in 1914 were paid. Commonly, these high arrears were blamed on absentee land owners, but as the Blairmore town council noted in 1916, "some of our most prominent citizens" were not "paying a cent." In fact, both residents and nonresidents often had high arrears. In Peace River, for example, about half the total arrears of $27,500 in 1918 represented only six accounts, made up of absentee and resident landholders, land companies and the ED&BC railway. At the 1919 year end, Blairmore had just over $31,000 in tax arrears, and of the 1919 levy of about $16,000, less than half had been collected.[49] Town councils were reluctant to alienate townsfolk by seizing property for tax arrears, which, in any case, was often a complex, lengthy and expensive process. Most towns quickly found themselves with more forfeited land than they could deal with, and more of it would not solve their need for cash.[50]

In light of such problems, towns had to find alternate sources of revenue. In 1914, local governments in Alberta tried to increase their income by claiming a percentage of the license fees and fines collected by the province in their communities. This attempt to raid provincial sources of revenue failed, but it marked an effort to gain greater taxing powers.[51] More practically, it was obvious that the tax system needed reform. Although Premier Sifton continued to defend the single tax system, by 1913 the province amended its legislation to allow towns to collect additional taxes, including poll and business taxes, and abolished the ceiling on tax rates in towns and raised it in villages. Thus, hated as they were by merchants, many towns brought in business taxes. Fort Macleod instituted one in 1915. While first set at 10 percent of rental value, it was subsequently lowered to 5 percent. Even so, it was still "bitterly opposed" by merchants who argued that they already paid too much tax. The council countered that business had to pay "something extra at least" to maintain the fire brigade whose efficiency had helped lower their insurance rates.[52] Blairmore introduced a business tax in 1917, as did Drumheller in 1919. As with other taxes, collection was a problem. In 1917 Blairmore collected only $178 of that year's business tax levy of $1,690.

Similarly, poll taxes were reimposed. In 1913, Blairmore and Coleman discussed implementing a poll tax. Blairmore expected to gain $2,000 from it, but it was recognized that both towns, so close together, needed identical tax systems to prevent the movement of people from the town with the tax to the one without it. These negotiations failed, but the matter was raised again in 1917. A poll tax was needed because, as was observed in Blairmore, "some of the pioneers and original 'land grabbers' cannot, or will not," pay their property taxes.[53] Poll taxes were also said to be fair because they spread the tax burden among all citizens. By 1920, most of the towns studied assessed a poll tax, or, as it was called in the Crowsnest Pass, an "educational tax."

Further amendments to the province's town legislation broadened the tax base by restoring the taxation of improvements. The single tax became optional in 1916 and was abolished entirely in the early 1920s.[54] Increased mill rates were also brought in. In 1921 the rate in Claresholm was increased by 10 mills, and while the town council had been elected on a promise of lower taxes, conditions were so bad that higher rates were needed or "another year like the present one and Claresholm will be forced to add its name to the list of towns already in the hands of the receiver."[55]

The changing methods of taxation from 1913 until 1920 created precedents for the operation of local government finance in the interwar years. Minor revenues, such as dog taxes, were vigorously collected—in 1929 the Drumheller town policeman went "house to house" searching for unlicensed dogs.[56] Business taxes remained common in the interwar years, and by the late 1930s, most Alberta towns had imposed them, although high arrears were typical. In Drumheller, for example, business tax arrears amounted to about $6,000 by 1931.[57] Poll taxes continued in use, especially in mining towns. In Blairmore, the poll tax produced about $1,000 in 1925. In Drumheller too, it had become an "important source of revenue for the town" by the late 1920s. In 1930, the town unsuccessfully attempted to have it raised from $4 to $6, a proposal the United Mine Workers of America opposed. Noting that most single mine workers spent much of their wages in Drumheller, it argued that they already contributed to the local economy. An increase in the poll tax was merely a ruse "to relieve property owners at the expense of single men." As for married men, it charged that since most paid "exorbitant rent," any increase in the poll tax should be matched with rent controls.[58]

In Drumheller, property taxes rose steadily. The mayor claimed in 1932 that taxes had increased to prohibitive levels in the previous decade, even doubling in some cases.[59] They continued to increase, reaching 60 mills in 1935. This rate was maintained until 1940, making Drumheller one of the most highly taxed cities in Canada. Even then, it ran a deficit of $12,000, but the council dared not ask for yet higher rates.[60] So too, property tax arrears continued to be a problem. In many cases, individual homeowners often had little or no cash with which to pay their taxes. These problems were particularly acute in the 1930s. One popular solution was to allow people to work off tax arrears. In 1936, Cardston allowed credit on tax arrears in return for labour in constructing a water reservoir for the town.[61] Drumheller had also instituted a similar scheme in 1933 whereby tax defaulters could work for the city to reduce tax and utility arrears. The programme was so popular that the city was forced to cancel it after running out of work projects. The next year, tax collections were even poorer, and it was intimated that people who were short of cash were opting instead to let taxes go into arrears in the hope of working them off and keeping their cash for other necessities.[62]

Local initiatives to meet the financial troubles facing towns were only part of the attempts to solve the financial crises faced by local governments during the 35 years following the collapse of 1912–13. The province also began tightening its control over local governments. Between 1913 and 1920, it established province-wide boards and commissions in an effort to cope with the problems of municipal finance. Among the most important was the Board of Public Utility Commissioners, an independent agency set up by the Department of Municipal Affairs. Established in 1915, it regulated all utility rates and approved the issue and repayment of municipal debt.[63] By 1920, further control came from the Municipal Finances Commission which had the power "to scrutinize expenditures, to revise tax and utility rates, and to supervise the financial management" of towns in financial trouble. It also negotiated with bondholders to reorganize debt repayments.[64] In the worst cases, pre World War I debenture debt was rescheduled so that at least some payment could be made. A number of Alberta towns came under the supervision of the Municipal Finances Commission. Fort Macleod did so in 1922, and for several years the Commission directed the town's finances and rescheduled its massive debt.[65] The Assessment Equalization Board was another provincial agency that dealt with the financial workings of towns. The centralization that these developments represented was necessary because of the gravity of the financial difficulties facing many towns, and they were said to be the true "beginning of the right of the Department of Municipal Affairs to step in and manage the affairs of a local authority when these got out of hand."[66]

This erosion of local government autonomy was confirmed through legislation passed in 1935 by the UFA government. Enacted against the backdrop of the extreme conditions created by the Depression, this legislation unequivocally made towns the wards of the provincial government. Under the *Department of Municipal Affairs Amendment Act*, the minister in certain circumstances gained the right to dismiss a town council and call for the election of replacements, remove town officers and appoint new ones, and "appoint an official administrator with powers of a council." And reflecting ongoing concerns about financing local government, under the *Alberta Municipal Assessment Commission Act*, the province was empowered to establish uniform assessments of land, buildings and improvements in urban areas and of land in rural areas. This act "struck at the very heart of local government finance" since the Commission had power to "hear and determine all appeals on assessments from a court of revision set up under the various local authority acts," establish "equalized assessments for all municipalities," and recommend to the Minister standards and methods of assessment that could be applied "province-wide."[67]

In addition, financial contributions by senior governments began to appear in the interwar years. At times of persistently high unemployment, many towns, even before 1920, had received some assistance from the provincial or federal governments to help meet their welfare obligations. These programmes often had stipulations designed to prevent abuse and reduce costs, and represented yet another erosion of local authority.[68] By 1931, many of these senior government programmes were ongoing because of the welfare problems most towns faced due to the Depression.

The tightening of provincial control over local government in Alberta had not occurred in a vacuum. The financial problems towns faced after 1912–13 resulted in part from their restricted tax base, which had been limited further by the province's imposition of the single tax system. Yet, local governments had endorsed and welcomed this system, which appeared irresistibly attractive during the speculative fever that gripped western Canada. Further abetted by the booster ethos that dominated their thinking, town councils fell easily into an uncritical optimism. Assuming that the economic boom would never end, they made decisions that seemed negligent to some contemporary critics, but now appear absurd. In any case, the combination of an insufficient revenue base with a parochial understanding of their own place in the national and provincial economy meant that the ability of towns to shape their own destiny was inherently limited. The attraction of the booster rhetoric about the possibility of unlimited growth and self-control over the economic future further ensured that town councils were poorly equipped to cope with events that lay beyond their control. For local authorities, the consequence was predictable: having proven their inability to conduct themselves reasonably, the province assumed more and more direct control. By the end of the 1930s, this helped to bring the finances of most towns under control. The economic boom that came with World War II and then with postwar oil discoveries, and the increased willingness by the province and the federal government to make direct grants to local governments, meant that the crisis that had begun in 1912–13 had been surmounted and largely forgotten by the 1950s.

4

SHAPING

LOCAL

PRIORITIES

Every town had a board of trade at one time or another. Each also had a newspaper. Both agencies represented different aspects of an effort to promote town economic growth and to link the town with outside events and forces. Each also expressed values about town life. Boards of trade were voluntary bodies that tried to support local business and encourage economic growth. Often seeing themselves as a form of local government parallel to the town council, they acted as the self-appointed voice of town business ambitions and as teachers of the civic virtues endorsed by business. In some respects, they aimed to build a community that accepted the values of the business class. After World War I, they became more concerned with a wider range of social issues, although their central concern remained the health of the local economy and the entrenchment of business leadership of the community. Newspapers too saw promotion as part of their function, but their role in town culture was always more complex because they expressed not only commercial objectives but broader social and cultural ones as well.

BOARDS *of* TRADE

Although historians have ranked boards of trade as important forces in Canadian city development, their significance in smaller centres has been less commonly recognized.[1] The earliest boards of trade in Canada appeared in the early 1800s, but their number increased dramatically in the late nineteenth century. All were dedicated to promoting economic growth. Motivated by a belief that "what was good for business was best for the community," they were initially concerned with transportation developments to "widen or protect their trading hinterlands." These priorities subsequently broadened to include attracting industry and government institutions to enhance the local economy. They also aimed to "reinforce the loyalty of the citizens to their community" and, after 1900, promoted civic reform to stimulate civic efficiency and project a progressive town image.[2] Where establishment of a board of trade preceded incorporation as a village, such as in Fort Macleod in the late 1880s and in Coleman between 1903 and 1907, they also served as a substitute for local urban government, organizing street cleaning and even attempting to promote the district to settlers and investors.[3] And their role in local government did not disappear with a centre's incorporation. In southern and central Alberta before 1920, they often prepared, in conjunction with town councils, advertising material about the town and district in an effort to attract services, industry, investment, and settlers. They also defended merchants against transient traders and catalogue competition, and promoted better transportation services to stimulate economic growth. In this sense, they created an interface between the town and the outside world. As well, they were commonly involved in more purely local concerns; in villages, they lobbied for incorporation as a town to facilitate the installation of utilities, and worked for lower fire insurance rates and street and sidewalk improvements.

These concerns reflected the needs of business, which boards of trade typically defined as civic welfare. In 1910, the *Cardston Alberta Star* noted that despite public ignorance of the function of a board of trade, it was "just as much a necessity as a town council" because it defended the interests of local business and the district generally. It had important functions "peculiarly its own which usually are outside the functions of political parties or town councils." As a public service and an element in local self-government, the ideal of the board of trade was to link together the citizens and the town council and to speak as "the voice of the ratepayers." Thus, the board of trade was seen as nonpartisan, democratic, and representative of community interests; similar in theory to the ideals that inspired local politics. It was an ideal of enlightened self-interest. As the Cardston board observed in 1913, its members worked for the good of the community "at the same time we are working for ourselves and those nearest and dearest to us."[4]

These beliefs were manifested in various ways before World War I. In Lacombe, an identity of purpose between the town and its board of trade was demonstrated in the co-ordination of their advertising programmes designed to attract settlers and industry. In 1914 Drumheller's board of trade carried out projects on behalf of the town council, thus indirectly shaping the town's priorities and policies. It took the census of the village and also investigated and prepared guidelines on a utility franchise. In 1919, it corresponded and negotiated with provincial authorities about Drumheller's participation in the federal housing scheme—a programme which would have brought financial and town planning obligations to the town.[5] In still other cases, as at Drumheller and Cardston, boards of trade performed actual local government functions such as road maintenance and snow ploughing to draw shoppers to town.[6]

In addition, boards of trade saw themselves as formative in shaping town culture. Faith in positive thinking and loyalty to the town, doctrines central in the booster ideal of town life, were often seen as special board of trade concerns. As noted in Claresholm in 1913, "the board of trade should keep burning in the hearts of the citizens of this town the loyalty and courage that inevitably dies unless constantly rekindled." By organizing such "fighting units," a strong "force for the offense and the defensive" could be maintained.[7] This nurturing of town virtues applied to average citizens and business owners alike. It seemed that some business people were not innately town boosters and needed to develop "a thinking, reasoning loyalty to the town." Sometimes town councils too had to be reminded of booster manners; the Fort Macleod board of trade criticized the town council in 1914 for its "gloomy views and pessimistic remarks" about the economy. In such ways, boards of trade aimed to promote, what in Grande Prairie in 1917 was called, "organized optomism [sic]." As the *Macleod Gazette* argued in 1901, while the people of the town needed "a certain amount of bracing up, a tonic as it were," they were not "unenterprising and lacking in public spirit," needing only "directing" and "concentration of purpose" through a board of trade.[8]

These objectives and programmes often earned boards of trade financial support from the town. The Lacombe board received a $500 grant in 1909 to assist its work. As was remarked in Cardston, such subsidies were a mark of "family pride." The board was said not to be a mere charity that should have to beg for money. It looked after the town's interests, and "it is up to everyone to either make or mend everything within our gates or take our share of the blame for any failings."[9] The Cardston board received a grant of $200 in 1912, a sizeable amount considering that the town spent less than $400 on health and relief the same year. When the grant was suspended in 1913 because of hard times, the board invoked the commonly made argument that it was not a sectoral organization, but a public service that would now have to be supported "practically upon the charity of the businessmen along main street."[10]

Boards of trade were not consistently successful before 1920. Most went through a period of initial enthusiasm, then staggered, and finally collapsed from apathy. Often, the middle stage was marked by all of the work falling "on the shoulders of a few conscientious ones whose ardor" soon cooled when they found the burden too heavy. Following a hiatus, often of several years, the board was re-established, and sometimes this process was repeated several times. This was said to be typical everywhere on the prairies.[11] This instability was often tied to general economic conditions. Although it has been argued by some historians that boards of trade were creators of economic growth,[12] in small town Alberta they were more often the byproduct of economic growth and optimism. Conversely, tough economic times were often hard on them, and by 1912–13, the boards in Cardston, Claresholm and Fort Macleod were all in trouble.

In addition to general economic conditions, a number of other factors had a negative impact on boards of trade. Since boards of trade often saw promotion as the realization of self-initiative, a circular definition of success was created in which the mere act of lobbying or advertising became an accomplishment. Boards of trade were also weakened by a tendency to take credit for developments they did not bring about, and a penchant for exaggerated rhetoric. The Lacombe board's promise during its 1913 membership drive that "for every dollar paid we will return one hundred dollars in the increased value of your property and in the increase of your business" likely created little public faith in the organization. While such exaggeration was more common in the boom years before World War I, it was a habit hard to shake. The *Drumheller Mail* editorialized in 1931 that the local board of trade was "no longer even a mutual admiration society" but only "an atrophied member of the body politic." Although its accomplishments in the year had been "nil," a "ponderous tome will be laid before the membership in which a colorful account of progress will appear."[13]

More importantly, many boards of trade failed to attract a balanced membership. While the first board of trade in Peace River in 1912 encompassed all the business owners in the town, this did not last. Although boards often represented only business interests, this focus was sometimes narrowed even further by a board's domination by special interest groups. For example, the board of trade in Fort Macleod was taken over by realtors during a time of intense real estate speculation in 1911. It had been inactive, but the newly formed Macleod Real Estate Association organized a meeting for "revitalizing" and "converting" the board into "a more efficient instrument to promote the town's interests." The town's mayor supported this development, even advising the new board to ask the town for a grant. The request was successful, and over the year the board received grants totalling over $2,300, a clear signal of both the town council's priorities and realtors' influence. Realtors also captured the Cardston board of trade in the same year, and although many business owners belonged to the board, they were "not sufficiently interested" in the organization to challenge this development.[14]

Such events were damaging because there was much public suspicion about the motives of real estate promoters during the boom years. In Cardston in 1913 street gossip had it that the president of the local board of trade, a realtor, benefited unfairly from his position on the board by directing inquiries about real estate to his own firm. Indeed, some "prominent citizens" believed that a realtor should not even be on the executive of the board of trade. Thus, the president of the Lacombe board of trade insisted in 1913 that those inquiring about subdivided land in the town be told the truth about falling land values, even though land promoters would whine that this was "knocking the town."[15] Such concerns led to proposals that the board of trade set up an office where the public could obtain information about the town and district. [16] A few boards hired promotional agents (usually called a "publicity man"), who worked exclusively to promote the town, but most had only an office and a secretary who was paid an honorarium.

These tactics were rarely successful for long; speculation was too seductive and too central in the economic system to be so easily controlled. In Peace River, the board of trade came under the control of oil promoters during the early 1920s. In 1922 it censured its secretary for telling a correspondent that stock in a firm involved in local oil exploration was speculative and ordered that all future inquiries be handled by the board's "oil committee" so that the "stability of oil companies will receive every encouragement." Revealing significant rifts within the town's business community, this move by the "oil slate" was disastrous for the board of trade. Since most business owners refused to pay membership fees to support "the wildcat boomsters," membership dropped and the board temporarily collapsed.[17]

The need for a balanced membership did not refer only to town businesses. In agricultural service towns, boards of trade invariably claimed that they spoke for both town and country and that they recognized the importance of farmer participation in town affairs, especially in the board of trade. Nevertheless, such membership was often limited. While the Fort Macleod board of trade in 1888 had included ranchers and farmers, this balance was soon lost and was not regained until after World War I. In 1929, the Cardston board of trade, which aimed "to create a feeling of fellowship" between town and country, had 111 members, all but four of whom were townspeople. And the board of trade in Peace River in 1940 could not attract any local farmers although it made frequent statements about agriculture and tried to encourage farm members with a special low membership fee. In Drumheller, where agriculture was an important local industry, a farmer was not elected president of the board until 1939. In some cases, however, especially after World War I, farmers did participate in boards of trade. By 1941 the Fort Macleod board of trade had an extraordinary 268 members, of whom 167 were from out of town, and the Lacombe board of trade and the Claresholm Men's Club (its board of trade) also had a significant number of farm members.[18]

The increased presence of farm members on town boards of trade in the interwar years was reflective of basic changes taking place in town life. Elizabeth Bloomfield, in her study of the history of Canadian boards of trade, contends that as a result of the "loss of decision-making power by small communities, as well as changed perceptions" of their effectiveness, boards of trade came to involve fewer wealthy business people and community leaders after World War I. As senior governments exercised more control over local government, and growth of chain stores led to a decline in the number of independent businesses, boards of trade became "less concerned with public policies" than with recreational and social services to members.[19] While boards of trade before World War I had occasionally been involved with building parks and other amenities, these activities were usually only an adjunct to real estate promotion. It was assumed that civic life and pride were built through economic growth and by language stressing community loyalty. By the end of World War I, however, social activities had come to be seen as one solution to the apathy and divisiveness that so often brought boards of trade to crisis.

Once the settlement period had ended, and especially after World War I when it was recognized that major industries were not going to set up in their towns, most boards of trade in southern and central Alberta shifted their attention to social issues. Since there was not enough for a board of trade to do in small agricultural service towns, it was concluded that such an emphasis could give the organization vitality and keep it intact. Thus, they brought in speakers and worked on projects such as building swimming pools, sport facilities and playgrounds, and sponsoring children's events and organizations like the Boy Scouts. These projects often were justified on economic grounds, but they also expressed a changed sense of community, which perhaps arose from the challenge raised by service clubs that were beginning by the interwar years to appear in most towns. By the late 1920s the Lacombe board of trade, demonstrating a union of country and town, was holding an annual banquet at which the district's "champions" in farming, sports, school, culture, and business were honoured. This was a significant change from pre war board of trade activities. In its statement of objectives in 1928, the Grande Prairie board of trade stated that it aimed to provide liaison with the outside world, serve as a clearing house for all community activities, and act as the focus for building community spirit.[20] While there was no mention of business needs, they remained important. Earlier concerns with economic growth were now expressed through programmes to encourage tourism, attract government services, promote the town's mercantile health, and encourage highway improvement and agricultural stabilization.

While involvement in community social issues was greatest in southern and central Alberta boards of trade, those in the Peace River district, where settlement was underway, were still largely involved in advertising and encouraging industry and settlement, just as boards had been in the south during the major settlement phase. They did, however, feature some social and entertainment activities. By 1922, board of trade meetings in Grande Prairie were organized as luncheons with songs and skits as well as board business. Meetings lasted two hours, and though "considerable" of this time was spent in "merry making," much business was also accomplished. These activities suggest that the parameters of activity for boards of trade had changed everywhere by this time and were not only the byproduct of a community's stage of development.[21]

These changing goals and activities were demonstrated clearly in Claresholm. There, the board of trade had an uneven history before the 1930s, but in 1934 a combined service club and board of trade was formed with "greater emphasis on the social side" than on board of trade issues. Since the new organization hoped to represent both town and country, it avoided calling itself a board of trade, a term traditionally associated with town affairs. Instead it took "the very neutral name of Men's Club." In the following decade, it successfully combined social functions and an interest in community projects with traditional board of trade concerns about roads, business and the economy. The club dealt with freight rates, highway improvement, marketing of agricultural products, and local business promotion, and, during World War II, it built a recreational hall for airmen stationed in the town. As well, it furnished a ward in the Claresholm hospital, sponsored grain shows, brought in speakers, gave funds to the library, built a paddling pool and raised money for a swimming pool. Funds were raised through amateur concerts and a carnival.[22]

Carnivals were a popular fund raising technique used by service clubs, but more than just the style of the service club was being copied. The model itself was being used, and boards of trade and service clubs often had a close relationship. Yet, the move during the interwar years to social concerns and a broader membership base was a reworking, not an abandonment, of booster ideals and business priorities. Boards of trade continued to endorse the prewar booster faith in self-help, self-initiative and positive thinking. Because of their publicity, economic development and road programmes, some boards continued to receive annual grants from the town.[23] They continued to speak for and promote business interests, and part of their educational effort in this direction was sponsorship of junior boards of trade, or junior chambers of commerce, for those 18 to 30 years of age. These organizations were designed to tranfer the values of the earlier generation to the upcoming one. A junior chamber of commerce was formed in Lacombe in 1936 and at its first annual banquet, the new organization was lauded for building up "executive ability" and teaching business practices to the young.[24]

ASSOCIATED BOARDS *of* TRADE

The wider focus of boards of trade during the interwar years was paralleled by an increased integration of town boards of trade into national and provincial organizations. This was an important change over earlier times when they had been largely autonomous and local. In the earlier period, the assumption that towns were locked in a merciless competition for trade, industry, and population, when coupled with the belief that a town was successful only in proportion to the personal initiative and community co-operation shown by its citizens, had often acted as a barrier to the creation of federated boards of trade.

Even so, efforts were made to form associated boards of trade that could speak systematically on district and regional issues. Among the earliest was the unsuccessful attempt by the Calgary board of trade in 1904 to organize an association of all boards of trade in the Northwest Territories and eastern British Columbia.[25] More modest in scale was the Associate Boards of Trade of Southern Alberta, first established in 1908. Although it quickly fell apart, it was re-established in 1911 with about 20 member boards, giving it a broad clientele throughout the territory south of the CPR mainline. Headquartered in Lethbridge, its objective was "to look after and advance the interests of Southern Alberta." It expressed a "desire to boom Southern Alberta," as well as more particular concerns such as hail insurance and lobbying for a national highway across the prairies from Winnipeg. The organization was soon torn by dissention; Taber and Fort Macleod withdrew, ostensibly because the association hired a secretary instead of using a volunteer, but the dissent more likely was fuelled by resentment over Lethbridge's dominance of the organization.[26] It was moribund by World War I, although another organization of the same name appeared for a time in the late 1920s.

In contrast to such broad federations, single issue organizations were more successful. Some were organized to promote a single event, such as the "Settle the South Conference" organized by the Lethbridge board of trade in 1926. With members drawn from a number of local boards of trade, the project tried to co-ordinate the promotion of immigration to southern Alberta. Others were formed with long-term goals, although still of a relatively narrow focus. In the early 1920s, the Tourist Association of South Eastern British Columbia and Alberta was formed to stimulate tourism by promoting joint board of trade programmes for distribution of maps and tourist literature. Similarly, the Foothills Group of Associated Boards of Trade was formed in 1937 with nine members. While having a number of district concerns, its primary objective was to lobby the provincial government to hardsurface the highway between Calgary and the United States border. It also attempted to fight the rerouting of highways away from main street (then a theory popular among town planners) to ensure that tourist traffic would benefit main street businesses.[27]

In contrast to the single issue organizations and approaches in southern Alberta, a somewhat different pattern emerged in the Peace River country where a greater sense of isolation and distinctiveness created greater unity. An associated board of trade for the Peace River country was formed in 1921, but it did not last. Greater success attended the organization in the late 1920s of another district association to deal with issues common to the area. Such an organization, it was said, was in keeping with the spirit of the age: "when men of capital, men of industry and labor men speak today, they do not speak as individuals but through their respective organizations. This is the modern and effective way of doing business, a system that is here to stay." In 1931, these sentiments led to the formation of the General Council of Associated Peace River Boards of Trade. Copying precedents from Saskatchewan and Ontario, the organization was formed upon the initiative of the Beaverlodge board of trade and included boards in both the Alberta and British Columbia sections of the region. The council's constitution recognized the delicacy of an organization made up of potentially competing towns. To ensure that there was "no coercion...nor any swamping of minority opinion by majority vote," it took a public stand only when there was unanimous approval. Otherwise, it acted simply as a liaison committee to pass information to member boards which could then take independent action. The overall objective was "to promote good will between districts" because "nothing is commoner than for neighbouring towns to develop towards each other a petty, bickering spirit of jealousy."[28]

The general council was a success. There was a willingness to cooperate and, more importantly, a recognition that individual and district needs were part of wider issues affecting the whole Peace River region, regardless of provincial boundaries. The association's primary concern was transportation—especially the building of a railway to the Pacific coast—but it also was concerned with general matters such as flood control, highways, and agricultural problems unique to an isolated frontier area. In 1947 it entered a new phase. Reflecting the large territory it represented, three district councils were organized to represent more localized needs at the General Council.[29]

Peace River was unique in the success of its district board of trade. Indeed, until the late 1930s, attempts to form a provincial association were singularly unsuccessful. In 1920, the Associated Boards of Trade and Chambers of Commerce was established in Edmonton with the goal of creating a unified approach on legislation affecting business, promotion of highway improvement, co-operation between agriculture and commercial enterprises, and development of "community spirit and good citizenship within Alberta." Although some towns were interested in joining, it did not find sufficient support to continue.[30] It did, however, represent an emerging trend. By the 1930s, provincial and national organizations were beginning to play an important part in co-ordinating board of trade activities and defining their concerns. It appears that organizations with the broadest geographical scope had the greatest chance for success, perhaps because they avoided local entanglements and rivalries. The Canadian Chamber of Commerce was formed in 1927 and rapidly became an influential national force, recommending national policies and programmes and keeping an eye on government affairs to prevent the enactment of legislation detrimental to business. Yet, its policies did not always find support. In the early 1930s, for example, its emphasis on reduction of government expenditures, as a means of coping with the Depression, was considered by the Peace River Associated Boards of Trade as "ill advised" and a harsh misreading of the cause of the Depression. Nevertheless, by the end of World War II it had become an influential national group with 340 member boards. It provided guidelines for effective organization of chambers of commerce, advised on the role such groups should play in their communities, and urged co-operation among district boards of trade as well as provincial and national ones.[31]

At the same time that this national focus was developing, a provincial one was also beginning to emerge. In 1938 the Edmonton chamber of commerce spearheaded the formation of the Alberta Board of Trade and Agriculture. While its provincial focus arose largely from the economic challenge of the Depression, it also was responding to other "unsettled conditions," which referred directly to the policies of Alberta's Social Credit government.[32] Edmonton's board attempted to enlist boards of trade in smaller centres to support its political and economic concerns, and speakers from city boards of trade addressed town board of trade meetings with an increasingly partisan message. The Edmonton board launched a province-wide campaign against the government and asked town boards of trade to support its legal and political challenges to Social Credit's debt and monetary legislation. Although this did not meet resistance in most towns, it was not always welcome, and some concern was expressed about the increasing political partisanship that was infusing boards of trade.[33]

By the end of World War II, the policies of Social Credit had changed sufficiently that it was no longer seen as a threat to business. Instead, left wing parties like the CCF were characterized as the primary threat. Like the movement against Social Credit, this concern was often expressed by city groups which gained access to townfolk through the local board of trade. Their increasingly important role in shaping town opinion was demonstrated by a series of speeches given in Grande Prairie in 1947. In one speech, a representative of the Edmonton chamber of commerce gave the Grande Prairie board of trade a "solemn warning" about "the threat to our democratic way of life." The speaker saw "no difference between Communism and Socialism, both were for government ownership, operation and control of distribution and financing. This could only end in dictatorship." Since the Canadian Chamber of Commerce soon planned to publish a book on "communistic activity in Canada," he "urged all to read it." In a second speech, a representative of the Canadian Chamber of Commerce warned again of the same "forces that are at work in Canada seeking to destroy our democratic way of life and Canadian enterprise system." Such threats could "best be combatted by positive leadership in each community by the boards of trade and by co-operating with similar organizations through membership in the Canadian Chamber of Commerce." In yet another speech, the president of the Grande Prairie board of trade contended that a changed role for government was a threat to business. He observed that it was a "right of free citizens to conduct their own business. We disagree that governments have the right to set up businesses in competition which are tax free." Since "chambers of commerce help to further free enterprise," he contended that boards of trade at both a national and local level should fight such developments.[34] In part, these speeches were techniques of recruitment—they pointed to dangers that membership in the organization could theoretically combat, while simultaneously expressing the social and political views of business.

NEWSPAPERS *and*
TOWN PROMOTION

The first town newspaper in what would become Alberta (and the third to be set up in the Northwest Territories) was the *Macleod Gazette,* established in 1882. Cardston's first paper appeared in 1898, while Claresholm had a paper by 1904 and Drumheller had two by 1918. As elsewhere on the prairies, these newspapers were operating within a few years of the first white settlement, usually predating the incorporation of the town or village.[35] Most were modest weeklies, with the first page and usually three additional pages containing local news, advertisements, and a limited amount of provincial and national news. The balance was boiler plate or, as it was also called, "ready print" material. Printed elsewhere, it often differed in type face from the rest of the paper. It carried general articles about world news, nature, and sometimes serialized stories, as well as advertisements for nationally available products, especially patent medicines.

Boiler plate material was unpopular with editors. In 1910, the *Macleod Gazette* proudly announced that it was dropping it in favour of local news and advertisements, which demonstrated both the paper's success and that of the town. But the experiment did not last; sure signs of financial difficulty soon were in evidence; boiler plate pages had reappeared, and the same syndicated article was being run more than once. By the 1920s, boiler plate material had disappeared for good from Alberta newspapers. A great deal of syndicated material, especially national and international news, was still used, but it was now usually set in the same type as the rest of the paper. Other nonlocal material included comics and wire service photos. The *Grande Prairie Herald* dropped boiler plate in 1926, replacing it with local news and syndicated material chosen by the editor. This was both less expensive and more popular since the boiler plate material was often stale by the time it was printed. Moreover, it was sometimes said to be "inimical to the interests of the Peace River country," a clear indication of the paper's ambition to express local priorities.[36]

Such local character was significant in a newspapers' appeal, and almost all were owned by individuals resident in the town. A few were owned by joint stock companies or groups such as the Alberta Stake of Zion which owned the paper in Cardston for a time before World War I.

| *Since the newspaper in Peace River was established in 1914 before the railway reached town, transporting the heavy presses was a difficult task. Archives Collection, A5458, PAA.*

| *The press of the first newspaper in Peace River in 1914 was run by an ordinary steam traction engine. Archives Collection, A5459, PAA.*

Paralleling other business activity, a newspaper was often established in one town, only to be moved elsewhere to seize emerging opportunities. In the Drumheller Valley, a paper was established at Munson in 1905, but, reflecting Drumheller's development, the paper moved there in 1913. Similarly, Walter Bartlett, who owned the Frank newspaper, moved to Blairmore in 1910 when it became apparent that Blairmore had become the major centre of the Pass.[37] Indeed, the transfer of a newspaper from one town to another was an important indication of town growth or decline.

Like any other business, newspapers existed to make money for their owners. But they were a special type of business. Like city newspapers, they served important and unique functions in promoting the town and in providing news, commentary, and entertainment. Although these broad functions were inseparable, emphasis on a particular function varied with each paper's editor. Many often argued that the newspaper's first duty was to provide news and that promotion of the district was secondary.[38] Nonetheless, boards of trade saw newspapers largely as town promoters. For example, the Fort Macleod board of trade argued in 1923 that a newspaper was important as a vehicle for local advertising and for enhancing the town's status and image as an urban place.[39]

Such attitudes shaped the fortunes of some newspapers. In 1913, the *Claresholm Review* noted that most towns were too small to warrant having a newspaper. However, "the petty jealousies" among towns made it impossible for "one paper to serve a reasonable district, because business men will not give patronage to a paper published anywhere except in their own hamlet. They will leave no stone unturned to get a paper of their own started and want the best brains and equipment in the land." This connection between boosterism and newspapers was sometimes demonstrated in small but significant ways. The *Cardston News*, established in 1925 by four local business men, renumbered its publication to volume 28 a year after its founding. This was intended to show that there had been a newspaper in the town since 1898 (though it had not been the *News*) and that Cardston was well established. On the surface, this was a specious bit of boosterism, but it demonstrated the view that the local newspaper should function as a town promoter.[40]

This, as well as the need for revenue, led many owners to justify their newspapers as advertising mediums. In 1916 the *Claresholm Review Advertiser* observed that "if the local paper serves any purpose at all, it is as a medium of information between the town and country, between the merchant and his customer or prospective customer."[41] In 1918 the mast-head of the *Drumheller Review* carried the slogan "Best Advertiser in the District." While newspapers often claimed that advertising made a vital contribution to the town's economy by increasing patronage of local business, it was simply an economic necessity. Subscription rates remained at approximately $2 per year from 1882 until World War II. Further, circulation was relatively low. In 1936, the *Drumheller Mail* sold about 1,000 copies per week, mostly within a 20 to 30 mile radius of the town. This was probably the highest circulation of any paper in the towns studied; by contrast, the *Claresholm Local Press* had only 300 sub-scriptions as late as 1942.[42] Even then, payment was often difficult to collect, and one of the commonest pleas of editors over the years was for subscribers to pay their accounts.

Since delinquent subscribers were often kept on mailing lists to justify higher advertising rates, advertisers naturally saw prepaid subscriptions as the best measure of circulation. While most papers in the 1920s aimed for 100 percent paid in advance circulation, this was impossible to secure. After World War II, however, most town newspapers used this system because it was easier to manage and was more insistently demanded by advertising agencies.[43] During the interwar years, circula-tion campaigns were popular. Usually arranged by outside agencies, prizes were awarded for the highest number of new subscriptions sold by a contestant. Greatest reward was given to those who secured paid in advance subscriptions for up to five years, and the prizes were often spectacular for the times: diamond jewellery, trips to places like California, a car, and cash.[44] Though they were popular methods for increasing circulation, some contended that the result was not the "qual-ity" circulation of established readership, and advertisers were naturally suspicious of "spectacular 'jumps' [in circulation] accompanied by increased advertising rates."[45]

Advertising followed various formats. Flyers had become popular by the interwar years, especially in the grocery trade, and were usually printed by the local newspaper. Calendars for store give-aways at Christmas or New Year were popular in the nineteenth century and had become a staple advertising feature of small business by World War II. These "useful and artistic bits of paste board" came in standard designs on which the local press printed the name of the business.[46] More impor-tant was regular weekly advertising in the newspaper, and all papers printed continual advice about its value. Much of this was self-serving, especially since advertising was the first expense businesses cut when money was short. In 1917 the *Cardston Globe* suspended publication because of a lack of advertising revenue, and such problems were compounded in towns where two or more papers split the market. When one paper closed, as invariably happened, advertising in the remaining one increased. This was the case in Claresholm in 1916 when the *Review* (established 1904) amalgamated with the *Advertiser* (established 1914), and the same process was repeated in 1928 when the *Review Advertiser* was absorbed by its new rival, the *Local Press*.

Arguments in favour of the value of advertising built upon the booster ethos that claimed that business success resulted from self-initiative. Treated as a form of self-help, advertising was thus not merely a business practice but became a confirmation of ideology. Newspapers often used blunt tactics to persuade local businesses to advertise—the *Blairmore Enterprise* could state without a hint of awkwardness in 1912 that those who advertised were "live business men" while those who did not were "dead men...only fit to inhabit cemeteries and not attempt to run a business." As well as such rhetoric, the public was often advised that advertising was a sign of a business's "respectability."[47] Such statements about the value of advertising were strongest in the period before World War I, or during economic hard times.

Newspapers also employed several other methods to generate revenue. Clubbing offers, in which a subscription to the local paper was offered in conjunction with a national magazine or newspaper, were popular before World War I. Most newspaper offices also sold a range of preprinted products like Christmas, birthday and greeting cards and stationery products like paper and typewriter ribbons. And pointing to the truly marginal profitability of town papers, a popular sideline for newspaper offices in southern Alberta around World War I was the sale of cut flowers and bedding plants. The most important of this type of activity, however, was job printing.

There were few businesses in the territorial period that did job printing exclusively. Most was done by newspaper publishers, and in smaller Alberta centres this remained the norm until at least the end of World War II. Even in a small town, printing needs were considerable, ranging from butter wrappers to invoice books, posters, letterhead, envelopes, and local government publications. There was some competition in this field, varying from travelling salesmen to those making hand-made posters. The latter were of little practical consequence, although the 1913 federal government ruling that no private posters were allowed in post offices was welcomed by one newspaper as doing away "with the cheap advertising which covers the walls of country post offices," thus eliminating this "poor rival of the weekly paper." The most significant competition came from transient traders, and local newspapers fought them vigorously. They demanded enforcement of local licensing designed to curb transient trading and attacked in print anyone who purchased such printing. When the Grande Prairie town council sent its financial statement to Edmonton for printing in 1946, the local newspaper indignantly noted that it, unlike the Edmonton print shop, paid taxes in Grande Prairie and should have been asked to tender on the job: "the town council has the right to ask for 100% co-operation from *The Herald Tribune*, which has always been freely given, and now we get this deal."[48]

The centrality of town promotion and the need for advertising created a certain uniformity in the nature of town newspapers. Yet, many had an individuality that stemmed from the character of their editors. In the towns studied, all editors were male and many had come from eastern Canada where they had gained skills in their craft. While there was sometimes high turnover in the business, many editors had remarkable staying power: C.E.D. Wood edited the *Macleod Gazette* for most of the period 1882–1903; C.W. Frederick owned the newspaper in Peace River from 1914 until 1939 and for a time also owned the *Grande Prairie Herald* and a short-lived paper in Waterhole (near Fairview); Walter Bartlett ran the *Blairmore Enterprise* from its founding in 1912 until his death in 1946; and C.B. Halpin edited the *Lacombe Western Globe* from 1906 until 1935.[49] In addition to gathering the news and writing, editors often performed the manual tasks of printing, like page layout, and sometimes ran the presses as well. Usually, they did not obscure their individual interests when putting together the newspaper—their pet concerns and projects made their way into the paper in editorials or news reports or in special features. The *Grande Prairie Northern Tribune*, for example, was eager to promote Esperanto, then seen as a possible route to world peace and understanding. From its establishment in 1932 until 1934, it ran articles on Esperanto, even printing articles in the language.

With few staff, news gathering depended on the editor's initiative. Often "correspondents" in surrounding villages and communities were used to gather local news, usually about weddings, deaths, and community and family gatherings. In return for this work, the "correspondents" usually received a free or discounted subscription to the paper and a commission on any subscriptions or advertising they sold. Such local news columns were a standard feature of town newspapers, one that big city papers sometimes mocked. But as the *Drumheller Mail* retorted, at least the local news columns were democratic; everything was reported.[50]

Most newspaper editors entertained the hope that their paper would be a focus for free speech and social comment. One element of this was the letters to the editor column, but as the *Macleod Gazette* found in 1882 and most papers would find subsequently, people did not "come forward as we should like them to do." Even so, many editors encouraged debate. In his first editorial in 1882, C.E.D. Wood promised that the *Macleod Gazette* would be nonpartisan and would promote free and unbiased discussion. "It is a great mistake," he wrote, "for people to think that, in a community or district like ours, only the bright and polished side of its social and everyday life should be open to view. It is quite as necessary that what is evil and corrupt should be fully spread out to the general sight." In expressing such hopes, Wood was very much a part of the new journalism that was emerging in Canada in the late nineteenth century.[51]

While such sentiments were sincere, they did not preclude a general support for the status quo and local business interests. The hatred of socialism and communism expressed by the papers in Coleman and Blairmore in the 1930s was an extreme example of this general pattern. Yet, support for the country's dominant economic system and form of government did not prevent efforts for social and economic change and against local political corruption and civic immorality. For such stances, editors were often severely criticised. In the late 1880s, for example, C.E.D. Wood campaigned in the *Macleod Gazette* for substitution of mixed farming for ranching in southern Alberta. This brought him into direct conflict with local ranching interests. By 1890, the paper was in financial trouble—not an unusual problem for early newspapers, though in this case it was exacerbated by declining advertising revenue from the local ranching community. In 1892 Wood relinquished the editor's chair and began selling real estate. In his farewell editorial he wrote that "in the newspaper business, more than any other, a man is bound to make enemies." But he was unapologetic, for "anything I have done, I have done in the way of what I firmly believed to be my duty." His successors had less courage, and when the paper closed temporarily in 1894, the final issue's editorial contained an apology to those that had been offended.[52]

Wood remained a potent force in the town; he was connected with F.W.G. Haultain, a powerful political figure in both the town and in the NWT, and when the paper was subsequently reorganized as a joint stock company, Wood was hired as editor, a position he held until 1903 when he moved to Regina to join Haultain's law practice. He ended his career on the Saskatchewan bench.

While Wood's political connections may have been unusual for a town newspaper editor, his experiences were not. Thinkers who went against the grain were never popular, and pressure to conform was strong in Alberta towns. Almost 50 years after Wood tangled with the ranchers of Fort Macleod, Archie Key, the editor of the *Drumheller Mail*, had a similar experience. Unlike Wood, Key did not mount a direct challenge to the economic life of a local elite. Rather, he challenged an even more powerful foe, the idealized image of small town life.

In 1929, on the prompting of the painter A.Y. Jackson, Key wrote an article about prairie culture for the *McGill News*. He rather naively circulated offprints of the article to his town "friends." It was a highly positive look at prairie social life and culture, but his references to Drumheller raised a storm. "I say we live in a town of shacks," wrote Key. He also stressed that the town had considerable cultural vitality although it had a bad, though increasingly undeserved, reputation for crime and vice. Such statements led to a "whispering campaign" against him and an attempt to organize a boycott of the paper. Part of this apparently was a settling of scores over past quarrels, but as Key phrased it, he was accused of "double-crossing the town, of hitting below the belt, of biting the hand that fed me, of preaching treason, arson and revolution." While some board of trade members were "highly indignant at the alleged knock to the town," and some businessmen took exception to parts of the article, the campaign against Key fell apart. The owner of the paper supported him, and Key forced the gossip into the open by directly challenging his critics, "whose massive intelligence failed to grasp the significance of the article." No doubt, his contribution to the social life of the town also stood him in good stead. He had helped to organize the library, and drama and music festivals, and, among other activities, had chaired the local town planning commission. When he left the *Mail* in 1933 to set up his own paper, his parting editorial quoted Franklin Delano Roosevelt: "I ask you to judge me by the enemies I have made."[53]

These examples indicate the way in which newspaper editors could come into conflict with town society. Yet neither Key nor Wood had breached the unwritten code of behaviour that guided most prairie newspaper editors. One of the elements in this code was the imperative of the editor to speak his mind on important local issues. Over the years, both Key and Wood expressed the typical contention that they had a right to champion what they thought was best for the town and district. In Lacombe, this position brought C.B. Halpin, the editor of the *Western Globe*, into conflict with the Klu Klux Klan which was recruiting in the district. The Alberta organizers of the KKK came from Saskatchewan, where they had enjoyed some success in preaching hatred of Roman Catholics, Jews, liberals and all non-Anglo-Saxons.[54]

While some other editors in Alberta were in conflict with the Klan (it burned a cross on Archie Key's lawn in Drumheller), Halpin's quarrel with the Klan escalated into a personal crusade. Debate began in 1929 when a reader wrote to say that the *Western Globe's* report on a Klan meeting was unfair. Customarily, editors did not respond in print to letters to the editor, but Halpin replied with a scathing rebuttal characterizing the Klan as a relic of "the dark ages," whose hate propaganda and vigilantism threatened to tear society apart.[55] The dispute continued in the spring of 1930 when the Klan tarred and feathered a local blacksmith it accused of immoral behaviour. This was typical Klan vigilantism—part of its self-professed mission to impose its version of morality and law and order on society. Halpin was outraged. "Mob justice is not justice," he contended, and demanded that "these hooded hoodlums" be "exterminated without the slightest compunction." The Klan responded by sending Halpin a threatening letter, which he then published. It warned that his editorial was "exceedingly displeasing" and that it would not stop the Klan's "mission" to create "a high standard of morality and integrity in our land." Claiming that its "Justice is meted out swiftly and surely," it claimed that the victim of the tarring and feathering had offended "in one way. YOU ARE OFFENDING IN ANOTHER WAY. Through your meddlesome tactics you have brought suspicions upon innocent men. That is a grave offence in our sight." And then the threat:

> The next issue of your paper will be watched with exceeding interest and your street utterances closely checked by an Emmissary [sic] of the K.K.K. now in Lacombe for that purpose. We will bear no more obstructional and defamatory conduct on your part toward the K.K.K. If your present conduct is persisted in you will be severely punished therefore. Your place of business will be burned to the ground. You

will be glad to leave Lacombe before the K.K.K. is through with you if any further slanderous statements are indulged in.

In reply, Halpin wrote of the "rotten doctrine" of these "hooded cowards" and the Klan's history "interwoven with crime."[56] And in subsequent issues in 1932 and 1933, he continued to report critically on the Klan's tactics in Lacombe and on its leader's trial for slander in Edmonton. Of course, it was high drama, but Halpin's defense of what he believed to be right was an important measure of strength of character and integrity. His actions, along with like-minded individuals elsewhere in the province, helped deny respectability and legitimacy in Alberta to the Klan and its gangster approach to political and social life.

Another more mundane but equally important aspect of newspaper ethics concerned gossip. While there was usually no need to print it since it could easily be heard on the street, small town newspapers usually refused to print any form of gossip. Even court cases were usually not reported before 1945, although in the 1880s Fort Macleod's paper reported, as a deliberate policy, the arrest of bootleggers and gamblers since they were said to be damaging society for profit. Nor would newspapers print material that might embarrass the innocent. This suppression of news not only expressed the ideal of the town as a caring place, but it also served a social function in protecting the innocent and helped sustain the editor's dignity. Editors were commonly asked not to report news that reflected badly on an individual, and as the *Blairmore Enterprise* noted in 1915, "so far as we are concerned, we get beastly tired of the 'favoring-by-suppression' business, but we continue to do it— probably for the reason that we still have a heart." And when four adolescents were arrested in Lacombe in 1920 for breaking into the Legion hall and having sexual intercourse in the bedroom set up for visiting veterans, the *Lacombe Western Globe* noted that, in consideration of the parents, it would not print the names, although everyone in town knew their identity anyway.[57]

Still another important element in this code of behaviour concerned politics and elections. These formed a major part of local news and were events of significance as well as entertainment. By 1900, it was no longer acceptable for a paper to be "bought" by a political party during an election. In denying rumors about the paper during the bitter 1911 federal election over free trade, the *Lacombe Western Globe* noted that while it "could have made money" this way, it would have been unethical. This did not, however, mean that newspapers were politically neutral. The *Macleod Gazette* was a Tory paper, but as Wood observed in 1903, good newspapers "never let go of the right to place the interests of their country above mere party. Independence and neutrality are two totally different things, and the latter in a newspaper is contemptible. Any paper which gives a general support to the party it believes in, while preserving the right to criticize its friends and praise its opponents, is independent enough for a new country."[58]

Much of the concern with politics focused on how government policies affected local needs. This was particularly well illustrated in the early 1930s with the rise of Social Credit. Many editors expressed the hope that it would solve the economic problems of the province, and those opposed to the party remained willing to discuss the issues it raised. The lack of antagonism to Social Credit in small town papers was notable, especially in comparison to much editorial opinion in Calgary and Edmonton newspapers. But Social Credit destroyed the sympathy it enjoyed when it proposed in 1936 to licence the press to counter what it perceived to be anti Social Credit opinion. For editors who had been hostile to Social Credit from the beginning (such as Charles Frederick in Peace River), the proposed legislation only confirmed their opinion. For others, such as the *Cardston News* and the *Drumheller Mail*, which had generally been sympathetic to Social Credit, it turned them firmly against the government. As the *Drumheller Mail* asked, "if Premier Aberhart intends to license the press against liberty of expression, how much more is the need to license individuals against freedom of speech?"[59]

Town priorities and culture were shaped directly by boards of trade and newspapers. The promotional objectives of boards of trade expressed the belief that a town could shape its future by enhancing business activity and attracting industry. However, few boards of trade could command sufficient resources or influence to realize this ambition. Thus, their significance was not in redirecting or determining local economic growth, but in expressing and shaping town culture. In this they were commonly supported by town councils, and newspapers were equally important in providing a forum for disseminating these views and in acting as a town voice.

In many ways, most boards of trade by the mid 1920s were different organizations than they had been 15 years earlier. A recognition that economic growth and stability depended on more than mere promotion necessitated a more sophisticated approach. The objectives of town cohesion and economic growth were combined with a new emphasis on social issues. Acceptance of a more limited future than booster ambitions had foretold before World War I also forced towns to look more seriously at their rural hinterlands. Thus, the growing inclusion of farm people on boards of trade in some towns during the interwar years represented a maturation of town culture. While it was popular to hold that population could be retained, and possibly expanded, through improvements like swimming pools, playgrounds and tree planting, it was also accepted that an enriched community life would create a better living environment. The advantages of the city were forcing towns to become more urban, and such urban amenities provided a better place to live and enabled small towns to counter the draw of the cities.

At the same time that the city was influencing the town through its example, outside forces like provincial and national associations were helping to shape town attitudes and opinions. The growth of the Canadian Chamber of Commerce was one example, as were parallel provincial organizations, which helped connect the town to wider issues. Newspapers also played a similar role in town culture, although they usually expressed a wider, and sometimes a more sophisticated, political and cultural sense. While newspapers could be as mindless in town promotion as the most committed board of trade, much of this may have reflected a need to accommodate local business opinion in a quest for advertising revenue. Yet, there was a promotional language and attitude that most papers shared, especially before 1920, which indicated the existence of a common approach to reporting. Nonetheless, some articles linked the town with the wider world, and some editorials expressed a vigour in economic and political questions that no town board of trade could attain. At their best, town newspapers demonstrated that the dissemination of news and political views was not always hierarchial; they did not merely transplant the views of the largest urban places to the smaller ones, but often expressed local concerns and opinion.

5

TOWN

ECONOMIC

GROWTH

Alberta towns were neither economically self-sufficient nor isolated. From the beginning, most were outward facing, with their continued existence dependent on the wider economy. As economic intermediary points, their success was also linked to their hinterlands. This dual focus meant that improvements in transportation remained paramount for those concerned with town development. As well, small town spokesmen saw manufacturing, processing, mercantile, and service sector development as essential for growth. In theory, this meant that towns could act as agents of economic change by attracting development and encouraging improvements in transportation, as well as by adhering to the booster ideals of unity of purpose. In reality, these efforts brought minimal results, suggesting that either their logic was flawed, or that the parameters of economic growth lay outside town control.

RAILWAYS *and the*
GROWTH *of* TOWNS

Urban economies were directly shaped by the extent and nature of their zones of influence. In the core area immediately around it, a town experienced almost no competition. A larger transitional zone lay beyond this. It was still tributary to the town but there was some competition from smaller centres, and from larger ones on its outer boundaries. Range of services as well as other advantages were important in determining the size of this zone.[1] A town's economy in part depended on the strength of its core area, but becoming a central place for the transitional zone was equally important for expanding trade. This was a complex process and changed with various economic and social factors, including the lessening of commuting time between centres because of changes in transportation.

Transportation was a key element in town economic growth, both for hinterland trade and in connecting towns to the national economy. Rail transportation was especially important for town growth and continuity before 1920. It tied the town to the wider economy and extended its hinterland. As was noted in Claresholm in 1909, farmers needed railways and good rail service, and "everything which helps the farmer helps the towns."[2] Nonetheless, the size of a town's hinterland along existing rail lines was fairly rigid because other towns placed equidistantly along the line also competed for trade. The greatest advantage, therefore, was to expand into a wholly new territory, where an existing town's commercial head start would allow it to serve as a distribution point for incoming goods and the export of local products.

Thus, demands for extension of rail lines were common. Lacombe was typical in this respect. It was on the main line between Calgary and Edmonton, and while there was initially some hope that it would supplant Red Deer as the midway point, it was quickly realized that the town was too far north for this to happen. This was especially evident after 1908 when Red Deer became the divisional point on the line, boosting its economy with a monthly payroll of about $5,000.[3] Lacombe then set its sights on becoming the centre for the largely unsettled area to the west around the hamlets of Bentley and Rimbey, then served only by trails. If this territory could be tied to Lacombe by rail, it was reasoned that it would become the entrepot for the whole area between Red Deer and Edmonton. These hopes seemed close to realization in 1911 when the CPR line running west from Moose Jaw reached Lacombe and joined the Calgary-Edmonton line.

Lacombe's position as the terminus for this line gave it some advantage in capturing trade east of the town, but this was constrained by existing towns such as Stettler. Its transitional zone hinterland was cut off to the south by Red Deer and to the north by Wetaskiwin. Thus, Lacombe's major advantage was as the transshipment point for goods going west by trail. Lacombe's promoters urged the CPR to build to the west, but the

CPR seemed content with Lacombe as its terminus. Nevertheless, Lacombe continued to argue that a line westward to Bentley and Rimbey was needed. The area was sparsely settled, and the Lacombe board of trade and town council threw themselves into lobbying for a line that would bring more settlers to the area. In 1909 a local company was chartered to build this line, and by 1912, the prospect raised great hopes in Lacombe because "everyone will agree that the building of the line from here to Rimbey will mean that Lacombe will treble in size and population within a year or two, and that the value of farm lands along the route will double in value at once."[4] A few miles of line were built by a company with local capital, and a few more were built by another company with shareholders from Lacombe, Bentley, and Rimbey. The line finally reached Bentley in 1917. The province took over the line in 1918 and pushed it on to Rimbey, and in the early 1920s it extended the line northward.

The difficulties associated with the completion of this western line showed that town authorities often had little effect on rail expansion. Although Lacombe's ambitions were clearly and energetically stated, they did not persuade the CPR to build westward beyond the town. Local efforts to build the line were also unsuccessful due to insufficient capital, and the town could not subsidize the line because the *Town Act* expressly prohibited the giving of bonuses for railway construction. The line was completed only with provincial assistance. This extension was doubtless facilitated by the area's MLA, John Brownlee, who became provincial attorney general in 1921. Thus, transportation developments that simultaneously entrenched and expanded Lacombe's western hinterland resulted from a number of factors, of which hinterland politics and needs were as important as Lacombe's ambitions.[5]

Similar factors were at play in the Cardston area. The Blood and Peigan reserves north and west of the town formed a barrier to continuous Euro-Canadian settlement, thus creating a sub-region in the southwest corner of the province between the reserves and the United States border. Cardston was at the core of this area, and its dominant position was further enhanced because it was the religious centre of the Mormon settlements in southwest Alberta. In 1907, when the railway reached the town, it had "no healthy competitors" to the south of the reserves. It was surrounded by smaller tributary settlements, giving it, in its boosters' words, "a commercial standing of no mean eminence."[6] Its religious importance was solidified in 1913 when it was selected as the site for the only Mormon Temple in Canada. There was some debate that the Temple might be located in Raymond, an aspiring town about 60 kilometres to the east, and there was great celebration in Cardston, not only for religious reasons, when the church chose it as the site for the Temple. Yet the outcome was never really in doubt; Cardston was the terminus of the line from Lethbridge, but more importantly, as the first Mormon settlement in Canada, it had an unchallengeable symbolic and political advantage.

Cardston's fortunes were further enhanced by the development of irrigation. There had been limited irrigation around Cardston from the late nineteenth century, but around World War I, the United Irrigation District was formed around the village of Glenwood, northwest of Cardston on the western boundary of the Blood reserve. By 1925 there were about 36,000 acres intended for sugar beet production under irrigation, but a railway was needed before extensive production could begin. The CPR and the Utah-Idaho Sugar Company favoured such a line, and while there were some in Cardston who opposed it in order to force "all and sundry...to come to Cardston to do business," the Cardston board of trade wisely supported it, arguing that it would increase the wealth of the whole district. Cardston's economic head start in the area and its religious importance allowed it to benefit because the people of the United Irrigation District were tied "socially, religiously, and politically" with Cardston.[7]

Like Cardston, Grande Prairie benefited from a period of isolation in which the town established itself and gained a head start in the area. When a rail line reached Grande Prairie in 1916, it provided connections through Edmonton to the rest of Canada. The line went no further into the fertile areas to the west until 1928, making Grande Prairie the end of steel for over a decade. Yet the railway had no sooner reached the town when demands began for its extension to the west. While Grande Prairie's boosters reasoned that this would increase settlement and enhance the town's commerce, their failure to achieve this goal proved, paradoxically, to be crucial to the town's success.

Grande Prairie's advantage as the head of steel was demonstrated by the fate of one of its rivals, Lake Saskatoon, a settlement about 20 kilometres to the west. In 1912 and 1913, Dun and Bradstreet Commercial Ratings reported that Grande Prairie had two businesses (one a branch of an Edmonton firm) while Lake Saskatoon had none. By 1914, Grande Prairie had 10 businesses, including Revillon Frères, a major fur and wholesale supply company. However, even more dramatic growth had occurred at Lake Saskatoon which had 14 businesses, including two lumber companies, a sash and door factory, a restaurant and a tinsmith. While Grande Prairie had an important advantage because the land titles office and immigration depot were located there, it was apparent that people considered Lake Saskatoon a serious rival: the Hudson's Bay Company opened a store, as did Revillon (though it kept its store open in Grande Prairie), and a flour mill operated by an Edmonton firm opened in both towns. A board of trade was established in Lake Saskatoon in 1915, the same year as in Grande Prairie, and the village put on a three-day celebration for Dominion Day (Canada Day) in 1914. By all conventional measures, the town had a promising future.

With the approach of the railway, however, Grande Prairie surged ahead. In 1915 Dun and Bradstreet rated 28 Grande Prairie businesses and only 15 in Lake Saskatoon, and in 1916, the year the rail reached Grande Prairie, Lake Saskatoon's growth began to slow. In Grande Prairie, there was rapid development, "quite unlike anything that had been experienced before the arrival of the steel." Even a disastrous fire did not slow its growth.[8] The ending of steel in Grande Prairie confirmed its head start as the metropolis of the south Peace River country, the richest agricultural section of the region. In 1916, the number of businesses rated in Lake Saskatoon declined to 11 while those in Grande Prairie increased to 31. Although the number of businesses rated for Lake Saskatoon maintained this level, and even increased slightly until 1920, the number then steadily declined, falling first to five and then to one by 1926. By 1929 none were rated. In Grande Prairie, the number of rated businesses increased dramatically, reaching 42 in 1917, 60 in 1919 and 75 in 1920, all stimulated by the boom created by the arrival of the railway. There seems to have been considerable over-expansion, since the number of businesses then began to decline, reaching a low of 46 in 1926. They then began to increase steadily. In the end, the railway dealt Lake Saskatoon a double blow: by ending at Grande Prairie it had given this rival added economic growth for 12 years, and when it moved on, it bypassed Lake Saskatoon. It stopped instead at Wembley (a competing settlement that had been moved in order to be located on the line), which then experienced rapid growth after 1928.[9] Grande Prairie promoters now realized the advantage they had enjoyed, and the president of the Grande Prairie board of trade worried about "what will Grande Prairie do when the steel moves on?"[10] There was little reason for concern. Its advantage as end of steel for 12 years had made it the major centre of the south Peace River, a status that was not challenged once the rail line moved on.

For the Peace River country, rail lines were not only of concern for the growth of individual towns. Because the ED&BC originated in Edmonton, the region became part of Edmonton's hinterland, but many people in the Peace River country argued that it should not be the hinterland of a single city. Thus, almost simultaneously with the completion of rail connections to Edmonton, demands for a competing line to the outside began. The favourite proposal was for one running west through the mountains to British Columbia. This became known as the "coast outlet," a powerful phrase in an area highly conscious of its isolation, and it rapidly became the panacea for the problems the area faced. It was firmly believed that the coast outlet would lessen the costs of importing consumer goods and exporting staples. There was a belief in the Peace River country that Edmonton opposed the coast outlet for selfish reasons and that Vancouver favoured it. In any event, Peace River wanted to have a choice, or at least wanted to be able to play one metropolis off against the other. Although Edmonton's board of trade generally supported development of the Peace River country, one editorial in an Edmonton newspaper in 1925, alleging that the coast outlet campaign was a "conspiracy" to cut Edmonton off from the Peace River country and supplant it with Vancouver, confirmed opinion in the Peace River country of Edmonton's "sickening" parochialism and selfishness.[11]

While the lack of a coast outlet remained a central grievance of the Peace River country in the interwar years, it did serve in principle to unite town and country. Yet details of the route to the coast created tensions. The north Peace River country, especially the town of Peace River, opposed the route favoured in Grande Prairie because it appeared to give Grande Prairie an advantage which could make it the entrepot of the whole Peace River country. By 1933, the coast outlet campaign had produced no results, and since "half a loaf is better than no bread," the cheaper alternative of a highway to the coast was favoured as a temporary expedient. In 1937, both the highway and railway proposals were admitted to be "a dead issue," although the war for a time revived them and gave them a national impetus that they had formerly lacked.[12]

| *Stage service connected Fort Macleod with other settlements in south-western Alberta in the late nineteenth century. This 1890 photo shows the stage leaving Lethbridge for Fort Macleod. Archives Collection, A3959, PAA.*

ROADS *and* OTHER

TRANSPORTATION SYSTEMS

The emerging alternative of highways formed an additional element in plans for town economic growth. Before the railway, trails and wagon roads had connected inland towns with their neighbours. In the 1880s, a trail ran from Fort Macleod to Lethbridge, and the ranching areas were similarly linked to the towns. These trails were established by use, and there was no legal authority to enforce a public right of way on them by 1893, the year the trail between Fort Macleod and Lethbridge was "closed up by the owner." A new trail had to be cut around this land, which caused great anger in Fort Macleod because it had been the main trail to Lethbridge since settlement began. Overall, there was little provision for roads by the territorial government, and by 1900 demands that it build roads to replace the rough trails were common.[13]

Crude as they were, these trails were important for trade. By the early 1890s a stage ran between Fort Macleod and Pincher Creek, and also to

Lethbridge, with scheduled stage service to Cardston beginning in 1899.[14] This raised hopes in Fort Macleod of drawing business from the southwest. Another concern at Fort Macleod was the construction of a bridge over the Oldman River to tap the trade of the area north of the river. A bridge had been built in 1891, tenders being let in the midst of the federal election campaign, but by 1905 it needed to be replaced if Fort Macleod was to keep its trade. While many people north of the river preferred shopping in Fort Macleod, the problems associated with the bridge forced them to go to Claresholm, a practice that needed to be reversed if "we wish to hold our trade and induce people to come here."[15]

The importance of roads grew with the advent of motor vehicles in Alberta around 1912. Ultimately, they had a revolutionary effect. By increasing the speed and flexibility of movement, they marked the beginning of a changed relationship among towns and cities and their hinterlands. They decreased the time required to travel between places, effectively bringing them closer together. This had an important impact on town economic policy. While railway companies could theoretically be lured to a town or city with promises of free land and no taxes, motor vehicle transportation required no terminals or divisional points, and towns had neither the authority nor the money to build highways. Instead, they could only lobby the province for highway construction and improvement. The granting of railway charters had always been a political matter, and highways continued this tradition, although the focus was now almost totally on the provincial government.

In 1918, the provincial government set out for the first time different categories of highways and priorized their construction. Of highest priority were main highways connecting cities and towns, then came market and other highways important for transporting local produce, and the last group included roads of a purely local nature. Such priorization was of lasting significance because, as in Ontario, it confirmed the economic and political advantages inherent in larger centres' head start. Further, as David Bettison noted in his history of local government in Alberta, this highway legislation gave the province the power to apply general principles based on provincial rather than local priorities. Indeed, he contends that in this sense Alberta was becoming a "province" instead of a collection of local authorities and private companies, "each seeking to use the provincial government for local advantage."[16]

| Good roads became a concern of town promoters because
automobiles created new opportunities and new challenges for town
businesses. In this photo, a road near Claresholm is being graded.
Not dated. Archives Collection, A20095, PAA.

Despite the advantage that provincially directed highway development offered to some communities over others, it was believed that towns
could generally meet the changes brought by motor vehicles. By 1932,
the trend towards fewer towns was clearly recognized as a fundamental
change in provincial life which had been "planned for horse drawn vehicles." The result was a drain of population from "those towns and villages which lacked strategic locations." Fewer towns led to the widening
of the core trading area of those remaining, and the centralization of
medical, educational and business services, making them more of "a real
community centre." As part of this competition, it was believed that
towns which were "progressive" and gave good service and good prices
would grow, while "backward" towns would "slowly perish by the roadside."[17]

The new role that private transportation was assuming in the economy
was quickly recognized. Auto clubs promoting road improvement and
providing a focus for auto enthusiasts were formed in many towns. One
of the earliest was in the Crowsnest Pass in 1913. Another was organized
in Cardston in 1916, and with about 150 members, it was anticipated
that it would "become a 'power in the land'."[18] But the main onus for

promoting good roads still fell upon boards of trade and town councils. Roads were often blocked with snow for part of the winter, and some boards of trade helped keep them open in winter, as well as grading and maintaining them in summer. The province began to assume these tasks systematically only in the late 1930s. More broadly, however, every board of trade was concerned with highway development, each demanding upgraded roads or the designation of a particular highway as a "trunk" or an arterial road to link the town directly with its hinterland, a larger centre, or some site with tourist potential.

Initially, the campaign for good roads was relatively casual. The disappearance of horse-drawn vehicles was gradual, and trains also remained important until the end of World War II. In 1929 the *Drumheller Mail* could editorialize, without creating a stir, that given low government revenues, highway expenditures rather than those for health or education should be cut. With such a choice, "we prefer to take the train once in a while, or walk, or stay at home." These attitudes soon changed. In 1939 it was noted at Claresholm that people had become "real snooty" about roads. Although the highway had been hard surfaced for less than a year, people now became impatient the moment they left the surfaced highway to drive on a gravelled road. This change in attitude did not go unnoticed by politicians. As the *Drumheller Mail* editorialized in 1936, while it often disagreed with the Social Credit government, it liked its generous road building programmes.[19]

While Social Credit knew its constituents, the economic importance of roads had long been a doctrine of boards of trade, town councils, and town promoters. When John Hanna, secretary of the Calgary board of trade, told the Drumheller board of trade in 1925 that good roads were "of very great importance to every board of trade," he was only confirming what it already knew. As Hanna observed, automobiles were changing the economy and hinterlands of towns. "Bad roads were an economic waste and people would go miles out of their way to another town...rather than drive a few miles over bad roads." These circumstances sometimes brought town rivalries into the open. As only one example, Cardston demanded that the highway from Lethbridge to Cardston be designated a trunk road and gravelled, and that it bypass Fort Macleod to draw tourists directly to Cardston and area. At the same time, improved road travel could also create a deeper recognition of district interdependence. In 1925 the major issue for the Drumheller board of trade was the condition of roads in the valley. Residents of Wayne

were demanding road connections with Drumheller, and their representatives joined the Drumheller board of trade in traveling to Edmonton to
lobby the provincial government to build the road. Their return empty-
handed raised "quite a storm," with resolutions drawn up by nearly all
the organizations in the valley, including branches of the Women's
Institute, the miners' union, Drumheller retail merchants, and some valley town councils. Perhaps to confirm district solidarity, the Drumheller
board of trade announced its support for a United Mine Workers of
America recommendation that all road workers receive union wages.[20]

The debate over roads in the Drumheller valley illustrated that highway development, like railway development, was relevant for town and
country alike. Yet while hinterland demands for ready access to towns
were an important element in efforts for road improvement, this co-
operative action still represented only a coincidence of interest. Towns
were primarily concerned with their own interests, and Drumheller was
no exception. In its 1927 report on progress on the construction of the
road to Wayne, the Drumheller board of trade clearly focused its concern
around Drumheller's needs. As it noted, efforts in lobbying for roads,
encouraging district co-operation, sponsoring sports days, and helping
establish a board of trade in Wayne had "encouraged everything which
would tend to make Drumheller more and more a centre of everything
for a large area."[21]

Because of their size and population, most towns did not consider
inter-urban transportation service as an essential element in town
growth. In the Crowsnest Pass and Drumheller, however, unique settlement patterns stimulated different responses. The earliest of these was
the incorporation in 1912 of the Crow's Nest Electric Railway Company to
provide service between Blairmore and Coleman. The company was chartered with W.A. Beebe as manager, and both the board of trade and the
Blairmore town council endorsed its construction. While some individuals found the project "a huge joke," the Blairmore board of trade thought
it showed the area's great future as it would bring "together the great
returns of the ten great coal mines and other vast industries of the Crow's
Nest Pass." While the project never got off the ground, its planning illustrated the unity of the area, where towns were close together and
stretched one after another through the Pass. By the early 1920s, taxis
and buses provided most Pass towns with regularly scheduled service.[22]

The Drumheller valley also had a network of towns, but they were
more spread out than in the Crowsnest Pass. A local transportation system

| Air travel created new economic opportunities for towns, especially those like Peace River in northern Alberta. Not dated, but before 1937. Archives Collection, A2589, PAA.

for these towns was provided as early as 1920 when Drumheller Bus Lines began carrying passengers and small freight to the Monarch and Newcastle mines for 15 and 25 cents respectively. It was a rather informal system; the waiting room for the bus was in a tailor shop in the Whitehouse Hotel block at the end of main street. Because valley roads were poor, the Drumheller Bus and Taxi Company bought a 25-seat bus with "special shock absorbers" in 1928 to run scheduled service in the valley.[23] Over the years, bus service from Drumheller was expanded, serving to confirm the town as the most important urban centre in the valley.

Other forms of transportation, notably by river and air, were of less general importance in the province before World War II. Among the towns surveyed, river transport was significant only for Peace River, which had a natural advantage as the centre of navigation to Fort Vermilion in the north and Hudson's Hope in the west. While the importance of river navigation for Peace River steadily decreased until 1952 when it was discontinued, it gave the town a locational advantage over its immediate neighbours, and also created some employment in shipping and boat building.[24] A greater impact came with air travel. By 1929 the Cardston board of trade surveyed potential sites and was lobbying for a landing field in the town, although a decade later it had not yet succeeded in this plan. Aviation facilities were also pursued in Grande Prairie and Peace River where the potential of northern air service was evident. Grande Prairie had a small airport before 1939, and a large airport was constructed by the Royal Canadian Air Force during World War II. There was much anticipation that aviation was the way of the future, although it was generally felt that the area needed to continue to concentrate on achieving the coast outlet. By 1947 the airport's role as a refuelling point for civilian air routes between Edmonton and the north and to British Columbia gave Grande Prairie some advantage in passenger and freight. So too, its location on the Alaska Highway, a legacy of wartime construction, gave it an important land connection. By this time as well, the beginning of two air service routes between Peace River and Yellowknife presented an opportunity for Peace River to capture the northern trade from other centres, especially Grande Prairie and Edmonton.[25]

Attracting Settlers

Improvement of transportation systems was one means to stimulate economic development by expanding both a town's core and transitional trading areas. Other efforts to increase the population and wealth of a town's hinterland were also pursued as a strategy of growth. One attempt to do so in Fort Macleod and Cardston before 1920 took the form of lobbying for sale of the Blood and Peigan reserves that lay between the two towns. Despite considerable shopping by Natives in both Fort Macleod and Cardston, it was argued that the use the Natives made of their land did not benefit the towns sufficiently. In 1898 it was suggested that the part of the Blood reserve abutting the northern boundary of Cardston should be sold to white settlers. The Bloods had much land, "but all we want is only a very few of those thousands of acres." Indeed, the "Indians would never miss it and the settlers would use every acre of it for ranches, farms and gardens." When a portion of the Peigan reserve was sold a decade later, the Fort Macleod newspaper pronounced it a "step in the right direction" and demanded that the Blood reserve also be opened for settlement because the benefit to "the Macleod district will be enormous." Subsequent efforts in this direction were fruitless, although the Fort Macleod board of trade continued to demand sale of reserve land until at least the end of World War I.[26]

A more conventional approach to stimulating hinterland growth was advertising for settlers. Central to these efforts were pamphlets, newspaper advertisements, and, among others, displays at fairs promoting the town and district. These projects were often major undertakings: the distribution by Lacombe's board of trade in 1909 of 5,000 folders about the town and district was not unusual. Most of these campaigns ended in southern and central Alberta with the economic collapse of 1912–13, but they continued in the Peace River country. In 1927 the Grande Prairie board of trade replied directly to 505 inquiries from Canada, the United States and Britain about land or business opportunities in the district and distributed 1,000 booklets and 500 "homestead sheets." The latter featured Herman Trelle, a Wembley farmer who had won the Grand Championship for hard spring wheat at Chicago from 1926 to 1928.[27]

Since production of such advertising was expensive, an alternative was to send information to leading North American newspapers in the hope that it would be printed as news. It was of no consequence whether this material was "of the boosting kind or just news, for every time a municipality is mentioned it means so much in its favor."[28] This "news" rarely made it into print, but real news did get printed, and events like Trelle's success in Chicago were doubly welcomed as free publicity. Political conflict also had the same effect. As was noted in the Peace River country in 1927–28, an effort to create a separate province in the region gave it free advertising in the nation's papers within 48 hours.[29]

While the effect of such advertising techniques cannot be gauged, it has been noted that few agricultural settlers were likely drawn by advertisements since the number of farmers in an area was ultimately a product of "the ability of the land to support them."[30] But advertising was part of the contemporary style of town promotion and could not be ignored because "from Winnipeg to Medicine Hat, from Lethbridge to Edmonton, broadsides of literature and scoopfuls of dollars are being directed at the advancing host with telling effect."[31] Proof of its effectiveness, however, was dubious. In 1909 it was observed in Claresholm that if cities like Winnipeg, Calgary and Vancouver found extensive advertising "of vital importance," then it was much more valuable for a small town, "one even with great possibilities such as ours." City size was evidence of its efficacy, for in every successful town and city in North America "a programme of advertising and publicity has resulted in the material development of the town."[32]

ATTRACTING INDUSTRY

The campaign for settlers was only part of the effort to stimulate economic growth. Industry was also courted, and two areas of production were targeted: local agricultural processing and nonagricultural manufacturing. While the two were only different aspects of the same ambition, they often provoked different reactions.

The attempt to attract agricultural processing sometimes created tension between town and country. Processing was believed to be of greatest potential in tandem with mixed farming, which necessitated a change in agricultural practises in some places. At Fort Macleod, for example, ranching had appeared by the late 1870s. Most of this production was purchased locally by the federal government to support the police or the Natives, although cattle were driven out to market as well. Ranching in southern Alberta operated on land leased from the Canadian government. Many leaseholders were wealthy eastern capitalists with political influence, and any threat to ranching challenged powerful interests.[33] Ranching involved a high ratio of land to production and population, and some people in Fort Macleod recognized that its substitution with more intensive agriculture would benefit the town. It was assumed that mixed farming would replace ranching; the substitution of one monoculture for another was not anticipated. By the late 1880s the *Macleod Gazette*, which until then had supported the ranching industry, began campaigning for mixed farming. In 1888 it editorialized that "drastic measures" were required because the development of the country had "gradually but surely come to a standstill." It demanded that leases be cancelled and the land distributed as homesteads, a stance that naturally brought it into conflict with ranchers.[34]

The main objective in encouraging mixed farming was to attract settlers and diversify agricultural production so that processing would take place in Fort Macleod. Thus, efforts to attract facilities such as a grist mill to process wheat into flour were integral to the campaign. The *Gazette* estimated that between $25,000 and $30,000 worth of flour was imported each year, and this money would be kept "in the district" if flour was produced locally. It would also create a spiral of growth: demand for wheat would increase, then for labour, and finally for settlement. "No country can expect to prosper when everything is imported and nothing produced," and the *Gazette* computed that the district spent about

| Lacombe, as shown in this 1908 photo of "hog shipping day,"
benefited from the economic activity created by mixed farming.
Archives Collection, A9008, PAA.

$79,000 for various goods "which can easily be supplied at home, if the producers only get up and rustle." This not only required an end to the lease system, but ranchers' arguments that the rainfall and soil of the area were unsuitable for farming had to be disproved. Accordingly, the *Gazette* glowingly reported the size of vegetables produced in local gardens and the potential for hog raising, dairying and grain farming.[35]

The farming (or "open settlement") side of the debate gradually defeated the ranchers after 1900 and much of the land around Fort Macleod was taken up by farmers. The town's demands may have played a role in this, but it was more important that the Liberal government in Ottawa, especially with Frank Oliver as minister of the Interior, favoured homesteaders and not Tory ranchers. In any event, it was a pyrrhic victory. By 1911 the suitability of the area for farming was being questioned and farmers were abandoning their land. Nor were farmers practising mixed farming since they steadfastly resisted its labour and time demands and instead opted for wheat production. This created some antagonism in the Fort Macleod district—the board of trade urged farmers to adopt mixed farming, while farmers resisted and accused the board of being "dictatorial."[36]

The theory that mixed farming was beneficial for town growth was not unique to Fort Macleod. The same arguments were made in all agricultural towns. In both Claresholm and Cardston, it was argued that mixed farming would eliminate agricultural instability and enrich the towns. Yet the conflict between town and farm over mixed farming before World War I was focused largely in southern Alberta since mixed farming already generally characterized the rest of the province. Lacombe was a rich mixed farming area and town and country had few differences about agricultural development. The Lacombe board of trade and town council worked to stimulate agricultural production in tandem with local farmers; it sponsored livestock shows and promoted the agricultural production of the area. After 1920, conflict between town and country over types of farming had also disappeared in southern Alberta. For example, the Claresholm board of trade by the interwar years had accepted, and even welcomed, wheat monoculture.[37]

Efforts to encourage mixed farming went beyond gratuitous advice to farmers. Marketing was important, and farmers' markets were part of the hope that mixed farming would benefit the towns. In Claresholm in 1909 it was hoped that a farmers' market (also called a country or a public market) would attract farmers to town. While it might take business away from stores selling produce, it was reasoned that a market would benefit the town by drawing farmers to Claresholm rather than neighbouring towns. The *Claresholm Review* warned that "the people living here must not forget that every new town in this district menaces to a certain extent the trade of Claresholm." The "only...way of keeping the trade" was to recognize "that the business life of the town is dependent on the farmers." A market would also stimulate market gardening, mixed farming and dairying.[38]

This argument was also made in Cardston, but a farmers' market was attempted only at Fort Macleod. A.H. Allen, president of the board of trade, noted in early 1913 that the market for local produce was small because most stores sold imported goods and only bartered for local produce. Since farmers often ended the year with a merchandise credit which was "absolutely useless" to them, mixed farming could only expand with a cash market for produce.[39] The next year, a farmers' market was established in Fort Macleod under the sponsorship of the board of trade. A committee was created to operate the market. Cut meat could be sold only in large pieces, presumably to pacify the butchers who were complaining about the market, and Chinese were barred from selling anything. The market was located on a vacant lot downtown. It was held once a week for three hours, with the last hour reserved for merchants to buy supplies. Surplus produce was sent to the Calgary public market for sale.[40]

Local merchants were unenthusiastic about the market, but the board of trade was dominated by realtors, and merchants had little voice in its market scheme. Moreover, few were probably willing to challenge the official rhetoric about the need for agricultural diversification which the market supposedly promoted. But silence was not consent, and their attitude was much like that of other Canadian merchants in similar circumstances. As a representative of the Retail Merchants Association of Canada advised Fort Macleod merchants in 1913, they should fight the farmers' market because it would hurt their business during the summer, leaving them only the winter trade when produce was hard to come by and of poor quality. Early the next year, Reach and Co., one of the largest stores in town, foretold that the farmers would sit all day waiting to sell their goods but "what you have left over don't bring it to us. We do not want the left overs." While only the town's two butchers and Reach and Co. were described as "antagonistic," no merchants "appeared very enthusiastic." Even so, most promised not to "buck the proposition" and several said that they would buy supplies at the market. The committee asked farmers to bring good quality produce and urged townspeople not to be "shy about carrying your basket to market. It is a new thing in Macleod, but an old established custom in older and larger cities elsewhere."[41]

The first market was highly successful and restrictions on cut meat were removed and Chinese were allowed to sell vegetables. But it was soon argued that the farmers' prices were too high and the market committee began posting the prices realized at the Calgary market for guidance. Disposing of surplus was also a problem. Worst, the number of customers fell, and those who came expected unreasonably low prices. By September the market was failing, and it was not re-established in following years.[42] It had demonstrated the limits of such retailing in a small town. The farmers' hopes of selling directly to the consumer and setting their own prices foundered because of the town's small population. Further, the market was feasible only in the summer and fall. The demand by townfolk for unrealistically low prices alienated farmers, and the silent hostility of the merchants doubtless also limited its success.

Local marketing of mixed farm products was ideally supplemented with "industry," a loosely used but emotionally charged term that meant any activity in which processing added value to a product. It could include processing meat from local livestock or manufacturing products such as wood building supplies, bricks and glass. Solicitation for industry was combined with the advertising for settlers put out by boards of trade and town councils. This was also supplemented in some places by the use of publicity agents. The Lacombe board of trade hired a "publicity man" in the spring of 1912, and town business owners pledged $10 per month for six months to pay his salary. Enthusiasm was so high that sufficient pledges were secured in a few days to hire a Mr. L.H. Mason from Chicago at $200 per month on a six-month contract. He was a "first class publicity man" who had "some fame as a promoter of industries." While his recruitment was a logical extension of the faith in promotion, results were negligible. The Fort Macleod board of trade also hired a "publicity man" in 1912, and by the time it fired him about six months later, it was the only town in the province that still employed an agent. With the exception of a brick yard, "he had not landed a single industry for Macleod. For this he is censured and probably branded as a time server."[43]

The objective of all this activity was to stimulate economic growth by creating a balanced economy. Some also contended that it would lower the cost of living. As it was remarked in Peace River in 1922, freight rates and costs of distribution were "killing this country; we ship our goods out to be manufactured and we ship them back to be consumed, and the railway takes the profit. By manufacturing our own products we could cut this expense in half, and increase the population to three times what it is now." As well, it was assumed that if industry was attracted to a town, growth would become self-sustaining. Fort Macleod promoters argued in 1913 that the town "will never grow unless there is a payroll to make it grow." In Grande Prairie in 1916, the heady year when the railway reached the village, it was remarked with an extraordinary casualness that the town needed to produce "as nearly as we can, every article that will be used on the farm." If the town was to become "a city, it must be made up of a manufacturing as well as a mercantile population."[44]

The belief that urban growth was possible only through a diversified economy was not as persistent in nonagricultural towns as in those dependent on agriculture. In the Crowsnest Pass, for example, there had been some hope before 1912 that the economy would expand beyond coal mining; in 1911 Coleman was said to be well positioned for a range of manufacturing because it had the "raw materials" for a glass factory, machine shop, brick plant, sugar mill, pulp and paper mill, sash and door factory and an iron shop. But the pursuit of manufacturing in the Pass was weakened, not strengthened, by the rich resources of the area. As R.W. Coulthard, general manager of Western Canadian Collieries, said in 1912, the immense coal resources of the area provided "a veritable clear profit from the earth."[45] There was little need to look further afield for wealth, and the Pass soon settled into an acceptance of its future as a coal mining and not a manufacturing area. Reflecting a more varied local economy, and perhaps a less wealthy mining sector, Drumheller was always more committed to diversifying the local economy through a marriage of mining and agriculture.

In the search for industry, the proximity of natural resources was nevertheless commonly cited as a benefit. This had been part of the lure of the west—its natural wealth had become legendary in the minds of immigration promoters who argued that only energy and vision were needed to exploit it. Since there was plenty of wood around towns like Peace River, furniture factories were seen as a potential industry. Similarly, furniture manufacturing and cereal processing were said to be logical areas for growth at Fort Macleod. These plans assumed that industries chose a location primarily because of its natural resources and not its proximity to markets. If a transportation system was in place, it was assumed that the framework for industrial development was present. This often led to demands for further railway construction. At Fort Macleod, it was argued in 1914 that yet more rail lines were needed to accommodate the area's expanded potential because of the opening of the Panama Canal. The town was "in the centre of the greatest wheat belt the world has ever known," close to the timber resources of the mountains, and at the "entrance of the Crow's Nest Pass with its wealthy territory beyond." Thus, if additional transportation facilities were built, it would "readily demand recognition as a manufacturing and distributing centre." The board of trade was busy advertising these advantages and sanguinely contended that it could "do a great deal, if it had the strength of united citizenship behind it, towards raising Macleod to the pinnacle of cityhood."[46]

Whether or not its citizens were united in favour of town growth, such policies made little difference in attracting industry. While town leaders consistently tried to attract industry, their plans were sometimes poorly formulated. Although there was little dairying at Claresholm, the board of trade placed an advertisement in 1908 in the *Commercial*, a Winnipeg business magazine, urging investors to establish a creamery in Claresholm. This was a popular proposal in most towns, and the board was probably following the current fad. In any event, some board members pointed out that since steam engine owners in the district had to send away for repairs, a foundry and repair shop would be more beneficial than a creamery. The *Commercial* was instructed to advertise for a foundry instead of a creamery. By 1911, opinion in Claresholm had not yet decided what industry to seek out. It was still felt that mixed farming would create some important spin-off manufacturing, "but beyond asking for a flour mill, no one has a suggestion to make."[47]

The randomness of such efforts no doubt contributed to poor results, but more fundamental reasons lay behind this general lack of development. Infrastructure like water and electricity was rudimentary or lacking; capital was difficult to secure; local economic conditions limited local processing; and big cities proved better able to attract industry which demanded infrastructure as well as financial concessions. Recognition of the importance of these factors grew, and in 1912 the Lacombe board of trade resolved that, despite its earlier efforts, it was "useless to work for industries for which we have no real inducements." Instead, it decided to focus on the area's good land to attract agricultural settlers. However, while the town was "not doing very much for factories" immediately, it would lay "the foundation" for them by securing "cheap power." This recognized that energy was fundamental in industrial development, and similar views were expressed in other Alberta towns as well. The next year, it was noted in Fort Macleod that a prospective investor's first question was the price of power, "and until we can compete with Medicine Hat or Calgary, it is almost useless to answer their enquiries."[48]

Initially, most power plants were locally owned and operated. As elsewhere on the prairies, some were established and operated by the town, a development which was justified as a mark of urban "progressiveness." In other cases, local investors secured a franchise from the town, raised some capital and bought generating equipment.[49] In 1907, an electrical plant was built by private investors in Claresholm. It was argued that ownership by local entrepreneurs with "an interest in the town" protected "the best interests of the citizens."[50] The plant burned shortly after it opened, and the town remained without electricity until 1912 when the town built a plant.[51] This pattern was typical, but whether privately or publicly owned, generating plants were often poorly capitalized and their operation suffered from a lack of operating and management experience. Many plants offered only limited and often erratic service, and most were unprofitable. By the 1920s, many small private plants—those in Lacombe and Grande Prairie were typical—had come under civic control in order to ensure continued electrical service. In theory, this also served private commercial interests by enabling the town to set low rates for manufacturing.[52]

Once a town acquired a plant, it was usually forced to invest in new equipment. But like their predecessors, towns often were unable to cope with steadily increasing demands for electricity and rarely had the expertise needed to operate the plants. Further, costs had to be borne through debenture debt, which was costly to secure after 1913. Town political life added further complexity because councillors were reluctant to force ratepayers to pay their utility account arrears. All of these problems created much discussion but no long-term solutions. With ratepayers complaining about electrical plant operating losses, and general complaints about service, towns eagerly sold their plants to large companies with central generating plants such as Calgary Power and Canadian Utilities. By the 1930s, most towns received their power supply from these companies, which offered better service. They also provided lower rates to commercial users, but these rates generally applied across the company's grid, giving no special advantage to a particular town.[53]

The financial difficulties facing both civic and privately owned local electrical plants reflected the general problem of attracting capital for construction and operation of industry. One widely recommended approach was to seek out local capital. In Lacombe in 1912 it was argued that instead of using the board of trade publicity agent as "a haphazard scout for outside capital" in a "hopeless" competition with cities, he should act as an "industrial organizer for his district." Ontario's industrialization was said to have resulted from the investment of capital savings of farmers and townspeople in local enterprise, and Alberta needed to follow this model as well.[54]

Even so, raising local capital was difficult. In 1888, it was found that construction of a grist mill at Fort Macleod would cost about $13,000.

Capital from banks and loan companies was impossible to secure in the Northwest in the late 1880s because of "the unsettled state of the country," and this may have explained the formation of a joint stock company to raise local capital. About 60 percent of the stock was quickly subscribed, but when the call for payment was made, investors were less certain about their commitment and the project collapsed.[55] Twenty years later there seemed to be more local capital available. In 1907, the Canadian Society of Equity, a farmers' organization, formed a joint stock company, Equity Co. Ltd, to build grist mills, elevators and other grain handling and processing facilities. Using local capital, the company undertook construction of a mill at Fort Macleod. The town provided free land, water, a tax exemption, and low cost electricity, but the company went into receivership in 1908, causing local investors to lose about 20 percent of their capital.[56]

Such problems strengthened the belief that outside capital was necessary for industrial development. Towns offered what concessions they could, and industry used the rivalry among towns to extract as many concessions as possible. Industries looking to locate, and towns wanting industry, scouted for suitable partners. Most of this came to naught in the smaller centres, and Fort Macleod's experience was typical. In 1913, a town representative travelled to seven Ontario cities seeking investment. As well, the board of trade received numerous inquiries from manufacturers looking to build. It replied to these proposals, and there the matter usually ended. In other instances, demands for concessions were so great they could not be met. Fort Macleod's hopes for a sash and door factory were dashed by a Milwaukee firm's request for an $18,000 loan; a candy maker wanted the town to take $1,000 in stock in the venture; and numerous others "wanted capital." While such demands were an obvious barrier, the town's ambitions were sometimes unrealistic as well. In 1912 the board of trade participated in discussions about a flour mill, but the proposed mill was too small "to merit anxiety on our part." Instead, it negotiated with another party which proposed a larger mill, but nothing came of the talks.[57] By 1913, efforts spanning 15 years had produced little. The only manufacturing in the town was a brick yard and the McLaren lumber mill, which had been established prior to the board's efforts.

The McLaren mill had, nevertheless, received public support. It was built in 1888 as a branch of an Ottawa Valley lumber concern to process timber floated down the Oldman River to Fort Macleod from the foothills. The lumber was used locally or was shipped to Lethbridge by ox team. The mill burned in 1894 and McLaren postponed its rebuilding. In 1896 he was persuaded to do so when the town offered $1,750 in cash, paid over ten years without interest. This was a goodly amount of money for Fort Macleod; in 1896 the town's total receipts were about $3,700.[58] The McLaren bonus became a one mill charge on local taxes and the plant received further subsidy by being exempted from property taxes. It operated until about 1911, when it was moved to Blairmore. It became one of the largest lumber firms in the Pass, where it operated until the early 1930s.[59]

True to the tenets of positive thinking, the failure to attract industry was usually blamed on others who had more to offer; rarely was it attributed to more fundamental economic or social conditions. The bonusing of industry was a contest that towns could not win. Most cities were not prevented by their charters from doing so, while towns were limited in this respect. In 1894 the Territorial government had placed restrictions on bonusing by towns and also required that any exemption from taxation be approved by a two-thirds majority vote of the ratepayers. Alberta maintained these provisions in 1905 and further required that exemptions from taxation could only be granted on a year-to-year basis. Many prairie towns opposed the use of bonuses since they could not compete with large cities. Some critics also argued that bonusing benefited only real estate promoters who gained from immediate increases in property values when an industry did move to a town. The bonuses that attracted it were paid by the ratepayers.[60]

Nevertheless, bonusing did have its proponents, although its local benefits were not always long term. As one study of the benefits of city bonusing policies in the Lakehead has concluded, while incentives immediately attracted industry, long-term survival depended more on locational factors and the area's suitability for a particular enterprise.[61] The importance of these factors in the success of manufacturing was illustrated by efforts in agricultural processing, one of the main industries in most towns. Creameries and meat packing plants were popular projects, yet success depended on local markets and supply of raw materials. Reflecting a solid mixed farming hinterland, Lacombe had a creamery before World War I, as did Cardston, which had a long cheese-making tradition. The first cheese factory (a co-operative) was established in 1890 and Cardston cheese was sold in Fort Macleod and other centres in southern Alberta by the mid 1890s. In 1911, a co-operative creamery was established at Mountain View, near Cardston. As a co-operative, it directly involved local milk producers, giving them an incentive to produce consistently. It was successful and continued in business until at least World War II. In contrast, a creamery at Fort Macleod was established about 1911 but closed in 1913 because it did not have a regular supply of cream. Farmers refused to form co-operative dairies—which the creamery operators believed were necessary to ensure enough cream for commercial production. The same problem was encountered in the Peace River country. In 1931, a creamery was proposed for Peace River, but some critics noted that several local creameries had already been "forced to suspend business owing to lack of the cream supply, while those few which are still operating are only running at a fraction of their capacity."[62]

While processing plants exported some of their production, local consumption was significant, and it was encouraged through advertising and promotion. For example, baking contests which used local flour were popular, and one held in Drumheller in 1934 using the local product, Blue Star flour, drew 258 entries.[63] Distance from large centres also encouraged local consumption by limiting competition for local industries. Meat processing plants were one example of this. While local butchers processed meat, some on a fairly large scale, most meat processing in Alberta by World War I was concentrated in larger centres. The only successful processing plant in the towns surveyed was in Peace River where the Peace River Meat Co. opened an abattoir in 1938. The plant cut meat and also made cured and cooked meats which were sold throughout the Peace River country. It was small in comparison to city plants (in 1945 it could process 150 hogs and 25 cattle per day), but it reflected the role of locational factors in success.[64]

The connection between a community's stage of development and broader economic factors was shown in the manufacturing of building products, another industry common in Alberta towns before World War I. Most of the towns surveyed had a brick yard, and many also had a sash and door factory (or a planing mill as they were later called).[65] Indicative of the forces governing manufacturing in small places, these operations were successful as long as settlement created demand for building products. Since they were tied to growth, the slump of 1912–13 bankrupted many, World War I finished off others, and the hard years following the end of the war eliminated most others. The only ones with a chance of success produced specialized materials and were also part of a vertically integrated business. One such business was a sash and door factory owned by Enrico Pozzi, a Blairmore builder, which produced a range of products, including cafe booths and church pews.[66]

The same cycle was apparent in the Peace River country. Lake Saskatoon had a sawmill in 1914, and a sash and door factory by 1916, and after 1917 a planing mill operated by H.R. Walker of Calgary. These plants supplied local needs and were welcomed because "it was impossible to order the mill work from Edmonton and have it arrive here on time." Overall, building product manufacturing had longer success in the Peace River country than in the rest of the province, likely because settlement was ongoing throughout the interwar years and the relative isolation of the area gave local manufacturers some protection from city competition. A brick plant using local clay was established near Grande Prairie in 1935 and was still operating in 1947. Other building product firms received a boost from the demand created by wartime construction needs.[67]

In many agricultural service towns, however, prospects for manufacturing had become remote by the interwar years. While the well-being of farmers had long been recognized as important for towns, a greater appreciation of the role of agriculture began to develop. Typical of this view was the assertion in Cardston in 1939 that the town's "future regardless of what may occur in the location of minerals or other natural riches is bound up with agriculture. This is our great source of wealth. Around it and its related industries must revolve the life, happiness and fortune of nine-tenths of the citizens of Cardston and the surrounding district."[68] Fort Macleod also saw a resolution of most farmer-town disagreements about agricultural practices after World War I. Both groups came to see irrigation as the solution for the agricultural problems of the district, and in 1922 the South Macleod Irrigation district was formed. Irrigation districts were co-operatives formed by a vote of the farmers to issue debentures to finance construction of irrigation works. For Fort Macleod, it was the 1880s again. In its campaign for approval of the scheme, the Macleod Times denounced dry land farming with the same energy and arguments that its predecessor, the Gazette, had used against ranching in the nineteenth century. Dry land farming was wasteful of land and resources, it was unstable, and it represented a capital drain. And to the contention that irrigation, being so productive, would only create oversupply, the Macleod Times argued that "large amounts of money have been sent to outside points, and large amounts paid to the C.P.R. for freighting" goods like potatoes and butter which could be produced locally. While the vote to form the district passed, the necessary construction did not proceed. Fort Macleod's demands for agricultural diversification, which had begun in the late 1880s, had not ended, and as late as 1944 the board of trade was calling upon the province to construct irrigation works in the district.[69]

In the 1920s, the advent of co-operative marketing also helped to stabilize agriculture. While most boards of trade did not play a direct role in this development, they welcomed it because, as was noted by the Cardston board of trade, co-operative marketing of dairy, poultry, livestock and grain benefited the town because it "had a tendency to steady the market" as nothing else had before. Some marketing pools spread payments throughout the year and "stabilized the inflow of money to a certain extent."[70] In this context, a popular project in many towns towards the end of the 1930s was the establishment of cold storage locker plants where farmers had meat processed and rented freezers for storing meat and produce for personal use. This met farmers' needs and kept them coming to town to pick up stored produce. In 1940, the Claresholm Men's Club was promoting a co-operatively organized locker plant, and similar projects were underway in many towns.[71]

These growing concerns with agriculture did not mean that towns entirely discontinued their efforts to attract industry. Familiar attitudes continued to shape these ambitions. In 1946, it was remarked in Claresholm that the town should benefit from the anticipated surge in the postwar economy but "it depends on what the town itself does about it." Many of the same promotional techniques also continued in use, and the Lacombe board of trade, for example, received a $2,000 grant from the town in 1936 to encourage "expansion of new industries."[72] Many centres also continued to try to attract industry by promoting the resources of the area. Drumheller hoped that its incorporation as a city in 1930 would give it greater scope to attract industry and economic growth. In an attempt to co-ordinate activity, members of the city's finance and land committee sat on the board of trade industrial development committee. The city promised concessions to firms seeking to establish in Drumheller, but few opportunities came along. By 1934 Drumheller still had no manufacturing plants except a flour mill, although it had two mine equipment distributors, a lumber wholesaler, and 10 mining companies. At the end of World War II, with prospects looking brighter than they had for some time, the city established an Industrial Development board to attract new industry and expand existing ones.[73]

In Drumheller, like all coal mining towns, an important economic issue was the well-being of the coal industry. Politicians frequently spoke about marketing Alberta coal, and town councils and boards of trade willingly added their names to petitions demanding exclusion of American coal from Canada. As well, efforts were made to amend freight rate tariffs to give Alberta coal a better advantage in the Canadian market.[74] In addition, efforts were made to meet the challenge posed by truck transport. As the president of the Calgary board of trade told a Drumheller audience in 1933, the competition of trucks and buses with trains was unfair because truckers used public highways without charge.[75] A more fundamental worry was that trucks were gas powered and were replacing coal fired locomotives. In the Crowsnest Pass, boards of trade, other local organizations, and newspapers formed an unusual alliance with mine workers to urge local stores to use rail instead of trucks to bring in their goods. The railway created local employment and, more importantly, it stimulated coal consumption. As the mine workers argued, "we dig coal, not gasoline."[76] Such concerns paralleled those of agricultural service towns with agricultural marketing, and both were meaningful indicators of the focus of economic concerns in Alberta's staple dominated economy.

Towns *as* Service *and* Tourist Centres

In addition to various types of industry, town promoters saw the public service sector as having significant potential for the local economy. Land registry offices, court houses, and hospitals would contribute to the expansion of the town's services, leading to increased population and the number of visitors drawn to the town on business. Since such facilities were provided by government, it confirmed a view of politics as a game of rewards organized by the party system. This view was reflected in Grande Prairie in 1913 in the observation that the constituency needed an MLA who was a full time "pusher and a hustler" who would "get for us" roads, bridges, railways and government offices.[77] When such buildings were planned, politicians were further pressured (as they were on highway construction and maintenance projects) to ensure that local workers and firms were hired for construction.[78] The partisan nature of this decision making was clearly understood. In 1910, the province planned to build an agricultural college at the University of Alberta, in the Premier's riding. The Cardston board of trade objected to this slight to southern Alberta, and organized a protest campaign. It asked other boards of trade to join the protest to force the government to locate the college in southern Alberta. The Fort Macleod board of trade refused to participate, observing that since it wanted a government demonstration farm located in the town, it dared not alienate the Premier.[79]

In light of such conditions, politicians commonly promised, at least during elections, that a town would get its wishes. Before World War I, many town authorities lobbied for land registry offices. They argued that it was expensive for homesteaders to travel to Calgary and Edmonton, where the main registry offices were located, and that such a facility would create a few jobs and increase trade in the town. For the same reasons, government found it difficult to close such facilities after they had been established, as was the case in 1933 when the province moved its land office from Grande Prairie to Peace River.[80]

The same considerations applied to the location of other government facilities. Court houses, like registry offices, were also in popular demand in all towns because they created some employment and brought people to town. In 1909 the province voted funds for a court house in Claresholm. This created great hopes in the town and the *Claresholm Review* warned land owners against greed. The building would be important for the town, and putting the matter bluntly, it pointed out that "this is not the occasion for some private individuals to unload."[81]

The court house was not built, and when the province announced plans in 1911 to build a demonstration farm in southern Alberta, Claresholm loudly reminded the province that it had been betrayed over the court house. Fort Macleod and Cardston, among others, actively campaigned for the farm, both for the jobs it would create and because it might stimulate mixed farming in the district.[82] Claresholm won the contest, largely, the neighbouring town of Carmangay claimed, by whining about losing the court house and through political pressure. And politics were important: while the Claresholm board of trade was "moving heaven and earth to get the farm," it was frankly admitted that the deciding factor was that Claresholm had a government MLA while Fort Macleod had returned one from the opposition.[83] By the 1920s, the students (who boarded in town) and the staff of the demonstration farm (now called the school of agriculture) had brought considerable economic benefit to the town. By the late 1920s, it was rumoured that the school would be closed. The Claresholm board of trade fought this "sinister proposal" by lobbying the government and attempted to increase enrolment by advertising for students. While this specific intervention failed, the building was turned into a psychiatric hospital, which continued to benefit the town's economy.[84]

Claresholm's greatest prize in government facilities came in 1941 when a wartime air training base was set up just outside the town. While the town paid for the installation of electricity at the base, it got the "benefit of all salvage" after the war. Within a year there were 1,500 men at the training base, plus their families in town. Business boomed, and many residents took in boarders and rented out rooms, complaining bitterly when the town came under federal rent controls.[85] The base was a blessing after the rigors of the Depression, and people in Claresholm enjoyed it, and some abused it. Although the Claresholm Men's Club opened a recreational hall in town for servicemen in 1943, some airmen claimed that the town's welcome in other respects was less than cordial, charging that Claresholm businessmen were "out to stick" them. There were air training bases in various parts of Alberta, and every town wanted one. The Drumheller board of trade began lobbying in 1940 for an air training base, but by 1942 it would have been satisfied with any type of "war industry." Local business owners "reviewed Drumheller's effort" and asserted that its generous response to recruitment and war bond campaigns "certainly entitled" it to "consideration by the government."[86]

Wartime facilities were important temporarily, but the local economy benefited more from permanent facilities such as consolidated schools or hospitals. While hospitals often received public grants before World War I, they were essentially run as local charities or by religious groups. In 1918, one or more municipalities were allowed to "petition themselves into a hospital district and appoint a provisional board" which devised a hospital scheme. After the scheme was approved by a two-thirds vote by the ratepayers, a hospital board was elected to build a hospital or work out an agreement with an established one in a neighbouring city or town. These hospitals were financed by debentures, requisitions on participating municipalities, provincial government grants, and patient fees.

By 1928, there were 19 hospital districts in Alberta, although fewer were organized in the 1930s because of difficulties in selling debentures.[87]

Like court houses or registry offices, hospitals were enthusiastically supported by town promoters. In addition to the health benefits brought to townspeople, they helped make the town a central place for the district. While the provincial government had a say in the selection of the site, the largest centre usually won if the voters could be got out, and boards of trade often arranged transportation to the polls for their townspeople. In 1918, a hospital district was formed in Drumheller, overcoming opposition in Delia, a smaller neighbouring centre. As the *Drumheller Review* jubilantly claimed, "there is weeping and wailing and gnashing of teeth in the Delia district, thanks to the splendid efforts of workers in the Drumheller Hospital District."[88] It was not mere promotion, however, that had decided the matter. Drumheller had the infrastructure to support the facility and it was central for most valley coal mines, making it a more efficient site to treat mine accident victims.[89] In a similar contest among Grande Prairie, Sexsmith and Clairmont, the telling factor in Grande Prairie's favour was that only it had a water and sewage system, fire protection, electricity and resident doctors. In other cases, where local opposition was stronger, the politics of hospital location could be bitter. For example, while smaller towns in the Crowsnest Pass did not care where a hospital was located as long as it was built, the issue caused such wrangling between Blairmore and Coleman that a compromise site was finally selected midway between the two towns.[90]

Despite the energy invested in the pursuit of such facilities, the public service sector was a relatively inelastic part of town economy. A more open-ended prospect for economic growth was tourism, which gained lustre in the interwar years, often, it seemed, as an alternative to industrial development. Part of its attraction was that it needed only minimal public infrastructure. As was remarked in Cardston in 1930, every dollar spent by a tourist was "found" money.[91] In the Crowsnest Pass, tourism was thought to have potential even before World War I when it was hoped that tourists would come on the train. But in the Pass, as elsewhere, motor vehicles changed such forecasts.

In the 1920s and 1930s, demands for road improvement were often linked with promotion of tourism. Auto clubs became involved in tourist promotion by preparing tourist maps and pressing for road improvement. In part, hard-surfaced highways were said to be necessary to attract American tourists.[92] In 1928, it was said in the Peace River coun-

| *This arch was built on Peace River's main street to welcome tourists and other visitors. Not dated. Archives Collection, A10643, PAA.*

try that "thousands of tourists are looking for new places to visit" and the novelty of the Peace River country would draw them if roads were improved. Tourists also needed maps and road signs, for which local boards of trade happily contributed funds. Maps were usually prepared by boards of trade, each sharing in the costs of the general tourism campaign. In 1929, for example, the Blairmore board of trade distributed $800 worth of maps of the Red Trail Route (Winnipeg to Vancouver via the Crowsnest Pass). Large road signs were put up to advertise the route at Yahk, British Columbia and at Cardston.[93] Signs were usually put up at the entrance to the town or at highway intersections to give directions to a town and indicate the facilities it offered tourists. Since road signs were not provided by government, their absence often meant that tourists did not know the name of the town they were in, which gave town boosters "a mild shock."[94] Facilities for tourists, especially "auto parks" where they could camp, were also needed because hotels were rarely used by ordinary tourists. Usually provided by the board of trade, they featured a cooking area, tables, benches and potable water.

Cardston and Drumheller were especially concerned with tourist development—the Mormon Temple and the town's proximity to Waterton National Park drew many visitors to Cardston, and Drumheller's palaeon-

| *As this 1936 photo illustrates, the grandeur of the Mormon Temple in Cardston made it an important tourist attraction. Oblate Collection, OB248, PAA.*

tological resources provided a unique attraction. In addition to the usual maps, signs and auto camps, both towns tried to create an environment to stimulate tourism. In 1930, plans were made in Drumheller for a small display of dinosaur bones at the library, and local tourist publicity provided guidance to nearby deposits of petrified wood. Recognition of the value of tourism increased steadily at Drumheller. Using the commission earned by selling war bonds, the Drumheller board of trade in 1944 produced 10,000 car windshield stickers featuring a dinosaur to advertise the palaeontological sites in the area.[95] Similarly, Cardston's view of its tourist potential grew during the interwar years. It was said to be "favored with more visitors than is common to towns of our size" because of the Temple which opened in 1921. In 1929, for example, 300 American Mormons travelled by auto to Cardston to visit it. By 1932 the town kept flood lights on it at night, which "truly distinguishes Cardston as The Temple City." In 1936 the board of trade put up a sign at the Temple directing people to the main street because "hundreds of cars have been getting as far as the Temple and going on through town."[96] As the site of significant church events such as marriage, baptisms by proxy for the dead, administration to the sick, ordinations and other gatherings of the priesthood, the Temple was an important centre.

While no other town had comparable facilities, a Seventh Day Adventist College established near Lacombe in 1916 made a significant contribution to that town's economy. In 1930, it created about $40,000 annually in benefits for Lacombe through the purchase of supplies and staff and student shopping.[97]

Early twentieth century town promoters were no doubt correct in seeing manufacturing as crucial for growth. While service centre functions had created growth in places like Fort Macleod at the beginning of Euro-Canadian settlement, by the twentieth century this function could only serve to hold population, not increase it.[98] The general inability of town promoters to shape economic conditions forced them continually to readjust their approaches for encouraging economic growth. The economic collapse of 1912–13 and the general failure to attract industry forced towns to look more seriously at public service institutions like hospitals or to tourism for economic growth. So too, it led to a more realistic view of the role of farming in their economies.

Transportation, industrial and agricultural development, public sector services and tourism were interconnected but separate components in the drive for economic diversification in towns. Such diversification was, however, only marginally realized. This failure in part resulted from the nature of manufacturing. By the early twentieth century, most manufacturing was complex, needing specialized knowledge and materials, large amounts of capital, and extensive public infrastructure. Thus, it was unrealistic to hope that factories making furniture, for example, would locate in a town whose only advantage was local lumber supplies.

Further, the financial crisis facing most civic governments by 1913 meant that town councils were handicapped by a lack of funds to install the necessary infrastructure or provide the concessions demanded by private industry. Of equal importance, they were also unable, even before the economic collapse of 1912–13, to compete with cities in attracting industry. They could not match the better infrastructure of the cities, or their strategic locations in the national transportation system. By the interwar years, patterns of urban dominance had largely been set. New cities such as Drumheller, for example, found that attaining city status gave them little advantage in pursuing industry.

The assumption that lack of growth resulted from the inability of local elites to focus the town's energy and purpose is thus of little benefit in understanding the failure to achieve diversification. H.C. Pentland's observation that economic development in the North Atlantic world was dependent on resources, capital, and labour, "but not upon promoters, who are always in excess supply," precisely summarizes economic development in Alberta towns.[99] As geographer E.K. Muller has noted, while the varied reasons for urban growth remain imprecisely understood, they can be "conveniently grouped under the rubrics of initial advantages, transportation, central place relationships and manufacturing."[100] Further, senior government policies favoured certain places over others for partisan reasons or broader provincial or national goals.[101]

While factors affecting urban growth reinforced each other, broader developments in transportation were especially important in changing a town's economic zone of influence by altering the time-distance relationship between places. With the completion of the C&E, Calgary and Edmonton were only 11 hours apart by rail in the 1890s, and this travelling time was reduced further by the time of World War I. The same change naturally also affected smaller centres. By 1930, it was possible to accommodate an eight-hour stay in Calgary by leaving Cardston at 5:30 A.M., arriving back in Cardston at midnight. It was a long day, but "Calgary is getting closer."[102]

6

Doing
Business *in*
the Small Town

Commerce was central to town life. It justi-
fied the establishment of most towns, whose continued health depended
on the success of their businesses. Only in the coal mining towns was the
mercantile rationale for town existence challenged by other economic
activities. In all cases, however, town businesses were increasingly integrated into the wider economy. Local control was threatened by chain
stores and franchise operations, and by competition from mail order
retailers, itinerant traders, and, in foodstuffs, from farmers. While various strategies were employed in an attempt to limit this competition,
town businesses increasingly were affected by outside forces that they
could counter only marginally.

Town Retail Trade

In its first years, a town's retail outlets were
general in nature. In the 1870s, Fort Macleod's major businesses included
two general merchants, a hotel and a blacksmith. Once the town was
moved off the island and became a permanent settlement, there was
rapid growth. By 1887 it had 26 retail and service businesses, including
five general stores, four hotels, four drug stores (most selling liquor), two
barbers, two boot and shoe makers, two blacksmiths, a hardware store
and assorted other businesses including a bank, a furniture dealer, a livery, and a harness maker. The same expansion took place in all towns. In

| *Among the first businesses in Claresholm was a general store run by the McKinney family. Archives Collection, A5476, PAA.*

1902, at Claresholm, William Moffat (later mayor of the town) "piled lumber on the prairie and sat on the top of the highest pile and watched for buyers." And they came. Within a year there were 16 retail, service and professional businesses in the town, roughly of the same nature as those in Fort Macleod in 1887. Claresholm, however, had two lumber yards and two farm implement dealers, reflecting different building technology and standards, and a stronger farm service sector. By 1910, Fort Macleod had 51 businesses, and Claresholm had 50, including a wide range of retailing and service.[1] As well, the adoption of automobiles added new types of businesses, but also marked the start of a decline of those associated with horse power.

There was rapid turnover of businesses, especially trades and services, in the first few years of settlement. Major businesses like hardware and general stores showed greater stability from the start. Sufficient capital was important in setting up a business that would be successful, but so were skill and an ability to make the correct decision in a highly uncertain and rapidly changing environment.[2] Some businesses followed the railway, continually establishing themselves anew at each railhead, settling down at the end of the line or at some point which appeared promising. Many of these merchants had stores elsewhere, and were testing potential new markets. J.E. Thomson, owner of a hardware store in Edson (then a supply point for the south Peace River country), visited

Grande Prairie in 1915. He planned to build a store "at steel head this winter and later on move to some point in the immediate vicinity." While he also visited Lake Saskatoon and Beaverlodge, by September 1916, when it was evident that the steel would not immediately move beyond Grande Prairie, he had set up a store there. At first, a branch of his Edson operation, he closed in Edson and concentrated on Grande Prairie where he soon became prominent in the town.[3]

Most often, branch operations were simply an effort to expand business. Although branches were set up in almost every type of business, they were most common among general stores, drug stores, clothing shops and bakeries. Rarely, however, were these branch stores successful. Spencer and Stoddard, Cardston hardware dealers, had a branch store in Kimball, but closed it in 1908. Similarly, Campbell's Furniture, a large Edmonton retailer, opened a branch in Grande Prairie in 1937, but had closed it by 1939. While conditions varied with each circumstance, small independent businesses were difficult to operate from a distance because they were not sufficiently profitable to support experienced salaried management. Running stores in different towns with the same management tended to drain both operations, and as was emphasized when Spencer and Stoddard sold their Kimball store, they could now "concentrate all their efforts in one place."[4] In other cases, changed transportation affected branch stores directly. Branch bakeries, for example, became obsolete when baking, done centrally, could be distributed by truck. The Bellevue Bakery in 1931, for example, supplied all Pass towns as well as Pincher Creek by truck, and by the late 1930s, a "growing number" of bakers delivered bread to neighbouring villages and hamlets in Alberta.[5]

Who were the people that ran these businesses? Most tended to be eastern Canadian or American settlers of British origin who came with some capital.[6] In some places, the ethnic make-up varied somewhat: Norwegians (mostly arrived via the United States) were prominent in Claresholm business, and in the Pass towns there was a significant number of Italian merchants. The few business people of non-European origin were usually Chinese. Initially operating small general stores and laundries, they soon began operating cafes. The hostility that they endured in the prairie west is well known, and the call for whites to boycott Chinese-owned businesses in Fort Macleod in 1901 was not unusual. Although they continued to be outsiders in town culture, the passage of time lessened overt hostility. Chinese also gained some sympathy from anti-Japanese sentiments in the late 1930s. Efforts, often spearheaded by city Chinese organizations to raise funds and inform the public about Japanese military aggression in China, gained some support among white townsfolk for Chinese in general.[7]

In addition to being white, most people in business were male. All the professionals in the towns studied were male, and most prominent retail businesses were also run by men. Although their wives often worked in the store, only the death of the husband brought women into public control of such businesses. Exceptions to this rule before 1920 included millineries as well as boarding houses. Later, women also operated beauty parlours, ladies wear shops, and sometimes cafes or tea shops.

Millinery shops were usually open only in the fall and spring. While they primarily custom-made hats and sold ready-made ones, they also sold yard goods, table linens, baby clothes, and sometimes did custom tailoring. Victims of changing styles, these stores had largely disappeared by the mid 1920s. Changing fashions opened other opportunities, however, and by the 1930s women were running beauty parlours catering exclusively to women. As well, women had established a greater presence in ladies' and children's clothing. Yet they were still marginalized in business life since stores selling both men's and women's wear remained male dominated. The situation in Lacombe in 1929 was typical. There, six stores sold clothing. Three sold both men's and women's clothes, two sold men's wear and boots and shoes exclusively, and one sold only women's clothes. The latter was the only shop owned and operated by a woman.[8]

Women in business typically catered to other women. This general rule did not apply to men, and there were numerous successful ladies wear shops owned by men, an example of which was Tony's Ladies Wear in Drumheller in the early 1930s. Little is known about the women who were in business. Like their male counterparts, they tended to be Anglo Saxons, but few of them were highly successful. Their pecuniary strength and credit rating by Dun and Bradstreet were usually low. Most lasted only a few years in business, and then disappeared from business life, perhaps marrying or moving to another place. By the interwar years, some women's wear stores were owned by wives of town businessmen, but many others were independent. One such store was set up in about 1923 in Coleman by Mrs. H.E. Gate, who had been a traveller for the Spirella Corset Company.[9]

Millinery shops and women's wear stores exemplified the retail specialization that appeared as towns developed. Even so, general merchants and hardware stores remained central to town mercantile life. These stores sold a broad range of goods. In 1909, Ouimette, Wright and Co. of Coleman sold groceries, crockery, furniture, flour, feed, clothing and boots and shoes.[10] Some hardware stores also manufactured articles for sale. Mark Spencer began manufacturing tinware in Cardston in 1898 and about two years later entered into a partnership in a general store. There he continued to make some of the tinware he and his partner sold. In Blairmore, a tinsmith and plumbing shop were also part of a hardware store.[11] While the combination of manufacturing and retailing had historically been widespread in tin smithing and harness making, it was never a strong tradition in Alberta and by the 1930s had largely disappeared. Settlement in Alberta was taking place at the same time that factory production of most goods was beginning to penetrate the whole economy. This ended the practice of tradespeople selling their own production through their own shops.[12] These developments increasingly made retailers into middlemen and paralleled the growing importance of nationally advertised products.

The greater role of brand names in retailing created opportunities for independent merchants to join associations using centralized wholesaling and distribution of named products. Among the earliest of these was Rexall, a druggist co-operative whose members were independent retailers. With about 3,000 members in the United States and Canada in 1914, it manufactured an extensive line of medicines. The name, it was said, stood for "King-of-All," and all stores offered a money-back guarantee, a considerable "innovation" given the bad reputation that patent medicines had given drug manufacturing. A Rexall store opened in Fort Macleod in 1911, and by the end of World War I they were appearing in most towns. The Rexall stores sold the same sorts of goods traditionally sold by drugstores, which before World War I included cosmetics, soap, stationary, tobacco, and chemicals, medicines, and health sundries. Rexall built on this tradition by increasingly providing some of these goods, as well as medicines, under its brand name.[13]

While Rexall's use of name recognition in advertising and store signs was among the earliest examples of this business trend in Alberta towns, hardware stores soon began to engage in similar practices. In 1936, W.H. Wilson Hardware in Peace River became associated with Marshall Wells, a wholesale house. Ownership of the store remained in local hands, but when Marshall Wells became its exclusive wholesaler, its name became part of the store's identification. After World War II, Marshall Wells gained its first associated store in southern Alberta in Drumheller.[14]

While such franchising of names and products represented a penetration of town business by outsiders, the earliest important example of this phenomenon occurred in banking. Reflecting the use of a centralized branch system, Canadian chartered banks quickly opened branches in prairie towns. The first bank in Lacombe opened in 1901 and in Claresholm in 1904. By assessing credit risks and in transferring funds, banks were essential mercantile agencies.[15] But as well, the coming of a bank was always heralded by local promoters as proof of the town's potential. It was said that bankers, supposedly conservative and possessed of a steel-like rationality when it came to money, would never locate in a town without a bright future.[16]

Chartered banks did not usually replace locally owned financial services because there were few such businesses in Alberta towns. Exceptions were the private banks of C. Edgar Snow and the Cardston Loan Company in Cardston and the Cowdry Brothers in Fort Macleod. Snow opened his bank in 1895 and it operated until about 1909. He was succeeded in private banking by the Cardston Loan Company which operated until 1930. The Cowdry Bank was established earlier, opening in 1886. Originally from Ontario, the Cowdrys had been associated with the Canadian Bank of Commerce. As an unincorporated bank, Cowdry's bank was not governed by Canadian banking regulations, but it performed banking functions such as taking deposits and lending money. It continued its close association with the Canadian Bank of Commerce, using it as its banker. The Cowdry bank opened a branch in Pincher Creek in 1899 and in Cardston in 1900, but closed the former the next year when a Union Bank branch opened there, and sold the Cardston operation to the Union Bank in 1902. While the Union Bank also opened in Fort Macleod in 1897, there was enough business for both, and the Cowdry bank was able to benefit from its local business and social connections. Ultimately, this could not sustain the business against chartered bank competition and in 1905 it was sold to the family's old mentor, the Canadian Bank of Commerce.[17]

The centralized control that characterized the chartered banks was also a feature of some retail operations. One of the earliest of these was I.G. Baker and Company, a Montana retail and supply company, which had trading posts in southern Alberta before 1874.[18] The most famous of these late nineteenth century chain operations, however, was the Hudson's Bay Company. For a time, it had retail outlets in Grande Prairie, Peace River, and Fort Macleod. At first, these stores combined fur and hide buying with retailing, specializing in sales to Native people. In Fort Macleod, its major competitor was the I.G. Baker Company, which it bought in 1891. Subsequently, it changed to conventional retailing, closing its small town operations to concentrate on the emerging city market in the west.

Centralized ownership also characterized the meat trade. P. Burns and Company, a large Calgary packing plant, operated butcher shops in many towns, combining wholesale and retail operations in a single outlet. Some of these stores also purchased livestock for processing in the company's plant in Calgary. P. Burns and Company established an outlet in Fort Macleod in 1902, and, with only minor interruptions, it was still operating in 1945, a record matched by no other butcher in the town. By 1909 Burns had stores throughout British Columbia, Alberta and Yukon, and from 1910 to 1925 it operated stores in most of the towns in the Crowsnest Pass.[19] The meat trade tended towards chain operations because entry into the business was difficult since meat markets often kept their own livestock to butcher and process for sale. The complexity of producing and marketing cured and cooked meats probably also encouraged centralization, as did the need for solid capitalization because the trade was highly seasonal; best in summer and weakest in winter.

Lumber yards were another business in which chain operations were prominent. During settlement, local saw millers supplied local needs, but lumber yards selling imported lumber soon appeared. In 1909, of the three lumber yards in Claresholm, only Moffat and Sons was an independent, reputedly the only one south of Calgary. Among its competitors, the Crown Lumber Co., owned by the CNoR, claimed to be "Western Canada's largest building supply concern." While some independent lumber yards, such as Whitlock and Company in Drumheller, were successful in the interwar years, the chains continued to dominate the retail lumber trade. Some were large operations; Crown Lumber remained significant, but the Beaver Lumber company, which by 1917 had a yard in Claresholm, grew to be a major player. Imperial Lumber Yards Ltd., which had 65 yards in Saskatchewan in 1918, also expanded into Alberta after World War I, including a yard at Drumheller. In contrast, other

| Safeway, which used the same style of buildings throughout the West to assert its corporate identity, had appeared in many towns by the early 1930s. This undated photo is of the Safeway store in Lacombe. Photo courtesy of Maski-pitoon Historical Society, Lacombe.

lumber yard chains were smaller. The Advance Lumber Company had yards in seven centres in southern Alberta in 1931, and the Frontier Lumber company operated in six towns in the Peace River country in 1929.[20]

Much of the impetus for chain store methods in the lumber trade lay in the control exerted by these large players. Prior to 1908, a combine including about 90 percent of lumber dealers in Alberta controlled competition by preventing sawmills in British Columbia from supplying retailers outside the combine.[21] Although this ended by 1908 because of legal action against participating lumber associations by the Alberta government, a pattern had been established. As well, the nature of the lumber industry favoured those buying directly from millers.[22] Other products, especially groceries, were also subject to monopoly. In 1908, a Grocers' Guild apparently controlled wholesale prices in sugar, canned goods, and various grocery lines in Alberta.[23]

While affecting prices, this had little impact on ownership of grocery stores, most of which were independently owned. During the interwar years, however, the grocery trade in small towns came almost entirely under the control of several chains, notably Safeway, an American company, which had moved into Canada in 1929. By 1934, it had 184 stores in western Canada, including 35 in Alberta. Jenkins, an Alberta owned grocery chain, was also common. Partly to meet the challenge that the chains posed, some independents joined associated groups of stores using a common name and wholesaler. These included Red and White Stores, Associated Grocers, and Piggly Wiggly, which was bought by Safeway in 1936. Like the chains, they emphasized nationally advertised brands. By 1932, 70 percent of grocery stores in Alberta were chain or associated stores. The opening of a chain store in a town often led independent stores to sell out to the chain or join an associated operation. In Drumheller, Jenkins opened in about 1925. Shortly thereafter, two locally owned stores joined Associated Grocers. This trend continued with the opening of a Red and White store in 1931. The local Jenkins's manager thought these grocers showed "vision" by realizing "that the days of the individual grocery store were numbered."[24]

Style was an important part of the attraction of the chain grocery stores, and their reputation as trend-setters gave them an important advantage. Their architecture and store layout contributed to this image, as did their promise of good service and improved quality. In 1932, the manager of the Drumheller Jenkins grocery store claimed that when his chain had opened in the town, "almost every local grocery store started house cleaning." Their appearance had improved "since Jenkins Groceteria opened here. We have cleaner, brighter stores with fresher stocks displayed in a better manner." While quality of fresh produce improved because of more centralized wholesaling and shipping, it was also assumed that extensive advertising and brand recognition were equivalent to a qualitative improvement. As Jenkins Drumheller manager argued, "the best brands of groceries today are nationally advertised and their names are soon familiar to all shoppers." The chains stressed these products, which were advertised in national magazines and through new forms of communications like radio, and they could supply them without interruption. The associated stores also competed by stocking nationally advertised brands.[25] Consequently, the impact of metropolitan forces on local business, and the centralization of control, were not only a matter of corporate structure and economy of scale. They were also the product of consumer conformism and standardization created and promoted by well capitalized, vertically integrated companies that could operate and promote themselves more efficiently because of changes in transportation and communications.

CO-OPERATIVE RETAILING

In addition to independent and chain stores, co-operatives existed in most towns. A number of early efforts to form co-operatives drew members from various groups. Under the encouragement of the Mormon church, The Cardston Company, the first store in Cardston, took the form of a co-operative in 1888. Ethnicity was a focus for others. In Coleman, an Italian co-op was formed in 1914, a Polish one in 1917 and an Italian-Belgian one in 1918. Farmers, however, were the most active group in co-operative associations. Among the earliest was one formed by farmers in 1899 in the Lacombe district to sell dry goods, groceries, clothing and agricultural equipment.[26] Also common were car-lot buying clubs in which a group purchased goods by the carlot and then split them among the participants. These were not, however, true retail co-ops, which were governed by their members and paid dividends on the basis of purchases.

In Alberta, farm organizations like the UFA (established in 1909) were interested from an early point in co-operative retailing to lower farmers' costs of consumer and farm supplies. In Alberta towns, co-operatives elicited mixed reactions. As in Britain and the United States, retail merchants in English Canada were traditionally hostile to consumer co-ops.[27] The Retail Merchants Association of Canada fought co-ops, arguing that they aimed to do away with private retailers, and it publicly congratulated itself in 1913 for breaking co-ops in Toronto. It worked to the same end in the rest of the country, telling Fort Macleod business owners, for example, that co-ops were "downright robbery" because dividends and lower prices were only possible by robbing the customer.[28] Such hostility existed from an early date. A petition circulated in Fort Macleod and Pincher Creek in 1890 demanded that the government refuse the incorporation of The Cardston Company because it would concentrate power and wealth into "a more co-operative, corporate, political and religious unit than they now are." Aside from expressing anti-Mormon sentiments, it was believed that co-ops challenged the individualism of town life and

business. Nor did the braggadocio of farmers and their organizations mit-
igate such worries. As the *Farm and Ranch Review* editorialized in 1910,
cutting out the retailer, which it called the "middleman," was "one of the
greatest testimonies to the advantage of co-operation."[29]

Although retail co-ops existed in many towns and operated their own
central co-operative wholesale agency, the UFA began competing with
these stores by organizing its own co-operative stores in each constituency in 1931. A Provincial or Central Co-operative purchased car-
load lots of goods like grease, lumber, flour, potatoes and other staples
for distribution to newly created UFA stores. Any member of a UFA local
was entitled to shop there. Each local ordered its goods and remitted cash
to the Central Co-operative for its purchases. Some town spokesmen welcomed this development; in Peace River it was viewed as a way to lower
prices and give people greater control over their lives. In Cardston, it was
noted that co-operation was a trend. Farmers were co-operating to sell
their products through the Pools, and now they were co-operating to
buy goods. Farm organizations had long wanted co-operative retailing,
and while it represented a big adjustment for small town business interests, some people argued that it was better to accept it than to force farmers into more extreme reactions.[30] Nonetheless, town merchants opposed
the UFA's policy. They saw it as unwelcome competition, as well as a
threat to the collection of money owing by farmers since they now had
an alternative to the private stores where many were up to their credit
limit. Retail merchants in southern Alberta, through the Retail
Merchants Association of Canada, announced in late 1931 that they
intended to confirm their "right to exist" in the face of the UFA's merchandising efforts.[31]

Despite the fears of merchants, co-ops did not represent a long-term
challenge. From 1913 until 1923, 165 co-ops were formed in the province,
but less than 10 percent of them were in operation 25 years later. Given
the hostility of the private sector, co-ops had difficulty finding wholesalers to supply them. As well, they only emphasized price advantages
and neglected to educate their members about co-operative principles.
Co-ops were also less successful in Alberta than elsewhere on the prairies
because there was less co-operation among retail co-ops. The involvement of the UFA after 1931 in co-operative retailing of farm supplies, for
example, was in direct competition with local co-ops and their central
wholesaling agency which were selling the same goods.[32] Such competition among co-ops ensured that their success in Alberta was minimal.

ITINERANT *and* MAIL
ORDER RETAILING

Competition in town retailing existed not only among independent merchants, chain or franchised operations, and co-ops. In farm service towns, grocers and butchers also competed with farmers who sold meat, poultry, eggs and produce door-to-door. While little is known about this informal trading, it seems to have varied with the state of the farm economy. Farmers had traditionally bartered produce with merchants, but it was an unsatisfactory system. The Fort Macleod farmers' market in 1914 suggests that farmers were not averse to direct sales, but they disliked selling produce door-to-door, doing so mainly in hard times.

Itinerant businesses were also active in Alberta towns. Before World War I, dentists, optometrists, and occasionally doctors, usually from larger centres, travelled on a regular circuit, setting up in a hotel for several days to see patients. Such visits ceased as resident professionals settled in the towns. Transient salesmen also made an early appearance. Most seemed to earn only a marginal income and, as in the rest of Canada, were involved in a survival type of existence.[33] Nonetheless, they were seen as a threat to town retail trade. As early as 1886, a transient trader representing an Ontario jewellery firm set up in rented space in Fort Macleod for four days during the fair and then moved on. Most, however, sold door-to-door, and their number increased during the interwar years when cars and trucks allowed more extensive canvasing of towns and farms. Many of these salesmen worked on their own, although by the 1920s the Watkins Company and the W.T. Rawleigh Company had commission salesmen on the road selling brand name goods door-to-door. While the total number of itinerant salesmen active in Alberta is unknown, Rawleigh and Watkins alone had about 150 to 200 in the province in 1928. By 1940, they were reported to be the only ones selling directly from a vehicle to consumers in Alberta.[34]

Of greater significance in town retail competition were mail order sales. As late as 1913, most Blairmore stores stocked little more than basic staples, and the public relied on catalogues for other goods.[35] The most important of these was Eaton's, which had produced its first catalogue in 1884. At first, goods were ordered from Toronto, but in 1905 a warehouse and sales office were opened in Winnipeg to supply the western market

| *Itinerant sales services were often seen as a challenge by small town businesses in the interwar period. This photo is of the Rawleigh salesman in Cardston. Not dated. NC-7-716, GAI.*

more efficiently. While Eaton's was the clear leader in Canadian mail order retailing, the Robert Simpson Company of Toronto also issued catalogues, and by 1903 was producing a 200-page catalogue. Huge numbers of catalogues were sent out: in 1908, Eaton's distributed 1,000 fall catalogues in Fort Macleod and district alone.[36]

Like the national mail order houses, city department stores often issued mail order catalogues. In 1918, James Ramsay, an Edmonton department store, issued a special Christmas catalogue, plus three others—one for groceries, another for wallpaper, and its ninth annual spring and summer catalogue.[37] As well, smaller stores offered mail order service to remote areas; settlers in the Peace River country during World War I, for example, could purchase goods from Edmonton, Edson, and other places by mail. Sales were stimulated further when shipping costs fell with the inauguration of parcel post in 1914. In the early 1920s, greater sales also came because of the cash-on-delivery system in which the receiver paid the retail value of the article plus shipping and handling charges, thus saving the cost of money orders.[38]

The mail order business expanded during the interwar years. While small city operations continued to service out-of-town customers through mail order, Eaton's remained the industry leader, followed closely by Simpson's, which by 1916 had also opened a regional office in Regina to serve the western market. Probably of equivalent standing to Simpson's on the prairies, Army and Navy Stores (British Surplus Supplies Ltd.), established in Vancouver in 1917, moved their head office to Regina in 1925. By 1932, the company had retail stores in Vancouver and Regina, but its strength lay in its catalogue operation, which sold dry goods, clothing, shoes, and some hardware and farmyard items. Among the best known mail order businesses in western Canada, in 1932 it did over $1 million in business, mainly in Alberta and Saskatchewan, and issued 600,000 catalogues twice a year.[39]

The catalogue retailers promoted themselves through illustrated advertisements in magazines, although reputation and word of mouth were probably as important. Eaton's used a display at the Calgary exhibition in 1910 to promote its offerings, and ran advertisements in regional and national publications announcing its latest catalogue. Advertisements in town newspapers were never an option since they refused to carry such ads in an effort to protect town merchants. Army and Navy stores also used radio advertising and billboards. But the greatest advertising was the catalogue itself: "attractive and alluring," it promised material satisfaction and fantasy.[40]

By the interwar years, the country was "under a deluge of artistically illustrated well-printed books of 500 pages each...inviting even the most remote prairie settler to send his money away to Winnipeg for whatever he may require." As in the United States, by helping to create and shape a large consumer market, mail order retailers were significant in changing Canadian consumers' expectations as well as the way that business in general was conducted.[41] They did an immense business and the number of catalogues distributed testifies to their reach. In 1926 it was claimed that Eaton's alone sent 2,000 catalogues to Drumheller, and in 1925 the *Hanna Herald* wrote an editorial (reprinted or plagiarized by every newspaper surveyed for this study) expressing outrage at "three tons of mail order catalogues for Hanna!"[42] As early as 1909, post office receipts at Fort Macleod showed that money orders totalling $105,000 were issued there, and most, presumably, were for catalogue shopping. In 1938, the Drumheller post office issued 2,744 money orders, most for catalogue purchases, and this would not have included the more extensive cash-on-delivery business done.[43]

Out-of-town competition was most severe from catalogue retailers, but cities also drew trade away from town businesses. This increasingly became an issue during the 1930s, when improved roads and private transportation allowed people from further afield to shop in larger centres. Cheap weekend railway fares drew shoppers from Coleman to Calgary by 1936, and by the same time, Claresholm, Fort Macleod and Cardston found that Calgary was absorbing some of their trade. Similarly, Lacombe residents were making trips in the fall and at Christmas to Edmonton for shopping. Cardston additionally suffered competition from United States stores. In 1937, the first good crop in eight years gave people some cash, and they spent an estimated $50,000 in Montana stores.[44]

REACTIONS *to* OUTSIDE
COMPETITION

While mail order houses, chain stores, itinerant traders and farmers selling produce had been part of retailing from the beginning of settlement, such activities were always portrayed by town spokesmen as a new and unwelcome threat to town merchants and the future of the town itself. It was commonly argued that people should not buy from the catalogue or transient traders. This drew upon booster doctrines that the town could be built up through the unity and loyalty of its citizens who owed the home town respect and commitment. The best way to show this was to shop at home. A typical contention was that a dollar circulated 15 times in a community before its "earning power" was exhausted. If the dollar was sent "away," this earning power benefited someone else and weakened the home town.[45] The town further suffered because catalogue retailers and transient traders created no local employment, nor did they pay taxes to support local services. While the same arguments were made in cities in Alberta as late as 1920, the issue was always more poignant for small towns. Their very existence was said to be at stake, for mail order houses, along with monopoly in manufacturing, favoured the growth of "a few large and vigorous centres of population with their big stores and big factories."[46]

To protect local merchants, the Territorial government in 1883 passed an ordinance licensing door-to-door sellers and auctioneers. Other transient traders, except those selling liquor, were unregulated. For some observers, this was unsatisfactory. In 1886, it was demanded in Fort Macleod that all transient traders be restricted "in the interest of legitimate trade and business." Such demands continued to be voiced. In 1935, with a rhetorical flourish that had by then become standard, the *Coleman Journal* called for control of such "chisellers on local trade."[47]

Licensing of transient traders lay in the hands of local governments that also had authority to license some resident businesses. Licensing bylaws were passed soon after incorporation by most towns. At one time or another, almost every town business wanted protection: drug stores demanded that only licensed pharmacists be allowed to sell certain products, coal dealers wanted seasonal coal sellers controlled, general merchants supported restricting any outside competition, and dance bands were even licensed in Drumheller in 1936 to protect local musicians.[48] Most often, this control was exercised through a general tax on transient traders. Fort Macleod's license bylaw in 1915 required that hawkers and peddlers pay $10 per day for selling in the town. In other cases, residency determined the amount of the license fees. In 1910, a resident real estate agent in Coleman, for example, paid $15 per year, while a nonresident paid $100.[49]

Licenses were also demanded of auctioneers, pawnbrokers, and secondhand dealers, largely to control the sale of stolen goods or new goods masquerading as pawned or secondhand goods. Licenses were also required for some trades, as well as for morally suspect businesses like poolrooms, bars, cafes, and travelling amusement companies. They were not usually assessed for professionals, such as lawyers and doctors, even when they were itinerants, nor were they usually required for hardware, grocery or clothing stores. Later, the province also licensed transient traders, as much, it seems, in search of revenue as to protect town businesses.

As in other matters, towns were not free to license as they wished. The *Town Act* prohibited license fees that prevented transients from doing business at all. Fees could be set for revenue only, not for regulation. Nor could towns license individuals selling agricultural goods they had produced, or those selling a list of specified articles deemed to be important for farmers, such as sewing machines, farm implements, and, among others, educational books and periodicals.[50]

Throughout the prairies in the interwar years, the pressure by town merchants for control of transient traders increased.[51] In 1920, the Retail

Merchants Association of Canada argued, as part of its Alberta membership drive, that it wanted retail trade "confined as far as possible to legitimate retailers," but that this objective was difficult to meet because of limited local jurisdiction.[52] Such views helped create tension between transient traders and towns, and between towns and the province. Rawleigh company representatives fought an ongoing battle with towns over license fees during the 1920s and 1930s. In 1930, the company noted that while licenses cost as little as $3 per year in some towns, others charged $25 per year, which was "tantamount to a prohibition of the business of a peddler."[53] Towns resisted attempts to limit their jurisdiction or to lower their fees. In 1930, the Department of Municipal Affairs advised Grande Prairie that its high license fees could be successfully challenged in court. The town retorted that it would willingly defend its fee structure because town merchants "pay a good deal more in Business Tax than the amount of the Hawker's and Peddler's license" and did more to build up the town than did transient traders.[54]

Higher fees and greater licensing powers could not solve the problems of town merchants. Enforcement and collection of fees were difficult since itinerant salesmen spent only a brief time in a town before moving on. Moreover, despite merchants' demands for protection, they too used itinerants. In 1928, LaFleche Brothers, an Edmonton custom tailor, observed that eastern ready-made clothing firms had transient traders throughout the west working in association with local merchants. While LaFleche was defined as a transient trader and had to be licensed, the eastern salesmen were not restricted because of their association with local merchants. Similarly, in 1921, full-time insurance agents in Claresholm found it difficult to compete because most merchants in town also sold insurance. Representatives of "some cheap insurance company" would visit town and "peddle their supplies to a party who has a side line of insurance, but whose business is entirely out of line with insurance."[55]

This debate over licensing was further complicated by farmers who sold their produce in direct competition with town grocers and butchers. Despite the provisions of the *Town Act* and the *Village Act*, one farmer informed the Attorney General in 1913 that town and village merchants and boards of trade commonly tried to stop farmers from selling their produce in town. Since the village got "its whole support from the farming community around it," he believed that it should recognize farmers' needs. Representing a fundamental political issue for farmers, he argued

that restrictions of trade created monopoly, and, as independent commodity producers, farmers had the right to sell produce as they
wished.[56]

This issue remained significant in the 1920s, and its solution, in the
popular language of the day, was said to lay in co-operation between
town and farm. Since farmers needed markets for their produce and merchants needed trade, each had to patronize the other to create a strong
community.[57] This expectation, however, ignored that such interests
were not inherently mutual, especially during hard times like the 1930s.
Farmers were told by Peace River merchants in 1931 that they could not
sell butter, milk or cream in the town without a license. The *Peace River
Record* noted that since an earlier "attempt to intimidate local farmers"
had failed, "it would seem that the methods of Tammany Hall or Al
Capone's gangsters are to be applied. The danger from citizens who
would resort to such methods differs from that of the Chicago gangsters
only in degree." Farmers had a right to sell their produce as they wished,
and Peace River needed their patronage.[58]

In this dispute, the greatest tensions were between farmers and butchers. In Drumheller in the 1930s, butchers argued that farmers and out-of-
town butchers, both of whom sold meat house-to-house, had to be
stopped. Farmers saw this as an attack on their interests. One observed
that if butchers paid a fair price for livestock, they would not face competition from farmers because no farmer "would peddle if he got a decent
price for his stuff from the butcher." He suggested that if farmers could
not sell meat in Drumheller, they would sell it in Calgary, where they
would shop as well, causing "a few more of the [Drumheller] business
men [to] go with long faces." By 1938, when the issue of farmers selling
meat came once again before the city council, the mayor remarked that
the issue was becoming "a chronic" one. This issue led many centres to
pass a bylaw stipulating that only meat inspected by the town could be
sold. When implemented, however, it proved too expensive since the
province required that such inspection be conducted by a veterinarian.[59]

Licensing was not itself sufficient to prevent consumers from exercising choice in where they shopped. In this respect, moral suasion was the
only recourse for town spokesmen who waged an unremitting verbal war
against transient salesmen and mail order retailers. As early as 1896,
Eaton's was a sufficiently important player to be attacked in the *Macleod
Gazette*, which argued that people should buy at home where they could
examine personally the goods they were purchasing, and not send capital

away from home. In addition, transient traders were portrayed as dishonest and shabby individuals who sold over-priced, shoddy goods and whose business drained capital from the town. Thus, as the *Peace River Record* observed in 1931, people should "sic the dog on all peddlers and smooth tongued sharpers."[60]

During World War I, such arguments were enriched by an appeal to patriotism. It was said in Claresholm that peddlers should be in the army and their presence in the town and district showed why conscription was needed. The mail order houses too were disloyal. Eaton's refused a request for a donation to the Lethbridge Red Cross, arguing that it could not contribute to every Red Cross local in the prairies, and instead donated in Winnipeg where its western offices were located. An account of the incident, printed as a syndicated newspaper item in every town surveyed, accused Eaton's of cold mercenary motives and, by implication, of disloyalty.[61]

Guilt was also used to persuade townsfolk to patronize town merchants. It was commonly said that it was rude and shameful to carry a mail order parcel into a local store and showed disrespect to the merchant. As the *Claresholm Review* editorialized in 1912, it knew of "men in this district" who would not have been able "to live and eat at all" during years of crop failure if local merchants had not generously given credit. In contrast to this philanthropy, mail order houses were said to be avaricious and exploitative. People in Fort Macleod were told in 1909 that, by patronizing them, they permitted "Toronto department store magnates to run steam yachts and maintain country places in England." As early as 1900, it was said that Eaton's low prices were possible only by using sweated labour. This argument was revived in 1934 when evidence from the House of Commons inquiry, and the follow-up Royal Commission on Price Spreads and Mass Buying, revealed appalling working conditions at various factories, including Eaton's and Simpson's. These findings were printed in many newspapers to show that catalogue "bargains" were possible only through "agony and human suffering."[62]

However it was achieved, the mail order houses did present a real challenge in their pricing and range and quality of goods. This took advantage of the weakest elements in small retail business. It was commonly said, especially before 1920, that prices in small towns were too high. In 1909, for example, the *Macleod Advertiser* editorialized that some local prices were "absurdly high" because when "a shirt worth 50 cents is retailed for $1.50 something is the matter." It seemed that some merchants wanted high profits on a few sales, rather than a lower margin on larger volume. Two letters to the editor reiterated this argument by stating that Fort Macleod prices were high—often double those in Calgary, Lethbridge, or in the catalogue. The *Advertiser* concluded that these findings were a "severe indictment against the merchants of Macleod." Thus, as it was observed in Cardston in 1916, local businesses were often thought to be "responsible for the conditions that exist" because they had "probably taken more profit than was necessary."[63]

Not all merchants ignored the threat that catalogue pricing represented, and some attempted to meet catalogue competition directly. Some of the larger merchants responded by producing their own catalogues. The Cardston Implement Company, for example, produced a seasonal catalogue of household goods and hardware in 1935. More importantly, many local retailers tried to compete on price, and by World War I it was frequently claimed that local prices had fallen to some extent because of mail order competition. One Claresholm jeweller promised that he would meet or better Eaton's prices if purchasers brought him the catalogue for comparison pricing. This was, the *Claresholm Review* noted, the best way to "beard the mail order houses." But central to this competition was the matter of credit, which local retailers often offered but mail order houses usually did not. As Spencer and Stoddard in Cardston noted, if customers brought in the catalogue, it would match its prices, but on the same terms: cash only.[64]

Despite such efforts, it was evident that the challenge presented by mail order houses demonstrated a changing economy and urban structure. Local solutions were therefore inadequate, and many merchants contended that mail order houses should be regulated by the state in the interests of small business. They charged that mail order retailers did not pay taxes to the province in which they sold goods, and throughout the interwar years retail merchants and their associations demanded that catalogue sellers be licensed and taxed. As the Retail Merchants Association of Canada argued in 1926, a special 10 percent tax on mail order houses should be levied by the federal government and distributed to each province according to the amount of mail order business done there.[65]

In comparison to mail order retailing, small town merchants found it more difficult to criticize chain stores because they paid property and business taxes and created employment in the towns in which they operated. Still, while chain operations like the Hudson's Bay Company escaped criticism, others, such as the lumber companies which participated in the combine before 1909, caused much public anger. In 1908 the *Claresholm Review* urged local shoppers to support Moffat and Sons, the town's only independent lumber yard, instead of the other lumber yards in town which were part of the combine, and which were attempting to break Moffat through a price war. Thus, people were told to look to the future, pay Moffat slightly more and give him a chance "to live" and to keep prices in line in Claresholm through competition.[66]

Hostility to chain stores was especially intense during the 1930s in Alberta, as well as in most of Canada and the United States. The chains were said to create unfair competition because of mass buying and low profit margins. Given the early emphasis of the farmers' movement on the evils of monopoly capitalism, such concerns found a ready audience among Alberta farmers, although they were highly attractive to small town merchants as well. The arguments against chain stores in the 1930s drew upon both the social and economic objectives of town life. In 1931, a correspondent in the *Cardston News* contended that chain stores were bad because "any kind of business which causes power to be centralized in a few hands is not of value to Society." Chain stores threatened the individualism of small town life, for any business run by employees and not owners was a social "menace" that "must be fought and destroyed." The next year, the manager of the Jenkins Groceteria in Drumheller attempted to respond to such opinions by remarking that radio programmes which claimed that chain stores harmed small towns were slanderous. Even so, the testimony of certain witnesses before the House of Commons committee on mass buying in 1934 was given wide coverage in town newspapers. It was alleged that branches of American chain stores operating in Canada cheated customers by giving short weights and diluting products like milk and vinegar. In the testimony of former chain store employees reported in a syndicated article in the Lacombe newspaper, "each admitted he was an honest man until he entered the employ of a chain store." And in case local readers missed the point, the paper added that this proved that one should patronize local independent merchants who kept capital in the town and helped "you in times of stress."[67]

Such beliefs were widespread. The Alberta branch of the Retail Merchants Association informed Premier Brownlee in 1927 that the chain stores were a "sinister" form of merchandising because they aimed to destroy independent merchants by selling goods below "fair selling price, which it defined as "cost plus a fair compensation for services rendered." The public also became habituated to the chains' lower prices and the use of loss leaders (a limited number of goods sold below cost to draw customers). This damaged the reputation of independent merchants, who were seen as gouging the public with high prices, even though they could not afford to meet the chains' prices because of lower volumes. One merchant told Premier Aberhart in 1936 that chain stores were forcing the profit margins of independent retailers so low through quantity buying and "secret rebates," that they were "gradually killing us off. Yes sir, business is simply hell for the little man, now days." In the year before, his general store had a gross profit of barely 18 percent.[68]

In response to these conditions, many appealed for a provincial tax on chain stores. Unlike some places in the United States,[69] this was not implemented in Alberta. Nonetheless, the complaints that such competition was harming business, the farm economy, and society itself led the province to propose regulation of business. The UFA government created the Department of Trade and Industry in late 1934. The department had several functions, including the promotion and development of Alberta's resources and, most radically, the regulation and control of trades and prices. With this legislation, "government was moving concertedly into the field of regulated marketing and industrial incentives."[70] It could now establish "codes" for industry, to regulate "cut throat" competition and "unfair business practices" that hurt small merchants and tradesmen. It was proposed that these codes would cover various trades and businesses to establish a minimum and a maximum that could be charged, as well as "fair" wages. The minister of the new department was given powers to impose a code on any industry.[71]

It was extensive and powerful legislation, which, if fully implemented, would radically have changed the methods of determining wages and prices. As a measure of the discontent of farmers, labour, and small businesses with the market economy in Alberta, the bill was welcomed by many. While some town merchants (such as in Lacombe) were opposed, the Alberta Retail Merchants Association cautiously endorsed it, and merchants in Cardston "saw in it one fighting chance to keep in business and regulate unfair competition and cut-throat business which is forcing every merchant to bankruptcy." The local board of trade "naturally" agreed with these sentiments, and urged the province to pass the bill because "towns are non-existent when the merchants cease to exist in them." The Cardston UFA local saw the bill as one step nearer the "planned economy" which is the ultimate solution of the mess things are in at present. With 5 percent of the people controlling 85 percent of the wealth, and the other 95 percent...cutting each other's throats fighting for the 15 percent of the wealth there is left...conditions have arrived at such a point, today, where if something is not done to control prices and regulate industry and business, then civilization is doomed.[72]

Opinion in the cities was less favourable; the *Calgary Herald* called it dictatorial, bureaucratic meddling that neglected the needs of consumers. Farm and small town opinion was sufficiently favourable that the bill passed, although the province stated that it would not initiate any "codes" for industry until "a thorough survey of the industrial situation of the province had been made."[73]

The UFA government was defeated in 1935, but the succeeding Social Credit government picked up the task and in 1936 began implementing parts of the legislation, especially those pertaining to wages and qualification of trades. Merchant opinion remained divided on the issue, but popular opinion in the Peace River country apparently held that "the small merchant and the working people" were "very much in favor of the codes as they realize that there is too much waste under the present destructive competition."[74] In any event, Social Credit subsequently took its own approach to the problems of competition, but these UFA initiatives were nonetheless significant as an expression of the frustration and difficulties experienced by small merchants as well as farmers in the 1930s in the face of a market economy increasingly dominated by monopolistic players.

Doing Business

The broadening of provincial regulation represented by the establishment of the Department of Industry and Trade took place at the expense of local initiative. It assumed that local control could not address the scale of change that was occurring in provincial social and economic life. In the same sense, retail merchants increasingly supported organizations that represented their interests at the provincial and national level. Initially, however, retail merchant organizations tended to be local. Associations, such as that of teamsters and draymen in Fort Macleod in 1911, aimed to set a common fee schedule in an effort to limit price competition and stabilize the business in general. Similarly, the Macleod Business Men's Association was formed in 1911 to create a system for credit checks to keep track of the "dead-beats and never-pays who so infest this newly settled region."[75]

Such objectives had formed part of the rationale in the formation of the Retail Merchants Association of Canada in 1896. An Alberta branch, the Alberta Retail Merchants Association (ARMA), was formed in 1898. At first, it had few members outside cities, but chapters were formed in Blairmore in 1912 and Fort Macleod in 1913 in the hope of limiting losses from bad credit risks. In Blairmore, it was claimed that losses were high because individuals obtained as much credit in one town as they could, then moved to another town and repeated the scam. ARMA planned to publish "a 'black book' for reference of members of the association all over the province" to prevent such fraud. Also representing a wider objective, the association planned to publish a monthly magazine to give "new ideas in connection with the retail trade" and "expose whenever necessary any fraud" that hurt retail merchants.[76]

These ARMA chapters were short-lived. Independent merchants were difficult to organize because they tended to offer their support only as long as the organization was meeting their immediate concerns. Thus, worries about credit might lead to the organization of a chapter, but once this concern had passed, the chapter fell apart. There was little sense of an ongoing commonality of interest, and efforts to organize province-wide were unsuccessful before the 1920s. The challenge of chain stores and mail order retailers, however, apparently convinced many merchants to support organizations that promised to help in meeting this competition. While ARMA, like its national parent organization, had made these concerns a priority since the late nineteenth century, widespread membership in Alberta came only after World War I. By 1931 it had staffed branch offices in Edmonton, Calgary, Lethbridge, Medicine Hat and Drumheller, with chapters operating in many smaller towns. It provided its members with a range of services. It petitioned government to attend to retailers' problems such as credit and competition, and it kept watch on legislative matters "to guard against legislation detrimental to retail business." It also had a legal department to provide advice to members and gave assistance in filling out income tax returns.[77]

The centrality of credit in the early concerns of ARMA pointed to its importance in the retail trades. The amount of credit extended by town merchants was high. In 1889, credit in Fort Macleod, like the rest of the Territories, was said to be out of control. This pattern persisted, and the Toshach store in Drumheller, which sold clothing, boots and shoes, estimated in 1935 that 30 percent of its business was on credit. In Claresholm, one grocery store before World War I apparently did half of its business on credit.[78] While these were high levels of credit for small merchants to carry, credit was necessary in a farm economy, and it was also a way of competing with cash-only mail order houses. But it had its drawbacks—accounts were usually carried interest free, and not all accounts could be collected. Hence, demands for cash-only shopping were common among retailers. From the late nineteenth century, North American merchants (probably like merchants at all times) had tried to abolish credit. Ironically for small town merchants, Timothy Eaton had been one of the great successes in this effort.

Over the years, numerous efforts were made to institute cash-only shopping. Usually, this necessitated a common front by all merchants in a town. Despite compelling reasons, such co-operation was rare. In 1907, eleven of the largest businesses in Cardston agreed to sell for cash or produce only. The agreement was to run for two years, and violators would be fined $200. Citing Manitoba precedents, it was said that this was a fitting response to the "ungratefulness of farmers" who asked for credit from local stores, but patronized a mail order house when they had cash. Cash-only shopping was lauded as being an "up-to-date, economically satisfying" practice in comparison to "antique, expensive, misleading" credit. These alliances never held together, but they continued to have appeal, especially in times of high credit. In a call for a province-wide agreement by merchants to sell only for cash, it was noted in Peace River in 1929 that banks, and not retailers, were in the business of credit. As late as 1931, ARMA continued to promote such agreements among its members, or as a minimum, that they use only "a very restricted policy of short-term credit."[79]

Despite such arguments, credit could not be avoided. It was a primary means of meeting competition, and it was especially needed in farming areas where income was seasonal. This became another argument for economic diversification, and as Reach and Co. of Fort Macleod noted in 1908, in a town without a payroll, merchants could not have a cash only business. "You either have to have a small peanut store with no clerks, no plate glass windows, no electric lights, no improvements" and little business, or, you had credit. Credit was essential in a place like Fort Macleod where farmers and ranchers received income only twice a year. These comments drew an approving response from a farmer near Granum who observed that "this cash cant is getting on the nerves of some of us farmers." Granum merchants had gone on a cash-only system, "jumping straight from six or twelve months credit right into paying spot cash." As a result, he refused to shop there, going to Fort Macleod instead.[80]

While credit was necessary, stores periodically curtailed it when trade was poor or when it was rising out of proportion to cash sales, and restored it when conditions improved. Even so, merchants walked a fine line. Almost all goods were bought from wholesalers on credit, usually on 90 day terms. While they usually had an adequate cash flow to meet these terms, this whole balancing act fell apart during the Depression. In 1931, farmers alone were estimated to owe Alberta retail merchants about $10 million. Five years later, this debt was estimated by the Alberta Debt Adjustment Board at $40 million.[81] Bankers and wholesalers tightened their lines of credit, creating a chain reaction and catching merchants "between the nether and the upper stone. They cannot collect from the farmers...and they are pressed by wholesalers, manufacturers and banks on the other hand to pay for those goods." Moreover, merchants extended credit without security, while banks and insurance and mortgage companies did not, allowing them to share in bankruptcy distributions and provincial debt adjustment rulings. Since merchants did not enjoy the same protection from creditors as did farmers under provincial debt adjustment statutes, this also added to the difficulties they faced during the 1930s.[82]

While the question of credit was particularly difficult, a broad range of solutions was proposed in respect to other areas of competition. For one, hours of business were regulated through bylaws in accordance with local agreements as well provincial and federal legislation. This helped ensure that no business gained an unfair advantage by opening when others were closed. In other cases, it was suggested that merchants change their whole approach to business to remain competitive. In 1921 it was observed in Claresholm that most merchants attempted to be all things to all customers, and tried to "handle some line of goods that is, or should not be, in conjunction with his particular line of business." In 1938, in response to complaints about Lethbridge grocery stores, which were apparently offering prices 20 percent lower than in Claresholm, it

THE CARDSTON MER. CO.
SALE

Tell It To Sir Wilfred Laurier

Whale Prices on

Trunks
Valises
Carpets
Rugs
Linoleums
Art Squares
Oil Cloths
Furniture
Largest stock of Shoes all at Whale Prices.
Felts
Slippers
Overshoes
Rubbers
Cordoroy Pants
Good mens suits first floor
Dressers
Stands
Tables
Chairs
Beds
Springs
Mattresses
Groceries all reduced

Tell it to Premier Sifton, tell it to the A. R. and I. R. R. men—tell it in the Assembly Hall—tell it to the mounted police—tell it to the doctors and lawyers—tell it to the school t..ers—tell it to the ranchers—tell it to th farmers, to the wheat growers, to the cattle raisers, to the elevators. Have Ln. Weeks recite it—tell it in the banks and in the hotels—whisper it to the station—tell of it in the Halls. Have J. Banner put it to music and have one the Cardston School of Music students sing about it   Tell it across the country to Spring Cool.e—let ..oes and Kimball know about it and speak of it in Taylorville, Leavitt and Beazer—phone about it to Mountain View and send messengers to Raley and Spring Hill—Glenwood should know of it too—tell it to 'he passengers who arrive in on the trains—tell it to the constable—tell it to .r. Ardiel—tell it to the bishop—to the Cardston boosters—let Dr. Lynn, Mr. Leavis and W. S. Johnston, the Mayor and school trustees, and don't forget to tell Miss Gundry about it—and Mr. Bailey will be interested too.

In fact tell everybody that THE FIRST WHALE OF A

SALE ever held in Cardston is on at the Pioneer Mercantile store

in Cardston—that there will be something doing every 5 minutes

for the next 14 days to interest everybody—Men Women and

Children at

Whale values on

Sheep lined Coats
Coon Coats
Fur Coats
Ladies and Childrens Mantles
Bear Skin Coats
Caps
Hats
Priestly's Dress Goods
Silks
Trimmings
Corsets
Underwear
Mitts
Childrens Underwear
Skirts
Costumes
Furs
All at Whale reduction for 14 days

Card. Mer. Co.
THE EVELY SALES CO. IN CHARGE

Sales services, such as this one in Cardston in 1911, were often hired in an effort to stimulate sales. *Cardston Alberta Star*, January 27, 1911.

was observed that "good stores could not be developed locally if every merchant was going to try and sell everything from soup to nuts."[83]

Promoting sales was another means of responding to these problems. It was frankly admitted that advertising helped turn wants into needs or created needs where none had existed before. "The reader may at first feel no need of the article referred to in the advertisement," wrote the Claresholm newspaper in 1913, but once the need was stimulated, advertisements could convince the shopper that the need could be satisfied only by purchase of "the particular make or style which the advertisement has been repeatedly advising." Once this was achieved, "the reader is now ripe for the salesman." Town newspapers continually tried to convince local merchants that such advertising would help counter slow sales and competition from mail order houses and other towns. All town newspapers argued that they were doing their part by refusing to carry advertising for mail order retailers. As the *Cardston Globe* argued in 1914, this loyalty had to be repaid with regular advertising by local merchants.[84] This combined warning and promise remained standard among newspapers until at least the mid 1940s when some began to carry discrete advertisements for mail order houses.

Another means of promoting sales included special promotional sales and techniques. While merchants rarely held sales of out-of-season goods before World War I, they were becoming increasingly accepted as a good business practice.[85] In addition, sales service companies, which offered merchants a package of advertising, pricing, staff and accounting, were used in Alberta towns by 1910. Utilizing extensive advertising hype, such services continued in use until World War II. While they were sometimes used simply to turn around slow sales, retailers often employed them on the orders of their wholesalers and bankers, and their employment by a business was often a sign that it was in major financial difficulty.[86] By the interwar years, some merchants had kept pace with technological change in promoting sales. In 1931, Trainor Hardware in Peace River put two salesmen on the road in a light truck to demonstrate home electrical equipment and appliances. The salesmen also sold "everything in the lines of hardware and groceries." Other promotional events were tied to seasonal needs, especially Christmas, which in the interwar years was being increasingly commercialized. The Toshach store in Drumheller regularly featured Santa at Christmas. Each child received a balloon, a dish of ice cream, and a chance to talk to Santa. In 1931, 600 children showed up. Similarly, the Cardston Implement Co. opened a

| Christmas events, such as a visit by Santa to the Toshach store in Drumheller in 1935, helped make main street a focus for seasonal events. Drumheller Mail, October 25, 1934.

"Toy Town" for Christmas in 1939, featuring a display of toys of "city proportions in a setting of green and silver decorations."[87]

Community events, in which a number of merchants participated, were also held in an attempt to increase sales. The challenge of competition and improved transportation was forcing greater co-operation among merchants. ARMA was a strong proponent of sales weeks using joint advertising, but it counselled that staple articles should not be put on sale, or only at a "small" discount.[88] These events were becoming common in all towns in the interwar years. They attempted to create a sense of occasion and make shoppers feel special, a tactic developed to its highest level by city department stores where shopping extravaganzas were used to create "excitement" about consumer commodities and make shopping a form of entertainment.[89] In keeping with this model, Grande Prairie held a merchandise "carnival" in 1925. It was described as "one of those rousing big sales such as is staged in the larger cities, with its free offerings and ridiculously low prices." Townsfolk were advised to welcome shoppers through courtesy, good values and to leave their cars at home to make parking available downtown. Another promotional technique commonly used was to hold a special sales promotion at the same time that other events brought visitors to town. In 1932, for example, Drumheller merchants offered special prices at Farmer's Shopping Week, which they mounted in conjunction with a UFA rally.[90] There was great variety in these events, but special Christmas attractions were used in all towns by the 1930s. Late night shopping, decorated streets, free movies and treats for children helped draw farm visitors to the town. As remarked in Cardston in 1938, the "big Christmas tree" put up downtown was a means of drawing the farm trade. In Peace River in the same year, the Christmas promotion was a six-day event with special hotel and railway rates for out-of-town visitors. A Santa Claus parade was featured in many places, and in Lacombe, Santa had a "headquarters" on main street where children could pick up his reply to their letters.[91]

Special merchandising events were also tied to the increasing importance of brand name goods in retailing. The technological change in kitchen equipment brought by electricity and gas was promoted heavily by appliance manufacturers and utility companies. The public's acceptance of technological change was not merely a process of passive social adaptation. In 1930, Canadian General Electric's home economist gave demonstrations in Lacombe's Comet Theatre on the economy and speed of "cooking electrically" and the benefits of refrigeration for food storage and preparation. Door prizes were given and the town's mayor introduced the event. The next year, a specially fitted railway car touring western Canada showing appliances manufactured by General Steel Wares stopped in Lacombe for a day. It gave the "merchant and his customers an opportunity to look over these lines and see what invention is doing to lighten the burden of householders in the home, whether they be in the city or in the country."[92]

In a similar fashion, campaigns were held to persuade the public to buy Canadian, British empire, Alberta, and sometimes locally made goods. Before World War I, buy-Canadian goods campaigns were popular and were tied to the "Made in Canada" train. Railway cars containing exhibits of Canadian industrial products were used to stimulate consumption of Canadian products. Among many other centres, the train visited Claresholm in 1912. This campaign used the common rhetoric that it was patriotic to buy Canadian goods because it increased employment and retained capital in Canada.[93]

During the interwar years, broader loyalties were also emphasized. Already in use in Australia, the West Indies, and the United Kingdom, in 1928 Empire shopping week became a feature throughout the British empire to stimulate manufacturing in the empire. While first held at the end of April, it was soon moved to coincide with May 24, the patriotic holiday honouring Queen Victoria. In 1932 it was characterized as a time "to strengthen the Bonds of Empire." Given this objective, it drew support from a variety of organizations, and in Drumheller the patriotic women's organization, the Imperial Order Daughters of the Empire (IODE), helped sponsor the event. Drumheller stores participated with special displays of empire-made goods and decorations of flags.[94]

Empire buying weeks were not, however, meant to encourage the purchase of non-Canadian-made goods at the expense of local loyalties. While most towns did not have sufficient production to sponsor major events such as the Made-in-Calgary campaigns of 1914 and 1916, most found it an appealing concept.[95] It was patriotism writ small: shopping at home built up the home town. As the *Cardston News* noted, it was good citizenship to build up one's town, province, and country. "It is good sound sense, for only that which Alberta produces builds Alberta."[96]

Such sentiments soon were expressed as a regular feature of retailing in the province. The first of these campaigns was launched in 1931 by ARMA to fight the Depression. Modeled on the Buy-British campaign in the United Kingdom, it aimed to stimulate consumption of Alberta-made goods. Merchants were encouraged to mount special displays of Alberta-made goods at special prices. By 1933, the campaign had become a co-operative venture between the provincial government and ARMA, with other organizations, such as the Canadian Club and the Women's Institutes, assisting in organizing local campaigns. Meetings were held in 47 towns and cities, where people were told how the purchase of Alberta-made goods stimulated provincial employment. A long list of Alberta-made goods was advertised, which the public was encouraged to buy. As well, the province's trade commissioner noted that the campaign would help overcome Albertans' "inferiority complex" since they believed "that products made on the outside must be better than those made right at home."[97]

The Alberta-made campaigns received added government support with the election of Social Credit in 1935. It favoured local industrial production as part of its remaking of the provincial economy. The Treasury Branch system, begun in 1938-39, played a part in Social Credit's plans in this respect. It used a complicated system by which purchasers of Alberta-made goods received vouchers for redemption at the Treasury Branches. Participation of a more directly partisan nature also occurred in these campaigns. The Social Credit women's group in Drumheller, for example, organized an Alberta-Made Goods Supper to mark the end of Alberta-Made goods week in 1941.[98] This politicization of home-buying campaigns complicated matters for those who did not support Social Credit.[99] But for many retailers, these campaigns were good for business. One Cardston merchant was eager to make the public "more Alberta conscious," and like many merchants, he participated in the campaign and found it profitable to incorporate its slogans in his advertising.[100]

THE PROBLEM *of*
COMPETITION

The threat from mail order houses, chain stores, farmers and itinerant traders led many merchants in Alberta, as elsewhere on the prairies, to conclude that the whole system of free market competition was destructive.[101] In 1934, the *Grande Prairie Northern Tribune* editorialized that the theory that supply and demand governed prices of manufactured goods served only to reduce workers' wages and the prices farmers received for their commodities. In the latter case, either farm prices had to rise or the prices charged by monopolistic manufacturers had to come down "if society is to carry on." This rejection of the market system had been voiced by merchants at an early date. For example, the 1925 convention of ARMA endorsed the national organization's policy of "price maintenance," by which manufacturers would be forced to set standard retail prices for all commodities. This would not, it claimed, reduce competition or raise prices, but would "eliminate the inefficient retailer, prevent profiteering, and at the same time ensure a reasonable margin of profit." The damage done to independent merchants by chain store competition was said to "indicate why the state should be prepared to regulate all merchandising of goods and services when individuals or aggregations of capital are pursing practices which are...tending to crush fair competition and fair prices in the Community." ARMA also wanted all businesses to be licensed and prohibited by law from selling below cost. As well, it believed that businesses should be required to charge a minimum percentage for cost of operation, that secret discounts should be prohibited, and that inspectors should be appointed to enforce these regulations.[102]

The essential element in this was to define "fair" profit. ARMA contended that it was the same amount that was paid on bonds.[103] The issue was, however, a murky one. It was continually argued in towns that retail stores were not making excess profits. In a simplistic statement of this view, it was argued in Peace River in 1938 that local butchers gave a "fair deal" to both producers and consumers as evidenced by the fact that "none of them have become wealthy." While the debate about "fair prices" had been politicized under the UFA, it became even more partisan with the coming of Social Credit whose policies in favour of a "just price" aimed to give something to everyone. Producers would receive a "fair return" while consumers would pay a "fair price" on their purchases. In this way, purchasing power would be stabilized and money kept in circulation, creating full employment. The obvious question for some was whether this could be created within capitalism, and Pat Conroy, a Drumheller labour leader, wrote that the answer to the question was "very emphatically NO!" In any event, it was never clear if the "just price" represented only price controls, or if it also meant a fundamental restructuring of the price mechanism. From the beginning, there had been a contradiction on this point in farmers' economic theory because, as C.B. Macpherson argued, they "accepted the liberal ethics of individual competition, while rejecting the ethics of monopolistic competition. The impossibility of rejecting the one while accepting the other was implicit from the outset."[104] Social Credit was no better able to resolve this issue than was the farmers' movement.

The second issue, though one of easier resolution in some minds than the thorny problem of "fairness" of prices, was the role of the merchant in creating wealth. In this, the farmers' movements were clear; it was primary producers, like themselves, as well as processors and manufacturers, who were the only creators of wealth. This equation led some farmers to charge that retailers and wholesalers were economic parasites. There was a continual effort in the 1920s by merchants and their spokesmen to convince the public that they were not "middlemen," because they added value to goods, such as "time" and "space," and supplied goods when and where they were wanted and needed. The *Cardston News* carefully made this point in its statement that "the Retail Merchant is not a middleman. His services are equal in value to those of the manufacturer, for he solves the problem of distribution."[105]

The demand by small merchants for limits to competition were part of a general revolt against the economic system in western Canada during the interwar years. While continuing to espouse the doctrine of free enterprise, it was evident that small merchants did not believe that they could live by it. In their demand for limits to competition, small merchants were closer to the ideology of the farmers' movements than they often admitted. Yet, the ideology of each drew upon different traditions. In late nineteenth century Britain, merchants had attempted to restrict competition by law and through association. Similarly, Canadian merchants of the same period were often, as Michael Bliss has shown, uncomfortable with competition, and even resentful of it. Many of these arguments retained their currency in the twentieth century west.[106] While farmers' discomfort with the market system drew upon different concerns, an attack was mounted on the competitive system by farmers and town business people alike.

The radicalism of farmers and merchants was more illusionary than real; both wanted to preserve private property and the market system except when it compromised their own objectives. Both brought a sense of moral righteousness to their arguments. The merchants' demands for restrictions on competition were, in effect, an attempt to create an oligopoly in which entry to merchandising would be limited and in which profit would be guaranteed and regulated by the state. This would have preserved their private interests at public cost. The tendency to monopoly so marked in advanced capitalism would not be eliminated; only its impact would be regulated. The charge of unfairness was entirely self-interested; unfair competition for merchants represented a social injustice, yet merchants wished to maintain a direct relationship with consumers, albeit with minimum prices, and resisted any suggestion that they be required to pay minimum rates for labour or farm commodities.

PART

III

THE DEVELOPMENT
of MAIN STREET

7

TOWN PLANNING

and ITS IMPACT

on MAIN STREET

The location and layout of a town developed directly from the motives of town founders and the general system within which they operated. In general, Canadians copied the American system of free homesteads and used public lands to subsidize construction of railways and the purchase of existing interests, such as those of the Hudson's Bay Company. Also like the Americans, and like colonizing settlers from the time of the Romans, they used rectangular or square grid surveys. Since this was an easy system to administer and survey, it was inexpensive, and in a market economy, the land so surveyed was simple to describe and sell. It was also an infinitely expandable system, and it perfectly supported the dominant view that land was another commodity, albeit a valuable one, with which to make money. There was often little concern for the natural advantages of a site in laying out a town. The CNoR located its towns on the basis of "price and the lack of encumbrances," and since poor quality land could be bought cheaply, its towns were frequently located in low lying wet areas or on other undesirable land; a practice that nicely met the company's ambition to make money as quickly as possible. The GTP, in contrast, tried to locate towns on level, well-drained land that was not too heavily treed and had access to good water.[1]

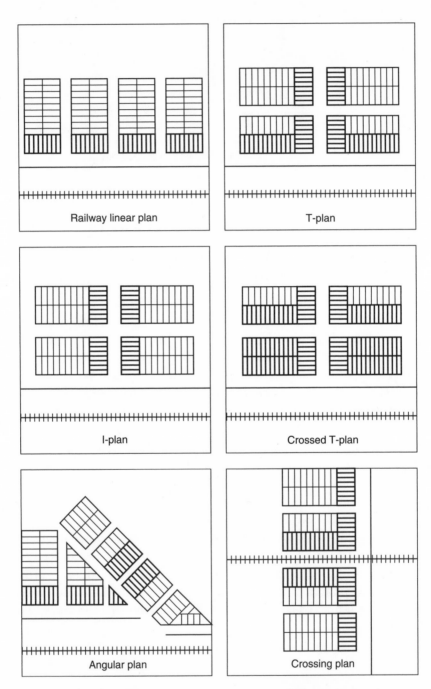

| FIGURE 7.1: *Railway Townsite Form in Alberta. (Narrow lots represent commercial use). Adapted from Ann Holtz, "Small Town Alberta: A Geographical Study of the Development of Urban Form," p. 88.*

TOWN LAYOUT

In the late nineteenth century, most town surveys made no distinction between commercial and residential lots. It was accepted that purchasers would "determine the purpose of their lots and ultimately the structure of the town."[2] Fort Macleod was surveyed as a grid made up of rectangular blocks divided into rectangular lots of equal size, and streets of equal width. Since the main street was the same width as other streets, it developed where business congregated. Lots in Fort Macleod went on the market in the summer of 1884, and by the fall the main street had emerged: "one street is now pretty well defined by the buildings on either side. This is 25th street, and from the present indications, it will be the principal street in the town."[3] By the early twentieth century, however, such random selection was unusual. Townsite promoters could charge more for commercial property, and the main street was surveyed as the widest street, usually between 80 and 100 feet (24.3 and 30.4 meters) versus 66 feet (20.1 meters) in other areas. As well, a townsite developer sometimes identified the business section of the town through rudimentary forms of zoning to guide land use.

Railway companies alone are usually blamed for the rigid layout, the lack of public space and amenities, and, often, the resultant ugliness of many urban places on the prairies. As the architects of this planning, such criticism is merited. Yet towns were designed within a cultural milieu that accepted that these centres were money making propositions—not just for railways, but for everyone associated with them. The railways recognized that investors made choices based on their assessment of potential growth, and therefore towns had to appear to have a future. T.D. Regehr's suggestion that railways in Saskatchewan were popular because they offered a crucial service to farmers and businessmen can be applied equally to Alberta. Thus, the design of a town ranked well down on the list of what people expected to gain from the railway. Few merchants located in a town because it was on a well drained or attractive site, and the relative success of towns like Claresholm, located in a sloughly area, suggests that it was the town's economic potential that counted. A town that looked like every other one had the virtue of being familiar, which gave it an aura of safety for investors and settlers. The look of success was thought to be that of prosperous western railway towns in the United States, or the settled towns in eastern Canada. A town therefore had to meet public expectations for uniform layout. In 1882 the *Macleod Gazette*, anticipating the development of a town on the mainland, editorialized that "there is a great deal in the way a town is laid out." The streets should be laid out "in regular order, houses built in a line, and in fact the whole town planned with every regard to method and regularity."[4]

The tremendous unity in the feel of towns in prairie Canada is not accidental. Yet, as Ann Holtz discovered in her study of town formation and layout in Alberta, there were variations in layout among different promoters and surveyors. As shown in Figure 7.1, she found that six forms were used widely by railway companies in Alberta. While none used one form exclusively or consistently, some companies favoured different ones at different times. Even so, all used a square or rectangular grid, but the way the town was then laid out appears to have been the product of a particular surveyor's preference. Although more imaginative plans were available, such as ones using curved streets, radial streets, and, among others, central squares, they were unusual and reflected unique conditions or demands. In general, they were seen as unmarketable. "Current ideas" about different urban designs had "little impact on the majority of town plans" in Alberta.[5]

Of the six town layouts commonly used in Alberta, each had advantages and disadvantages, but none was overwhelmingly inferior or superior to the other. Although there were some variations, the CPR tended to use angular and crossing plans before 1900 and railway linear and T plans after 1900. The angular plan created some variation in layout, but, as was the case in Lacombe, it did not clearly define the main street. The crossing plans created a large business district, but also created traffic problems at the end of main street and split the town once it had expanded to both sides of the track. The CNoR preferred the I plan, except in divisional points where a crossing T plan or a crossing plan was often used. The GTP used an I plan for its towns east of Edmonton, while those to the west were laid out on a T plan or a crossed T plan.[6]

A square plan was most often used by Mormons in southern Alberta. The Mormon block, or the "Plat of Zion," was based on a stipulation that urban centres be composed of units of one square mile, divided into blocks of 10 acres. Each block was further divided into four residential or twelve commercial lots. The streets were to be 80, 100 or 132 feet wide (24.3, 30.4 and 40.2 meters wide), intersecting at right angles and aligned to the cardinal points of the compass. This plan was not followed exactly in the LDS settlements in southern Alberta, but many, like Cardston, featured wide streets and square blocks. Of the 19 LDS settlements in southern Alberta, 10 were laid out in this manner. Square block plans were not, however, exclusively used by Mormons. They were used widely in the United States in the nineteenth century, although the lots were much smaller and usually were rectangular. This approach was applied at Frank, Blairmore, and Coleman, probably because they were laid out by an American surveyor.[7]

Of these plans, the Mormon block was the only one deliberately designed to reflect social rather than economic needs. While it, like others, paid no heed to local natural features, it was designed to preserve community cohesiveness. In 1899, it was noted that while Fort Macleod lots were 66 x 99 feet (20.1 x 30.1 meters), in Cardston they were "big enough to admit of a dwelling and a hen house being built on one lot without the odor from the one interfering with the comfort of the other." Indeed, in Cardston, "people seem to be utterly oblivious as to the money value of the earth's surface and have appropriated as much of it upon which to erect their dwellings as seemed necessary and desirable."[8]

The Mormon survey was not a mere pursuit of comfort but aimed to enhance Mormon social organization. It created community by breaking down physical isolation.[9] In 1899, 109 residents of Cardston petitioned the Territorial assembly to exempt the village from certain provisions of the *Village Ordinance* that regulated the distance between haystacks and buildings containing stoves or fireplaces. The residents argued that their success in bringing poor agricultural land under cultivation resulted from their social and land organization, for "the cultivation of as small an area of land for the support of one family is much better than trying to cultivate too much, therefore our people do not scatter out, but centralize their efforts." Every farmer owned property in the village or hamlet, and in the winter moved there "for educational, religious and social advantages." This had been a Mormon custom "ever since we became a people," and they could not comply with the village ordinance because "our lots are not large enough to allow us to have our hay stacks the prescribed distance" from houses. These and other special needs were recognized in the incorporation of Cardston by a special ordinance of the Northwest Territories in 1901.[10]

GROWTH WITHOUT PLANNING

Initially, those laying out or surveying towns had to meet only very broad legal planning requirements. Alberta's first legislative action affecting town layout was the 1906 *Land Titles Act*. While it stipulated width of streets and lanes and that lots had to be accessible from the rear, developers were otherwise left to their own devices. While cities like Edmonton, unlike most towns, had some subdivision controls, their development was usually as unplanned as most towns because existing regulations were often ignored.[11]

The territorial and provincial governments exercised additional control by approving incorporation of urban areas. Initially, the minimum population density necessary for town status was low. The *Municipal Ordinance* (1883) allowed the incorporation of a town in any area up to four square miles with a population of 300, or a population density of 75 persons per square mile. The area that a town could occupy was subsequently decreased, and population requirements increased to 700 by 1912. With the formation of the province in 1905, expansion of urban areas continued to be approved with little question, but the province began to exhibit a willingness to regulate after the economic collapse of 1912. In 1913, for example, it denied Lacombe's request to annex fringe areas of the town. The town argued that people living there were "obtaining all the benefits of the improvements which have been made in the business part of the town," but paid no taxes. Since Lacombe had neither water nor sewer, and provided almost no services to its residential population, its argument was tenuous indeed. The province denied permission, noting that the population living in the fringe was very small and annexation was not in the town's interest.[12]

Once built up, the basic form of a survey could only be changed with great difficulty. While the gridiron survey permitted almost infinite expansion of urban areas, most main streets were relatively compact. By the 1930s, Cardston's business area took up four blocks, and Peace River's and Coleman's encompassed 5 blocks each. Drumheller's was the largest, taking up eight blocks in total. As in most centres, this area was the only part of the town that was fully built up. Here, buildings abutted each other or were separated by small gaps of as little as 500 cm. The main street of Peace River was closely built up by 1930, but the immediately adjacent area, like the rest of the town, was not. Houses in most towns

In most towns, the area immediately around the railway station
saw intensive business development, as demonstrated by this 1921
photo of Drumheller. The station is situated just out of view to the
left. Archives Collection, A6087, PAA.

In 1907, Claresholm's main street was nearly built up and business
development had begun on a side street. Buildings were scattered
throughout the rest of the town. Archives Collection,
75.170/6, PAA.

As this 1914–15 photo indicates, Blairmore's main street developed along one side of the street facing the railway. Archives Collection, A19700, PAA.

were separated by vacant lots, although there were exceptions, such as Blairmore and Coleman where residential areas were well built up by World War II.[13]

Main street lots generally filled up quickly; by 1913 it was reported that Cardston "businesses are commencing to segregate into separate entities, and the class of buildings now being erected is of much higher order." By the end of the boom in 1913, most main streets had attained a density that remained approximately the same until the end of World War II. This growth was often a rather mechanical filling of available lots along the main street. Except in places like Cardston and Fort Macleod where main street buildings predated the railway, those lots easily accessible to the railway station were usually built on first, and this often defined the central section of the main street. This gave an important economic advantage to those who acquired such lots when the town was established. In towns which had more than one railway line, like Drumheller, the railways were pressured to build "union" stations so the commercial focus of main street would not be fragmented. In Blairmore, which had a single sided main street, there were about seven buildings on the main street in 1903, all relatively close to the station. There, buildings appeared first on the corners of blocks, and subsequent construction filled in the areas in between.[14] This seems to have been a general pattern in most towns, and development usually proceeded apace on both sides of the street. In some cases, however, double sided main streets filled in first on one side and then the other. By 1915, Cardston's main street had developed solely along the west side, and buildings began to appear on the east side only in the early 1930s.[15]

Mercantile operations were almost exclusively concentrated on main street, although in the interwar years there was some minor development, usually small grocery stores, in residential areas. Land use on main street was highly mixed, with service, professional, mercantile, commercial, and residential uses interspersed. In the early years of a town, a single building often housed several uses. In Claresholm in 1904, one main street building contained a church and the lodge rooms of the Canadian Order of Foresters on the second floor, while its main floor was occupied by a restaurant, bakery, a hardware store and a "tin shop with implement house attached." As more buildings were erected, many businesses moved into their own buildings, although the overall land use remained highly mixed. In one part of Lacombe's business district in 1909, a butcher shop, photo gallery, secondhand store, several houses, and a hotel were in close proximity to each other. Similarly, on Peace River's main street in 1915, a rooming house was next to the cinema, which was next to a hardware store. Adaptation of a building from one use to another was equally flexible; a milliner could occupy the space vacated by a butcher, or a cafe could replace a general store. In 1924, after the Home Bank failed, its building in Blairmore was "annexed" to the Cosmopolitan Hotel and became a beer parlour.[16]

By the 1930s, houses had usually been converted into stores or had been moved from main street, but much residential use on the street remained. Although there was a rooming house on Grande Prairie's main street in 1936, residential space was more typically located on the second floor of commercial blocks. While the upper floors of many two-storey buildings continued to serve as professional and business offices or as fraternal lodge halls, a greater number were used as dwellings. Banks always used the second floor of their buildings as residential space for their employees, and rooms above cafes were typically occupied by the cafe owner, or were rented by the night or week. The Dallas Cafe in Drumheller had 35 registrations in December of 1938, while three of the eight rooms above the Depot Cafe in Lacombe were used by the cafe owners as a dwelling, with the balance rented to "transients of the tramp class for about 30 cents a night." Even when the main floor of a building was vacant, as was the case in one building in Coleman in 1941, the second floor remained in use as a residence.[17] In addition, dwellings were sometimes located at the rear of ground level shops.

During the interwar years, it became popular, as part of the justification for town planning, to contend that towns in Alberta had developed randomly; the favourite analogy was that towns were like "Topsy, who just growed." This observation contained much truth, but it obscured the fact that the main street had often "just growed" as a result of the actions of the most powerful individuals and groups in the town. In 1912, West Canadian Collieries moved several houses from the abandoned mining town of Lille to its "new townsite" at the west end of Blairmore's main street, where it planned to open a mine. The term "new townsite" revealed that it was not viewed as part of the town but a distinctive urban unit. Earlier in 1912, the company had built sidewalks in the subdivision, a small but sure sign of the company's ambitions. This was spelled out more clearly later in the year when the company offered Blairmore a free site in this subdivision for the town's proposed fire hall. It was an obvious attempt to draw the Blairmore main street westward, instead of concentrating development in its existing location. This created a political crisis in Blairmore, with the mayor supporting the West Canadian Collieries site and the rest of the town council bitterly opposed. While the debate centred on the argument that it was absurd to have the fire hall located outside the central part of town, the real issue was the future growth of the main street. West Canadian Collieries was accused of serving its own "petty interests" in the west end of town. Yet everyone recognized that the broader issue was not minor. Blairmore's town council discussed nothing but the fire hall issue for months. Those wanting a compact main street won in 1913 when it was agreed that the fire hall would not be built outside of the business district. This was a set back to West Canadian Collieries' plans for its properties, but it did open its mine there in 1915, and ultimately succeeded in drawing the main street to the west through the construction of office and retail buildings in the 1920s. While these formed a separate business enclave at the west end of the main street, they ultimately helped to string the main street out even further, illustrating how powerful interest groups could shape the physical evolution of a town.[18]

PUBLIC BUILDINGS

Unlike most Alberta towns, Fort Macleod and Cardston had town squares. This reflected a popular nineteenth century urban design principle. The appeal of this ancient town form lay in its attempt to create a focused community, as in many European or eastern Canadian towns. In this central area would be located the most important of the town's buildings, including the town hall, the fire station, the post office and the court house, and perhaps commercial enterprises like a bank or a hotel.[19]

Such plans were never realized in Cardston or Fort Macleod. When the railway arrived in Cardston, the town asked that the station be located on the town square, but since this involved five street crossings, the railway instead located it at the end of main street. Subsequently, the town square was used for periodic public entertainment. Although it had no trees or landscaping, in 1912 the town built a 350-seat grandstand on the site, confirming its use for sports days. Then, in 1919 the town leased the square and the grandstand to an individual who stabled and fed livestock over the winter. In the spring, the place was "in a filthy state," leading to many complaints. In the 1920s, it developed into a children's playground, with play equipment installed by the board of trade.[20]

A similar process occurred in Fort Macleod. In the late nineteenth century, the town square, which was located one block south of the main street, was sometimes used as a camping site by Natives and other visitors, but the town made little effort to improve the square. In 1899, the town council proposed its subdivision and sale, but this was stopped by main street business owners who feared that rival businesses would set up there. Later the same year, it was proposed as the site for a town hall. The ratepayers agreed to a $5,500 debenture for the building, but the town council was divided on a suitable location; some wanted it on the town square, others on the main street. A public meeting was held and the public square location was approved, indicating some awareness that the square could become a focus for town life. Most business people and main street property owners, however, wanted it on the main street where it might increase property values and reduce the cost of insurance by creating a fire break. Similarly, others claimed that a main street location was needed to stabilize the street and make it "a bona fide street for all time to come." Not all business owners supported this view, arguing that its location on the square would make it "an ornament to the town." But mayor Cowdry, a private banker with main street property interests, announced that the town hall would be built on main street if he could "manage it, no matter where the majority of the ratepayers may want to have it." And so it was built on main street, even though its costs rose by an additional $400 because land had to be purchased. While it ultimately did nothing to reduce fire insurance rates on the street because of its frame construction, it was large enough for town offices and an auditorium which was rented out to help pay for the building.[21]

The town square came to public attention once again in 1904 when the court house was built there. While this sited what would be the town's finest building on the square, it was of limited significance in the evolution of the town's form because the main street was by then well developed as the centre of the town. The balance of the square was used as a sports field and the town's curling rink was later built there. While this created a minor community focus for the site, the presence of a town square generally was insufficient to redirect the shape of a town. Form did not direct function, nor could it challenge the supremacy of the commercial rationale of town life. Rather, the main street served as the centre for public life, simultaneously meeting the interests of a town's commercial interests and receiving greatest attention for infrastructure like sidewalks, lights and water. This further helped to assert its central role in town life and confirmed the marginalization of town squares. The concept that public buildings such as a court house and post office could be located together as part of a community centre was rarely a consideration in most towns. Such facilities were desirable because of their economic benefit, and it was usually demanded that they be imposing buildings to enhance the reputation of the town.[22] Usually located on or near main street, they were rarely sited in a configuration that linked them together as a public and community focus.

Of all public buildings, the location of the post office was considered to be the most important. There was always concern that it be close to the main street for the convenience of business owners. With the appointment of a new postmaster in 1914, it was proposed that the Cardston post office be moved from the centre of the business area, where it was located in a store, to another store on the northern edge of the main street towards the train station. Making the usual identification of business needs with those of the town as a whole, main street businesses petitioned against this move, arguing that it would inconvenience everyone, "there being neither business houses nor dwellings on the north of the proposed new post office site" which was "entirely out of the business district of the town." Similarly, business owners in Peace River complained that the post office was too far from "the business centre of town," but their concerns were not met until 1938 when a new post office was built on main street.[23]

Aside from this concern, it was commonly argued that the post office had to be a fitting structure to enhance the town's image. In 1918, it was contended that Drumheller needed a larger post office because the town had "grown beyond the country store size of a post office." By the late 1920s, growth again necessitated a new post office, and a "monster petition," got up by the town council, was signed by nearly every ratepayer. The local Member of Parliament also lobbied for a new building, and it was constructed in 1930. A new post office and customs house was built in Cardston in the late 1930s. It was located on a side street off main street, a relatively central location that aroused no controversy. "To Cardston, the modern town, postal service is highly important," and the usual concern about image was satisfied because the building was large, "handsome looking," and faced with "corduroy brick of variegated colors." It was noted with approval that "many of the Calgary churches are faced with the same beautiful material."[24]

In addition to lobbying for court houses, post offices and other public buildings, most towns had built town halls by World War II. Calls for such buildings were periodically made and those in Cardston in 1939 were little different than those voiced over the previous 30 years. It was claimed that a civic building for town offices and for rest rooms for out-of-town visitors ("who weekly mean so much to the town") was essential to symbolize the town's history, serve as a community focus, and stimulate "civic pride."[25] Such an awareness was slow to emerge, and perhaps was confirmed in part by the heavy base of rural shoppers, who did no business at a town hall and were therefore unconcerned with its function or symbolism.

Prior to World War I, most towns did not have civic buildings, except possibly a fire hall. The town offices and council chambers were sometimes located, as in Drumheller in 1919 and Blairmore in 1911, in rented space on the second storey of a commercial building on main street. And as late as 1946, Lacombe rented space for its town office and council chambers in a two-storey building formerly used as a service station. The town sublet the balance of the building at street level to a furniture store and the second floor as dwellings. Despite frequent demands, Cardston constructed a town hall only in 1940. It was just off main street beside the recreational centre, and it had a community focus since the town offices, library and police department were all located in the building. Before 1945, this was the closest that any of the towns surveyed came to creating a grouping of public buildings that might serve as a community focus. In most cases, the town hall rarely became a central focus or symbol of a town. Coleman built a combined town hall and fire hall on a side street just before World War I, but it was said in 1933 that the grounds had been an "eyesore for twenty years" and the building itself was not "imposing." Shortly thereafter, the site was landscaped and made into a memorial park as part of a relief project, but the town hall retained its "shack like appearance," and demands for its improvement were common. The next year, it was veneered with stone at the basement level and with cement blocks on the upper walls. The design was planned and contracted by J.S. D'Appolonia, a local contractor.[26]

Like Coleman, Grande Prairie had a two-storey frame building as a combined town hall and fire station. It was located on a side street where land was cheaper. As well, this location was favoured since it was difficult to get a fire truck quickly out of a main street building because of street traffic. As one town councillor recalled, "a side street was the proper place to build a town hall."[27] Nevertheless, when built in 1920, there was some hope that it might serve as a town centre and community symbol. There were plans to landscape the front with grass and flowers, although this apparently was not done. By the late 1930s, the town hall became more community focused when a rest room for rural women was located there, and the IODE set up a library in the council chambers two nights a week. While both developments represented an attempt to establish a community focus, lack of space elsewhere in the town was also a factor in their location in the town hall.[28]

FORMAL TOWN PLANNING

Prior to 1913, when Alberta passed its first town planning act, there was no coherent town planning legislation in the province. The 1913 legislation recognized local authority to regulate the layout of streets and lanes, the size of lots, the height and spacing of buildings, zoning and land use. As well, it recognized local authority in preparing general plans to guide all aspects of town development, including regional planning. Nonetheless, the province retained significant power. If a local authority failed to prepare a planning scheme when needed or demanded by land owners, the minister could call public hearings on behalf of the local authorities and implement a town plan. Nor could a town planning scheme be implemented or amended without the approval of the province. The 1913 legislation was another limitation of local government power, but it had no immediate practical impact. The economy had collapsed by the time it passed, and regulations under the act were not issued until 1915. Nor did the provincial government have the expertise to administer the legislation. Thus, no town plans were prepared under the 1913 act, and none were prepared until 1929 when the province introduced a new town planning act.[29]

While the 1929 *Town Planning Act* contained new provisions for urban transportation, preparation of general plans and regional planning, it largely reenacted the 1913 act. In 1929, planning objectives included improvement of traffic patterns for safety and efficiency, implementation of zoning to prevent incompatible land use and to promote public sanitation, and consideration of a site's natural advantages when designating land use. The legislation also governed building bylaws, laying out of parks for public enjoyment and town beautification, replotting (to cancel plans of subdivision from the boom years), regional planning, and, among others, tree planting.[30]

Town "beauty" was an important consideration in 1913, but it was of even greater concern in the 1929 legislation. In reference to Alberta's proposed legislation, Cecil Burgess, professor of architecture at the University of Alberta, argued that towns, to be good places to live in, "ought to be beautiful. Many great cities are so, ours are distinctly not so." Alberta was not "alone in this problem. It is one of the great problems of modern life. All over the world it is being recognized that a great menace of general ugliness is threatening our civilization. This problem is recognized and a machinery is being organized to meet it."[31] Reflecting such concerns, the 1929 town planning legislation permitted architectural controls and stressed tree planting and redesign of streets to enhance the natural beauty of a site. Especially important was control of highway billboards and gas station advertising which disfigured the landscape. In the United States and Britain there was significant public revulsion to highway advertising signs and garish filling stations. Many Canadians reacted the same way; Saskatchewan passed town planning and beautification legislation in 1928, and similar legislation was under consideration in British Columbia. Thus, Alberta's concerns were part of a general movement during the interwar years in Britain and North America. It was also a response to a lively group of town planning advocates, as well as Premier J.E. Brownlee's "vigorously expressed distress, after his European tour, at the debasement of the country-side in all directions by hideous advertising signs and by irresponsible building." As Horace Seymour, Alberta's first town planner, remarked in 1931, "beauty can only grow out of utility," but as Cecil Burgess pointedly commented, "opportunity is now knocking at the gates of the Western towns. Will they rise to take it? Or do they really care?"[32]

Under the 1929 *Town Planning Act*, towns could appoint town planning commissions to make recommendations to the town council about zoning and other town planning matters. While local planning commissions did not have legislative authority, town councils could delegate certain powers to them. Nonetheless, the province played a key role. The minister approved general plans and zoning bylaws and could also demand amendments. The province also provided expertise, advice, and approval through its newly established Provincial Town and Rural Planning Advisory Board. A nationally renowned town planner, Horace Seymour, was hired to co-ordinate the province's efforts and advise the board. He immediately began a publicity campaign on the benefits of town planning and visited towns throughout the province.

The prospect of rational town development was welcomed by many in Alberta. It seemed like an opportunity for a fresh start; a chance to undo the errors of the past. Clearly, attitudes were changing, and in expressing its support for the 1929 legislation, the *Drumheller Mail* made the typical analogy that "the majority of towns are true relatives of Topsy who 'just growed'." Drumheller was "suffering today because no zoning bylaw has ever been considered. The business section is still in a polyglot condition because building restrictions were unknown until a few years ago." If Drumheller's future development was planned, the town could be made beautiful. By realigning some streets, the hills around the town could become "a scenic background to the town itself." And expressing a common concern in Drumheller, such improvements might mean that the town would no longer be "looked upon as a mining camp."[33] Such views were significant in marking a changed attitude that recognized the town's setting as an important expression of its character. A similar concern about Peace River was noted by Horace Seymour in 1929 when he remarked that, given its beautiful natural setting, the town could become "an outstanding example for the whole province." Except for its main street and a few residential areas, Peace River was still at the stage of development where planning could be applied inexpensively. Playgrounds and parks could easily be laid out, and streets replanned and boulevarded. Picking up on Seymour's views, the *Peace River Record* argued that:

> despite the vast amounts involved in building costs and the provision of public utilities, the laying out of towns has heretofore been entirely without rhyme or reason, everything proceeding in the most haphazard way imaginable, each individual undertaking his own planning and building without regard to his neighbors or the general appearance of his community. With the assistance of the Alberta town planning commission much can be done in nearly every town to improve this condition. In Peace River particularly there is an unusual opportunity for this work.[34]

In keeping with such enthusiasm, a number of towns acted quickly. Drumheller, Lacombe, Peace River, and Grande Prairie appointed commissions in 1929 and Cardston appointed one in 1930. By 1931, 20 towns had appointed planning commissions, 11 of which were preparing zoning bylaws. Since they were advisory only, Horace Seymour believed that they could be given wide scope. However, he diplomatically observed that they should be "a body outside the council," since councillors "were constantly faced with current requirements and invariably had one eye on the tax rate." In any case, as Cecil Burgess remarked, there was "really more thought than money needed" to implement sound town planning.[35]

Most members of town planning commissions were local figures, often former mayors or town councillors. In addition, the current mayor and at least one councillor usually served on the commission.[36] In many cases, these commissions eagerly seized the task of attempting to plan and beautify their town. In Drumheller, the commission first tackled a zoning bylaw, and its preliminary plans included a civic centre, boulevarding, and opening up the street along the river to make a scenic drive.

Despite such enthusiasm and the province's initial commitment, the 1929 legislation rarely lived up to its promise. Only a little progress was made between 1929 and 1931 in the areas of street widening, correcting dangerous intersections, boulevarding streets, landscaping school and hospital grounds, replotting, and, less commonly, zoning. As with the badly timed 1913 legislation, the 1929 act was introduced on the eve of the Depression, and the province soon reassessed its commitment to town planning. In its cost-cutting, Horace Seymour's position was abolished in 1932, although the Provincial Town and Rural Planning Advisory Board continued to operate, albeit without technical advice. Similarly, planning efforts in most towns were stymied by the Depression. In Cardston, the town planning commission did almost nothing after its formation, and, as the chairman of the Lacombe town planning commission noted in early 1931, the Depression slowed town planning work in Lacombe, although he also significantly noted that town planning had been found to be "more involved" than expected.[37]

Part of this unexpected complexity arose because town councils' notions of town planning often turned out to be radically different than those of their planning commissions. For example, many town councils saw planning largely as a matter of making a town pretty. In Grande Prairie, town planning was absorbed by a tree planting campaign. Despite town planners' considerable efforts to educate townspeople, this apparently was a popular understanding of what was meant by town planning. Town councils were soon at loggerheads with their planning commissions over other matters as well. Many soon came to see planning as an expensive and unwarranted interference with private property. In less than a year after its creation, the Peace River planning commission was fighting with the town council about solutions to the "generally unsatisfactory condition of the town." It argued that the council's lack of co-operation amounted "almost to direct antagonism" to its efforts in "enhancing the appearance of the town's streets, river frontage and other public places." The commission resigned in protest, noting that the expenditure of town money on a town planning scheme was "not in the public interest until such time as the town council is willing and ready to lend an intelligent interest to the work." Although the commission was soon reappointed with the same members, town planning in Peace River had begun poorly, and planning efforts there before the end of World War II were desultory. Much the same pattern was apparent in Drumheller—although the conflict between the council and its town planning commission was not as direct, the council stalled the implementation of many of the commission's recommendations.[38]

ZONING

When railways were creating and laying out towns, land use controls were occasionally applied. The GTP used a form of zoning in its mainline towns, excluding "objectionable" uses such as livery barns and blacksmith shops from the main street. Minimum values, which varied from town to town, were also imposed for buildings on portions of the main street. The town was laid out on only one side of the track to prevent traffic problems and uneven main street development. The objective was to create an orderly town that would attract business. In order to promote public safety and local traffic needs, it became customary to locate grain elevators on the opposite side of the track to that used by train passengers. The same strategy was used in Blairmore where coal was loaded on one side of the track. This was done partly because of the location of the Greenhill mine, but it also served to preserve values on the built-up side of the main street. Usually, the switching of cars in the station grounds was also avoided so not to depreciate townsite land values.[39]

Such regulation of land use was one element of zoning. While the 1913 town planning legislation had allowed towns to impose limited zoning controls, Alberta's 1929 town planning legislation gave towns greater power to establish "building zones" for all or a portion of the town. In practical terms, many towns had been dealing with such matters in a piecemeal fashion for many years. For example, "many old buildings" on Blairmore's main street were built over the front property line and obstructed the "street lines." In 1912, a surveyor hired by the town set a bench mark to which buildings had to conform in set back and grade. By fixing a grade, it was said that the town filled "a long-felt want in connection with building on Victoria Street and is sure to save the town many inconveniences as well as being an act of economy." The same was done in Cardston in 1909. Building to a consistent set back, however, remained a problem in many places; in 1930 there was at least one building on Peace River's main street that was 20 feet back from the sidewalk.[40]

Other zoning-like regulations in Alberta towns before World War I consisted of bylaws which restricted the use and storage of inflammable materials or established fire zones in which buildings had to be built from materials like brick or stone. While the primary concern was fire prevention, consideration for the devaluation of property because of incompatible or offensive uses was sometimes implied. In some places, this gradually helped to eliminate liveries, blacksmith shops and laundries from main street. Service stations and garages created similar concerns about fire, and cars entering or leaving the site also disrupted street traffic. These were regulated by bylaws or agreements with the owners in question. For example, in 1923 the construction of a garage at a busy intersection on Blairmore's main street led the town to draw up an agreement with the owner "to safeguard the town against liability in case accidents should occur, due to the location of the garage."[41]

After 1929, Alberta's new town planning legislation enabled the implementation of coherent and co-ordinated bylaws in the place of these piecemeal zoning efforts. While fire zones to protect against fire hazards continued to be declared, coherent development through zoning controls was increasingly seen not only as a matter of convenience and safety but as one with clear economic benefits. As it was phrased in Drumheller in 1930, zoning would protect "property owners against depreciation in real estate values." The same argument was made in Coleman in 1936, when it was suggested that the town needed "certain building restrictions" to "improve the general appearance of the place and make it impossible to erect a shack next to a decent looking building. Mining towns as a rule have been very careless about appearances."[42]

Such arguments were compelling in theory, but their application was less straight forward. Even though the provincial town planning advisory board discouraged the passage of zoning bylaws before a general plan had been developed, most towns before 1947 adopted combined zoning and building bylaws but not general plans. It has been contended that this happened because the legislative process for adopting general plans was more complicated and "tied" the hands of town councils. Yet, there were important similarities in the process for adopting both zoning and general plan bylaws. The political dynamics of town life, as well as the inability of most towns to develop complex documents like general town plans, were likely more important in the adoption of zoning bylaws over general plans. The province kept control of the process by requiring ministerial approval of all zoning bylaws, and it gave considerable leeway to those attempting to defeat such bylaws. The minister could hear objections to a zoning bylaw following its appeal to the local town planning commission. Anyone could seek amendment or repeal of a zoning bylaw, and those hearing appeals were required to ensure "that substantial justice is done and that the interests of any individual are not unduly or unnecessarily sacrificed for the benefits of the community."[43]

The zoning classifications used in Alberta towns were relatively limited. The province distributed a model zoning bylaw which recommended that land use be classified as residential, multiple dwelling, local commercial, central commercial, industrial, and agricultural. In business districts, most zoning bylaws permitted businesses that were nonpolluting, involved minimal shipping and receiving, were quiet, involved minimal fabrication, and did not create a fire threat. This effectively helped to limit the main street to retail, office and commercial uses.[44] Although the Drumheller town council examined the province's model zoning bylaw in 1929, it instead proposed a plan with broader categories including residential, multiple residential (in the area adjoining the business district), commercial, and industrial. The zoning bylaw was slow to be adopted. It had not yet been passed by 1932, when a need for it was made clear once again with the construction of a natural gas distributing station in a residential area. The *Drumheller Mail* fumed that "Drumheller has more than its share of building atrocities which a happy-go-lucky administration allowed in the past." The town needed a policy "to protect" it "from the anarchistic designs of individuals who view issues only from their own personal angle and refuse to think in terms of community progress."[45]

Drumheller's zoning bylaw was adopted later in 1932, despite concerns that the restriction of "building in any way also restricted individual initiative." Such concerns were largely unfounded since the existence of a zoning bylaw did not mean that town councils were restricted in encouraging development. Well established customs, in which land development was governed by private need (sometimes carried out at public cost), continued to characterize development. In late 1944, Grande Prairie passed its first zoning bylaw which had been carefully drafted in consultation with the Alberta town planning board. Yet it provided only temporary protection. Within 18 months, the town council amended it over the protests of residents to allow construction of an auto repair garage in a residential district adjoining the downtown.[46]

8

BUILDING

MAIN STREET

The design and materials of construction of main street buildings were often viewed as the clearest evidence of a town's growth, prosperity, and future. The most expensive and fashionable buildings were commonly described as "a credit to the town," suggesting their role as emblems of civic growth. Building design was dictated by fashion, and by attempts to appear permanent, modern, and city-like. Since the initial growth of most towns was concentrated within the years between 1900 and 1913, many main street buildings were built at this time, giving them a similar scale and design and creating an integrated streetscape.[1] Equally important in the look of buildings was their capacity to generate revenue. Certain architectural styles were thought to enhance the profitability of a building, and signs and interior layout made a contribution as well since it was believed that "modern" buildings would stimulate trade.

MATERIALS of CONSTRUCTION

The first buildings in all towns were wood structures. In some communities like Fort Macleod, Cardston, Peace River, and Grande Prairie, log was the first building material. In Peace River, all buildings were log or frame construction, and some continued in use for many years. One of the oldest log buildings in the town, the Peace Hotel, was demolished in 1937. Built around 1912, it was later covered with lumber siding, and in 1929 it was commented that "very few people knew of the primitive method of architecture employed."[2]

Milled lumber construction soon replaced log; in 1915 much building was underway in Peace River, and among the new structures were "several excellent buildings, which, though frame, are good permanent places which add materially to the town." In centres like Claresholm, where timber was scarce, milled lumber construction predominated from the beginning. Most of these early wooden buildings were unpainted. As late as 1929, it was commented in Peace River that "the weather plays havoc with buildings, particularly of wooden construction, and neglect of a period of years had brought the inevitable result—a drab, neglected appearance." With a sense that a significant and permanent shift had taken place, it was noted in 1916 that a main street building, for the first time in Grande Prairie's history, had been painted immediately after its completion.[3] Nonetheless, building owners often needlessly feared that painting would lead to increased property assessment and higher taxes. Still, owners were continually urged, most often as a part of clean-up campaigns, to paint their buildings. As was noted in Cardston in 1919, despite the popular attitude that paint was "more or less of a luxury," it helped to preserve wood and enhanced property values.[4]

Of equal importance, painted buildings contributed to a positive town image. In Claresholm in 1928, "a shabby unpainted neglected looking collection of buildings" did not impress shoppers or prospective new citizens "as being the home of up-to-date merchants" who offered good value. The next year, it was argued that Coleman's "very dowdy and run-down appearance" could be reversed with paint because "new paint, like new clothes, creates a mighty good impression." A similar motive inspired the *Grande Prairie Herald Tribune* to advise townspeople in 1947 to "splash the paint on in bright, gay colors that will give a lift to the town's drooping spirits. Don't repeat the old drab colors. They belonged to the dreary thirties. These are the dashing forties. Away with the gloomy, sombre roofs and walls. Try out daring color combinations that will look happy even on a dismal day."[5]

Wooden buildings remained a significant part of the building stock of most main streets. By 1936, Coleman's main street had seven buildings of brick, while the rest were wood frame, and in the same year, 95 percent of the buildings on Grande Prairie's main street were wood frame, with the balance either brick or brick veneer over hollow tile. While many wooden buildings remained along Peace River's main street by the 1930s, an increasing number of those being built used hollow tile covered with brick or stucco. A few of solid brick were also built; the first appeared on main street in 1932. In contrast, such materials were in wider use in other towns. The majority of buildings on main street in Lacombe, Blairmore, Fort Macleod, and Cardston were brick, stone, cement, frame or hollow tile covered with metal siding, brick veneer or stucco. Most of these buildings had been constructed before World War I during the settlement boom.[6]

In Fort Macleod, the Cowdry Bank (1901–2) and a building constructed by D.G. Grier were among the town's earliest brick buildings.[7] The latter, rented by the Great West Saddlery Company, featured a pressed metal facade. Produced in St. Louis, Missouri, the metal was laid over the brick as a decorative feature. Although such prefabricated metal facing was popular in North America after the 1880s, it was unique in Fort Macleod. It featured traditional architectural decorations, including an elaborate cornice.[8] The use of brick and stone, primarily sandstone from local quarries, increased in Fort Macleod after fire in 1906 wiped out many of the wooden structures along main street. In addition, the speculative frenzy from 1911 to 1913 also stimulated construction of many brick and stone buildings.[9] By this time, brick buildings were also going up in other centres. Fire had also destroyed many frame buildings on Lacombe's main street in 1906 and by 1907 their replacement gave Lacombe a whole block of masonry buildings. By 1910, stone, cement block, and brick buildings were also completed or under construction on Cardston's main street.

Brick and stone were permanent, noncombustible, high status materials. Their expense confirmed that the town's future was secure and warranted investment. Despite much talk by merchants about plans to build buildings of brick, or, better still, of stone, it was remarked in Fort Macleod in 1899 that even one building "built now of stone and brick would do more for Macleod's immediate good than fourteen business blocks" in the minds of promoters who should "drop the fire trap business and lead the way to brick and sound stability." This concern about permanency was partly the product of the newness of Euro-Canadian settlement and a desire to create a future in the West. As well, it grew from competition among towns; a town with good prospects had to look the part to attract settlers and investment. These concerns were evident when the Milnes block, a solid brick building, and then the best structure in Claresholm, was completed in 1910. It was "erected to stay built," with a foundation strong enough to permit additional storeys in the future. It was as fire proof as possible, and was fully modern with hot and cold water and steam heat. In addition to such features, many of these buildings were constructed of locally made brick. As observed in Blairmore in 1910, the town's new buildings were "not all frame" but included some of brick, and adding to pride and confidence, "of our own manufacture."[10]

These materials continued in use after 1920, and the view that they were an asset to the town persisted. Claresholm's brick buildings were said in 1921 to give the town "an air of permanence."[11] Stucco over hollow tile also became popular, and cement block, which was inexpensive and fireproof, also gained in importance. A "sensational new" building material that came into use in some towns by World War II was cinder block, which in southern Alberta was manufactured at Raymond. Made of crushed cinders, sand, and cement, it had high compression strength and good insulating qualities. It was usually stuccoed and, like hollow tile, was often used as a veneer over wood frame.[12]

ELEMENTS of DESIGN

While materials of construction contributed to the image of main street, the look of buildings was also a product of architectural fashion and business needs. The design of main street buildings responded to the fashions popular in larger, wealthier, and, in the eyes of townspeople, more successful urban centres in North America. Demonstrating that such design ideas had informally spread throughout the society, most of these buildings were constructed without the involvement of architects. Instead, local builders, brick layers, and stone masons, familiar with contemporary fashions, designed and built most of them. Architects designed these buildings in a few cases—the Edmonton firm of Rule and Wynn, for example, designed some stores in small towns, including a new grocery store in Grande Prairie in 1940.[13]

Fashion and the needs of merchandising exerted a powerful influence on the look of main street buildings. The basic design parameters were that a building had to make its public statement within the confines of a narrow lot, where only the facade was visible from the street. The design also had to allow for large windows facing the street to let in light and to display merchandise. As well, concerns about fire exerted some influence. In cities, fire bylaws have been credited with directing construc-

These two views of Lacombe in 1900 (top) and 1910 (bottom) show the effects of a decade of infill construction and renovation of earlier buildings. Archives Collection, A11263, PAA (top), Archives Collection, A11276, PAA (bottom).

| The earliest permanent buildings on Coleman's main street featured
historicist architectural designs. Photo from about 1912. NC-2-336,
GAI.

tion towards stone and brick. While concerns about fire affected construction in towns as well, the role of local government in forcing these changes was minor. Most brick and masonry buildings in Coleman, Claresholm, and Cardston were constructed before the towns had passed building bylaws, and enforcement of building bylaws in many towns, like Fort Macleod and Lacombe, was so poor as to be meaningless during the period of major construction before 1912. Rather, efforts to obtain lower insurance rates, the prestige of building with such materials, and the possibility of obtaining a higher rent for such buildings were more significant in encouraging high building standards.

The earliest wooden buildings on main street were utilitarian and met the straightforward need of sheltering business. Despite the popular image that early main streets were immediately built up with false fronted buildings, the first commercial buildings tended to be gable-

roofed structures, with the gable usually facing the street. These buildings were later renovated by applying a false front. This fashion
appeared everywhere on the North American frontier. Whether in southern Alberta or in Idaho, most early buildings were gable or flat-roofed
structures with false fronts, sometimes with a stepped or round profile or
a small centrally placed pediment.[14] The construction of such a false
front on one store in Fort Macleod in 1885 was described by the *Macleod
Gazette* as being "different from anything yet put up in town, the top
being rounded instead of pointed" [i.e., gabled]. Some attention to
design was apparent since "a half circle let into the front, above the door,
will have the name of the firm inscribed on it."[15]

On these frame buildings, windows and doors were usually built flush
with the wall, and the flatness of the facade was reinforced by using
shallow facings. This lack of depth created a somewhat monotonous
streetscape, but this was soon superseded by more complex design. Most
buildings, regardless of material of construction, were relatively small,
usually one or two storeys, although some towns had a few three-storey
buildings, one of which was usually a hotel. Favoured design elements
for all these buildings until about 1930 featured architectural decorations
"borrowed from the architectural styles of the past, usually in more or
less new combinations." This broad design approach has been described
as "historicism."[16] Within this tendency, a varied range of stylistic elements were applied: sometimes classical influences such as columns over
a symmetrical facade, other times Renaissance revival influences such as
decorative cornices, and at yet other times Romanesque influences such
as rough dressed stone and heavy rounded arches. These were modest
expressions of the same designs used in city buildings, and they
expressed the popular view that familiarity and standardization indicated success and a town's uniformity of purpose.[17] As well, these historical styles, or elements of them, expressed popular notions of beauty and
the linking of the past and present. As Cecil Burgess, then the newly
appointed professor of architecture at the University of Alberta, told a
Fort Macleod audience in a 1913 lecture, beauty was inherent in good
craftsmanship and good architecture expressed human genius. A society's buildings, he contended, were a permanent record of civilization
that linked the present with the past.[18]

Cornices of pressed metal were one popular application of these principles. Sometimes featuring classically inspired garlands or simpler decorative devices like geometrical shapes in relief, they were mass produced

and commercially available in Alberta by 1900. They may also have been manufactured in some Alberta towns. For example, while nothing is known about his production, one Cardston tinsmith in 1909 called his business the Cardston Tin and Cornice Shop.[19] Wherever they were manufactured, cornices were commonly used in Italian Renaissance Revival style, an academic style that was popularized at the Chicago World's Columbian Exposition in 1893. Within a decade, this style had inspired the design of small and large commercial buildings throughout the United States and Canada. Its rapid and widespread adoption reflected the growing interconnection of communities. Since so many towns in the Canadian west were in a rapidly developing phase when it was popular, aspects of this style were used widely. It was said to have many attributes, and as has been argued in the case of one important Winnipeg commercial building, asserted refinement and stability as a signal of corporate legitimacy and security.[20] In towns in the United States, it has been contended that when applied to small commercial buildings, "it was an interpretation of the Renaissance as ordered beauty." Of greater importance, such buildings were stylish and "proclaimed the modernism of the block and presumably the goods to be had inside."[21]

The use of these styles sometimes came to be associated with those who employed them. By using similar designs across Canada for post offices and other government buildings, the federal government created recognizable state building styles. Large companies like railways and banks also often used standard designs in their corporate building style across the county. The Bank of Commerce, for example, favoured neoclassical styles which, with pediments and columns, projected a serious and stable appearance. Many of these designs were scaled down versions of those used in big city branches.[22] Among the finest of these classically inspired buildings in Alberta was the Merchants Bank of Canada in Lacombe. Constructed in 1904 at a cost of $30,000, it was located on the triangular end of a downtown block and featured a classically inspired facade with a corner entrance, blind columns and a fine cornice.[23]

These historicist designs gave way by 1930 to an entirely different approach in which building facades were pared down and decoration was eliminated or abstracted. This produced streamlined buildings, often referred to as Moderne style. The architectural historian Dorothy Field has noted that this style "owed much to the new field of industrial design, which, by the thirties was producing 'aerodynamic,' 'streamlined' designs for everything from cars to vacuum cleaners. With its clean, uncluttered 'stripped down' appearance, Moderne architecture was in keeping with this widespread enthusiasm and romance with the future." Moderne buildings featured flat roofs, rounded corners, a horizontal line, and geometrically shaped windows. Favoured materials included chrome, stucco, glass blocks, and various manufactured building materials marketed under names such as bakelite and vitrolite, a bright shiny material.[24]

These buildings represented a significantly changed attitude. Instead of appealing to a historical continuity, the future was divorced from the past. This was part of the intellectual and design revolution taking place during the interwar years in the European world. Functionalism became a primary definition of beauty, making the principles that had inspired the earlier historicist designs irrelevant in a machine age. Moderne was stimulated by the designs shown in 1925 at the International Exposition of Decorative Arts in Paris and rapidly spread to North America.[25] It was promoted through magazines and movies. Through the movie *Our Dancing Daughters*, for example, people in Drumheller in 1929 were exposed to forms of "modernist" architecture. According to a local review, the film had "exotic settings" with "an amazingly symbolic style of architecture and interior decoration. Throughout the modernistic motif employed by the M-G-M art expert, sweeping curves, abrupt angles and futuristic geometrical compositions are predominating features."[26]

Since they were linked to modern machines and technology and had "a futuristic element," many cinemas, gas stations and car dealerships employed the Moderne style.[27] Oil companies also used it as part of corporate identification. The Texaco station built in 1932 in Drumheller was a stucco building "similar in architectural style to the Texaco stations in larger centres."[28] As part of the image of speed and efficiency, many of these Moderne gas stations featured gas pumps under covered driveways. This allowed a motorist to "drive in, order so many gallons and drive on with little delay."[29] Moderne's appeal, however, was broad, and it was applied to almost any type of building. While new construction by the 1930s tended to be at the margins of the business area because most main streets were by then fully built up, Moderne was usually applied in any new construction. Thus, the burning of one part of the Alexandra hotel in Drumheller in the 1930s created an opportunity for applying the new style on main street. The new addition featured many Moderne elements; its corner location permitted it to be wrapped around the corner, and its round windows, horizontal lines, and stucco cladding marked it as a progressive and modern building.

Once objects of admiration, the older historicist designs were now often spurned. While elements of historicist styles were often retained for buildings such as banks and government buildings like post offices, designs for commercial buildings generally began to respond to the influence of the pared-down designs of Moderne. Coleman's newspaper was critical of the town's main street—which had a number of older buildings in a range of historicist designs—because it did not give a "very favorable impression owing to its handicaps and grotesque styles of architecture and store fronts."[30] This view was general, and older buildings were often renovated in the new designs. While this usually involved little more than stuccoing the exterior to cover up any decorative elements, this worked to give the old building a "really modern appearance" and, on a more practical level, to make wooden buildings more fire resistant.[31] In 1938 the Soby store in Claresholm was renovated by installing "an almost continuous plate glass display front" surmounted with buff coloured awnings. The building's exterior was stuccoed, making it "attractive and in line with modern architectural ideas."[32]

While the historicist and Moderne designs were dominant everywhere, they did not represent the entire architectural vocabulary of small towns. In both Blairmore and Coleman, where Italian builders were prominent, a number of buildings demonstrated other design influences. In the early 1920s, a group of commercial and office buildings called the Greenhill Addition was constructed at the west end of Blairmore's main street. They were built and designed by Enrico Pozzi, who as an adult had immigrated to Canada from Italy. Showing an unusual measure of design independence, they featured stucco exteriors, but were not precursors to Moderne. Rather, they evoked the feel and mass of vernacular buildings of northern Italy. Similarly, when J.S. D'Appolonia renovated a derelict building at the end of Coleman's main street in 1934 for the Italian Society, what was called "mission stucco" was featured. Two blind columns ran from the ground level to the gable end and a large sunburst etched into the plaster was featured in the gable end facing the street. Steel ornamental balconies were constructed on the front and side of the building. As well, the area around the windows was inset with "colored Victrolite."[33] It was a highly mixed architectural statement: California influences, then highly popular in domestic architecture in Alberta, were apparent in the ironwork and the rough stucco, Moderne materials were shown in the Victrolite, but the massing of the building and the sun burst in the gable end showed independence of such fashion. These latter features, like those of the Pozzi buildings in Blairmore, would also have been at home on the plains of northern Italy.

BUILDING INTERIORS

While exterior facades of buildings were changing in response to Moderne influences after World War I, interior spaces were also being altered because of changing fashions, competition, and theories about merchandising. In 1906, Fort Macleod merchants were criticised for their "dilapidated and disreputable" buildings, which had neither good interior design nor the "attractive and inviting appearance from the outside that so successfully entices purchasers within and induces them to purchase." It was well known that appearances counted in attracting business, and if the design of Fort Macleod's stores was improved, "there will be less ordering goods by mail." Indeed, the public was beginning to refuse to shop at businesses that "have so little regard for appearance, so little regard for the convenience of their customers, so little regard for the welfare of the town as to persist in doing business in such places as some of the merchants do to-day." Merchants had to respond "to public opinion and erect places of business according to modern ideas or else make way for others who will." One merchant claimed that there was no incentive for him to put up a "respectable building" because people in Fort Macleod would only buy from him when they wanted credit. This reasoning did not convince the *Macleod Gazette* editor; "people would not go into his dingy old place if they could help it and we do not blame them very much."[34]

The standards of acceptable interior design changed continually. Before World War I, most stores had counters along each side of the room, behind which were high shelves holding goods. The public was served from behind the counters, which often contained display cases as well. Heavy goods were displayed in the centre of the room. It was a tightly organized system based on the presumption that customers were relatively passive and wanted to be served. This approach was thought to be respectful and dignified, and was often reinforced by the solemnity of interior design. Wood treated with clear finishes was usual, even in food stores. When McInnis and Company renovated their meat market in

| *Before World War I, store interiors were designed so that customers were waited on at the counter by staff. This 1912-13 photo is of the general store in Drumheller. NA-2389-5, GAI.*

Fort Macleod in 1901, the interior walls and ceiling were finished with red and white pine, "set alternately."[35]

These approaches to merchandising soon changed. By the interwar years, openness and lightness had become increasingly important. In general, the objective was, as it was said in Cardston in 1926, to create the look of a "modern department store." The "balcony style" for store interiors, a city-like design, was used in some two-storey stores. The centre of the store was the full height of the building, creating a large open space. A wide staircase, usually at about the centre of the main floor, led to the second level which featured a wide balcony running along the sides, front and back of the building. Both floors were used for merchandise.[36] A light and bright interior was crucial in defining these buildings as modern. Light colours, smooth surfaces, and natural light provided through plate glass windows contributed to the look, but electrical lighting was used as well. The adoption of fluorescent lighting in the interwar years was important in meeting these needs, and its installation was commonly noted as a significant sign of modernity. By World War II it had become common to leave lights on in stores all night, partly for security, but more importantly to project a modern image and to advertise goods. In 1945 it was remarked in Coleman that one newly renovated store on main street now featured open shelves and displays. Along with the large display windows, the fluorescent light in the store "at night fills the interior with dazzling light thus aiding in the floor display."[37]

This use of open display reinforced the overall design of the store and projected a sense of approachability and a democracy of material consumption. As in many towns, the Toshach store in Drumheller adopted "open display of merchandise for the inspection of the customers" in 1934.[38] The 1938 renovations to the Soby store in Claresholm, part of which included the installation of a modernist exterior on the building, also involved changes to the interior. Formerly, the store had contained two distinct areas separated by a large staircase, with drygoods on one side and hardware on the other. The staircase was removed, creating a single large room. This allowed expression of "the latest ideas in displaying merchandise." As it was explained:

> Nowadays the merchandise is laid out in attractive bins in easy handling range of the prospective customer. The psychology is that the eye of the buyer is interested and he often is encouraged to buy when suddenly confronted with something attractive or what he needs but has for the moment forgotten about. Anyway, the result has been to step up this big store to par with some of the modern city shops. Results are already seen in...increased trade volume.

Thus, modernity was used in an effort to encourage impulse buying, although this was often couched in terms of offering greater choice to the customer.[39]

This move towards open and accessible building interiors was also evident in grocery stores and the grocery sections of general stores. Moderne influences were evident in streamlining and the use of light colours and smooth surfaces which were judged to promote cleanliness. The chain stores, like Safeway and Jenkins, were leaders in applying these new interior designs. Safeway, which advertised itself as an "ultra modern food store," emphasized well lit and open interiors, although the stores were not overly "modernistic" and were never radical in their design. While the interiors were modern, and the exterior of the stores featured large plate glass windows, the facade of the buildings employed

| By the end of the 1930s, store interiors, such as Reginald Smith's grocery store in Cardston in 1941, stressed self-service and openness. NC-7-707, GAI.

quaint but fashionable Spanish California features consisting of a stumpy fixed tiled awning across the facade and small pilasters topped with tiled cross gables at the corners.

Nevertheless, the trend was "modernistic" and it was copied by many stores that sold food products. The Peace River Meat Co. store used fluorescent lights, electric cutting equipment and stripped down design to promote public "confidence" that their products were clean and of high quality. In 1942, another private grocery, the Foodland Store in Drumheller, opened a store with similar features. The store was "modernistic in design" and brought "a new type of merchandising to the city, in that citizens help themselves to their goods." Laid out in a "modern manner," it had open shelves and "islands" on which goods were displayed. "As far as possible, all goods are wrapped in cellophane to allow the customer to see what he or she is purchasing." This allowed reduction of staff, and therefore lower prices, and people were also "better able to obtain their needs as no high-pressure salesmanship will be used to make them purchase more than they need or things which they do not want."[40]

WINDOWS

While architectural design served to advertise a store's modernity, it was often employed merely to create a facade, a mask to promote business. In 1936 it was observed that three-quarters of the frame buildings on Grande Prairie's main street were in disrepair. "The shop fronts" were "the only substantial part" of the buildings, and the alleys behind were a chaos of storage sheds and outbuildings. Such conditions pointed to the acceptance of architectural design as a cosmetic technique to make an immediate statement and to promote business. In this, the use of windows to display goods and attract shoppers was fundamental. They were, as the historian Keith Walden has argued, a "discourse about the character of modern life," and expressed "a language of modernity." Window displays were thought to be essential for sales and to encourage impulse buying. In keeping with this view, it was argued in 1916 in Fort Macleod that good window displays would help get the thoughts of residents "away from the distant mail order houses."[41]

The first stores, such as those built in Fort Macleod in the 1890s, tended to have small rectangular sash windows, or else ones made up of several panes of glass. While this allowed display of merchandise to pedestrians, a view of the goods was broken by the muntins. By the 1880s, plate glass was coming into use in Canadian cities for shop fronts. This trend intensified by the 1890s, and merchants increasingly demanded glass fronts to permit better display of goods.[42] This practice appeared in Alberta towns during the first decade of the twentieth century. It was judged to mark a town as city-like, and represented the penetration of a more intensive consumerism in small towns. It has been suggested that in the United States the extensive use of glass windows, as well as glass display cases inside the store, "mediated between people and goods in a new way, it permitted everything to be seen and at the same time rendered it inaccessible."[43] This was an element of modernity, and the construction in 1911 of a Fort Macleod store front which was "practically of solid glass" was said to give "a most attractive effect. It is altogether a most modern and up-to-date front."[44] Flush to the sidewalk with only a small indentation for the entranceway, these glass fronts changed the look of the street from a relatively closed to a more open and welcoming one.

| From an early date, display windows were used to promote sales. Windows such as these in Fort Macleod in about 1899 were later replaced with single sheet plate glass windows that allowed greater scope for window decorating. SABR R-B1546.

Greater changes in the display of goods occurred by the 1930s when designs featured a much more deeply recessed entranceway lined with show windows. This beckoned pedestrians inwards to the store and also allowed expanded window area for display. This system was in widespread use throughout the province. When it was installed on the J.D. Levesque clothing store in Peace River in 1932, the *Peace River Record* commented that Levesque had always "led the town as far as modern building conveniences are concerned, and from this recent improvement, apparently intends to uphold the slogan, 'Levesque leads.'"[45] This style dominated for a short time only; by the early 1940s recessed fronts were being removed to give a flatter facade and more interior space.

Until the late 1920s, displays were usually mounted only in the available window space. The back of the display window was usually closed off from the rest of the store, although wire screen was sometimes used instead so that flies could not get into the window display area. These techniques helped keep the goods on display free of dust, focused the attention of pedestrians on the display itself rather than the store interior,

| *Recessed entrances lined with plate glass display windows lit with electric lights were popular in the 1930s. By 1934 it was featured on Toshach's store in Drumheller. Along with an electrically lit store sign, it presented a fashionable look. Drumheller Mail, October 25, 1934.*

and prevented "people inside the store from staring" at window shoppers.[46] By the late 1920s, electricity created new possibilities. In 1930, Lyne's Meat Market in Grande Prairie used coloured lights for its Easter window display, and "the effect was so striking that not a few got out of their cars in order to get a close-up of the window."[47] Of greater importance, electricity lessened the emphasis on the store window. Barriers between the back of the window and the store were removed to display the store interior. With good lighting at night, the whole sales area was put on display for the entertainment of pedestrians in the evening and as passive advertising.

While these changes permitted greater emphasis on the store interior, window displays remained important. Nonetheless, they were sometimes criticized for their poor presentation. In Claresholm in 1911 it was remarked that while "one of the most valuable assets a merchant has is his opportunity to make his window sell his goods," in "too many cases the window display suggests a junk shop and is a hindrance to business rather than an aid." In general, window displays in town stores were usually quite modest, displaying wares in a straightforward manner. Most tried to suggest a bounty of goods: piles of fruit, candy, vegetables, and canned goods, as well as clothing on mannequins. In a competition held in Blairmore at Christmas in 1912, the winning display was that of a meat market, which set out a "display of birds and beasts, catchingly displayed," while a general store was commended for its display of "a great pyramid of dainty chocolates surrounded by all kinds of confections." In a few cases, more elaborate window displays were mounted. Tableaus were especially popular with the public and newspaper reporters. In 1902 in Fort Macleod, A.F. Grady built a boat from various articles of hardware he stocked, and in 1910, Fisher's Hardware in Claresholm featured a display of locally manufactured brick made into a small house with green lawns and all the "attractiveness of a wealthy farm home." It was "admired by hundreds." Such displays relating to settlement and home building were popular. The Hudson's Bay store in Fort Macleod in 1908 mounted elaborate displays that drew much attention and favourable comment. One, which was "beautifully got up," featured paint and painting products. The bottom of the display "is an excellent representation of grass, while a commodious house in the background is made up entirely of paint cans. Rabbits and children are to be seen on the paths while lawn sprinklers and hose keep the grass watered. The rest of the display is made up of Varnishes, Enamels, Brushes, etc. On Saturday night there was a display of the new electric sparklers in the way of illumination which attracted a large crowd."[48]

Window decoration was an art in many big cities, and in 1921 the *Grande Prairie Herald* reported with pride that the display of cosmetics in a local drugstore showed that the owner had, like city merchants, "taken some pains to make his window display to attract attention." While competitions were occasionally mounted before World War I to stimulate effective window displays, they had become more common by the interwar years. Large Canadian manufacturers mounted window display competitions to promote their products. Lux soap ran one such campaign in 1927. Although it did not win a prize, the Coleman Trading Company mounted a display which nevertheless attracted public attention and during "the first day the display was in the window, five cases of soap were sold." Miller Electric in Peace River had better luck in Canadian General Electric's 1935 national window display competition when it won second place and put Peace River "on the Canadian mer-chandising map."[49]

Special events in a business's history also stimulated window displays; in a statement about the public debate over prohibition in 1915, Mike Rossi's liquor store in Blairmore mounted a display featuring bunches of grapes beneath a maple tree. In the tree sat a bird "looking dryly at the assortment of booze underneath, and wondering as to whether it would be safe to return to Alberta for another year." Special events in the com-munity also prompted noncommercial window displays. Of course, coro-nations and patriotic and historical celebrations were an occasion for window displays too. Other events were also promoted in this way; stuffed wildlife and forestry products were used in a store window in Blairmore in 1926 for Save the Forest Week, a display in 1943 connected with a war stamps savings campaign in a Grande Prairie store created an "unusually decorated window" featuring flags and photos of men from the district killed in the war or serving in the armed forces, and a display in Peace River in 1945 featuring a pair of Dutch wooden shoes sent home by a local soldier brought home the role Canadian troops were playing in the liberation of Holland.[50]

Christmas usually called for special effort as well. While most stores had special Christmas displays of goods, most were not decorated before the interwar years. For example, all stores in Fort Macleod in 1886 had special goods on display, but only one store decorated its premises, using evergreen boughs and wreaths. This changed during the interwar years when Christmas displays were used in response to the common concern about catalogue shopping. The Cardston Rotary Club gave a $10 cash prize for the best decorated Christmas store front and window in 1937. The *Grande Prairie Northern Tribune* advised its readers in 1935 to walk down the main street to look at the displays which compared "favourably with those in the larger Canadian cities. Not only are the various displays artistically arranged but they include a wide range of goods which makes it unnecessary for buyers to send out for their Christmas gifts or needs." Especially noteworthy were the lighting effects which added "further to the beauty and attractiveness of the window displays of Grande Prairie's up-to-date stores."[51]

An adjunct to large windows was an awning that kept the sun off the goods on display and provided some shelter to pedestrians. Consisting of cloth over a retractable frame, awnings had become common by World War I. The first awning in Grande Prairie went up in 1916 on a general store, and by 1923 the town, like most others, had passed a bylaw governing height and construction of awnings.[52] By the end of World War II, awnings were still common, but fashion was shifting towards fixed metal canopies. The Jenkins Groceteria in Drumheller, for example, installed a new facade on its store in 1940. "The front is ultra modern," reported the *Drumheller Mail*, "having a large marquee, made of stainless steel and glazed opalite glass, decorated with brilliant neon signs." It was said to make a positive contribution to Drumheller's business section.[53] This change represented a significantly different use for awnings. While the older types often had the store name printed in small letters on the fringe, they primarily sheltered goods in the windows and pedestrians on the street. The new ones, however, functioned largely as advertising features and mainly served promotional needs.

SIGNS

In 1932, many stores in Coleman did not have signs at all, and it was said that the "casual passerby does not know the peanut vendor from the liquor store."[54] Before the 1930s, signs were very modest. Most were painted boards, mounted flush to the wall above the windows or hung at a ninety degree angle from the building on a bracket. Many of these signs used a considerable amount of text. This, along with their size and discreet nature, demonstrated the pedestrian orientation of the street. It also indicated that most trade was local in nature, dependent on custom, habit, and an intimate consumer knowledge of the town.

The 1930s saw an increased use of larger and brighter signs. While there was a perceived need for quick store identification because of greater travelling speed and increased tourism, this change also indicated a more intrusive commercialization of everyday life. Signs had become more than a means of identification; they were a mark of style and suggested a high level of activity. The *Coleman Journal* argued in 1932 that a sign-filled street would "enliven the business section" and demonstrate that merchants had pride in their business because "a good sign is an invitation to enter." Thus, when "travelling sign painters" visited the town and painted a number of store signs, the *Journal* welcomed the change because it enabled "strangers to know who's who and what's what." Further, signs helped increase business, which "has to be gone after more keenly now than ever before, for in times of depression even people with money have an aversion to spending it."[55]

The connection between signs and sales was strengthened through technological change. By 1930, modernity demanded electrically lit signs. Incandescent bulbs hung or placed to illuminate the sign were commonly used, but neon was also growing in popularity. By 1929, Drumheller had three neon signs, which were described as being "the most economical form of sign illumination known." Many of these neon signs were generic ones, such as those supplied by tire and automobile manufacturers, and simply included the brand logo and name. Others were more individualized. Among the first "independent" neon signs in Blairmore was one mounted on the Cosmopolitan Hotel in 1935. To some, this was a component of urban beauty and progress. In 1937, the erection of additional neon signs in Grande Prairie prompted the local newspaper to note that the town could now "boast two Neon signs" on a single building. The "rapid increase of Neon signs in Grande Prairie as a decorative medium for business house lighting, constantly strengthens its fame as the bright town of the North." In this, there were no inherent limits, and when a Grande Prairie jewellery store installed a neon sign measuring 5.5-by-1.5 metres in 1946, it was approvingly said that "this means another added flow of light to the street." As A.G. Baalim, a prominent Lethbridge businessman, told the Cardston board of trade in 1931, Cardston's economic potential could be realized by making it a "beautiful" town. In this connection, he asserted that "modern signs operated by electricity are deserved by Cardston instead of the old hand painted boards." Along with new store awnings, painted buildings, and other improvements, the town could "live up to the name of the Temple City." Such views had a broad appeal—in 1938 it was observed that the progress of Cardston's main street included, among other things, five neon signs decorating the business area, "while two years ago there were none."[56]

The appeal of more noticeable and "up-to-date" signs was demonstrated in 1935 by the construction of large advertising sign boards on the main streets of Drumheller and Blairmore. The signs were put up by Neolin, an out-of-town firm. Each sign board was made of metal and had spaces on which the names of local businesses could be inscribed at a cost of about $40. The signs were lit at night and each featured an electric clock surrounded by neon tubes, as well as a huge thermometer. In Drumheller, it also featured the slogan "Welcome to Drumheller." While the sign was generally welcomed, the editor of the *Blairmore Enterprise* foretold that the neon tubes would not last six months given the number of "destructive boys who delight in throwing rocks at anything and everything."[57] Boys, however, proved not to be the problem. In Drumheller, when the company sponsoring it "did not come across with the second month's light account, the supply of electricity was cut off, the clock stopped, and the sign went without lights." The same thing happened at Blairmore. The signs were torn down in both towns in 1937–38, having never been fully operative for more than a month. The *Blairmore Enterprise* interpreted the sign's fate as "a monument to a number of business people who just simply had the money to throw away...for something that never was worth a solitary cent." It showed that many Blairmore businessmen were "first water goats," although they were not alone since "other towns in Alberta appear to have been similarly victimized."[58] While the subscribers appear gullible in hindsight, the incident revealed a growing belief that advertising might increase business, and advertising in a contemporary format might increase it even more.

The Neolin experiment also illustrated the increasing impact that advertising was having on the landscape. There was some criticism of large scale advertising before World War I. In 1909, the Claresholm town council made a "vigorous protest" about Calgary advertisers "plastering the sides of [Claresholm] buildings with soap and jewellers ads." The signs were said to be "a disfigurement to the street" and "ugly from every standpoint," although this protest was likely also an effort to protect local merchants from city competition. By the interwar years, other signs, like billboards, were coming into use—in 1934 the Toshach store in Drumheller had billboards within a 30-mile radius of the town which announced the number of miles to the store.[59] Criticism of such advertising was mounting, however, as was evidenced by the 1929 town planning act restrictions on roadside billboards. In 1929 Cecil Burgess observed that "we are destroying the beauty of the world" with poor architecture, shoddy town design, and advertising billboards.[60] The year before, while calling for a public boycott of stores using ugly signs, he had remarked that "advertising has become a real disease with us. It has its uses, its place, its proper forms, but it has ceased to recognize all of these. Much of our advertising is of no use, goes quite out of its proper place and takes forms that are an offence."[61] Nor did his criticism weaken —in 1947, he argued that most signs in Alberta towns and cities were too big and were placed incorrectly on buildings. This was due to various factors, one of which was an effort by merchants to overpower neighbouring signs. This was vulgar, Burgess thought, since "we do not admire most the man who shouts louder than his neighbours. A decent degree of self-restraint is as attractive in business as in private life." He proposed that the basic principle for all signs should be that they *"be arranged so that the building shows itself."*[62] But poorly designed signs were becoming so prevalent that they were setting the standards of popular taste; "atrocious signs are hailed with delight on account of their sheer badness and boldness, much as smart or bold criminals enlist a certain amount of public sympathy and admiration."[63]

Such fashions in signs, coupled with those in building design in general and the obsession with modernity, meant that the landscape of most towns did not evolve incrementally or express continuity with the past. The streetscapes that had evolved before World War I possessed a continuity and unity because of similar architectural designs and building scale. This particular feel and sensibility was sometimes lost in subsequent development. It is often assumed that it was not until the 1950s that the historical fabric of main street was threatened by incompatible development, spurred on by a craze for fashion. Such development, however, often occurred much earlier. After World War I, it was increasingly accepted that buildings with traditional styles were either irrelevant or embarrassing. These attitudes governed the aesthetic standards of towns, and when old buildings were renovated to obscure their original architecture, or were torn down, it was often welcomed. When the Anderson house, once one of the town's "best" residences and a feature of the Cardston main street, was torn down and replaced with a service station in 1933, it was noted that the service station would be "modern" and would "make this corner one of the most attractive pieces of business property in the town."[64]

The American geographer, Pierce Lewis, has contended that such attitudes reveal a weak sense of community self-esteem and self-worth, and a belief that the only valid economic standard is growth.[65] Such an explanation is attractive when these attitudes are placed within their cultural framework. They were perhaps inevitable in light of the assumption that what was commercially defined as "modern" and "fashionable" was progressive, and that progressiveness was profitable. In terms of architecture, this ethos was confirmed by the absence of a standard of architectural taste that was independent of fashion; few people had a benchmark by which to judge buildings. They were content to ape the current fashions, and incorporated whatever contemporary stylistic elements were fashionable and defined as "modern." What mattered was that the building represented economic progress. Even when a building was of markedly better design than most of its neighbours, its economic value was its most compelling justification. In reporting on the completion of the Milnes block in Claresholm in 1910, the *Claresholm Review* editor confessed that he did not have "sufficient knowledge of the technique of architecture to give a detailed description of the building, but we can say that it is a handsome structure and a distinct credit to Mr. Milnes and to the town of Claresholm. In building it Mr. Milnes had invested a large amount of money and has shown in a practical way the faith he had in the future of the town."[66]

9

"SOURCES *of* COMFORT *and* CONVENIENCE": THE IMPROVEMENT *of* MAIN STREET

In 1912, it was said in Blairmore that good streets were "a source of comfort and convenience to every town." This was especially so with respect to the main street, which ideally had an all-weather roadway, good sidewalks, and lighting. All of these enhanced business and property values.[1] During the interwar years, the automobile stimulated further demand for street improvement. Water and sewer systems, which promoted health, economic growth, and fire protection, were also a significant part of this modern street infrastructure. All of these developments were a conscious rejection of conditions from the late nineteenth and early twentieth centuries, when Alberta towns had typically been dark and dirty, with sidewalks and streets impassable in wet weather and littered with garbage and manure.

In pursuit of such street improvements, towns rarely strove to integrate their surrounding topography. Instead, they drew upon contemporary definitions of progress and fashion and the demands created by automobiles. Indeed, the only influence that a town's geographical location had on its appearance was the rather accidental one resulting from its potential as a newly formed settlement.[2]

| As this *1915 photo of the visit of the Governor General to Coleman shows, construction of sidewalks and road improvement were under way in the town. NC-54-746, GAI.*

SIDEWALKS, LIGHTS,
and STREETS

Initially, individual owners constructed sidewalks in front of their businesses. In Fort Macleod in 1884, the I.G. Baker Company laid a heavy plank sidewalk to connect its store and warehouse on main street and enclosed the space between the two buildings with a high picket fence. Continuous walks were not laid in Fort Macleod until 1896, four years after incorporation.[3] Until then, wet spells meant that pedestrians had to wade through mud before coming upon another piece of walkway. It was graphic evidence of the absence of collective purpose or need. Each store was autonomous, having little connection with the rest of the street. On the whole, the settlement was still a collection of buildings sheltering individual trading interests.

The greater sense of urbanism emerging in towns by the early twentieth century meant that amenities such as sidewalks were increasingly attractive. Planking was used to build the first civic walks in all towns, but these walks often were not level and were "stepped up and down as builders placed their bets on where the street grade would finally be settled."[4] While town boosters were fond of warning that the town would be sued for personal injury if these walks were not improved, they also pointed out that good walks would project an aura of modernity and stability and enhance property values.[5] Hence, many towns built continuous plank walks, and these remained in use in some places, such as Peace River and Grande Prairie, for many years.

Cement walks, however, brought much greater status. By 1913, property owners along Blairmore's main street were replacing the plank walks built by the town with cement ones. While a patchwork of plank and cement walks resulted, it was hoped the cement walks would be a precedent for other businesses to establish "the magnetism of the Metropolis." But precedent was a weak incentive, and town governments usually had to install cement walks. At this point, improvement charges could not be assessed for sidewalk construction, nor could a town force property owners to build a sidewalk.[6] Most towns willingly met such costs from general revenues. Lacombe was inordinately proud of the cement walks it installed on main street in 1910. Fort Macleod also built cement walks in its downtown area in the same year. While there was great debate about how wide the walks should be, they were said to have increased property values and took Fort Macleod "appreciably closer to the city class of municipalities and out of the towns."[7]

In residential areas, plank walks were replaced only gradually during the interwar years with concrete, shale, or cinders. Proposals for the use of Fort McMurray tar sand were common, but it was not often used because of its cost.[8] By this time, good walks in residential areas were recognized as a means of enhancing town business and entrenching the main street as the focal point of town life. In 1936, the Drumheller city council announced a plan to build cement walks in one residential part of the city. While they would be safer for children, it was also reasoned that residents would be drawn to the downtown, rather than shop from the catalogue, if they had "a decent sidewalk to walk on."[9]

Good lighting was equally important because dark streets were bad for business and dangerous for automobile drivers and pedestrians. Street lights were installed as quickly as possible after a town was estab-

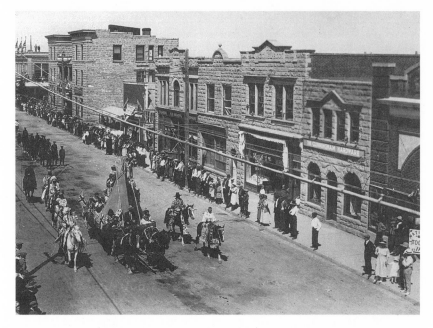

| *By the time Fort Macleod celebrated its fiftieth anniversary in 1924, its main street had been lined with cement sidewalks. Archives Collection, A20682, PAA.*

lished. Claresholm was typical in this respect when it installed ten street lights on the main street as soon as electricity was available. And their installation in Blairmore in 1912 was "hailed with satisfaction by all residents" because the streets were "dangerous to tread, fearing molestation by dogs or other creatures." Generally, streets were lit by arc lights, which projected from poles along the street, or were suspended on wire hung over the middle of the street. Only a few lights were used; Drumheller's new street light system in 1928 consisted of one light hanging in the centre of each intersection, plus one in the middle of each block. By the 1930s, such lights were criticized because they lit only the street, not the sidewalk and the building fronts. In 1938, it was argued that such lights in Lacombe provided "but poor welcome to the Saturday night shoppers." In 1940, new lights mounted on 30-foot poles were installed, giving the town what was considered a modern look.[10]

The ability to dispel darkness with electric light had a profound impact on people's sensibilities, instilling security instead of fear.[11] It attached people even more firmly to the technological change that electricity represented, and confirmed the advantages of urban life. Farm electrification in Alberta did not begin to any extent until after 1947, but while the country remained dark, the towns were lit, forming an oasis of light in a seemingly empty darkness. Consequently, towns without adequate street lights were not merely uncomfortable but backward as well. In 1938, it was remarked in Coleman that "one almost feels like apologizing" to visitors, "especially if the few lights we do possess are not on and the lurid light of the coke ovens is the only illumination."[12]

In contrast, Grande Prairie installed new lights on main street in 1930. They were kept burning 24 hours a day, giving the town its own "Great White Way." While some councillors had been concerned about costs, the visual trappings of urban progress were more appealing and the town diverted money earmarked for a sewer system to purchase the new street lights. In 1945 the whole system was upgraded with the installation of additional light standards and increased wattage. It was proudly noted that when driving into Grande Prairie at night, the dark countryside suddenly gave way to light when "you pop over the hill a couple of miles north of town." The town lay "like a lapful of sparkling gems, like twinkling stars against nature's backdrop of night." And flying into Grande Prairie at night was equally impressive: the town was "like a diamond girdle about the waist of a fair maiden." Such pride also presumed Grand Prairie's technological "progress" and advancement. In contrast, by 1947 most other small western towns did not have such extensive street lighting.[13]

Another costly project facing many towns was improving roadways, which was particularly difficult in some places because of their geological character. The soil at Fort Macleod was full of gravel and rock, and the traffic on main street continually brought boulders to its surface. In 1886 it was remarked that "if the whole country had been thoroughly searched over, no worse spot could have been found upon which to lay out a town site, so far as the ground alone is concerned." At Claresholm, the choice of a slough for the town site left a legacy of problems. In 1911 its streets were "a viscous sea of liquid mud," and on one downtown street the water was "green from stagnation." Indeed, "a sewerage system is imperative if our town is to assume a metropolitan appearance." By the end of World War I, the main street had been gravelled, but this alone could not correct the problem. The town could not afford a sewage system because the pipes had to be laid at a great depth to ensure adequate flow. As one engineer commented, "had any regard been taken of the topographical features of the ground when laying out the town in the first place, a great part of this expense could have been avoided." In 1935, it was noted that "again this spring we have experienced the 'floating streets' in the downtown section, with the occasional truck miring down and having to be dug out." The main street was part of a provincial highway, and usually the province paid a portion of maintenance costs. In Claresholm's case, however, the province refused the town's repeated requests to share the costs of hardsurfacing the main street because the high water table and the instability of the subsoil made it too costly. In better located centres such as Drumheller, Peace River and Grande Prairie, the province willingly paid its usual share of street surfacing.[14]

The need for gravelling or hardsurfacing was reinforced after 1920 by the growing use of motor vehicles. In 1916, "even horses" found it difficult to get through in places on Cardston's main streets, and automobiles could "only make a passage by adding hydroplane equipment." Although the streets were subsequently gravelled, they were still "rotten" in 1927, and were not improved until volunteers from the community laid sufficient gravel to stabilize the roadbed in 1929 and again in 1931. The main streets of Drumheller and Grande Prairie were gravelled at about the same time, but by 1940 Grande Prairie still "had no really passable streets" during spring thaw or wet periods.[15]

Motor vehicles also complicated improvements in street crossings. Efforts to keep pedestrians out of the mud led to the construction of elevated street crossings. In 1896, Fort Macleod had "ugly obstructions placed across the streets, across which horses have to be taken at a careful walk." In Claresholm in 1913, the same devices were "responsible for twisted backs and broken springs." To the disadvantage of pedestrians, street crossings were soon lowered to accommodate motor vehicles. In 1920, with mud over his shoe tops, "even the parson used strong language" when crossing an intersection in Claresholm, and in Lacombe, the sidewalks were coated with mud tracked onto them from the crossings.[16]

Motor vehicles also contributed to the problems of blowing dust, which was already a concern in most towns. In 1910, dust blowing in from the countryside was said to be ruining merchants' stock in Claresholm. In the Crowsnest Pass, dust and soot from coal mining and coking were everywhere. This was especially so in Coleman where a mine tipple at the foot of main street spewed out dust, which was carried by the prevailing winds directly onto the main street. Cars made these problems worse, as did the dry weather and soil drifting in southern Alberta in the 1930s. By this time, cars had become more powerful and driving speeds increased. In 1936, it was reported that most people drove at 65 kilometres an hour on Cardston's main street, raising choking clouds of dust. It was so thick that the town band, playing on the main street one Saturday afternoon, was forced to retreat. Store shelves and counters were covered with a layer of dust "that you can write your name on," while cars parked along the street were "filled with absolute dirt, not just plain dust." In some towns, the dust was so thick that certain lines of merchandise, especially in groceries, could not be displayed. Streets were often sprinkled with water, but this provided only temporary relief.[17] Instead, the most common approach was to spread oil on the street to stabilize the gravel. While this was done in many places, it was never satisfactory. The oil ruined shoes, car tires and paint, and tracked into homes and stores. Because the gravel was only oiled on top, it was easily disturbed by cars skidding to a stop or accelerating quickly. As well, unoiled gravel tended to rise to the surface, creating the dust problem anew. The only solution was hardsurfacing, and by the 1940s a number of towns had hardsurfaced their downtown streets, giving them "a more modern outlook."[18]

TRAFFIC and PARKING

The need for street surfacing demonstrated the increased public costs brought about by privately operated motor vehicles. None of these problems or costs were regretted, however, and as was said in Grande Prairie in 1927, "traffic problems" proved that a town "has arrived."[19] While provincial legislation governing motor vehicles, first passed before World War I, applied both to towns and highways, these provisions were often too broad for use in towns. Councils therefore passed additional regulations to regulate driving and parking.

Of course, horse traffic had also been regulated. By 1912, general street bylaws banned horses from sidewalks, riders and drivers were required to keep the horse's pace at a "moderate rate," and horses could not be broken, bred, or left untied on the street.[20] Hitching posts, usually built by merchants in front of their stores, were a feature of every main street. In Claresholm, most were not flush with the sidewalk, which made the roadway narrower, and in 1911 the merchants replaced them with ones of "uniform size and appearance." They were painted green to add some colour to the street. While horses were being replaced by motor vehicles by the end of World War I, they were still in use in the late 1920s. Nevertheless, their decreased importance was signalled by the removal of hitching posts on many main streets. The last such post in Drumheller, a metal one in front of Toshach's store, was dismantled in 1928. It had "provided loungers with a substantial arm rest for many years," but its demolition showed that "Drumheller has safely emerged from the cow-town era." Yet such self-congratulation was premature. By 1930, the use of horses was increasing because of the Depression, and hitching posts were re-installed in Drumheller by 1932, and a watering trough for horses was built downtown in 1934.[21]

The major traffic issue of the 1930s was not the resurgence of horses but people's driving habits and the availability of parking. It was readily apparent that the automobile was not simply a new form of transportation. It also changed people's behaviour; high speed was fun and stylish. In 1927, it was observed in Cardston that it was "astounding" how irrational "otherwise sensible men" became when driving and how society was "almost conscienceless about driving crimes. We tolerate anything."[22] Similar reports and complaints about reckless and fast driving, by adults and children, appeared in all the towns studied.

By the late 1930s, most towns had traffic bylaws regulating turning at intersections, keeping to the correct side of the road, and permissible speed. Size of commercial trucks allowed on streets was also restricted. While many of these regulations were obeyed, many drivers were difficult to control. In Drumheller in 1936, most drivers ignored the stop signs and speed limits, and "the observation of the 'no U-turn' is probably the only regulation that is almost one hundred percent regarded." Cardston passed a traffic bylaw in 1937 but did not begin enforcing it until 1939. It then found that elderly drivers in particular resented controls and argued that "since they have been driving without any regulations for many years, there is no need for any regulation now, at least not for them."[23]

In an effort to regulate traffic, stop signs were put up on many main streets by the late 1930s. In Drumheller, it was proposed in 1937 that a couple of "ditches" be dug across the main street to create a "speed trap" to slow traffic; a system that, as the mayor noted, was hardly necessary given the ruts in the street. In an effort to control traffic flow, many towns, such as Grande Prairie in 1928, installed a "silent policeman." This was a cement pyramid or pillar placed in the centre of an intersection, which forced turning vehicles to slow down to navigate around it. It also helped keep traffic in its proper lane. Since drivers tended to hit them, especially at night, the silent policemen were painted with white stripes and reflectors were mounted on top. This made little difference. Because they were "a menace to life and property," Blairmore and Drumheller dismantled them in 1937, as did most towns by 1940.[24]

Cars were usually parked at the curb, although parking in the centre of Grande Prairie's main street was permitted before 1939. Whatever the parking arrangement, people tended to park "at every conceivable angle." This lessened the availability of parking, and many towns tried to enforce angle parking at the curb as a solution. As was commented in 1928, "limited parking space in the centre of town is one handicap that must be overcome if residents of surrounding communities are to be encouraged to patronize Drumheller stores." Shoppers resisted walking any distance and insisted on parking as near as possible to the place they planned to visit. In Lacombe in 1938 it was contended that when parking spaces on main street were filled, instead of parking on side streets, many people would rather drive "to the next town" to shop.[25]

There were several ways in which main street congestion was addressed. Townspeople were asked to leave their cars at home, especially on Saturday when farm people came to shop. Limits on the length of time a car could be parked were instituted, and public parking lots were built. All of these efforts foundered because they challenged the cultural attributes of car ownership. Both townspeople and farmers liked to park on the main street on Saturday to watch "the crowds go by." Business owners insisted on driving to work and parking in front of their stores instead of in the alley behind the store or on a side street. It was an expression of commonly held beliefs about the success, status, and convenience that cars brought their owners.[26] These factors ensured that appeals for voluntary parking restrictions failed. Similarly, bylaws setting parking limits, usually one hour, were unsuccessful. Once again, people refused to give up the entertainment of parking on main street on Saturday, and farmers resented the regulations, claiming that they were not given enough time to shop. Indeed, the fining of 40 farmers for violating the one hour rule in Drumheller in 1937 led to such an outcry by merchants that the bylaw was suspended. Public parking lots also failed for the same reasons. Lacombe tried this approach in 1938 to "prevent congestion on down-town streets" on Saturday nights. Even though the parking area was a graded lot close to the main street and was lit and supervised by the police, the public refused to use it. It stood empty while downtown streets became "overcrowded with cars, people and horse-drawn vehicles."[27]

The role of the car in entertainment, in defining personal self-worth and pride, and in the town economy also had to be confronted in other attempts to regularize parking. Parking bylaws, such as provisions prohibiting parking in front of cinemas and hotels, were not enforced in Grande Prairie in 1947 and main street was crammed with cars. To provide additional parking, the city replaced 45 degree angle parking with 20 degree angle parking. This met demands by merchants who believed that farmers would not come to Grande Prairie to shop on Saturday night "unless their wives and children can sit in the parked cars" on the main street. Similarly, business usually resisted the re-routing of highways even though it would lessen congestion on main street. By 1930, town planners were arguing that highways should bypass smaller centres to promote safety and lessen street congestion and the costs of maintenance and construction of streets and highways. Alberta's town planner argued in 1931 that tourists could be drawn to the main street by developing an attractive town entrance. Whenever bypassing was proposed, however, such as at Claresholm and Lacombe, it was fought by town merchants who feared it would hurt business.[28] Town councils agreed, not only because they supported the merchants, but because they wanted the province's continued contribution to main street maintenance.

While the business lobby was an important factor in the failure of most efforts to deal with congestion, the attitude of the community at large was no less influential. Congestion was thought to be a symbol of success. Thus, even when the automobile created a decline in the quality of public life, it was excused. In 1937, the amount of traffic on Cardston's main street was said to be limiting movement and producing clouds of dust. Yet, "the fact is that Cardston is just suffering a few growing pains. We are proud of the growth and glad to keep abreast of the advancement taking place." Even so, the automobile did not reshape the urban form of towns in the same way that it did in cities. As a commercial strip, a town's main street already took one of the urban forms that automobiles would soon promote in cities.[29]

SANITATION *and* CIVIC CLEANLINESS

In the late nineteenth century, there was high public toleration of unsanitary town conditions. At the same time, emerging scientific understanding increasingly held that many diseases could be prevented through public sanitation. Given the increasing role of science in defining progress, it became more common to define a progressive town in terms of cleanliness. As such, it was typically foretold that filthy conditions not only encouraged disease but discouraged potential settlers and investors. Yet, despite numerous complaints, and the passage of legislation by the Territorial government permitting the enforcement of public sanitation, conditions improved only slowly.[30] In 1890 it was reported in Fort Macleod that:

walking about the streets of Macleod at night one's olfactory nerves are saluted with at least a hundred separate and distinct kinds of smells, each one worse if possible than the preceding. One gets them literally *ad nauseam*, and in this respect, Macleod is no different from a dozen other places that we know of. We have had the same experience in Lethbridge, we have smelt the same smells in Medicine Hat, aye, and Calgary too.[31]

Incorporation as a town brought little immediate change. By 1897, Fort Macleod was much as it had been a decade before. While it had a health bylaw, it was ignored. There were no sewer or water systems, nor garbage collection. As a result, the townsite was "one vast nuisance ground." As well, the livestock and poultry on Fort Macleod's streets in 1896 was said to give it "more the appearance of an immense barnyard than the flourishing and business centre that it is." The sidewalks were covered with manure, and one observer admitted that there was "more truth than poetry" in a Calgary newspaper's statement that Fort Macleod was building sidewalks "solely for the use of the town cows and other animals."[32]

Responsibility for public health and sanitation rested with local government. While quarantines were commonly placed on buildings such as houses and hotels to limit the spread of contagious diseases, local bylaws were often unenforced in the face of public hostility or apathy, and most townspeople saw the filth as familiar and expected. As in the rest of

Canada in the late nineteenth century, it contributed, in historian P.B. Waite's phrase, to the "elemental crudeness of much of life."[33]

By the early twentieth century, public attitudes were beginning to change. While the territorial government's major concern was the prevention and control of contagious disease and the construction of hospitals, it compelled all towns to appoint local health officers in 1897. By 1903, contagious disease was no longer blamed solely on population movement, but also on "the unsanitary conditions of many of the smaller towns."[34] Blairmore's overseer wrote in 1903 that conditions in the settlement desperately needed attention because "every street and alley is covered with old Fruit Cans and all kinds of *filth* and this hot weather is making them *steam*." By World War I, dirty and garbage strewn streets had come to be seen as backward and damaging to business. The Fort Macleod board of trade urged the local board of health in 1909 to take action about "the fever" which was "rampant in the Town," and which threatened to become a "general outbreak which would result in a great loss of life as well as being most detrimental to business." As was observed in Blairmore in 1912, while "the best advertisement any town can have is light, sidewalks and cleanliness...the greatest of these is cleanliness." Thus, the comment in Grande Prairie in 1918 that a clean town promoted health and impressed visitors represented an increasingly popular view, and people who were "filthy" were warned that they were living "in the wrong town even if we are on the frontier."[35]

Contemporary understanding of the cause and prevention of disease in part led to installation of water systems. Impure water caused much disease in towns before World War I.[36] Civic water systems promised to alleviate this, but the health needs of residential areas took a secondary position since such systems were installed first on main street as part of fire protection. This did not, however, lessen the growing acceptance of the necessity for public sanitation, as was reflected in Fort Macleod's new health bylaw in 1910. Pigs were no longer allowed in the town except "under certain rigorous restrictions," spitting on sidewalks was outlawed, and, reflecting that the downtown now had water and sewer, new buildings had to be connected to the water and sewer mains. It was hoped that this would clean up the town and gradually rid it of the "unsanitary wells" and the outdoor privies "with their unspeakable abominations."[37]

By the end of World War I, all towns had permanent boards of health and medical health officers, usually a local doctor, who recommended public health measures for the town. They also enforced bylaws concerning waste disposal and the cleaning of privies, yards, and public areas, heard public complaints about sanitation, and inspected public eating and gathering places. These local developments occurred in tandem with expanding provincial regulation. Under the *Public Health Act*, provincial inspectors also made regular inspections and issued orders for disposal of garbage, and the cleaning of privies, lanes, and places of business. By 1919, town councils were obligated to enforce these orders, and most willingly complied.[38]

While these changes in public sanitation were formalized through bylaws and infrastructure, it was understood that their effectiveness depended on changed public attitudes. In 1917, it was argued in Blairmore that the most important task in promoting public sanitation was to stimulate a "sanitary conscience" so that citizens would "positively do nothing which is even remotely likely to jeopardise another person's health." The influenza epidemic at the end of World War I clearly confirmed the public's role in preventing contagious disease. When it brought "heavy" loss of life in Drumheller, it was pointedly remarked that the town's wretched sanitary conditions had to be improved to prevent a recurrence. In contrast, it was recognized that the lower number of fatalities in Lacombe was due to less crowding, relatively good sanitation, and prompt medical care. The epidemic also demonstrated unequivocally that disease prevention overrode local jurisdiction. In an effort to contain infection, the province, followed by local boards of health, applied bans on public gatherings. In Blairmore, as in the rest of the Pass, the number of influenza cases was high and the town was quarantined by the local board of health. All places of business were closed, highways were barricaded, and no passengers were allowed to board or leave trains stopping in the town.[39]

Despite the systematic articulation of public health ideals and the appearance of infrastructure like water and sewer, a wide range of sanitary conditions remained in Alberta towns by the end of World War I. As was the case in many other places, a water system was installed at Coleman in 1924, but a sewage system was not installed until after World War II and the business area relied on several cesspools and a few outdoor privies. In 1946 the town's water supply was, as usual, unsafe to drink for several months, forcing residents to boil the water.[40] Claresholm could not afford to install a sewer system until 1945 because local subsoil conditions made it too expensive an undertaking. In the

Peace River country, lower incomes and recentness of settlement restrained development of such infrastructure as well. Visitors to Grande Prairie were struck, it was claimed in 1937, by "the primitive sanitary conditions that still exist here." The town began installing water and sewer the next year, but Peace River had neither until 1949.[41] In other places, however, sewer systems had gradually been installed or extended. A water and sewer system was installed in Lacombe in 1929. By that year, Drumheller's sewer lines were gradually being extended into residential areas, but showing an attachment to old ways, many people kept their outdoor privies even when their house was connected to the sewer mains, and garbage was routinely dumped in the lanes.[42]

Garbage disposal continued to be a problem in most places. While Blairmore had installed a water system in 1913, by 1919 it still did not have sewage or garbage disposal. Thus, people used outdoor pit privies, and since the nuisance ground was about a mile from town, most dumped garbage within the town limits. Most centres passed bylaws requiring residents to dispose of their garbage and to clean their privies. In 1917, Claresholm did not have any regular garbage pick up, even though "the private individual has not the equipment to do it himself and to have it done privately costs three or four times as much as it would if some one was hired by the town for this work." By 1934, Coleman had a "slovenly" appearance because it had no garbage disposal system, and individuals carted ashes and garbage in wheel barrows to "various dumps" around the town. When it appointed a scavenger in 1934, Coleman adopted a system widely used in Alberta. The scavenger collected a monthly fee from each householder as his wages. This cost the town nothing, but it was a chaotic system since the scavenger always had difficulty collecting his fees and refused to serve those in arrears. Nonetheless, Coleman, like other centres, used this system until after World War II.[43]

Despite such difficulties, health regulations generally were extended through local and provincial action. By 1936, most towns had bylaws requiring tuberculosis testing of cows producing milk for sale. As well, by the 1930s most towns were seriously trying to limit the keeping of animals in town to protect public health.[44] In keeping with these developments, rulings by provincial health inspectors were generally heeded. In 1928, the provincial inspector confirmed the finding of Drumheller's medical health officer that the town's lanes "were among the worst in the province," littered with garbage and lined with dirty and rundown privies, especially behind restaurants. He recommended that more civic collection of garbage be instituted and that businesses selling food follow better sanitation practices. A concerted effort to clean up the town followed, and by 1930 the contrast with conditions of two years before was striking. These gains, however, were eroded during World War II. In 1943 the Alberta Department of Public Health observed that another year of war "again resulted in sanitary conditions slipping backwards, essentially because of a shortage of manpower."[45]

While sanitation policies were primarily concerned with public health, they also brought related changes. Tidiness, although often of direct relevance to sanitation, was often treated as an aesthetic matter. In the early twentieth century, relatively little concern was expressed about litter, except that waste paper blowing about the streets frightened horses and caused runaways.[46] Just before World War I, however, many town councils began declaring clean-up campaigns and ordering the public to clean their property and adjacent public areas. For the first such event in Blairmore in 1913, a civic holiday was declared. Other places declared a clean-up week beginning on Arbor Day, a day in the spring dedicated to planting trees. Because clean-up campaigns were directly related to efforts to encourage public sanitation, they usually enjoyed the direct involvement of the local board of health, which often carried out an inspection of the town at the end of the campaign.[47]

Although some of these clean-up efforts were failures, greater success occurred in the interwar years when they were integrated with efforts to promote civic pride and prosperity, health, tourism, and fire prevention. This was evident in Grande Prairie in 1931 when it was contended that:

> a community can encourage prosperity through appearances. If everything about our surroundings looks threadbare, it is but natural to accept an attitude of discouragement...But if we can have our homes, gardens and premises looking spic and span, we can defy old man gloom to do his worst to continue the depression. It just can't be done when we have our surroundings bright and cheerful.[48]

Reflecting such views, clean-up week came to include such things as painting buildings. It became a highly organized event promoted by local businesses which offered special prices on garden tools, paint, and building supplies. Sometimes, service clubs and boards of trade mounted special promotional window displays, or sponsored and organized the event. Such participation and sponsorship were measures of the changed role that public sanitation and tidiness had come to play in town life. As well, tourist promotions were clearly easier if the town was attractive and clean. In Coleman in 1934, the main street needed to look its best because it was "the bright, well-kept front street which is the shop window of any town," and tourists would only stop in towns with a pleasing appearance.[49]

"MORE AFRAID *of* FIRE THAN BURGLARS"

Before 1948, each of the towns studied experienced at least one major fire which destroyed part of the main street. The burning of about one-third of Peace River's main street in 1932 was an extreme example of a common event. In this, Alberta was identical to the rest of the prairies and much of Canada. Losses from fire in Canada were dramatically higher than those in Europe—in 1914, the average fire loss per capita in Edmonton was $2.20, versus 93 cents in a group of English cities. In such an environment, it was not surprising that in 1909 Claresholm merchants were "more afraid of fire than burglars." Not unexpectedly, fire insurance companies demanded better fire prevention and protection systems to limit claims, and senior governments increasingly tried to contain the massive economic loss that fire in Canada annually caused.[50]

The cause of such fire losses in Canada was said in 1916 to result from "our so-called practical policy of allowing towns to grow up without proper control of their layout, and without proper regard to fire risk in connection with the erection of buildings." Before its incorporation as a town, Fort Macleod had no regulation of buildings, nor did it have any fire fighting equipment. In 1885, it was "perfectly powerless" against fire, and in the absence of local government, the *Macleod Gazette* proposed that a fire engine be purchased through public subscription. A meeting was held to investigate this proposal, but no agreement was reached. The settlement remained defenceless for the balance of the 1880s, and the *Macleod Gazette* warned in 1886, "so surely as there is a town called Macleod, just so surely will a heap of smoking ashes be all that is left of it one day." By 1892 the fire equipment owned by the

NWMP for protecting its property was used to fight fires in the town, but after incorporation, the town purchased its own equipment and organized a volunteer fire brigade. The latter was so poorly organized, however, that it did not even turn out for a fire on one occasion in 1897.[51]

While fear of fire was great, the burning of particular buildings or even whole sections of main street was not always viewed as an unmitigated disaster. When the Cosmopolitan Hotel and several other wooden buildings on Blairmore's main street burned in 1912, the *Blairmore Enterprise* observed that they would now be replaced with ones that would be "a credit to any modern city." Indeed, the replacement hotel was of brick and stone and was "one of the finest" buildings in southern Alberta. "'It's an ill wind that blows nobody good' is an old saying and fits well at present." The same year, Lacombe suffered its second serious fire in four years, but as the *Edmonton Journal* remarked, poor buildings had been replaced with better ones after the first fire, and the main street had gained in "substantiality and general attractiveness." The latest fire would bring "still further improvement." Indeed, a major fire was "an excellent test of whether a community rests on a solid economic basis or not. If it doesn't, it never recovers." Opinion in Peace River in 1932 was equally blunt. The fire there had cleared the main street of many old and "dangerous" buildings and "from the ashes will arise a first class set of buildings," bringing lower fire insurance rates and improving the street's appearance.[52]

The cause of fires varied. Arson was common, although it was difficult to prove in small towns, especially since arsonists sometimes seized the opportunity to set a fire while another building was burning. This seemed to be the case in Peace River in 1915 when fire broke out in a main street building nearby but unrelated to one already burning. The resulting blaze was "more the nature of gasoline explosion than of an ordinary fire." Investigation of such suspicious fires often became entangled in the personal and social rivalries they exposed, and many people seemed not to view arson as a serious crime. When a Blairmore Hotel caught fire for the third time in a short period in 1916, it was joked, "can it be the Germans!"[53] Indeed, when prohibition was enacted in Alberta, some insurance companies, with the benefit of their experience in Saskatchewan where sale of liquor had been made a state monopoly in 1915, temporarily cancelled all fire insurance policies on hotels in the province.

Of greater ongoing importance, the insurance industry, through the Western Canada Insurance Underwriters Association, demanded improvement of conditions to limit its members' losses. This especially applied to main street properties where fire spread rapidly because buildings were closely spaced and the alleys were cluttered with privies, storage sheds, and discarded packing crates. Town councils, often prodded by boards of trade, attempted to provide fire protection. In Claresholm in 1910, the town policeman watched for fires and sounded the alarm. When one town councillor argued that the residential part of town should have equal treatment, the local paper editorialized that "he couldn't have been really serious. All respectable people are in their homes at night and can watch their own property. The business section is deserted after midnight and that seems to be the usual time for serious fires."[54] Using general revenues, towns installed water systems and purchased fire fighting equipment. In 1912, Cardston installed a water system primarily in the business area, and during the celebration of the event, no mention was made of improved sanitation, only that the town now had "ample fire protection."[55]

While this bias in favour of protecting main street buildings was a product of local priorities, it was confirmed by fire fighting technology. By the end of World War I, fire fighting equipment available to most prairie towns consisted of hand operated water pumps and small chemical engines effective only in a limited area. This fire fighting equipment was operated exclusively by volunteer fire brigades which were usually formed almost immediately after a town or village was incorporated. As water and sewer services were extended to residential areas, many towns began replacing their existing equipment with truck mounted equipment that could serve the whole town, and even close-in rural areas. For example, truck-mounted fire equipment purchased in 1921 gave Drumheller's fire brigade greater range.[56]

Most Alberta towns, like others in Canada, also responded to the fire hazard through regulation. The earliest expression of this concern was the Territorial government's ordinance to control the construction of chimneys, but it had little effect in reducing fires. The sequence of events leading to passage of local bylaws was similar throughout the prairies. As in so many cases, local governments were rarely anticipatory in their legislation and responded only after a disaster, or more charitably, when a clear need was expressed or when a higher legislative authority demanded change. Thus, following a major fire (and an increase in insurance rates), better fire protection and bylaws to control construction and fire hazards were demanded.[57] For example, when a livery barn fire in Claresholm threatened the main street in 1910, popular sentiment suddenly endorsed a building bylaw, and one was passed about a year later.[58]

These bylaws were of two sorts. One was a building bylaw which required new construction in specified areas (or fire zones) to use incombustible materials like brick, stone, hollow tile, and cement. First-class fire zones were most restrictive, while new construction in second-class fire zones could be frame if clad with metal siding, brick veneer, or some other incombustible material. The common practice of moving shacks into the alley behind a business for storage purposes was usually prohibited. Main street was always in the first-class fire zone, while immediately adjacent streets were usually second-class zones. Residential areas were subject, at best, to weaker controls.[59]

Fort Macleod's first such bylaw was passed in early 1902, and even in the depth of winter, when construction was unusual, "there was a little rush of building...to get in ahead of the Fire Limit by-law." When the town passed a new building bylaw in 1912, the fire zone was extended and new regulations dealing with construction of chimneys and the moving and construction of new buildings were enacted. Controls were imposed to regulate "unsafe buildings or small buildings endangering or affecting surrounding properties, such as laundries, livery and sales stables, public halls, theatres and all places of amusement." In order to create fire breaks, the bylaw also prohibited the construction of wooden shacks on street corners and required that buildings at certain downtown locations be constructed of fire proof materials to create a series of "fire guards" across the business area. More often, however, fire walls were built between buildings to prevent the spread of fire. Ideally, each block had at least two fire walls, but even a single one helped to lower insurance rates. As was done in Blairmore in 1911 and 1912 and in Peace River in 1919, a fire wall was often placed between frame buildings when they were being constructed. In Blairmore, the town put $1,600 into the project with the costs recovered through a local improvement charge. The wall was of brick, 20 feet high and 13 inches thick (6 x 0.33 meters), running from the sidewalk to the lane.[60]

The second type of bylaw was a fire prevention bylaw. This banned storage of gasoline in the fire zone, required the removal of inflammable trash, and prohibited burning of garbage in laneways without a permit.

In some cases, towns had one or the other of these bylaws but not both. By 1930, it was becoming common for building and fire prevention provisions to be combined into one bylaw. Under the guidance of the provincial town planning board, towns like Grande Prairie, Peace River, Drumheller, and Cardston passed new bylaws combining fire prevention and building regulation. At the same time that they dealt with general zoning matters like set backs and density, they also created fire zones, regulated storage of inflammable and explosive materials, specified that new buildings in the fire zone had to use metal window frames and wired glass, and set out specified wall thicknesses. Usually, standards for electrical wiring and natural gas connections, if regulated at all, were treated in separate bylaws. [61]

While such bylaws were increasingly common, town councils were often unable or unwilling to enforce them. Since it was politically and economically impractical to demand renovation of existing buildings to bring them up to the new standards, a substantial stock of dangerous buildings remained. Ironically, they were eliminated only by fire since there was little expansion after 1913.[62] Unlike water systems and fire equipment, which were paid for with public funds, fire regulations restricted the profitability of private property for the common good. Such regulations often went unheeded, as was the case in Lacombe when one town councillor moved a wooden shack into the downtown in 1907. The same problem existed in Fort Macleod where there were many wooden, ramshackle sheds behind main street buildings in 1909. In 1920, when the Peace River town council discussed a building bylaw, one councillor opposed it because "fire proof" construction would hinder development since brick and cement were expensive, having to be imported from the south. Even those in favour of the bylaw agreed that "too radical a change cannot be asked for at the start," and the town did not pass a comprehensive building bylaw until 1930. In Lacombe, a bylaw requiring new buildings of solid brick or stone in the first-class fire zone was blamed in 1909 for "retarding the building up of the main portion of the town" by making construction too costly. If veneered buildings were allowed in the fire zone, it was claimed that "several good buildings would be put up in the near future to replace the unsightly frame shacks in the main portion of the town." In any event, the existing bylaw was ignored, and "it has got to the stage now where people do not even think it necessary to take out a permit to build structures of any kind."[63]

This pattern endured in the interwar years. In 1926, the provincial fire inspector found the stipulations in Grande Prairie's fire bylaw "of no value or importance whatsoever" for a town of its size. It needed a bylaw to regulate construction practices and establish fire zones. In 1930, Grande Prairie passed a new building bylaw using a model bylaw prepared by the provincial town planning board. It established first- and second-class fire zones, and also appointed a building inspector and an electrical inspector. However, as the provincial fire inspector discovered, "neither of them appear to have taken any action towards eliminating existing fire hazards." Further, "part of the first class fire limits were recently changed to second class limits to enable a prominent resident to build a large hotel there according to second class specifications." The lanes behind main street were cluttered with sheds, outhouses, and "dilapidated or scantily built ice storage sheds." Moreover, gasoline was stored in many main street buildings and sheds in contravention of the bylaw, and the inspector issued 25 orders to remedy these dangers. By 1947, conditions were still poor in Grande Prairie. The building bylaw had "not been rigidly enforced" and new buildings lacked fire walls, and old buildings "which should be condemned" were being covered up with "renovations."[64]

Many of these problems were gradually remedied. After the 1920s, regular inspection by the provincial fire inspector's office helped to improve conditions. The formation of the town planning board in 1929 also assisted towns to draw up bylaws that combined fire prevention and land use provisions. About the same time, the province also adopted the Canadian Electrical Code to establish a standard code for the province. Recognition that almost half of the fires in Alberta in 1940 were caused by faulty wiring led to better enforcement, in part because of increased efforts by the provincial wiring inspector who toured the province handing out remedial orders. The federal government also sponsored fire prevention campaigns to raise awareness of fire safety practices, and the insurance industry continued to exert pressure for improvements and prepared and distributed model building, fire and electrical bylaws. By the mid 1940s, the success of these efforts was becoming apparent. In 1946 the enforcement of bylaws in Claresholm was found by the provincial inspector to be effective and "the town was exceptionally clean and [it was] quite apparent that keen interest is taken by the local business men in keeping their places free from rubbish and inflammable material."[65]

Mundane as they now appear, sidewalks, street lights, roadway improvement, and parking were matters of central importance in contemporary definitions of a successful town. They were attributes of modernity that were believed to contribute materially to the success of business and the quality of town life. The initial concentration of this infrastructure on the main street showed its centrality in the town's urban form and its role as a focus of town life. It also demonstrated how business priorities and needs were universalized in town life and took priority in local decision making. The same bias appeared when infrastructure was installed for fire fighting. If this created discontent among the rest of the town's population, it was rarely recorded, although in 1926 it was commented somewhat resentfully that the residential areas of Coleman received fire protection and police service in return for their property taxes, but no street improvements, utilities, garbage pick-up, or even the planting of a few trees.[66] Partly because of this focus on main street needs, and a reluctance to infringe on the right to make money from private property, towns rarely took the initiative in regulation that served community needs. The province was also reluctant to encroach on such property rights, but it more often took a wider view and forced towns to accede to minimum standards in health and especially fire prevention. Similarly, insurance companies were a powerful influence in raising building standards. Thus, coerced by insurers and senior governments, local governments were more often followers than leaders.

MAIN STREET *and*
COMMUNITY LIFE

10

STREET

LIFE

Main street framed the public social life of townspeople and visitors. Gender, age, ethnicity, residency and class intersected to create a varied and often complex social environment on the street and in the town. Social life was idealized as an interwoven set of social priorities serving a quest for respectability, social order, morality and sociability. At times rowdy, streets had become calmer and more orderly by the 1920s, realizing a hope that town life would be peaceful, quiet, and dignified.

It was commonly believed that a varied and contemporary range of opportunities for social life and leisure helped to retain town population and attract visitors. This was especially important, it was said, because farm life was a "dry-as-dust experience."[1] At the same time that farmers gained a choice in where they shopped and spent leisure time because of motor vehicles, their new found mobility made town social life and institutions more firmly a part of their lives. It also changed public demands for leisure activities and shaped the interaction among farms, towns and cities. The popularity of Saturday evening shopping essentially paralleled the use of automobiles, which allowed one to get home easily the same day even if one left town late. Such trips to town were rarely single purpose and tended to combine shopping with visiting and catching up on local news and opinion. Stores were thus a focus for social life in the same way as cafes, poolrooms and movie houses.[2]

By the end of World War I, it was generally accepted throughout the prairies that recreation drew business to towns. This made it important for a town to offer "amusement and education" to farm people and to welcome them as friends since one was "apt to do business with those you know and like."[3] Consequently, competition was not as much between merchants as between towns. In Cardston in 1941, it was noted that "people are seeking entertainment and amusement in addition to their merchandise purchases and the towns that provide this will profit." Accordingly, the remark that even more farm trade in North Dakota would have gone to the mail order houses had it not been for the social advantages of a trip to town also applies to Alberta.[4]

MOVIE THEATRES

Movies were one popular recreational activity that drew farm families to towns. Not restricted in terms of gender, they appealed to all segments of society. Movies made an early appearance in Alberta towns, and like other entertainment businesses, they were usually located on the main street. In the early years, they were sometimes mounted by itinerant showmen, such as the one that put on scheduled programmes in 1908 in the second storey of a Cardston store. Movies were also often presented in opera houses and halls as one part of a variety show of drama, music, dance and other performances. Many towns had commercial opera houses and halls with a stage and moveable seats to free the auditorium for dances. These buildings provided a venue for performing arts events, speeches, commemorative events and movies. The Opera Hall in Blairmore was constructed in 1911 at a cost of about $12,000 by a local businessman. Seating 800 people, it had a balcony, boxes near the stage, and dressing rooms. Scenery, consisting of six hand-painted curtains, including one of asbestos, was purchased from a Minneapolis firm.[5]

In what was probably an effort to make these presentations appear like regular entertainment features, the halls where movies were shown were sometimes given theatrical names. The one in Cardston was called the Bijou, but it was only remotely similar to the movie houses that emerged after World War I. Movies were combined with dances, variety shows and other entertainment, and rarely was the building specially designed for showing movies. While travelling theatre companies played in many towns before World War I, movies soon became regular features and began to take over opera halls or occupy their own buildings. The Lyric Theatre in Fort Macleod, which opened in 1911 in a former furniture store on main street, represented this trend. The renovations were minor but provided a "modern style" movie theatre with "two aisles between the seats." The projector was located in an iron booth because of concerns about fire, made worse by the flammability of early film. In 1912 in Claresholm, there was no bylaw governing electrical wiring, fire protection, or safety exits in public buildings. Thus, the International Order of Forresters, which rented its hall for commercial entertainments, banned movies from its building. Such concerns were also prominent in the minds of the audience which often sat through a movie in fear of fire. When the Rex theatre opened in a new building in Claresholm in 1918, it emphasized that it was "practically fire proof." Along with comfortable seats, it "gave one the sense of security and restfulness necessary to the proper enjoyment of the entertainment."[6]

By World War I, almost every town in the province had a movie theatre where people could "spend an afternoon or evening of entertainment." The buildings were often simple structures, but children found the movies a "big event" and adults were told they had educational value.[7] Education was, however, a minor part of the attraction of movies, although they were used for educational purposes of a sort during World War I when war propaganda films were shown regularly in all town theatres. Similarly, in Cardston in 1913 anti Mormon films were shown to demonstrate "to what depths the enemies of 'Mormonism' will stoop" and the task faced by LDS missionaries "in the outside world." More often, however, the aim was entertainment. This drew people from surrounding districts and kept townspeople "from going to other places in search of amusement," all of which helped business. The screening of a film of Buffalo Bill's Wild West Show in Lacombe in 1911 was said to be "well worth driving miles to see." And in Grande Prairie in 1917, movies were held three times a week in summer and six times a week after harvest, suggesting a high level of rural patronage.[8] Especially popular movies such as the 1926 *Ten Commandments* or the 1928 *Ben Hur* brought long line ups and a flood of country people to town. As well, free movies at the local cinema were a common feature of Christmas sales promotions in the interwar years.

Movies were a complex form of entertainment. The province censored them to accord with provincial standards, and thus met, to all intents and purposes, any local concern about their moral impact. Rarely having any local content, films relied on their inherent magical qualities, their technology, and a star system to attract audiences.[9] In small towns, stars were promoted through newspaper reports and extensive advertising. The technology and design of cinemas became a sign of community advancement. In 1917, the Grand Theatre in Grande Prairie purchased a "moteograph" projector which gave a steadier image on the screen and provided local audiences with "moving pictures as they are shown in the best and most up-to-date city theatres." To celebrate the new machinery, the management put on a dance in the theatre after the last showing on Saturday night; indicating that the theatre had moveable seats (probably chairs) and a level floor. It also suggests that the tradition of combining a movie with other entertainment was not yet lost.[10]

By the early 1920s, with the maturation of the movie as a discrete entertainment event, cinemas in specially constructed buildings had become a prominent feature of main street. The Orpheum Theatre, which opened in Blairmore in 1921, was ranked as the most "up-to-date, comfortable and convenient theatre in the Pass." It had wide aisles, plenty of leg room, good ventilation, and two projectors, eliminating interruption of the film to change reels. With a four-piece orchestra to accompany the film and help "keep the place from being in an uproar before the performance," it was "a picture-house-supreme" comparable to any in the city.[11] By the time sound movies were introduced, movies were a regular part of town life. The talkies increased their appeal and confirmed town life as being in step with that of the largest cities.

While it was clearly implied that town cinemas were simply keeping up-to-date, they in fact had no choice but to keep up in technological terms if they wanted to show the newly released films audiences demanded. And the new sound releases were hugely popular. When the Boyd Theatre in Peace River installed sound equipment in 1930, it provided free stabling of horses at a livery, or storage of cars at a local garage, for those coming from a distance. Two cinemas in Grande Prairie installed talkie equipment the same year, and drew people from every part of the district, "many of whom had never heard and seen the talkies before." When the talkies opened at the Capitol in Grande Prairie, the theatre was "packed to the doors, with a long line waiting for the second show." The movie, *Hold Everything*, in colour, demonstrated the technological advance of the movie industry and Grande Prairie's part in a wider and glamorous world. As the audience was told before the screening, the movie had been shown only two weeks previously in a $3 million theatre in Los Angeles. Thus, when the theatre burned the following week, it was not just another fire, it was a blow to the town's prestige and sense of worth. The fire "cast a gloom over the entire community" because it had taken "a personal pride in the splendid new building and

The Avalon Theatre in Lacombe in 1934 sported a Spanish-Colonial facade which marked its fashionableness and its California-inspired glamour. Photo courtesy of Maski-pitoon Historical Society, Lacombe.

ultra modern theatre." This reaction was intensified since arson was suspected, and the local newspaper editorialized that if the villain "of such a fiendish piece of work" was found, he should "get the limit, including if the law so allows, the lash."[12]

The talkies stimulated changes in movie theatre design. Before the 1930s, the exteriors of town movie houses were rarely different from other buildings along the main street. By the 1930s, however, this was changing. Installation of a central entrance, similar to city cinemas, was popular. The Boyd Theatre in Peace River constructed a central doorway to replace the doors on either side of the building's front and stuccoed the exterior, giving it a more contemporary look. At street level, the Palace Theatre in Coleman in the late 1930s had central double doors with glass poster cases on either side. It was an image of sleekness and elegance.[13] So too, the city fashion of Spanish Colonial cinemas was copied in towns. Lacombe's Avalon Theatre in 1934, located in a traditional two-storey brick building with a pressed metal cornice, featured a California Spanish colonial design on the street level, with a narrow tile awning across the first storey. It had archways, bits of cast iron, and stucco. It was a clear and pointed statement that movies owed everything to California and nothing to the traditions of the more conventional neighbouring buildings.

The greatest changes after the introduction of the talkies took place inside the theatre. Some renovation was necessary to improve the acoustics for sound pictures, and initially most theatres hung curtains to deaden sound and prevent echoes. More extensive renovations soon took place, and those at the Boyd Theatre in Peace River in 1932 were typical. While a large electrically lit marquee outside marked a change to the street, the interior decoration and appointments caught the public's imagination. While the stage was retained and the floor remained level, everything else indicated a modern cinema. Modern electrical equipment and gadgetry were installed. Earphones were installed in the front row of the balcony for those hard of hearing, and a "crying room" (a separate glass fronted room for those with babies) was built. Light colours were used throughout and the walls of the auditorium contained false windows with curtains, fake window boxes and other "ornamentation." The lobby was an "attraction in itself." It was of a "drawing room" type with "a settee, fireplace, palms and whatnots, lighted by soft and pleasing colored globes." The walls were hung with photos of movie stars and posters of coming attractions. Change in taste came quickly, however, and in 1940 the theatre was renovated once again. This time, the stage was torn out and a sloping floor was built. "New and modernistic decorations," and "a silencing floor covering and draperies to prevent interruption by patrons coming and leaving" were installed.[14]

The new talkie equipment and the renovated theatres were costly in a business which had not been highly profitable. Prior to 1920, movie theatres in towns appeared and disappeared with extraordinary regularity, and owners changed even more rapidly. The Rex theatre in Claresholm changed hands six times between 1914 and 1916. Initially, movies were run continuously. Those at the Lyric in Fort Macleod in 1911 began at 8:15 p.m. and ran until 10:30 on weekdays and 11 on Saturday, and many people apparently sat through the whole evening watching the same movie at least twice; all for 10 or 15 cents admission.[15] By the end of World War I, prices had advanced to around 25 cents, not a substantial increase given wartime inflation. By the late 1920s, however, prices had almost doubled, and they rose still further with the introduction of sound movies. As in city cinemas in Alberta, reduced business because of the Depression forced many cinemas to cut prices and run special promotions to keep audiences.[16] In the late 1930s, conditions improved somewhat, but during World War II these gains were once again lost. This, according to some theatre owners, resulted because high wartime taxes cut profits, and in the Crowsnest Pass one theatre temporarily closed in protest.[17] The major theatre chains did not move into towns before 1947, suggesting that profit margins at town theatres remained too low for their expectations. Nevertheless, local theatre chains emerged. In 1927, the Brewerton Brothers of Raymond bought the Palace Theatre in Cardston, giving them control of the cinemas in the two most important towns in the area. Such ownership saved costs because the same pictures could be shown in more than one theatre. The Brewertons also owned five theatres in Montana. In the Peace River district, W.C. Boyd had theatres in Peace River, Fahler and Fairview by 1930. Similarly, in 1941 William Cole owned theatres in Bellevue, Coleman and Blairmore.[18]

CAFES *and* RESTAURANTS

Like movie theatres, cafes and restaurants were among the first businesses to locate on main street. After 1923, provincial liquor regulations required that every hotel with a liquor license have an eating place. Cafes were also independently located along the street. Their role in town life was diverse. They had a direct utilitarian purpose in serving food to the many commercial travellers, to farmers and their families in town for the day, and to local people without cooking facilities. The latter was commonest in the mining towns where many cafes catered to miners by selling meal tickets. In 1922, the Palm Cafe in Blairmore provided 21 meals a month for $9, or 39 cents per meal.[19] Little trade seems to have come from townspeople going out for dinner. Some restaurants periodically offered a Sunday dinner menu at a special price, but these efforts did not attract sustained patronage. Instead, cafes served as informal meeting places, providing an important social opportunity for townspeople and hinterland visitors. From the beginning, they sold tobacco, candy, soft drinks, take-out ice cream, and sometimes baked goods. In cafes run by Chinese before 1920, Chinese and Japanese decorative and fancy goods were also offered.

While cafes were among the first businesses established in a town, many saw a rapid turn-over of owners. For most, it was a marginal business, although some showed remarkable longevity under one owner. By 1934, the Wong Brothers in Grande Prairie, for example, were successful enough to build a solid brick one-storey building on main street which they rented to a hardware merchant. The usual pattern, however, was for owners to change relatively often. When a new owner took over, the place was often renovated and renamed. Opening events for a new cafe were an important part of a successful launch for the business, and certain conventions were popular. The first day's receipts were often given to a local charity like the hospital, and free ice cream was given to children. Some, especially in the Peace River country, put on a dance for the public.[20]

Until about 1920, the major design in cafes in the towns under study emphasized either a soothing and cosy atmosphere or one of privacy. An ice cream parlour was also often combined with a cafe and sometimes with a drug store. The Wisteria Confectionery in Grande Prairie in 1920 did so, and its garden-like design of lattice work gave a "cool appearance so necessary in the hot weather." Designs aimed at privacy emphasized high booths, sometimes curtained, although this was banned by the province in 1922 as part of enforcing prohibition. Even so, curtained booths remained in some places and disappeared only in the 1930s because of changes in fashion, which seems to have been a more powerful force than the law. The 1935 renovations to the Coleman Cafe were said to make it look like a city cafe. The "old curtained booths" were replaced with new "woodwork partitions painted and trimmed in modern style" and mirrored panels gave the cafe "an added touch of smartness."[21]

Such renovation to more contemporary styles was part of a radical shift in design which continued to influence cafe interiors until after World War II. While many restaurants in Alberta had carefully advertised their cleanliness, after about 1930 they also began to renovate to install contemporary electrical fixtures and appliances as well as designs intended to connote efficiency and sanitation. Bill's Koffee Shoppe, which opened on Claresholm's main street in 1938, used these contemporary design standards. The interior was painted with high gloss white paint with the trimmings done in red and black lacquer. Its layout stressed openness, with a semi circular counter with twelve stools upholstered in red leather plus four booths. The lighting was "of the very newest indirect type." The floor had linoleum in "Moderne pattern, blending with the general color scheme." Thus, its design emphasized easily cleanable and highly finished smooth surfaces, which looked clean and were easy to maintain. "But behind the counter" was the "real interest" of the new business. The Koffee Shoppe had a restaurant type "Frigidaire" with glass doors, an electric coffee percolator, an electric waffle iron, and a natural gas range.[22]

The tendency to renovate following a change in ownership was evident the next year in Claresholm when Charlie Lee, newly arrived from Canora, Saskatchewan, purchased the Claresholm Cafe. In keeping with the current fashion, he renovated by installing "modernist light fixtures, streamlined mirrors, chromium fitted tables," new chinaware, hardwood floors, a lunch counter and booths. He also remodelled the facade of the building with a "new brick-finish processed wall surfacing material" and, as the final touch, installed a neon sign outside. These modernist designs were in widespread use and served many purposes—they made a bold statement that ownership had changed and the new owner was in tune with modern ways, they met contemporary concerns about sanitation, and they helped to attract trade through a modern look. This often intersected with anticipated tourism. In Claresholm, the renovated Koffee Shoppe wanted to tap "the flood of tourist traffic that is bound to follow surfacing of the new highway."[23]

Another aspect of these modern cafes in the 1930s and 1940s was the common affectation of using the letter K instead of the letter C in the cafe's name. While the appeal of this fad remains unclear, few towns escaped it. It was taken almost to absurdity in Claresholm in 1946 by the Daisy May Coffee Shoppe which, while missing the opportunity to misspell coffee, advertised itself as Kleen, Kosy and Kwick.[24] The equally popular spelling of "shoppe" likely attempted to project a sense of cosiness, all of which was at variance with the sleekness of modernism and indicated that the old values of warm kitchens, compatibility, and charm had not been abandoned when the new look was taken on.

The socializing that went on in cafes was not always welcomed by town leaders who sometimes saw lounging around restaurants as a denial of the value of work and useful leisure. These concerns were given an added dimension because Chinese were prominent in the cafe business. It was a common charge that Chinese cafes were a place where "law breakers congregate and cause no end of disturbance and trouble" by gambling, drinking, "rowdyism and loafing."[25] There were, of course, cafes in every town that were run by non-Chinese, and these owners sometimes used racism to their own advantage by advertising that they used "all white help."[26] In light of these concerns, licensing was sometimes used to try and control the number of cafes in a town. Cafes, like poolrooms, required both a provincial and town license, and the provincial license was granted only after the local government approved the application. Unlike most other businesses, cafes received little benefit from town licensing because for them the common claim that it brought protection from competition was rarely meaningful. There was no transient competition, and in catering, competition came from church ladies groups, which were impossible to oppose.

While cafes had traditionally offered regular meals in the day and short orders in the evening and at night, eating establishments offering short order meals throughout the day had become common by 1940. Ye Waffle Shoppe, the first "light lunch counter" in Grande Prairie, opened in about 1933 and mainly served pastries and cakes along with short orders. Wartime restrictions had an impact on all types of eating places. During World War I, shortages and rationing of meat and bread forced cafes to adopt "beefless and baconless days" at least one day a week. During World War II, wartime rationing and labour shortages had the same effect. Shortages of food and quotas forced eating places to curtail hours of operation or to close temporarily. In Coleman, these conditions affected many miners who in 1943 appealed to their union for help because they had to find places to eat and to have their "buckets" made up. Subsequently, the federal government issued supplementary food quotas for cafes in mining towns, allowing them to keep regular hours, honour meal tickets, and fill lunch buckets.[27]

BARS, POOLROOMS
and BROTHELS

Liquor was readily available from businesses along main street from an early date. Until 1892, when drinking was restricted to licensed bars in hotels, saloons operated in towns like Fort Macleod. Patrons were male, but there were class divisions between

| Bars, like this one in Blairmore in the early 1900s, were centres of some men's social life. The animals, presumably killed by local hunters, were popular symbols of "manliness." NA-3903-28, GAI.

"respectable" bars and the "evil smelling and disreputable joint."[28] Sale of alcohol for private consumption was restricted to licensed vendors. These provisions were retained when the province was created, as was the territorial prohibition of liquor north of 55 degrees latitude. Thus, there were no bars in either Grande Prairie or Peace River, although there was some bootlegging and those of European descent could import liquor for their personal use. Elsewhere, prohibition could be imposed in a locality through local option if approved in a vote by 60 percent of householders. Such approval was narrowly defeated in a vote in Claresholm in 1908. In Cardston, because of opposition by the Mormon church, liquor sales were prohibited in the town from the time it was established.[29]

Demands for the restriction or total banning of liquor made liquor a political issue in both the territorial and provincial periods. Drinking was blamed for a multitude of social problems, including violence and disturbance of the peace, and it was believed that it needed to be controlled to create an orderly society. As in Fort Macleod in 1894, the anti liquor forces were co-ordinated through organizations like the Women's Christian Temperance Union and the Royal Templars of Temperance. Even so, prohibition was the concern only of a minority, albeit an influential and vocal one. When the federal government held a plebescite on prohibition in 1898, it carried in Fort Macleod by 52 votes to 48. Of the 363 eligible voters, less than a third had bothered to vote.[30]

The prohibitionists rejected freedom of choice when it came to liquor. They wanted it banned and the bars closed, and a provincial vote in 1916 outlawed the recreational consumption of liquor. This was directly related to the war effort and was presented as a patriotic issue. The strongest votes in favour were in the south and central parts of the province, especially in places with large Protestant and Anglo-Canadian populations. In 1917, Claresholm elected Louise Crummy McKinney, one of the most prominent prohibitionists in Alberta, to the provincial legislature. Only in the mining communities of the Crowsnest Pass were the drys out-voted. Initially, there was pride in the achievement of prohibition and the social improvement it had supposedly brought. In mid 1916, it was noted that drunks had been "pretty numerous on the Claresholm streets" before prohibition, but people were now spending more money in stores for "the necessities of life" instead of liquor.[31]

The appeal of prohibition soon waned, and illegal drinking was a continual issue. As the Peace River Social Service Council complained in 1921, there was an "increasing amount of intoxication prevalent in this town." Liquor came onto the market through bootleggers or for "medical" reasons.[32] When prohibition ended in 1923, public consumption was allowed in licensed beer rooms in hotels, while liquor for home consumption was sold only in government stores. Liquor licenses were also granted to private clubs, such as the Great War Veteran's Association, or, later, the Canadian Legion. In Coleman and Blairmore in 1926, each town had four licensed premises, three in hotels, and one in a veterans' club.[33] Bars were now also allowed in the northern part of the province, and in 1924 the first ones in the history of Grande Prairie and Peace River were opened. Only Cardston remained dry, although in 1926 there were complaints about bootlegging and drinking, as well as the almost equivalent vice of smoking, at dances. Neither was considered "a decent standard for a social party in our [LDS] communities."[34]

Cardston was not unique in its ongoing hostility to liquor. Canadian Legion branches, which applied for liquor licenses for their club rooms, often found themselves pitted against local anti liquor forces. This caused bitter public dispute in Drumheller in 1928 and in Claresholm in 1931. And memories of prohibition were still fresh enough in 1940 for the Drumheller Rotary Club to mount a parody of a favourite prohibitionist play, *Ten Nights in A Bar Room*. Making fun of the prohibitionists meant that they were still a residual force, and as late as the end of World War II, the construction of a new legion hall in Grande Prairie was controversial because of its plans to sell beer. Although public drunkenness seemed to have decreased overall, it was still frowned upon and drunks on the street were usually arrested and fined.[35]

Directly related to the liquor question was prostitution. In 1914 a brothel was established on a corner lot of Peace River's main street. This location, wrote the *Peace River Record*, suggested that the village council not only favoured vice, but fostered it by clearing away the brush in front of the brothel at public expense, "probably to give the girls a better view of the main business corner." Prostitution was quickly moved off main street, but its control remained difficult. Some towns attempted to suppress it by having the police run prostitutes out of town. A more practical approach was to allow a "segregated area" which kept it off the streets. In 1919, while it was "regrettable," this was thought to be "the only solution" in a mining town like Drumheller. Such areas operated in other places as well. In 1911 the *Fort Macleod Advertiser* denied there were brothels in the town. Its concerns were less with vice than with economic growth. "This paper believes in a clean town, as a business proposition, and, as far as can be ascertained, we have it." It was a disingenuous statement: Fort Macleod's "segregated area" was located outside the town limits.[36] In any case, concerns about prostitution were most common before 1923, after which it largely disappeared from public debate. The end of prohibition was one factor in this since brothels had often been involved with bootleg liquor. As well, the number of single, transient males in the province declined after World War I.

If the bar and brothels were one part of town culture for some men, poolrooms were another. Of the towns studied, each had at least two poolrooms on main street, and sometimes as many as five, with one sometimes located in a hotel. Their clientele was wholly male. In addition to pool tables, many had one or two bowling lanes as well as a barber shop and a sales counter for soft drinks, tobacco, and candy. Some, like one in Cardston in 1912, offered a shoe shining service and an "electrical massage apparatus."[37] In addition, many provided bathing facilities, usually in connection with the barber shop. The ethnicity of poolroom owners paralleled that of other businesses in the town. In the agricultural towns, owners tended to be of British descent, while in the mining towns they were often of central European and Italian descent.[38]

For moral and social reformers, such as the prohibitionists and the "respectable" class, the poolroom was part of the underbelly of town life. The mayor of Cardston called them "perfect hell holes."[39] There was much antagonism to poolrooms in Mormon towns, and local licensing powers were used in an attempt to restrict them. In 1909, Cardston raised its license fee to $300 for the first table, and $200 for each additional table. Those affected appealed to the courts, which quashed the fees as "prohibitive and intended to be so." Until this point, there had been little regulation of poolrooms by the province. In Blairmore they could be open all night if they wished, and prizes such as cigars were often given for high scores and tournaments.[40] However, the increased appeal of moral reform ideas caused a tightening of provincial regulations. Prizes were forbidden, closing hours were set, and a minimum age of patrons was stipulated. In 1913, Natives were prohibited from entering a poolroom, although this was lifted by the early 1920s.[41] During prohibition, poolrooms received greater scrutiny because of concerns about bootlegging. As was noted in Coleman in 1918, the poolroom's role as a male social centre had changed because of prohibition:

> Somebody sold liquor in a pool room because after the hotels were closed the pool rooms were about the only places in the smaller towns and villages where it was possible to sit down or get warm and feel at home. As a consequence, farmers waiting for their teams and almost everyone else, good and bad alike, made the pool room their headquarters when forced to wait in town. As a result, largely, of providing accommodation for the public, a new set of restrictions is in order and a number of them will be closed up.[42]

In contrast to many businesses, poolroom owners rarely expressed concern about making their places modern and up-to-date. Perhaps their appeal as a male preserve was served by keeping them dim, smoky and casual, and few efforts were made to bring them into line with contemporary fashions in building design and decoration. While usually located on main street, they were not always on street level. In 1910, for example, one poolroom in Cardston had the tables on the second floor, with

| Poolrooms, like bars, were often a focus for male social life and
some critics saw them as gambling dens and places of social
corruption. This one in Lacombe in 1906 featured a slot machine.
NA-1583-6, GAI.

the barber shop and bathing facilities on street level.[43] In 1918 some
design change resulted from new provincial regulations. To establish
greater control over patrons, candy and tobacco counters and barber
shops had to be separated from the pool tables by a wall, and the interior
of the poolroom had to be visible from the street. For a time, this eliminated poolrooms in basements or on second floors as well as blinds or
shutters on the street-side windows. While the level of control remained
significant, the end of prohibition lessened official concern and regulation became somewhat more lenient.[44] By World War II some poolrooms
were once again located in basements.

While bowling alleys were often part of poolrooms, they had emerged
as separate businesses by the late 1930s. Yet, there was still an association
between pool and bowling in the minds of some. Although Stoddard's
Bowladrome in Cardston was located next to a poolroom, it organized
leagues and emphasized the building's cleanliness, good ventilation, and
light to counter preconceived notions about such places. In 1945 in

Grande Prairie, Frank Donald, a prominent local hotel keeper, opened a "Recreational Centre" which featured a poolroom in the basement and a bowling alley on street level. While the customary linking of pool and bowling was apparent, the facility's name and design made special efforts to welcome women. For example, a restroom for women was located on the main floor so they would not have to use the restrooms (with their "shower baths") in the basement. Emphasis was placed on the bowling alley's fluorescent lighting and its "Mastic Flooring, a material new to this country, which prevents any noise and is easy to walk on."[45] Modern materials and appointments were being used to transcend the traditional association of bowling with poolrooms and to reverse the practice of excluding women.

CONTROL *of* STREET LIFE

In 1909, the Claresholm town solicitor was asked by the town council to prepare a bylaw "governing conduct on streets, sidewalks, and for the general preservation of order." The bylaw would "include nearly all the offences common to man." In their scope, these provisions were a microcosm of dominant views about the conduct of public social life. The street bylaws in Lacombe in 1907 and Coleman in 1911 shared identical wording and were probably drafted using a standard precedent. The concerns they expressed were not unique to towns; Edmonton's 1912 street bylaw contained similar provisions, and even some identical wording to those of smaller centres.[46]

These bylaws expressed social ideals. As such, they shaped the tenor of social life on the street more than they directed it. Many towns had police officers to enforce these bylaws and perform other functions. While "excellent order these past months" had been established in Claresholm in 1913 because "of a policeman on the streets," most towns had little need for extensive policing. Serious crimes were relatively rare. There were occasional thefts, and gambling was common in all mining towns. During prohibition, there was also much bootlegging. In the Crowsnest Pass, crime was typically blamed on "foreigners," and while the area had more reported crimes than agricultural service towns, the extent of criminal behaviour was commonly exaggerated. Much of this was stereotyping by members of the Anglo-Canadian dominant culture of those of non-British descent as criminal and radical. In a similar fashion,

Chinese were often blamed for gambling. This mindset was demonstrated when four Chinese and four Caucasians were found guilty of gambling in Claresholm in 1910. During the trial, the defence argued that the game was merely a party among friends, to which the prosecutor replied that the company of Chinese and "white men could hardly be that of intimate friends." Such ethnic and racial biases were common in the justice system. In 1913 it was said in Blairmore that police "efforts to preserve peace among the English speaking classes, who are known to shelter crime in its many milder forms," were relatively casual. In comparison, if a non-English-speaking person was "suspected, he is immediately made to defend himself as an illiterate before the courts."[47]

The relative peacefulness and order of town life led to strong reactions when serious crime did occur. The murder of a young woman in Drumheller in 1920 led to demands that the town "become clean and wholesome morally, physically and mentally." But more commonly, public perceptions about crime arose from gossip, a prurient interest in vice, and a general fear of disorder. In Grande Prairie in 1917, a police inquiry failed to substantiate claims about extensive bootlegging and gambling in the town. Similarly, in response to complaints to the Department of the Attorney General in 1917 about "rowdyism" in Peace River, the Alberta Provincial Police sergeant reported that a "good cleaning up here would do no harm and would meet with general approval." But he was unclear about what the public meant by rowdyism. "I think, probably," he reported, it meant "the number of gamblers, pimps and prostitutes in town, rather than any frequent disorderly conduct in public places." For those already concerned, anxiety increased in later years with newspaper and radio reports about crime in other places. In 1930, it was contended that Grande Prairie, which had two police officers (one of whom also looked after public works), also needed a night police officer. Even though the town had "been comparatively free of crime, if reports of what is happening in other parts of the west are anything to go by, it is high time" the town had "all night police protection."[48]

Reactions to disorder were not only the product of local gossip and moralizing or a fear that the town would be contaminated by outside forces. They also drew upon an assumption that a balanced restriction of behaviour was necessary to maintain social and economic stability. Such concerns were especially pointed when it came to children. It was generally accepted that crime prevention required the careful discipline and control of children. Crime, it was said in Cardston in 1919, was a "habit" that was easily acquired by boys and if "not nipped in the bud, will develop into serious proportions." For adults as well, such a view meant that even minor matters could herald social collapse. Seemingly innocent matters, such as the blowing of car horns on Cardston's main street by wedding parties, could thus be a force that weakened social order. It showed disrespect to the public, and although a small matter, it "grows on the community and acts much like an infectious disease."[49]

This example indicates the commonly held view that noise-making was a mark of disorder. A quiet setting defined a well-functioning society. While bylaws commonly restricted people from being noisy, technological change helped reorient such concerns. It was commented in 1935 that "nervous and mental disorders" were increasing in North America because of noise from traffic, radios and other sources. While worst in cities, noise was increasing sufficiently in Cardston "to wear a man's nerves to a frazzle, to say nothing of ruining his disposition." Yet at the same time, noise was welcomed as representing an advancing society. In 1937, John Woslyng, a town councillor and Cardston businessman, set up a "public address system" with speakers along main street as part of the town's jubilee celebration. He kept the system operating, and by 1940 its broadcasts helped keep "shoppers and visitors abreast of the news of the district and the world."[50]

It was not only human behaviour that shaped street life. Usually, animals created more problems for public peace than did most people. Throughout the 1880s, hogs wandered the streets of Fort Macleod and "people out after dark often stumbled over these living obstructions... the pigs usually getting the best of the encounter." A more lasting concern centred on roaming dogs. Reports of dog attacks on pedestrians were not unusual, and although all towns had bylaws requiring that dogs be licensed and controlled, they were only periodically enforced because almost everyone owned a dog and resented the town's efforts at control. While town police shot thousands of unlicensed and stray dogs over the years, the extent of the problem led some people to take matters into their own hands. Sometimes, noisy or dangerous dogs were shot by neighbours, but they were most often poisoned, and every town had its rash of dog poisonings from time to time. While such tactics sometimes earned cautious support, they were more often condemned as cowardly behaviour that robbed families of treasured pets and companions.[51]

THE NATURE *of* STREET LIFE

In many respects, main street was male oriented. Bars and poolrooms were especially important in these male activities. But loitering on main street was also central in many men's social life. By 1898, men customarily hung around outside the hotels in Fort Macleod. The hotel keepers did not object, indeed they saw it as a normal part of their establishment's function and ambience. Nonetheless, the town council asked the police to break up the crowd to keep the street clear. This caused much "friction" between the men and the police, and the town compromised by demanding that if the crowd became "too large or too boisterous," the hotelier had to quiet them down, disperse them, or, if necessary, call the police.[52]

Concerns about loitering continued to be expressed in later years. Various bylaws in Coleman, Lacombe and Drumheller, for example, all prohibited people from standing or sitting along the street if they obstructed pedestrians. While streets lined with lounging men were not conducive to business, these regulations generally reflected a hope for a decorous town life. Hence, the street bylaws of both Coleman and Lacombe also prohibited people from throwing snowballs or "any missiles dangerous to the public," and from running or racing on the streets or crowding or jostling "other foot passengers so as to create discomfort, disturbance or confusion." As well, there was a fear that loitering might turn to violence. Fighting on the streets seems to have been uncommon, at least it was rarely discussed by newspapers or police reports, and when it was noted, it was usually blamed on drunkenness. "Boisterous" singing, shouting and foul language (all prohibited in many town bylaws) were more common. Much of this foul language came from drunken men. In 1900 it was said in Fort Macleod that it was "almost impossible to pass along Main street late in the afternoon or in the evening without hearing someone under the influence of liquor shouting out ribald or obscene language at the pitch of his voice." In 1910 in Blairmore it was said that vulgar language offensive to women was unfortunately too common on the streets and in public places.[53]

Such behaviour indicated that main street did not focus on women's needs, which were often treated as incidental to those of men. No facilities catered exclusively to women, and women from the country often had nowhere to pass the time. Many of them spent their time in the

| *Loitering around hotels was a popular male custom in small towns. This 1890 photo shows men posing in front of the Fort Macleod hotel. Archives Collection, A3887, PAA.*

shops, often browsing for long periods until their husbands were ready to go home. With the adoption of automobiles, women and children could at least wait in the car and "watch the rest of the parade go by, while their husbands and fathers, are, well, just exactly where are they?"[54] Given these conditions, demands for public rest rooms were common. These were not merely public toilets, but a place where farm women could wash, visit, rest, change the baby, and, presumably, wait for their husbands. In the 1920s and 1930s, most trips to town were still a full day's outing, and as was observed in Fort Macleod in 1920, they were often the "only chance for a change" for many farm women. Even so, these outings were often miserable, and "nothing is more distressing than to see a mother trying to soothe or satisfy her fretful baby out in the open street." A rest room would make women's visits to the town more pleasant. And as was noted in 1909, since farm women did not rent a hotel room to rest, "no business would be interfered with and the comfort and shopping in Claresholm would be greatly increased."[55]

Unlike Manitoba, where rest rooms were a common feature of most towns, such campaigns were rarely successful in Alberta.[56] In 1918 a womens' rest room was established by the Fort Macleod branch of the Council of Women. Located on the second floor of a main street building, it was apparently soon closed. By 1920, the Women's Institutes of Alberta owned or operated a total of 48 rest rooms and social and recreational centres throughout the province. While it is unclear how many of these were rest rooms, all were justified as important for building "community."[57] Generally, however, rest rooms seem to have been short-lived projects. Year after year, town councils were urged to construct rest rooms in order to stimulate rural trade. The need for the facility was obvious, and as one Peace River woman, calling herself "Country Cousin," wrote in 1939, "if we go to a hotel, if not asked to move on, we know we are not wanted, and realize we are a nuisance, if we wait in a store we are in the way, if we wait on the street we feel uncomfortable, and soon wish we were home." To meet such needs, a rest room was established in 1946 in Peace River by the local chapter of the Women's Institute and the board of trade.[58]

The marginalization of women in street social life paralelled their role in the wider society. Similarly, the place of children and adolescents reflected their social standing and concerns about the need for proper upbringing. In part, children were controlled by curfews which were in place in all towns by an early date. Fort Macleod had one by 1903, and Claresholm's 1910 bylaw stipulated that between November and May children under 16 years of age had to be off the streets by 9 p.m. unless accompanied by a parent or guardian. Children violating the curfew could be fined up to $10 and taken home by the police, or locked up in the town jail if they resisted. The parents or guardians could also be fined.[59] With some variation, these provisions remained in place in all towns for the next 35 years. In many places, a siren or bell was rung to announce the curfew hour. Over time, there was a continual cycle in which curfews were announced, enforced for a time, and then ignored. Towns with only one police officer could not adequately enforce them, and most towns were unwilling to create the authoritarian system necessary for strict enforcement.

Curfews and other controls were intended to set limits on children's behaviour. One area of common concern to all towns arose in respect to bicycles, which made an early appearance in Alberta towns. The "bicycle craze" struck Fort Macleod in 1893 when the editor of the newspaper and the bookkeeper of the McLaren lumber mill each purchased bicycles from a Calgary supplier.[60] By the interwar years, they were more commonly used by children and adolescents, who not unexpectedly preferred to ride them on cement sidewalks rather than the rutted streets. In all towns, this brought complaints about danger to pedestrians and a lack of discipline. Thus, bylaws were passed to prohibit the practice. Raising similar concerns, another common but "very dangerous" game saw children who hung on, or attached a sled, to the bumper of a car while it was driven along the street in winter. Although demands for the police to stop this practice were continually made, it was never eliminated.[61]

Other areas of concern revolved around various forms of boisterous behaviour. Opinion on the matter varied over time, and in 1910 the arrest and fining of a group of some of Claresholm's "most respectable young men," for "shouting like maniacs" at 3 a.m. on the street, led to the accusation that the police officer was a spoil sport. He defended his actions by contending that they had disturbed the peace and had he not acted, "he would hear of it for some time and from the very ones who think the law was not made for them. It is the same old story: sack the other fellow but don't touch us." Another major concern was the "midnight frolic," or late night dances. It was widely believed that such events led to immoral behaviour among the young, and in 1933 Drumheller responded with a bylaw outlawing dances between Saturday midnight and 6 a.m. Monday. A related matter was the role of automobiles in adolescent entertainment. After Saturday night dances in Cardston in 1939, "cars race up and down the streets, honking at each other." Indeed, "if a person were to shout as loud as these horns honk, he would be arrested for disturbing the peace."[62]

Such "boisterous behaviour" generally did not include vandalism, but that which occurred was usually the work of boys and teenaged males. Scribbling on walls, committing minor damage to public buildings such as post offices, and shooting at street lights and glass insulators on telephone poles were most common. Reaction in Drumheller in 1939 to this "kind of fun" was typical—people demanded that it be stopped because it cost the public money. But more serious acts brought stronger reactions. For the second time in 1940, vandals tore down most of the signs on the buildings on a whole block of Grande Prairie's main street. The mayor announced that he hoped the culprits would be caught and jailed because "this kind of thing will not be tolerated in this community."[63]

| *Hallowe'en was a time to make jokes about public figures. In 1925, an outdoor privy was towed to Blairmore's main street and labelled "Blairmore's Houses of Parliament." NA-3903-21, GAI.*

These reactions were in contrast to those stimulated by the minor vandalism that was a part of Hallowe'en. As a time for pranks and the pillorying of adults, modest attacks on property and reputations were tolerated. In 1900, "a butcher's sign in front of Fowler's barber shop" in Fort Macleod on the morning after Hallowe'en "caused some little amusement" in the town. A privy dragged to the main street and labelled "Blairmore's Houses of Parliament" in 1925 earned the same response. The most popular Hallowe'en pranks from an early date included those of a "style that finds most favor with little boys." Soaping windows (and later of automobiles), removing gates from their hinges, dragging wagons onto the streets, and the inevitable tipping over of outdoor privies were all common until World War II. Yet, permissible behaviour on Hallowe'en was not left to chance. Children were controlled by enforcing the curfew for that night. In 1920, the Lacombe town constable arrested 47 young men for disturbing the peace and destroying property on Hallowe'en eve, or, "eves, this year the festive season having lasted nearly a week." The extent of the damage set another limit. The customary pranks were generally accepted, but when the damage cost too much to repair, the line had been crossed. In 1923, it was observed in Grande Prairie that Hallowe'en was usually a night of merry making but of late it had become "a night of wilful damage and mischievousness," with much damage to commercial property. World War II brought further limitations, and in 1942 Hallowe'en pranksters in Coleman were warned to "keep in mind that householders in these days of war are hard enough pressed...without having to pay for property damage which is not of their own making."[64]

Hallowe'en was a symbolic time of testing social limits, but greater attention was paid to disorderly behaviour attributed to outsiders or those not accepted by town society. During the 1880s and 1890s, for example, whites in Fort Macleod expected Natives to stay on the reservation and leave only with the permission of the Indian agent. In a typical expression of this view, it was said in 1886 that "these Indians have no earthly right to come and loaf about town" and "prowl around at all hours of the night." This demand had its effect and Natives were ordered to return to their reserves later in the week. In part, this attitude arose from fears about an uprising in southern Alberta in connection with the Metis rebellion of 1885, but it also represented a prevalent view that Natives were both a threat and an unjustified burden upon white society.[65] It was an attitude that the federal government endorsed with its unsuccessful efforts in the late nineteenth century to implement a pass system to prevent Treaty Indians from leaving the reserves.[66]

By World War I, town opinion had shifted in some respects. When the federal government attempted to stop Treaty Indians from attending fairs because it was said to make them "restless and neglect their farming," the Fort Macleod newspaper editorialized that Indians were picturesque and drew a crowd. Because they made the fair more exciting, "let them come." Native people often put on dances on the street of towns like Claresholm in return for a collection of money. This practice was restricted in 1933 when the Canadian government prohibited such performances off the reserve without a permit. At least, editorialized the Lacombe newspaper, this might help preserve a part of Native culture. Dances would now be held away from white society and freed from the "contamination of the market place" because "the white man...sooner or later finds a way of making money out of any spectacle he encounters."[67]

These changed attitudes did not translate into acceptance. If Natives were no longer seen as a threat, they were still often seen as a nuisance.

In 1917 the Claresholm town policeman "earned the gratitude of many" townspeople by ordering Natives who were begging on the street to leave town. The local newspaper editor argued that "charity has pauperized" the Natives, and that "the policy of 'work or starve' would be of undoubted benefit to the Indian." At least this put Natives on par with transient whites, who were also commonly driven out of town if undesirable. The difference, of course, was that Natives lived in the district whereas the others did not. Some towns, like Fort Macleod, had a resident Native population, yet Natives played almost no role in the published accounts of town life.[68] The assumption that they were not a legitimate part of the community was evident.

Those who appeared to be vagrants received much the same treatment. In Fort Macleod in 1886, the police rounded up 15 or 20 men "with no visible means of support," and those unable to give a "satisfactory account of themselves" were "given their marching orders." Such approaches were commonly used to rid towns of suspected gamblers, pimps, and prostitutes, but vagrants and wandering unemployed men were soon treated in the same way. Blairmore's 1918 vagrancy bylaw defined a vagrant as anyone who was "a loose, idle or disorderly person" refusing to work to maintain himself, or loitering around the streets and disturbing the peace by vandalizing property or insulting passersbys, or having "no peaceable profession or calling."[69] This encompassed a number of the stock apprehensions in Canada about the underlying causes of violence and social disorder as well as popular beliefs about the social virtues of steady work.[70] Christian charity could not, of course, be denied. As did many others, Claresholm's bylaw contained a provision prohibiting begging unless the beggar had a letter from a local minister testifying to his "worthiness" for "public generosity." As was observed in Claresholm in 1913, "there is only one thing to do with the man who won't work and that is to keep him busy moving. Pass them along." The widespread use of such policies meant that vagrants were continually moving among towns and cities. The Calgary police court, for example, passed in 1910 what were called "leave the city" sentences, which acquitted petty criminals if they left the city.[71]

While such policies maintained their popularity after World War I, by the late 1920s they were intentionally being used to counter demands for relief. In 1928, 200 men were "ordered to leave" Drumheller, with the result, it was reported, that there had been only one demand for relief.[72] During the Depression, this became more common. In one case in

Claresholm in 1937, about 100 relief workers were sent from Calgary to work on the harvest. Finding little work, the workers asked the town council for help. While it replied that welfare was a provincial or federal responsibility, the men were given "two bits each and told that it was the finish of Claresholm's hand-out." But it remained common to blame the unemployed for their own plight. Later the same year, it was remarked in Claresholm that while it was "tough to see the poor chaps wandering up and down the railways with their packs, sleeping in box cars and under culverts," there was work for farm hands in Ontario, showing that they used "little or no judgement in their ramblings." Soon, all charitableness was gone: a month later the Claresholm paper wrote that relief workers were spongers and the public that supported them were "suckers."[73] Such attitudes were widespread. In 1933, the Drumheller welfare board advised the public that it should not feed transients because "the government will take care of them" in the work camps. Describing the camps as warm, comfortable, and newly renovated, the board suggested that "trucks are leaving every day for the relief camps to take any transients who have no work and no home." There "the government can keep a check on them—when they are drifting about from pillar to post no one knows where they are from one day to another."[74]

The public was often warned not to be duped by requests for assistance. As it was phrased in Claresholm in 1929, "rather than pass over a deserving case most people freely donate, and as a result society has a throng of plutocratic parasites preying on its tender-heartedness." Yet many continued to be generous. One form of this generosity came in the numerous relief campaigns of the 1930s. Ethnicity sometimes focused these efforts: the Italian Society in Coleman, for example, paid out $27,000 in relief in 1933 to take care of local unemployed people of Italian origin. Broadly, appeals for cash, clothing and "other small comforts" for the local needy, such as in Claresholm in 1933, enjoyed full support. This generosity contrasted sharply with official reactions to the way that the transient poor, or those on relief, were treated. There was little opposition to these policies, suggesting that townsfolk generally supported them.

The contradiction between the official hostile reactions to the poor and evidence of individual generosity to local appeals for assistance is a revealing measure of small town culture. In the first place, the limited tax base of local government did not provide it with the resources to support relief. Only senior governments had such resources, and it was only with regular and planned involvement after World War II by federal and provincial governments that the problems of financing relief were surmounted. But beyond this basic difficulty, small town attitudes toward the poor encapsulated the view that a town existed unto itself and had almost no responsibilities to those from outside its boundaries. This parochialism was another, and less appealing, dimension of the consequences of encouraging "town pride" and community cohesion, and showed the limits of such a narrow definition of "community." It also demonstrated how a commitment to individual effort and personal independence could become a disparagement of the poor and the less fortunate. Yet, the poor had their uses, especially as cheap labour. As Lacombe farmers argued in 1939, keeping the unemployed out of the town made it difficult to find farm hands. Ultimately, farmers agreed to let the police know how many men were needed, and the police permitted that number "to leave the freight trains to fill the jobs."[75]

While it would be naive to contend that there were no people who were poor because of their personal habits or attitudes, arguments about the undeserving poor underscored the social attitudes of small town culture more than they did the reality of poverty and unemployment. The common view that the poor used relief as an excuse not to work rarely could be proved. The continual demands by the unemployed for work provides evidence against this view. So too, evidence is provided by a number of investigations about alleged abuse. In 1931, W.A. Beebe, a former Blairmore mayor, argued that some residents on relief had cash in the bank. An RCMP investigation found all the welfare recipients he named were destitute. Similarly, in 1942, the Drumheller city council asked its medical health officer to examine male indigent relief cases. He found that all but two were "unfit for any type of work." These two could perform only light work, and so were put to cleaning the streets.[76]

Street life was never separated from dominant views about the ideals of town life. Such ideals were often rooted in the preoccupations found everywhere in Alberta and the rest of the country. When applied to the main street, these social conventions became part of its character, in the same manner as its buildings and layout.[77] Businesses like poolrooms, movies, bars and cafes were important leisure activities for town visitors and residents. They helped define the town as urban, and a town without such leisure offerings could rarely have been successful. Because twentieth century leisure was so powerfully influenced and defined by technology and fashion, it became a primary focus in towns for the expression of modernity and fashion—for being "city-like." It also created a link between town and country that was not merely commercial and helped establish the town as a social centre for rural people. Yet, at the same time, these activities were seen by some as challenging the purity and ideals of town and country life. With the exception of movies, and to a lesser extent, cafes, the often marginal respectability, male orientation, and business objectives of much commercial leisure left many needs unfilled, which in turn stimulated leisure activities organized by voluntary and sectarian groups.

11

BUILDING
COMMUNITY
THROUGH LEISURE

The sense of community created by commercial recreational activities was developed more deliberately by voluntary groups like churches and service clubs, as well as by celebration of statutory holidays and various special and seasonal events. Many of these leisure activities and occasions—like their commercial counterparts—served the economic objectives of towns, particularly those of main street. Yet while they drew visitors and focused community life around business needs, they also served to unify town society through activities and projects that complemented the social ideals that governed town life. At the same time, and like commercial leisure, they sometimes reflected differing community points of view.

CHURCHES

Churches offered one route to creating a sense of community. Religious activity began almost simultaneously with the formation of a town. Usually first performed by itinerant ministers, services were held in private homes or public buildings like schools. Before a church was built in 1910 in the Crowsnest Pass, Roman Catholic priests performed mass in private homes. Protestant ministers followed the same practice, although adherents of different denominations often attended whatever Protestant service was closest. For some denominations, the use of an itinerant minister lasted for decades. In Drumheller

after 1911, Lutherans worshipped in several schools with the aid of itinerant ministers, but no formal services were organized until 1938 and a
congregation was only established in 1951.[1] For the major Anglo-
Canadian Protestant denominations and Roman Catholics, however,
churches were soon built and staffed with resident clergy. While often
supported by churches or patrons in eastern Canada or Europe, local
congregations gradually became able to pay their own way.[2]

Whatever their stage of development, churches provided a social
focus for their adherents, and as they became better established, this
social function expanded. Women's and youth's clubs were formed and
offered a variety of recreational activities. Dances, congregational din-
ners, plays, and musical evenings helped hold members and attract new
ones and, equally important, raised money for the church. These leisure
activities were sometimes controversial, especially among some
Protestants. Tension periodically existed between those who saw them as
useful tools for creating a community of church-goers, and those who
viewed them as inappropriate—if not counterproductive—church activities. In 1921, Methodists in Fort Macleod vigorously debated the merits
of church sponsored dances; resolving that while some dances (such as
folk dances) were acceptable, others were not.[3]

In any event, such church sponsored leisure activities rarely brought
the church and the whole community together. In Claresholm, the
Methodist church set up a reading and games room for youths in about
1906. Interest in it soon waned, and in 1910 the church tried again by
organizing a "group" Young Men's Christian Association (YMCA) to serve
a number of area towns. Usually, the YMCA operated in larger urban centres, but under this approach, local committees were formed in
Claresholm, Okotoks, High River, and Nanton. The Canadian West
Committee of the national YMCA provided financial assistance, and a
salaried manager regularly visited each town to organize activities as part
of a "Christian effort for the young men and boys of the community."
Rooms on the second floor of a main street building were fitted up as a
meeting and reading room which was open in the evenings. This experiment, like its predecessor, started "with a flourish," but was dead within
two months. The "tameness" of the activities could not compete with
commercial ones, since "young men who have enjoyed the fascination of
the pool table can hardly be expected to appreciate to any great extent,
the crokinole board." In denominationally fragmented towns, a recre-

ational centre that did not provide "ordinary every day amusements" was "doomed to failure."[4]

It was not only competition from commercial leisure that defeated efforts to tie the church more closely to its community. In most towns, facilities were limited since even the wealthiest churches had only a hall or the church basement for social events. More significantly, church attendance in most towns was usually low or erratic. Church leaders continually complained of public indifference to church matters and the difficulty of financing the church.[5] Overall, the problem was not in membership, but in attendance. The Grande Prairie Anglican church continuously faced serious financial problems, but as the church Rector observed in 1932, if the existing congregation regularly attended church, "the consequent collections would suffice for all needs of the church." But regular attendance could not be counted on, even from those belonging to the church clubs. In 1929, the president of the Grande Prairie Women's Auxiliary noted "the small church attendance and appealed to the members to make an effort to attend more regularly."[6]

Public indifference to formal church attendance did not translate into hostility or resentment towards the church or its clergy. Men of the cloth occupied a privileged, though perhaps unenviable, position as town moral guardians and social models of probity and spiritual values. Yet while ministers may have been esteemed, the public demanded that they have the same (or lower) financial standing as their parishioners. Moreover, ministers and churches were often viewed as a kind of public service to be used only when needed. As the Coleman newspaper editorialized in 1936, the public wanted a church for funerals, weddings and baptisms, but refused to attend regularly or support it financially.[7]

The origin of these attitudes to the church was perhaps part of the changed lifestyle and attitudes that came with settlement in a new land, but the persistence of these attitudes long after the vicissitudes of settlement had passed point to more complex social and intellectual processes. In the case of Protestant churches, these attitudes were compounded by denominationalism. In Claresholm in 1918, four churches were open for a few hours to serve about half the town's population one day a week. Because of "ancient rivalries," each congregation worshipped separately and "no community spirit is developed by these gatherings." Yet, cooperation offset some of these denominational differences. In the Crowsnest Pass before World War I, Methodists agreed to confine their

| *Cardston's annual "Pioneer Days" celebrated the history of Mormons in southern Alberta. Photo dated 1906. Archives Collection, A5642, PAA.*

activities to Bellevue and Frank while the Presbyterians restricted themselves to Coleman and Blairmore. The most well-known example of denominational co-operation was the formation of the United Church of Canada in 1926, but "local union" had been an even earlier feature in some towns. It had begun in Drumheller in 1920, and in Lacombe the Methodists and Presbyterians united (although each retained some autonomy) in 1922. Yet even after the formation of the United Church, the denominational map of Alberta remained complex. In 1931, there were 23 denominations in the Peace River country, while Grande Prairie alone—then a town of just under 1,500—had six resident ministers, plus two congregations visited by itinerant ministers.[8]

If the church demonstrated divisions in town society, its role in tying town and country together was equally problematic. Some churches were built in rural areas as isolated structures to serve the surrounding countryside, and ministers from nearby towns periodically held services at country points. For those who travelled to town to attend church functions, churches were usually located in residential areas, or at best at the end of main street, and rarely provided symbolic or actual linkages between main street and the country. In any event, an economic cross-over between church and town commerce was improbable since all busi-nesses closed on Sundays. Thus, except for weddings, funerals and other church events that might be held on a weekday and which brought country residents to town, churches did not contribute greatly to town commercial life.

An important exception to these patterns was found in Cardston and most Latter-day Saints towns. While churches in other towns were unable to become community focal points because of denominational dif-ferences and social attitudes, the Mormon church was highly successful. In Cardston, its facilities and community activities helped unify social life. The town's religious homogeneity reinforced this role, creating a highly structured and integrated religious environment unusual in other pioneer communities. By the 1890s, LDS social clubs and celebrations provided an opportunity for recreational activities like plays, variety shows and musical events. The installation of a new drop curtain and scenery for the stage in 1911 and gym facilities for basketball in 1914 in Cardston's Assembly Hall demonstrated the church's role in providing recreational facilities for its adherents.[9] The construction of such facili-ties was not solely dependent on local resources. In 1940, for example, a community hall was built in Cardston. The central church organization in Salt Lake City provided cash which the community matched with labour and materials. Attached to the Second Ward Chapel, just off main street, it had a large gymnasium as well as meeting rooms. When the building opened in 1942, at an estimated cost of $97,000, it was a unique church facility in small town Alberta.[10]

FRATERNAL, SERVICE *and* OTHER ORGANIZATIONS

In mining towns, unions were often a focus for social life and a sense of community, even though their function, as well as their political and organizational differences, meant that they rarely represented all workers. Nevertheless, union halls were rented for public occasions. The one in Coleman was built in 1908 and was particu-larly large and well equipped, and was often described as Coleman's "Opera House."[11]

In the early settlement years, fraternal orders like the Oddfellows, the Masons, and the Loyal Orange Lodge were of greater significance in shaping community social life and providing opportunities for leisure. These organizations were active soon after the founding of a town. Drumheller was barely established in 1914 when a lodge of Oddfellows was formed. These clubs emphasized fraternity among members, and also provided life and health insurance and death benefits for members. But they also provided a focus for town social life, and it was said in 1913 that "a good criterion of the life of any town" was "the number and size of its fraternal societies."[12] They were often cited by town promoters as attractions for potential settlers since they were familiar and comforting institutions.[13] At this time, they rarely emphasized community service as their primary objective, as did the service clubs like Lions, Rotary, Elks and Kinsmen which became popular in the 1920s and 1930s.

Fraternal and service club facilities were often used for public events. The Oddfellows and the Masons were usually the first to have a fraternal hall. Often a lodge constructed a building on main street, renting the main level for commercial purposes and using the second floor for lodge meetings. By the end of World War I, many Masonic and Oddfellows lodges had constructed buildings solely for use as fraternal halls, and most Oddfellows continued to let such facilities for public events. Service clubs initially rented halls from fraternal organizations for meetings, but they soon constructed their own halls. The Elks, for example, opened one in Grande Prairie in 1930.[14]

Women's auxiliaries, especially with the fraternal orders, were organized in many towns as well. There were also other women's organizations, the commonest being the Women's Institute and the Imperial Order Daughters of the Empire (IODE), a patriotic club that stressed the British connection. Nonetheless, the fraternal and service organizations, which had male only members, dominated, drawing upon the business and professional class in most towns. The Lions club in Coleman, for example, was organized only when enough businessmen had signalled an intention to join.[15] The Rotary and Kiwanis also aimed for "business and professional men of means," while the Elks club promoted itself as being for men of "ordinary means."[16] Not surprisingly, in the towns studied, the Elks were among the most active and widespread service club before 1947. They represented a wider spectrum of town population than many other service clubs. The one in Blairmore, for example, counted many

| *Fraternal club "carnivals," like this one in the Coleman rink in about 1935, featured games of chance such as Crown and Anchor (left) and raffles and general displays. NC-54-2001, GAI.*

miners among its members, and in 1932 it dissolved for a time when labour troubles deeply divided its membership.[17]

Among the service clubs that drew their membership primarily from the town business class, Rotary aimed to have "one active representative man from each line of business and profession in the community." It combined a pledge of community service with a promise to promote ethical business and professional conduct as well as personal development through "good fellowship" and by "making acquaintance of men you ought to know."[18] This business orientation often brought Rotary Clubs into a close relationship with boards of trade. This was a natural development because of the trend among boards of trade after World War I to view improved social and living conditions as important for attracting industry and stimulating economic growth. The service club fit neatly into such changing views about why towns were successful.

In Drumheller, almost all Rotary members also belonged to the board of trade. Showing an identity of interest, the two organizations sometimes held joint luncheon meetings. This common interest was also

demonstrated in 1934 when the Rotary Club built an auto camp to promote tourism in the area. Similarly, in 1936 the Cardston Rotary club
arranged for the town band to play on the street corners on Saturday
evenings as part of a shopping promotion. Their effort made the main
street "a place of business and pleasure combined." Such shared interests
were not exclusive to Rotary. The transformation of the Claresholm board
of trade into a Men's Club in 1935 also reflected this marriage of commercial and social interests. While it promoted the town in traditional board
of trade fashion, it also used service club techniques in promoting community development and fellowship.[19]

Service clubs were highly regarded by town promoters. In 1938 in
Coleman, they were "a desirable organization in a town" because they
promoted "the neighborly spirit of goodwill and friendship." They
offered sociability for members, public entertainment, and pledged to
work for community betterment. A popular route to these ends were the
"carnivals" that many of them mounted. In Blairmore, the Elks club put
on an ice carnival shortly after the club was organized. Including events
like fancy skating, skaters in comic costumes, and a carnival queen, it
helped raise funds and quickly established the club's community profile.
It was hoped that candidates for queen could be drawn from "each
nationality represented in our population," which in Blairmore would
have meant healthy competition.[20]

Carnivals had great variety and were used for fund raising. Games of
chance and raffles were almost always featured,[21] but also included were
midway attractions, sports, dances, sometimes a stampede, an amateur
show, and a drama festival. These events were immensely popular. In
1931, the Elks club in Grande Prairie sponsored a three-day carnival to
coincide with Dominion Day (now called Canada Day), with the usual
events plus a midway, games of chance, and "daring parachute jumps."
The club also organized a stampede in 1947 which drew between 5,000
and 6,000 people.[22] In contrast to these elaborate productions, other
clubs like the IODE used whist drives and dances as fund raising events.

The projects favoured by service clubs usually involved facilities for
children. The Elks in Grande Prairie built playgrounds, while the Rotary
Club in Drumheller, in addition to other activities, built a swimming
pool.[23] This emphasis on community building through volunteerism and
sociability coincided with the belief that town life was caring and socially responsible and that communities were made by individual effort and
community cohesion.[24] This achieved some genuinely valuable results

that transcended the ethic of growth for its own sake. Swimming pools, for example, though not vital for the community, were a welcome facility for children and were cited by town promoters as proof that their public services were comparable to those of cities.

These clubs also stimulated connections between towns. Fraternal clubs commonly held district, regional and provincial conventions and outings that brought members together. The Oddfellows in southwestern Alberta held their annual picnic in Blairmore in 1913 with representatives from Lethbridge, Fort Macleod, Claresholm, and other points. A street parade was held, including 900 lodge members as well as floats, some sponsored by Blairmore businesses. Sports, a picnic, and a dance followed.[25] All lodges used similar gatherings, and fraternity was further stimulated when members of one lodge attended meetings in neighbouring towns for installation of officers and conferring of degrees.[26] The service clubs copied these methods in building fraternity, but often added a community service component. Thus, when the 17 Elks lodges of the south Peace River country met in 1929, they also put on a community picnic and sports day for children.[27]

Objectives similar to those of fraternal clubs were also met by organizations based directly upon ethnicity. In towns with an overwhelmingly British population, clubs like the St. Andrew's Society were common, although their function seems primarily to have been to organize Burn's anniversary celebrations. In Claresholm, Norwegians were organized through the Sons of Norway, an American ethnic club. The club celebrated May 17, the anniversary of Norwegian independence, and provided social occasions for members. And when lodges of the Italian organizations, the men's Enrico Caruso Lodge and the women's Grande Consillio, were organized in Drumheller in 1934, lodge representatives from Lethbridge, Coleman and other Crowsnest Pass towns attended the inauguration.[28]

In addition to defending their members' interests, veterans' clubs also fulfilled a similar role for veterans by providing opportunities for sociability. There were a number of veterans' organizations operating in Alberta; one of the earliest and most widespread was the Great War Veteran's Association representing veterans of World War I. One was set up in Drumheller in early 1919,[29] but by the early 1930s, most veterans' organizations had been united in the Canadian Legion. The Legion played an active role in most centres, sponsoring the Remembrance Day service in November. It was one of the major public events in small towns in the interwar years, all of which had been touched by the calamity of 1914–18. Yet Remembrance Day did not emerge merely from a shared historical experience, but was deliberately fostered by veterans' organizations which believed that society was forgetting the war and its consequences. In the years immediately after the war, there was no public commemoration of the war, except for a national "Peace Day" in 1919. Instead, veterans met privately and commemorated the war.[30] By the mid 1920s, however, Remembrance Day had become a public event. The Legion sold poppies on the street and also co-ordinated Remembrance Day services in all towns. At first, these were often held in theatres or public halls, but by the 1930s many Legions, in concert with organizations like the IODE, had constructed cenotaphs which became the focus for such services.

The Legion was a complex organization. Its work on behalf of veterans gave it a precise function, but it often expressed a narrow view of Canadian identity. Its defence of the monarchy and "Britishness" was predictable by the late 1920s. Further, its opposition to left-wing radicalism in places like Drumheller and the Crowsnest Pass towns habitually posited that socialism was an act of disloyalty. The Drumheller Legion in 1925 characterised local socialists as "foreigners," while in the Crowsnest Pass the Legion was prominent in anti communist activities. Since many of its members were miners, this cost the Legion some members and/or split the working class, but the organization had sufficient breadth that it did not collapse under such strains.[31]

By the end of World War II the Legion was becoming more service oriented. The club in Claresholm, for example, sponsored a baseball team and supported other sports. As Claresholm members were told in 1946 by Owen Brown of the Legion's Provincial Command, the Legion needed to defend veterans' interests, but it had to abandon the attitude that "we are vets and we want this for us." Otherwise, the organization would fail. He pointed to the success that service clubs had found with children's projects and recommended that the Legion support similar activities. Organizations such as the boy scouts, girl guides, cadets and sports clubs were "bound to be well backed by the community and thus the prestige of the Legion would be raised higher."[32]

The Legion also became more involved in the community through participation in the construction of community centres. A popular idea in the United States by World War I, it was recommended that social centres also be built in Canada.[33] Often envisioned as containing a library, meeting rooms, a large hall for public gatherings, and sometimes sports facilities, they were promoted as fitting war memorials. Capital and operating costs of such facilities were difficult to raise, however, and before World War II only the largest and wealthiest centres could afford them.[34]

The idea of the social centre was revived after World War II as part of post war reconstruction. In 1945, Donald Cameron of the University of Alberta Department of Extension toured the Peace River country promoting this concept. It was well received because it reinforced a common belief that war memorials should be "practical" facilities that enriched community life. These "living war memorials" included hospitals, libraries and community halls. The latter were most popular. It was hoped they would be "removed from any commercialism" so they would be accessible to all classes in commemoration of those who had died in the war. In this context, the Legion club in Grande Prairie planned a memorial hall with three-quarters of the space for public uses.[35] But a voluntary club could not build or operate such complex facilities alone, and they were usually constructed only with town or provincial government assistance.[36]

HOLIDAYS *and* PUBLIC CELEBRATIONS

Holidays, celebrations, and fairs drew hinterland people to a town and kept townspeople and their money at home. In the late nineteenth century, limited transportation and few rival centres meant that Fort Macleod and Cardston experienced little competition for their respective celebrations. Fort Macleod's two days of sports in honour of the queen's birthday in 1883 attracted "about the greatest number of people who have ever been in Macleod at one time." Horse races, cricket, foot races, dances, and variety shows of skits and songs put on by members of the NWMP provided two days of sociability. Significantly, there was no mention that the celebration benefitted Fort Macleod's economy or status.[37]

Events in neighbouring towns and cities soon provided competition for such celebrations. As early as 1891, people from Fort Macleod attended horse races on May 24th in Lethbridge, while the 1907 Lethbridge fair attracted people from Claresholm who took advantage of special train fares. In 1908, no Dominion Day celebrations were held in Claresholm because the Calgary fair was on. Medicine Hat advertised its fair and stampede in 1917 in south-western Alberta and offered reduced charges for accommodation and special rail excursion fares.[38]

The draw of these out-of-town events increased with changes in transportation that allowed people to move around more easily and inexpensively. In this context, by 1900 holidays were no longer commonly described as just a time for sociability, but as a chance to promote the town. Thinking in Cardston was typical. There, it was argued in 1913 that the agricultural fair was "a decided business advantage to a more or less degree to every one of our merchants and business people." Similarly, the attendance of district people at Cardston's two-day Dominion Day celebrations in 1910 was seen as an opportunity for "forging a new link in the chain of good will that binds the towns and villages of this part of Alberta." By 1931, this rationale was still appealing, and as the board of trade argued, "we need a united boosting of the Cardston fair and all such fete days" to popularize the town as "a convention and sports centre."[39]

On statutory holidays like May 24th and Dominion Day, stores were closed, although cafes, poolrooms and bars were open. Retail business was captured the night before when stores stayed open, as well as on the day following the opening day's celebration since these events were often scheduled as two- or three-day affairs. Until the early 1930s, Dominion Day in Grande Prairie was customarily celebrated over two or three days, with a parade and patriotic events on July 1 and sports, horse races, band music, and sometimes a variety show performance on the following days. In 1924, on the evening before the celebration, stores "were all ablaze until a late hour, and business was good, the interior of the shops presenting a Christmas eve appearance." Merchants usually offered sale prices for fair week. Business was also furthered by events at the celebrations. The relatively new feature of a street parade at Fort Macleod's Dominion Day celebrations in 1905 provided some merchants with an opportunity to advertise themselves while entertaining the crowd, estimated at 3,000. At least one-third of all businesses in the town as well as the NWMP and Blood and Peigan Indians participated in the parade. The Natives, dressed in traditional clothing, "gave the people hours of entertainment such as many had not witnessed in their lives." Many of the mercantile floats presented displays of merchandise or patriotic tableaus.[40]

Local promotion was broadened beyond immediate commercial needs by agricultural fairs. They were held periodically in all the towns in the study sample, except those in the Crowsnest Pass. Exhibits of local agricultural produce were inevitably linked to local promotion. Fort Macleod's first fair was held in 1886, and while the exhibits were few, it was said that they helped prove the mixed farming potential of the district—an especially pointed issue at Fort Macleod at the time. Indeed, the use of the agricultural fair as an opportunity to boast about the productivity of the land often seemed to be of greater importance for townspeople than for farmers, the supposed beneficiaries of the event. Because the fair in Grande Prairie in 1916 was backed by local businesses as "an excellent advertisement for the wealth and resources" of the south Peace River country, it was criticized as being nothing more than "a big boost" for the town's merchants. But when a fair was unsuccessful, farmers were often held accountable. When the Claresholm fair of 1918 attracted only poor exhibits, the town blamed the farmers because they sped into the fair grounds in their cars "without bringing any exhibits" which they had formerly brought in wagons. By 1926, the Claresholm fair was back on track. With a midway, races and other entertainment features, it was able to attract a paying crowd and good exhibits.[41]

Claresholm's experience showed that entertainment was important for drawing visitors and exhibitors to fairs. Horse races were a traditional feature of fairs, but a popular entertainment event by the 1920s was a rodeo showcasing calf roping, bucking horses and similar events. In 1927, the three-day fair held in Grande Prairie featured a stampede as well as auto races, horse races, sports, and, for the first time in the Peace River district, a midway. Indeed, stampedes sometimes usurped agricultural fairs. Although it was claimed in 1933 that "the depression killed" Cardston's agricultural fair, it was actually replaced by a rodeo. The first was mounted in 1932, and it gradually took over at the expense of agricultural events. By 1937 the rodeo had become a distinctive event and its profits were used to purchase the fair grounds from the agricultural society and pay the debts of the fair board. In time, the agricultural fair was neither missed nor remembered. The rodeo had taken its place and brought Cardston "increased business and entertainment." In Coleman, which had never had an agricultural fair, the board of trade sponsored a rodeo in 1946 to publicize the town and raise money for a civic centre.[42]

The Calgary Stampede was an important inspiration for these rodeos. A stampede held in Calgary in 1912 drew so many visitors from Fort

Macleod that the town declared a civic holiday. The town band went along as well, and the travellers, in good booster spirit, planned to "advertise" Fort Macleod. After 1923, the Calgary exhibition was combined with a stampede. It was usually front page news in southern Alberta. Claresholm riders competed in the rodeo events and local organizations entered floats in the stampede parade. The Claresholm Sons of Norway float, a replica of Leif Ericson's ship that had been built for Claresholm's Dominion Day celebrations, won first prize in the 1933 stampede parade. By 1939, Claresholm looked like a "deserted village" during the Calgary stampede.[43]

In addition to meeting a need for sociability and promoting business, statutory holidays like May 24th and Dominion Day customarily had a strong patriotic element and served to legitimize and confirm the British nature of Alberta and its dominant culture. The 1927 Dominion Day celebrations in Coleman, marking the sixtieth anniversary of Confederation, featured floats, sports and a patriotic service. Equally important in these terms were the statutory holidays connected with events in the life of the royal family. The personalization of the monarchy occurring in late nineteenth century Britain, where the monarch and the royal family were said to embody Britishness and the nation, had also become a strong feature in Alberta towns by the interwar years. Before World War I, royal events were celebrated only randomly. Sixty years of a reign was a worthy cause to celebrate, and Queen Victoria's diamond jubilee in 1897 was honoured with two days of sports in Fort Macleod, with everyone in "holiday attire," flags flying from every building, and a "grand mounted review" of the NWMP at the sports ground. Yet, the king's birthday might be celebrated in one community but not another. When the king was crowned in 1911, only Coleman among the towns in the Crowsnest Pass celebrated the occasion. In Claresholm, no events were organized because people had other plans.[44]

By the 1930s, events connected with the royal family were uniformly observed as community celebrations. The silver jubilee, marking the 25th year of the reign of George V in 1935, was celebrated in most towns with patriotic services, parades, bonfires, and dances. In Peace River, the day began with school children, RCMP, and veterans parading to a community service consisting of hymns and speeches by the mayor and the Anglican bishop at the Boyd Theatre. Distribution of jubilee mementoes followed, and the rest of the day was taken up with sports. Throughout the country, bonfires were lit at the same time in the evening, and Peace

By the late 1930s, May Day was an important celebration in mining towns. This undated photo shows the May Day parade in Drumheller. Archives Collection, A2920, PAA.

River's bonfire on a hill near the town joined "the chain of bonfires from coast to coast."[45] The coronation of George VI in 1937 was another occasion for parades, sports, dances and fireworks.[46]

In all these celebrations, the monarchy did not merely provide colourful ceremony but confirmed social values. The silver jubilee audience at Peace River in 1935 was told that the colours of the Union Jack reflected the king's service, purity and truth. At the service held in Cardston on the same occasion, it was claimed that as the titular head of a great national family, the king had "the highest regard for the sanctity of the home, holding that disloyalty to the home, disloyalty to wife and children is the unpardonable sin of a true Britisher." Similar sentiments were expressed during visits of Governors General and especially when the king and queen visited Calgary and Edmonton in 1939. People flocked to the cities to see the royal party. Bleachers were allocated to towns along the processional route and special trains offering low fares ran to each city. In Drumheller, fund raising drives collected money to send children to Calgary. So great was the exodus from the town that on Friday morning the streets were "comparatively deserted."[47]

In the Crowsnest Pass, patriotic holidays became part of the area's political and labour struggles. Before the late 1920s, Dominion Day and May 24th were celebrated as elsewhere in the province. May Day, which of course was not a statutory holiday, was also celebrated by Pass miners at least by the early 1920s. Although not exclusively, it, rather than Labour Day, was celebrated by most socialists and communists. By the early 1930s, May Day had become a major celebration in the Pass and at Drumheller, reflecting an intensification of the struggle by labour for recognition, job security and better wages. In 1932, the communists organized the celebration in Blairmore, and a contingent from Coleman marched to the neighbouring town. They paraded behind a banner decorated "with revolvers and red paint to represent blood" and the slogan "Remember Estevan," where three striking miners had been killed by the RCMP. In Drumheller, Labour Day was usually celebrated only as a sports day in the 1930s, but the 1939 May Day parade drew over 1,000 people in an anti fascist parade down main street.[48]

With increased political radicalism among miners, Dominion Day, and especially May 24th, became a focus for anti communists. The British flags flown and carried in marches in the 1932 Dominion Day celebration in Coleman were said to be "an inspiring sight symbolic of unity and loyalty in which all classes of the community joined with enthusiasm." In Blairmore, May 24th celebrations were similarly used to promote the view that socialism was treason. The parade was said to be the largest ever held in the Pass. Instead of floats, there was a large crowd representing local organizations which promoted the Britishness of Canada. The Legion, the boy scouts, the girl guides, the IODE, and various individuals paraded down Blairmore's main street, gathering at the sports field where Union Jacks were presented to the Blairmore boy scouts "for safe keeping." The propaganda was as blunt as that of May Day, but if the message had been missed, the *Blairmore Enterprise* explained that the parade

demonstrated beyond the shadow of a doubt that true loyalty to Country and Flag existed in this district, despite what Communists and disloyal propagandists would say to the contrary. We have of late seen too many flags which are foreign to our general principles and well being in general, that it was quite apparent we as citizens should endeavor to show our hands and display in a definite form how we stand.

| *This detail from a 1930 photograph of Blairmore shows that parades, like this one mounted by a travelling circus, confirmed the main street as the centre of town life. NC-54-2224, GAI.*

The next year, Coleman anti-radical forces arranged for a carnival for the whole week of May 24th in an effort "to offset" the "rotten propaganda of disloyalty and rebellion fostered by traitors to Canada."[49]

Such appeals to tradition and history were not unique to royal visits or national celebrations, nor did they solely arise from the direct challenge of the left. By the 1920s, most towns had gained sufficient confidence and tradition to celebrate their own history. In conjunction with Dominion Day in 1924, the fiftieth anniversary of the arrival of the NWMP and the founding of the town "as an outpost of empire" was celebrated in Fort Macleod. The event took months to organize and cost over $16,000, but its success guaranteed that memories of it would "live for ever." The parade of Natives, floats, beauty queens, decorated cars and bicycles, Red River carts, cowboys and other personalities was the largest ever mounted in the town, taking 90 minutes to pass a viewing point. The celebration also included a stampede, a carnival, an "Indian village," sports, and four bands playing at various sites. Over 30,000 people, many from Lethbridge and Pincher Creek, attended the three-day celebration.[50]

Similarly, Cardston honoured its history in 1937, celebrating the fiftieth anniversary of the town and of Mormonism in Canada. The parade was described as "linking the past and present, the peoples of Canada and the United States, the white and red races." The parade by Natives "brought back vividly the days when they roamed the country in their wild and picturesque state." While white settlement had meant dispossession, this was resolved by an appeal to "the harmony which had always existed between our pioneers and their Indian friends."[51] At the same time, the inclusion in the parade of the bands and cadets from nearby Indian residential schools presented yet another view of the consequences of this friendship.

The main street was a primary site for all of these celebrations. The parades were a "public ritual" which helped convey the message of the event.[52] They launched the most important events and took place along the main street, confirming it as the heart of the town. Parades also served to link the celebration, which often took place on the fringe of the town at the fair or sports ground, to the main street. In keeping with the hope of projecting sociability and progressiveness, the streets were often decorated. For Cardston's fiftieth anniversary celebrations, the main street was oiled and buildings were painted, with the result that "there is not a shabby front on the whole main street. It is a joy to those of us who live here to be in such a progressive, clean beautiful town." Decorations were put up along the main street and "right here on Main street" were "hot dog stands, restaurants, concessions, fortune telling booths, ferris wheel rides, midway, Indian Village, and everything that goes to make up a real show." The historic Card house, the home of the founder of Cardston, was restored and made into a local historic site for the celebration. One visitor commented that Cardston had "been boosted ahead" 20 years by its "outstanding and splendid celebration."[53]

Such elaborate street decorations were common at the most important events. In honour of the coronation in 1937, Grande Prairie's streets were "flanked with waving flags, festooned bunting, heraldic crests, and backed with continuous store windows honoring King George and Queen Elizabeth in effigies enshrined in displays of royal colors." Similar use of window decoration appeared during Fort Macleod's fiftieth anniversary celebrations in 1924. The display in the windows of Ferguson's Drug store of historical photographs and artifacts was "a big centre of attraction, especially so to the many oldtimers," while the windows of R.T. Barker's Menswear store contained a replica of the old police fort.[54] Another popular street decorating scheme was to line the street with cut trees; usually conifers. While sometimes used at Christmas, this was also done at other events in both summer and winter. In Cardston, holes were drilled in the edge of the sidewalk in 1926 so flag poles could be put up for celebrations. Sometimes, lights were also strung across the street and were often cited as an example of the town's modernity and progress. As was said in Fort Macleod in 1924, the main street was "like Broadway, lights, laughter and merriment, and myriads of people."[55]

SPORTS

Sports days were popular events in the towns studied, and sometimes celebrations like Dominion Day and May 24 were little more than a day of sports. In summer, most towns had mid-week half-day holidays, which were also often justified as a time for sports. Claresholm, among others, observed Wednesday afternoon closing by 1910, but there was a general fear that nearby towns, which did not close at the same time, would pick up trade by default or that farmers would be irritated because the stores were closed. Peace River businesses, for example, only began closing Wednesday afternoons in 1932 when all other towns in the area had agreed to do so. A decade earlier, it had been argued in Peace River that such a holiday was needed because baseball games could not be held on Sunday without a "fight from the churches."

This was a common justification for Wednesday afternoon closing, but it also expressed a broader need for leisure. As was said in Cardston in 1915, "it is none too much fun that any of us gets out of life after we reach the working age and a half day a week is little enough." The half-day holiday broke the monotony and provided an opportunity for physical exercise. This was not a denial of work. The "inspiration of the freedom from the shackles" brought by a mid week break made people work "the more intelligently and more industriously."[56] By the late 1920s, such breaks were also provided by winter carnivals. Among the earliest were those in Peace River, Grande Prairie, and Claresholm. Typically, they featured dog races, skiing, hockey, curling, and, among others, skating.[57]

The justification of a mid week holiday in terms of sports and physical exercise, as well as their prominence in almost all public celebrations and holidays, revealed the importance of sports in town life. They were the most common form of recreation and were believed to create cohesion among townspeople. One resident of Peace River argued in 1922 that local people, rather than attending events in nearby towns, "should take more interest in their home town, and encourage sports, etc, for it all counts in making a town." Indeed, it was contended in Claresholm that organized sports created "a civic consciousness and civic community cohesiveness."[58]

The social benefits of sport also included character building, a notion that was widespread throughout Alberta and the rest of the country.[59] In Peace River in 1936, increasing difficulty in recruiting young players for the baseball team raised the spectre that an aging team had little future, as did a country which neglected sports. "In Old England, it is said, future battles are won on the rugger fields, and it is also true in a measure that the baseball fields aid materially in the development of young men." This inevitably led to the conclusion that sports prevented juvenile delinquency. "Devilishness" in boys, said the *Grande Prairie Herald* in 1928, was only "an overdose of health." They had a "certain amount of steam to let off," which if not released through sports would find "some other avenue." This familiar argument led some people in Lacombe to argue in 1942 that "planned sports have no equal in the building of both mind and body." Thus, better sports facilities and programmes were needed to counter a perceived increase in juvenile delinquency said to result from wartime enlistment and longer working hours.[60]

In addition to these social benefits, sports were said to contribute to a town's economic well being. The Drumheller senior hockey team, one of the most successful senior teams in Alberta in the 1930s, fell apart in the early years of World War II. This cost the town a source of entertainment, but Drumheller business owners also contended that the town had lost "an industry that is worth at least $35,000 annually" in players' wages and trade from visiting fans. Moreover, sports promoted a town as a central place, or as was argued in Blairmore in 1910, "a good team in any line of athletics is a splendid advertisement." The Drumheller board of trade in 1914 managed all team sports in the town, giving up the task only in 1919 when it was criticized for being little more than a sports club. This function was informally taken up again in 1925 when the town's businessmen subscribed $200 to purchase uniforms for the senior baseball team. Until then, the team's uniforms were "much like Joseph's coat, of many hues and textures," but in their new "natty uniforms with a big 'D' on the breast pocket, our bunch will be able to step out and trim anything in sight." Such bravado was confirmed when a league or provincial sporting victory created a permanent record of town success. When the Cardston team won the provincial intermediate baseball championship cup for the second time in 1935, it was hailed as giving the town "real fame" in Alberta's sport history. "Each year the name of the winning team is engraved on the cup, and Cardston's name now appears twice." Not coincidentally, the board of trade put on a banquet to toast the team's success.[61]

The emphasis on building community and promoting the town created an inherent bias in favour of team sports which in theory were thought to demonstrate social cohesion. Especially popular were curling, hockey, and baseball, although nonteam sports, such as lawn tennis, commercial boxing, and wrestling were also popular. With the construction of golf courses during the interwar years, such as the one in Lacombe in 1927, golf also emerged as a popular sport with middle and upper class townspeople. Many other sports, such as lacrosse, badminton, football, basketball, cricket, quoits and horseshoes, were played intermittently between 1900 and 1945 or found favour in one community but not in others.

The emphasis overall, however, was on team sports. While there were many women's hockey and especially softball teams, men's teams gained greatest exposure and support because they were most prominently organized by provincial and regional leagues. Individual success in a sport of course brought credit to a town, and individuals who won a provincial or national sports event were often feted.[62] But too much individualism was seen as a bad thing for a town. By 1932, organized team sports in Claresholm had dropped off badly in favour of "single family" outings like picnics. The local newspaper editorialized that while these might be "very enjoyable," they did not develop "inspiration or community spirit. Let's sacrifice a few of our individual enterprises and see if the interest of the community cannot be advanced by mutual effort."[63]

Public reaction to these team sports varied. At times, enthusiasm was very high and only a fine line separated it from disorder. In 1910, the mayor of Claresholm suggested that to sustain the town's reputation, townspeople's enthusiasm for the baseball team should be "confined to gentlemanly expressions." In the previous year, the crowd had shouted racist taunts at a visiting Metis player, and the mayor clumsily commented that "so long as he plays on a team he is one of the boys and is as much entitled to respect as any other player." Similarly, Coleman crowds in 1934 were told that "using obscene language and hurling abusive epithets at hockey players is unsportsmanlike and disgraceful."[64] But maintaining public enthusiasm for the games was equally problematic. In many towns, a team's success would gain public support, but interest would then wane and the team would temporarily disband. The Crowsnest Pass, where people tended to be obsessed with sports, was the exception, and team sports often focused rivalries between towns or political groups.

The intermittent support evident in many towns was partly related to financial and organizational problems. Successful teams could usually count on financial support through public subscriptions, but with failure, contributions dried up.[65] Businesses often sponsored a team, but they risked "being left very much out of pocket at the end of the season."[66] As well, teams were supported by service clubs, such as the Claresholm Elks club which funded the town's hockey team in 1926.[67] These approaches, however, did not provide secure funding from year to year, and this situation reinforced the primacy of hockey and baseball which were organized in local and provincial leagues. This helped draw large crowds and the gate helped to reduce sponsors' expenses. Professionalization also had the same effect, and as a result, senior men's amateur hockey was said to be surrounded by a "camouflage." Rules to discourage professionalism, such as residence rules, were evaded and ways were found to pay wages to players. This meant that senior hockey was feasible only in centres that could afford it. In 1938 it was said to cost at least $8,000 to field a team for the league, while one good enough to reach the national finals would probably cost between $20,000 and $30,000. "Winter employment" offers of $75 per month made by the Drumheller Miners in 1937 "found no takers" and these "wages" had to be increased. In such conditions, amateurism was said to be a sham. Similarly, both Blairmore and Coleman in the early 1920s imported hockey players, and once a team in a league adopted this strategy, it inevitably spread to others.[68]

While there were many efforts to organize sports locally, most proved unsuccessful in the long term. One commonly suggested approach was the formation of an athletic association. One citizen in Claresholm in 1911 argued that such an association with centralized fund raising would save each team the task of "harassing the citizens" for money. Similarly, in 1939 an athletic association in Peace River was proposed to create stability and to free individual sponsors from the burden of supporting the team. This would allow the economical distribution of funds and in the "long run" save "the merchant money."[69] The failure of such associations was perhaps due to a reluctance on the part of the public to make long-term financial commitments. More importantly, these voluntary approaches were unable to maintain themselves on a permanent basis in the absence of a local co-ordinating body.

This problem was demonstrated by the difficulty in maintaining branches of the Amateur Athletic Association (AAA), the central regulatory and organizing body for amateur sports in the province. A branch was formed in Blairmore in 1929, but it disbanded relatively quickly. Only in Cardston was a branch of the AAA successful. Formed in the early 1920s with the sponsorship of the Mormon church, by 1925 it was organizing local basketball, boxing, wrestling and track and field. The Cardston AAA raised funds through memberships, ticket sales and by organizing tournaments. It also held a carnival to raise money, but soon abandoned this approach because it involved gambling which was "degrading to the standards of good clean sport."[70] The success of the Cardston AAA owed much to the support of the Mormon church, and in towns without such a strong co-ordinating body, the AAA did not enjoy similar success.

The same limitations were experienced in providing sports facilities. Commercial boxing and wrestling—which were immensely popular— were easily accommodated in commercial theatres or community or lodge halls, such as the Opera House in Drumheller. Specialized commercial sports facilities, however, were rarely successful. The rink in Grande Prairie in 1925 was owned by a number of businessmen, but it was unprofitable. Similarly, Blairmore Arena Ltd., which began operations in 1923, was in difficulty by 1934. It had "not paid one cent in dividends," had large tax arrears, and the rink was in such poor repair that it was questionable if it could open for the coming season. In Drumheller, the private skating rink was successful as long as the senior hockey team did well, but when the hockey club collapsed in 1940, the rink began to lose money.[71]

In contrast to these private commercial facilities, those built by service clubs had better fortune. The clubs provided the necessary capital and sometimes operating funds, and the facility avoided property taxes since it was not for profit. Moreover, it was usually built on public land and received other public support. Swimming pools were the most successful of these facilities. They were major projects, involving considerable funds and complicated engineering. The Rotary club in Drumheller began construction of a swimming pool in 1926 and finished it in 1928. It raised about $6,700 for the project during construction and afterwards continued to manage and subsidize it when necessary. Slightly earlier, the Elks club in Coleman had opened a swimming pool at a cost of about $4,000, while the Claresholm Men's Club opened one in 1942. Pools were seen as valuable community facilities. They were fashionable and city-like, and gave children something to do during the summer and kept them off the streets.[72]

Sports facilities were also provided by volunteer sporting clubs. While private clubs ran golf courses in a few towns,[73] rinks built and operated by hockey or curling clubs which raised money by selling shares and memberships were more common. The most successful of these club facilities were curling rinks, which relied on participants rather than spectators for income. Curling was very popular among men and women, and the rink served as a meeting place.[74] Skating rinks were also built in the same way. The first ones were open air, often constructed by a club for one season on a vacant lot and moved the next year to a different location if necessary. They were often unpopular with spectators and players, and demands for covered rinks were persistent.[75] Since few clubs could afford more elaborate facilities, some towns built their own rinks and financed them through debenture debt. The popularity of team sports, and their perceived role in building community, legitimized such government expenditures. These rinks were usually located wherever the town owned land, usually near the edge of the town, although more central locations were used when available. Lacombe issued $6,500 in debentures in 1912 to construct a skating and curling rink.[76] A handful of other Alberta towns also had municipally owned rinks by 1930—Claresholm opened a municipal skating and curling rink in 1927. Fort Macleod opened one in 1930 on the Court House square, which had previously been used as a playing field.[77] By the 1940s, artificial ice was in demand in order to attract larger crowds and permit scheduled hockey games. This was justified in southern Alberta where chinooks could destroy a scheduled game in hours, but status also played a part. As the *Drumheller Mail* phrased it in 1947 when arguing for artificial ice in the civic arena, "our civic pride demands that we have an arena in keeping with a city of our importance."[78]

The appeal to civic pride often made in respect to sporting facilities demonstrated another way in which the booster ethos was integral to small town culture. With the exception of Cardston, the tendency of religious denominationalism to fragment rather than unify social life placed churches at variance with the booster values of social and cultural uniformity. Further, church attendance was usually too limited or irregular for the church to become a major unifying social institution. In any event, by the interwar years service clubs had become an alternative means of providing this focus. Although there were class differences among clubs, they had immense appeal because they were fashionable and they drew on booster notions about the inherent uniformity of the community and an identity of interest between business and the town. The fact that they combined fun with social purpose gave them further appeal. Public holidays were similarly incorporated into town ambitions. In all of these events, the necessity of combining "fun" with the pursuit of growth and social uniformity revealed the extent to which mass public leisure and its ethos had penetrated towns by the interwar years.

In this process, the main street retained its importance in town life by linking commerce with celebration and fun. Sports also demonstrated this link, especially through their promotion of civic pride and the financial support teams gained from town businesses. Yet sports also ultimately helped to diminish the role of the main street in town life. The cost of land and the location of town-owned lots were often the prime factors governing the location of rinks and playing fields, rather than their relationship to other town facilities. Because they tended to be located away from the main street, or were at its margins, sports facilities began to create a new dynamic and to challenge the main street's centrality in town life.

12

ENHANCING
the COMMUNITY:
PARKS *and*
HORTICULTURE

The concern with beauty expressed in the 1913 and 1929 planning legislation assumed that trees, gardens, and parks enhanced civic life. Parks were said to be places of "rest and beauty," especially for mothers and children. They were valuable for children's physical and moral development because their "surroundings have a large share in the making of their minds." These concerns posited that parks and beauty stimulated society to function at its highest capacity.[1] Such arguments were common everywhere in Canada from the late nineteenth century, but on the prairies, they had added force. In 1913, it was contended that Lacombe needed a "park and downtown gardens" to make the town attractive. Even towns "on the bleak prairie" and located in less fertile areas had such amenities. Land suitable for a park was available near the downtown, and it was recommended that parks be laid out in residential areas as well since parks would be "a splendid investment for the town."[2]

PARK DEVELOPMENT

The reaction of local authorities to the value of formal parks was generally positive, although park development was often stymied because land development emphasized individual profit-making and paid little attention to community social and aesthetic needs. Town surveys rarely included provision for parks until 1913 when the province required that reserves of land for public parks or public works be provided. All plans subsequently included park space, but it was usually located at the edge of the town instead of as an integral part of the town's design. Thus, parks generally were not a priority, an attitude demonstrated in Drumheller where park land had been reserved along the river east of the main street. Efforts to develop the site in 1918 caused grumbling about its cost, and volunteers could not be found to fence the site, clear brush, and build benches and swings. As the *Drumheller Mail* editorialized, it was no "wonder that our town is lacking in the little things that go to make life worth while," since "the fight for the almighty dollar takes up all the time at the disposal of our citizens."[3]

Such difficulties were not encountered everywhere, and parks were developed when they had the backing of an influential community group. A park was built in Lacombe by The Lest We Forget Club, a women's club formed among relatives of veterans and men killed in World War I. Opening in 1924 on land near the downtown, it featured lawns, shrubs, trees, flowers, and a statue inscribed with the names of men from Lacombe and district who had been killed in the war. It was said to provide a place for passive enjoyment and reflection, and this objective continued to define its purpose.[4]

In other cases, parks evolved into spaces with a more active orientation. This demonstrated a shift in popular views about the function of parks and the ideals of town life. In Claresholm, a park was developed as a place where the town band could put on public concerts. The band played on street corners, but in 1914 it built a temporary bandstand opposite the main street. It was "brilliantly lighted with electrical lights" and the music "took the monotony out of the whole evening." In 1917, the band attempted to lease land from the CPR for a permanent bandstand opposite the main street, but the railway "absolutely refused." This drew in the local branch of the IODE, which secured land from the town and planted grass and trees and built a bandstand. The bandstand was still in periodic use by the early 1930s, and the park was still seen as a place of rest—in 1932 the town prohibited baseball games in the park because ruined the grass. By 1938, however, athletic activities in the park had been confirmed: tennis courts and a wading pool for children were operating, and the Men's Club and the town jointly undertook to plant trees and re-seed the grass "to make the park a beauty spot as well as a playground for the children." This approach was taken further when the Men's Club began construction of a swimming pool. This too was located in the park, leading one irate resident to ask, "Why build it in the park? It is the only spot in the town which can be beautified, and why spoil it with an unsightly bunch of concrete?"[5] Such views were increasingly anachronistic. The park's dedication to children's recreation was logical in light of the historical justification of parks as playgrounds, and the installation of modern facilities like a swimming pool reflected changing objectives for public park space and approaches to building community.

The evolution of the park at Coleman was similar. A park was laid out in 1909 in a ravine on land donated to the town by the International Coal and Coke Company. It was called Flumerfelt Park in honour of one of the company's executives. From its beginning, the park served a dual function as a place of picturesque beauty and an athletic ground. It had a field for sports, as well as "shady slopes and winding woody paths." Development was handled by the town and the board of trade, which installed "permanent and artistic" improvements. The park was well used and generally well kept, although by the end of World War I the fence around the athletic field was "gradually disappearing, being carried away piecemeal," presumably for firewood. By 1928, the park was still considered a place of "natural beauty" and a sheltered spot "with the murmur of the stream to soothe the feelings." It also had tennis courts, and by 1947 the Lion's Club had proposed a paddling pool, and plans were also afoot to construct a civic centre there.[6]

The evolution of the parks at Coleman and Claresholm illustrated changes in public expectations about public space and leisure opportunities. By the early 1930s town planning commissions often proposed development of parks to improve civic life. These parks were usually dedicated to athletics, and as was commented in Grande Prairie, the town planning commission's recommendation for an athletic park deserved support because "wholesome games" encouraged morality. While sports had been one element of park design before World War I, the increased use of parks as playing fields showed a significant change in public expectations. Playgrounds for children continued to be a significant part of public parks, and most towns did not construct separate facilities for children. In Drumheller, however, E.A. Toshach, a local merchant, built a children's playground near his home in about 1929. With swings, slides, sand piles, and a skating rink lit with electricity, it was a unique gesture of community sentiment.[7]

In addition to public parks, bandstands also provided an area for public leisure. The development of a park specifically as a site for a bandstand, as at Claresholm, was unusual. Instead, they were commonly located on a small plot of land somewhere along or near the main street or on the railway right-of-way. At Blairmore, the strip of land between the tracks and the main street had often been described as an eye sore, and in 1921 it was planted with grass and a bandstand was built. Though it served as a place for local bands to entertain the public, it took on a quite different role during the labour troubles of the late 1920s and early 1930s. As a platform for labour and political speakers and a site for demonstrations, the bandstand became a community institution quite different than that originally intended.[8]

HORTICULTURE *and*
TOWN BEAUTY

The view that parks could improve character was part of a general belief that environment influenced character. Mimicking the rhetoric about parks and beauty, gardening and tree planting were linked with clean-up campaigns in an effort to beautify towns. As was observed in 1913 in Lacombe, "we unconsciously try to live up to our environment. If this is true of adults, it is doubly true of children." Gardening and tree planting were said to make the small town a refuge, confirming it as home to the upcoming generation and helping retain town population. As it was phrased in Cardston in 1914, the town should be beautified with trees and gardens to become "a centre of interest, taste and refinement so that none will care to leave us and outsiders will want to settle in such a community."[9]

Several studies have argued that a significant element in prairie landscaping efforts was an attempt to reshape the natural landscape in accordance with immigrants' ideals of beauty and memories of their former homes.[10] This reflected an often ambiguous definition of "home." It was the place from which immigrants had come, and at the same time it was the place where they were making a new life in Alberta. Trees, gardens and lawns were visual proof of stability and permanence. Reflecting a feeling that the natural landscape was alien, the prairies were popularly said to be drab and monotonous. In 1929 it was commented in Peace River that to understand the beauty trees provided, one only had to compare "an eastern town with its wealth of shade trees and a prairie town devoid of trees but heavy on packing boxes." The comparison was not based merely on envy, but also reflected a longing for a different history and former homes. In 1947 it was remarked in Grande Prairie that "nothing can take the place of trees to give a small town that air of gracious living." Those who remembered "the tree shaded streets of every village and town 'back east' will understand what trees do for a town. Those towns too were once bare and ugly. It took years for the trees to grow and mellow the harsher outlines. Never put off planting a tree for another year." Accordingly, tree planting was said to be a commitment to the future. When the Peace River board of trade began planting trees on boulevards and other public spaces in 1935, it observed that in 30 or 40 years people would "look back with pride and say, we are glad our parents planted trees in the proper places at the proper time."[11]

Such assumptions fit nicely with interwar rhetoric about civic pride and its connection to home, business, and town growth. In an expression of these sentiments, the *Coleman Journal* editorialized in 1938 that "if we have to live in a place, by all means make it as cheerful and attractive as possible, and set an example of progress. It would increase local pride." And an important reference for civic pride was the judgement of outsiders. In 1929 Drumheller residents were warned that visitors assessed the character of local citizens by the exterior of their homes and streets. Garbage littering the town indicated "slovenly inhabitants" while neat yards, lawns, trees, and flowers suggested "good citizens, interested not only in their own personal pleasures but with a sense of community pride."[12]

A unique expression of community pride occurred in 1934 when Blairmore's communist town council began the "beautification" of main street. The council changed the street's name from Victoria Street, presumably after Queen Victoria, to Tim Buck's Boulevard, in honour of the Canadian communist leader. New street signs were constructed, lights were placed down the centre of the street, sprinklers were installed, and trees and shrubs were planted. The sprinklers were apparently designed to settle the dust on the street. The redesign of the street honoured Buck and the communist victory in Blairmore's elections. It was also part of the campaign to have Buck freed from prison, where he was incarcerated because of his leadership of the communist party, an organization banned by the Canadian government at the time. The street was highly controversial and a source of much comment, but Tim Buck Boulevard lasted only about two years. It was expensive to maintain, and in 1937 the town council restored the historical name of the street and placed the light standards along the sides of the street to better illuminate the sidewalks.[13]

While the ideal town was lush with trees and vegetation, rapid development without attention to preserving or planting trees made later beautification difficult. In 1913 it was noted that the "numerous angles" of Lacombe's downtown streets had provided opportunities for a downtown park and tree planting, but "it is too late now for that" because the business area had been built up almost completely. In the Peace River country too, the towns were barren because the area had been methodically stripped of native trees. In 1935 it was remarked in Peace River that "we see in this northland a too frequent desire to destroy all and any trees in sight, with the result that much of the natural beauty has been marred." Most of these trees had been cut in the laying out of the town, but others had been used as street decorations for holidays and festivals. In Peace River there had once been "a great number of beautiful spruce trees" located in an area set aside for a park, but by 1935 "hardly a spruce can be found in the said plot. Why? Simply because the trees have been used to temporarily decorate the streets, and in a few days these same trees have been drawn away and burned or left on the ice to disappear in the spring."[14]

In addition to reasons of sentiment and emulation, tree planting was said to bring direct economic benefits. The value of trees in conserving moisture was an important argument in the late nineteenth century, especially in southern Alberta, and tree planting was routinely recommended as a solution to the aridity of the region. Generally, pleasant surroundings were also said to be conducive for business. In an attempt to make it clear that concern for beauty was not effeminate, it was remarked in Lacombe in 1913 that "a man can be more of a man" when surrounded by a beautiful landscape than "if surrounded by that which is unlovely and dreary. We drink in our surroundings, and to some extent become like them." Merchants in a beautiful town were "likely to be more pleasant to do business with," and more ambitious than if continually exposed to "tumble down houses surrounded by dirty yards." Moreover, visitors would speak well of a town, enhancing its reputation with settlers and investors. Increased tourism was also added to the arsenal of reasons for town beautification. As was remarked in Cardston in 1914, "make the place attractive, and they [tourists] will stay and spend their money here."[15] As part of an effort to make the town attractive for tourists, Lacombe main street merchants placed flower boxes along the street in 1935, and the Men's Club in Claresholm undertook a similar project. In Cardston, the excellence of the landscaping around the court house was likened to "a demonstration farm for the town."[16]

Another way to meet these objectives was to establish a garden at the town's train station. As the primary means of travel before 1920, this was important for town promotion. Travellers formed their first, and possibly their only impression of a town from the train. The CPR commonly laid out formal gardens around important train stations like Red Deer and Medicine Hat, but smaller centres also benefited from this policy. The gardens were welcomed and town boards of trade, such as in Claresholm in 1911, often urged rail companies to lay out gardens to make the approach to the town more attractive and to provide townspeople with a "pleasant place" for outings and community gatherings.[17] CPR gardens were located across the country and usually employed "geometrical, balanced and regular" designs. The one in Fort Macleod was "laid out in ornamental flower beds, and rows of trees four deep have been planted around the boundaries." It had a central circular garden with a 4.5 metre mound topped with a bandstand. The CPR continued to maintain most of these gardens until after World War II.[18]

While horticultural efforts represented a mix of personal, financial, aesthetic, and even overtly political objectives, there were several barriers to their success. Initially, it was widely believed that the climate of the province prevented successful cultivation of most flowers, fruit and ornamental shade trees. As well, some people believed that it was "too much trouble" since settlers had more important tasks than caring for trees and flowers.[19] Expense was another consideration, and plants grown only for beauty were sometimes thought to be frivolous. As the *Macleod Gazette* contemptuously observed in 1893, although the town was dreary without trees, many residents' "sole ambition and aim in this world appears to be the raising of cabbages and other garden truck." Perhaps such attitudes were inevitable during the frontier phase, and as was commented in Lacombe in 1913, "in a new country beauty has often to give place to utility. In a young town much that is crude and unsightly is likely to be tolerated, until what is absolutely necessary for present needs has been provided." But such justification was valid for only a short time. Although located in a fertile district, Lacombe had "a bare, almost barren aspect," especially in the business district. Clearly, part of maturity and success on the frontier meant overcoming necessity, but "the day has arrived for Lacombe to pay more attention to appearances than has yet been the case." Other towns were in a similar state. It was contended in Claresholm in 1909 that the town needed to pay more attention to horticulture because it, "like so many other towns in the west, is woefully bare of attractiveness. It's a place to do business in and that's about all."[20]

Efforts to overcome apathy and disinterest in horticulture gave rise to various proposals. If the expense of obtaining trees from nurseries was a barrier, it was commonly said that native trees could be transplanted at little cost, and this was indeed a popular and common practice.[21] Another tactic was proposed in Fort Macleod in the 1890s when it was recommended that a portion of property taxes be remitted to ratepayers who planted trees on their property. Bylaws to this effect were twice drafted and received enthusiastic endorsement from the local press, but they were both defeated by the town council.[22] A more popular approach was to institutionalize tree planting and gardening. Arbor Day was the earliest expression of this approach. It was set aside by the territorial government in 1886 as a public holiday devoted to tree planting.[23] Yet, as the *Macleod Gazette* observed in 1888, observance of Arbor Day did not suggest that trees should be planted only on one day in the year. Rather, it should be an inspirational event to stimulate tree planting throughout the spring.[24] In general, however, even the most optimistic proponents admitted that Arbor Day was poorly observed, although a handful of trees were usually planted. Complaints were made that the day fell too late in the season for successful tree planting in Alberta, but, more importantly, greater organization was needed. Thus, boards of trade and private clubs often established horticultural committees to promote tree planting and gardening. Given the economic justifications for tree planting, their involvement in such campaigns was logical. Other organizations were also committed to tree planting: in 1928, in an effort to beautify the approach to the town, the Grande Prairie Women's Institute planted poplar trees along the street from the station to the town, and the next year the Canadian Club planted maple trees in an effort to beautify the town and familiarize townspeople with the national symbol.[25]

A popular means of encouraging interest in tree planting and gardening was the formation of horticultural societies. As early as 1909, the Presbyterian Ladies Club in Claresholm organized a flower show. While such societies were functioning before World War I, their greatest popularity came during the interwar years. In an effort to make the town attractive, the Claresholm board of trade organized a highly successful horticultural society in 1928. A similar society was organized in 1918 at Bellevue in the Crowsnest Pass, and its annual shows and garden competitions became notable events for people throughout the area. Other efforts to encourage and educate the public about horticulture came from government agencies and private organizations. The horticultural work of the federal experimental farms in testing hardiness of plants and distributing seedlings was important, as was the work of the Canadian Forestry Association which mounted exhibits in a rail car during the interwar years. The Tree Planting Car toured the country and usually received a favourable reaction: by June 1938, mid way through its tour of that year, it had already visited 48 towns in Canada and had drawn an estimated 17,000 visitors. Its reception in Cardston in 1920 was much like that in Drumheller in 1942. Both drew good audiences to listen to lectures, watch films and look at displays about tree planting, landscaping, and gardening.[26]

In addition to voluntary efforts, town councils also undertook tree planting. The *Blairmore Enterprise* argued in 1921 that the town should emulate Calgary, which since 1912 had planted 29,000 trees, being "precisely 28,991 more than were planted in Blairmore in the same period." By the mid 1920s, however, Blairmore had planted between 600 and 1,000 balm of gilead along main street. Between 1925 and 1939, Drumheller also planted thousands of trees on boulevards and other public spaces. The town did not, however, provide routine maintenance for them, and residents were required to prune and care for trees planted in front of their property.[27]

By 1930, these efforts had brought results in many places. With few exceptions, however, individual businesses remained unresponsive to tree planting or other horticultural efforts, even though, as one Grande Prairie observer noted, landscaping by the Imperial Bank of its lot showed how easily a business place could be made "positively beautiful." Nevertheless, tree planting and horticulture were usually left to the town or to home owners. Claresholm had many notable private gardens, and Cardston, in comparison to a decade before, had been greatly enhanced through tree planting and gardening. Even so, there were a number of difficulties to be overcome. Weeds spread quickly because of poor maintenance of vacant lots, including those owned by the towns, and lax enforcement of the province's noxious weeds regulations. In addition, carelessness was often a problem. In Drumheller, for example, the habit of parking on the boulevards killed many of the trees planted there by the town.[28] The greatest threat to horticultural projects, however, came from animals running at large.

Before World War II, gardening was a highly risky venture since newly planted trees and private gardens were often destroyed by livestock and poultry. Gardeners became disheartened and gave up when "a herd of cattle or a team of horses spend the night on the front lawn" and chickens scratched up the garden.[29] Although cows were no longer wandering at will on the streets of Cardston in 1934, they were kept by many townspeople and were driven to pasture each day. And, "many a citizen these days is wondering. Wondering who has the right of way—the home loving and home beautifying citizen or the cow trailed by a playing boy who allows that cow to run over lawns and gardens with impunity, breaking off branches and often whole trees, and otherwise messing up the premises." Those who objected to such innocence were called "cranky and ill-tempered," but the matter so fundamentally challenged efforts to beautify the town that "sentiment must be cast to the winds."[30] While at least a moderate level of control was achieved during the interwar years, animals were still running at large in some centres as late as the end of World War II.

Despite the persistence of such problems, the results of tree planting campaigns had become evident by World War II when many towns had tree-lined streets. Yet the commitment to such beautification was always easily compromised. If trees interfered with sidewalk development or installation and operation of street lights, they were often removed with little reluctance. In 1940, for example, Lacombe cut down a number of trees because they shaded the new street lights.[31] Another factor that perhaps shaped attitudes to public gardening and parks was the nature of housing in Alberta towns. The great majority of people lived in detached houses, with yards that could be developed as private gardens. This, in combination with other factors, contributed to an emphasis on private rather than public gardening, illustrating how one aspect of social autonomy affected town development and the expression of community.

PART

V

CONCLUSION

13

TOWN LIFE

The history of Alberta towns contains parallels with David Rayside's findings about the contemporary political life of a small Ontario town which he describes as "the politics of consensus in which divisive and consequential issues are avoided." Instead, the "safe issues" in town politics are pursued—upholding private property, individual initiative, limited government, and unimpeded growth. Rather than interpreting this consensus as a "normal" state of affairs, Rayside sees it as a reflection of the ability of local business people to shape and determine the issues of town political life. This is achieved, he argues, not by collusion or by explicit pressure on municipal government, but because of the town's culture, its limited tax base and economy, and because of its economic and political dependence on outside investors and the provincial government.[1]

In many ways, Alberta and Ontario towns both bear the legacy of boosterism and point to common town culture in different parts of the country. Whether in its pre World War I versions or its later variants, boosterism combined with local business priorities to create a certain mindset. This encompassed the view that local government was the means by which a community gained the power to shape its future, enabling it to direct development and exploit the resources in its hinterland. The difficulty of realizing this objective created a tension that could not be resolved, and often shaped the culture and politics of small town life.

The play between local ambition and outside forces was evident from the earliest stages of town development. Railways, land developers, and government determined both where towns would be sited and how they would look. The placement of towns and the layout of their main streets often expressed metropolitan ambitions on the frontier. Towns were needed to organize local trade with larger, more distant centres. But towns were not only seen as intermediaries—they also generated a direct return to those who established them. Integral in this process was that they were laid out in advance of settlement to attract settlers and investment. Towns were economic institutions and their appearance reinforced this fact.[2] Because those who established them dictated their layout, a similarity in appearance emerged in all towns. This was perhaps the most graphic evidence of the power of these agencies. Yet, the ambitions this represented were fully accepted by the people who lived in the towns. Uniformity of appearance was not viewed as a liability but as a benefit. It simultaneously created and reinforced popular notions about the look of success and economic potential. In these terms, the aspirations of a town's leading citizens were symbiotic with those of railways and other agencies. Appearance was an economic, not an aesthetic or social issue. This attitude not only created the initial look of a town, but it was an ongoing force in shaping its appearance, and in large part accounted for the mixed results of later efforts to reshape town appearance through professional town planning. Similarly, definitions of urban priorities, expressed through such things as boosterism, incorporation, main street infrastructure and building design, and, later, leisure and social facilities, served these similar objectives and aspirations.

Once a transportation link with the provincial and national economy was established, a town's location was set, even though its growth remained uncertain. While there was sometimes minor conflict among them (except in the Crowsnest Pass where disagreements were greater), town councils, local newspapers, and boards of trade typically focused and structured economic and cultural ambitions. Town councils were dominated by main street merchants and professionals and council priorities revealed their political and social attitudes. Town councils served wider functions than just encouraging growth; their health and social welfare responsibilities are evidence of this, but even these efforts reinforced the objective of furthering the stability and economic needs of town business. In part, town councils promoted these needs by installing water, sewer and electrical systems, and by trying to attract industry and services to make the town a central place. These aspirations were often expressed through exaggerated anticipation of economic growth. Remaining a small centre was undesirable, and the language and activities used to foster growth included aphorisms and programmes indistinguishable from those used in other urban places of all sizes on the prairies.

If growth was the central issue for town promoters, it has been no less so for many urban historians who have often agreed that local entrepreneurialism helps explain urban growth, especially in a centre's formative years. This presumes that decision-making by business and government took place at a local level and was amenable to local influence, and that power was one directional. Yet, the similarity of small town and city rhetoric about the desire for urban growth raises questions about this assumption. If it is presumed that urban places with a unified elite and a coherent vision of their future, and which pursued policies to stimulate growth, grew to city status, it is equally logical to assume that such attributes were lacking in places which did not enjoy such growth. Yet, this was not the case. Towns and cities shared attitudes, language, and theories about growth, as well as the social organization that was said to be necessary to promote it.

Without denying the potential benefits of local initiative, town growth (or its absence) was more the result of a range of political, economic, and technological forces. Local authority to pursue economic objectives was limited by a lack of revenue because of limited taxing power and a cyclical economy, and by territorial and provincial government restrictions on local government. These limits on local autonomy arose from a centralizing tendency of the provincial government. Yet, at the same time, the erosion of autonomy also resulted from the habitual failure of local government to transcend immediate needs and local personalities. But most importantly, local power could not deal adequately with the growth of provincial population and expanding interconnections between places because of changes in transportation, deployment of capital, and the general nature of the economy. Thus, the erosion of local power reflected deeper currents in provincial life, which independently contributed to an inability at a local level to diversify town economies. As David Bettison observed in this connection, "local development by local initiative was being increasingly superseded by province-wide considerations. Public and private investment in the local community were becoming increasingly subordinate to the systems of relations which governed the larger political unit."[3] In the case of city growth, and especially in that of towns and other smaller communities, this conclusion emphasizes that a centre's wider political and economic context was formative. In fact, from the beginning, urban development in the prairie west was set within a national and international context which had initially stimulated the region's settlement by Euro-Canadians.

Yet a town's stage of development in the overall settlement of a district as well as other locational factors (such as natural barriers to communication and size and wealth of the immediate hinterland) were also significant in town growth. Locational factors were not, however, static. While head start could make a town a central place for a time, this position could be usurped by other towns because of changing locational advantages. Moreover, the importance of location changed with the emergence of new forms of transportation, and with the decline or ascendency in the importance of local resources. Generally, the success of the farm economy was uneven, and it suffered severe set-backs because of natural disasters. Moreover, a decline in the price of a commodity, or at the most extreme, a relative decline of its economic importance (such as coal versus petroleum), could shape a town profoundly. Urban advantage was therefore complex and varied, continually changing over time.

These broad conditions and economic cycles meant that while there initially was some diversification of the economy of most towns, it could not be sustained. Before 1912, the brick plants, sash and door factories, and building services that had developed in many places held promise of a more diversified economy. But this activity was premised on high initial demand for such products because of settlement, and on continued demand due to further settlement and the upgrading of buildings in a town and its hinterland. But it was a vulnerable sector, and the economic collapse of 1912–13 stymied such growth, as did the war years that followed. The economic collapse of 1912–13 was not just a temporary reversal but shaped long-term town development, and erratic economic conditions after 1919 reinforced its impact and confirmed most towns as service centres.

Yet the belief that economic diversification was attainable remained strong in the minds of many town leaders. Tourism held some promise in this respect, and this ambition was also expressed through the desire to see "modern" and "city-like" buildings and infrastructure like sidewalks, streets, sewers, and electric lights upgraded on main street, as well as the creation of services like hospitals that would attract investors and settlers. In this, state investment in the town economy through government offices and services—as well as infrastructure with wider economic implications, such as highways—became significant in attempting to elevate a town to the status of a central place.

For those towns that had begun as jumping off points for rural settlement and had evolved into rural service centres, the fate of their rural hinterlands had a direct impact on town development. Hinterlands also played a direct role by either resisting or agreeing with town ambitions, depending on whether or not their needs coincided with those of the town. While the relationship between town and farm was one of mutual dependence, farmers were not subservient to town interests, and their independence of a particular centre became greater as methods of transportation improved. The advent of motor vehicles was especially important and reinforced a town's emphasis on its main street infrastructure to attract trade. Alberta farmers (regardless of location or time) were rarely self-sufficient, and mail order shopping and transient traders offered alternatives to town stores. Motor vehicles increased their choices even further by giving them easier access to a greater number of towns for shopping. Thus, few farmers seem to have had reason to agree with the need to be "loyal" to the "home town," and efforts to attract their trade relied on sales promotions and special events that asserted the special advantages of the town. The ongoing contests over the sale of farm produce in towns, mail order shopping, and "cash versus credit" are evidence of this changing relationship and reveal the existence of some tensions between town and farm.

Economic parameters were only part of the rationale of town life and development. In addition, most towns, especially the many agricultural service centres, served as social centres for rural people. While towns asserted their own ideals—they sought, for example, to prevent loitering and vagrancy and to promote social order, quiet, and dignity as town characteristics—they also acted as cultural intermediaries. Although local rhetoric held that towns were special urban places—different in culture and quality of life from cities—city culture and standards were assumed to be normative, and most towns worked hard to emulate them. The same play between asserting local priorities and responding to wider forces operated in other cases as well. Town boards of trade drew upon the language and precedents of other places in defining and asserting town priorities, and they later became a conduit through which national organizations like the Canadian Chamber of Commerce could promote their economic and political ideas. The same process worked in many other instances as well: advertising, articles, and editorials in town newspapers asserted local needs and simultaneously transmitted outside standards and preoccupations to town and farm, while service clubs linked towns to national organizations and set new priorities. The town also brought commercial leisure activities such as movies to farm people.

While this gave the town less social cachet than cities, the excitement of these attractions nonetheless attached to the places where they were presented, no matter how shabby. In other respects, towns also provided more localized social opportunities through businesses like cafes, poolrooms and bars, or through charitable entertainment events like festivals, carnivals, and dances.

These activities collectively defined towns as both social and economic intermediaries. At the broadest level, the shaping of town life by outside social and economic influences had begun with the birth of the town: its layout, architecture, and infrastructure responded to the look of other places that were defined as successful and worthy of emulation. All of these issues were focused both directly and indirectly on the main street, the centre of town life. Through their domination of local government and their status as community leaders, main street interests shaped the economic, social and cultural priorities of towns. The fate of the town depended upon the economic well-being of its main street businesses, and almost all aspects of town life involved, in one form or another, the main street. Its physical appearance signalled the success and potential of the town, and its cultural and social advantages helped draw trade by providing sociability and recreation. In this sense, urban form helped to make the town. While urbanism is premised upon the gathering of people within a physical entity, its essence is a set of relationships. The strip of buildings that made up main street, although often so accepted and so ordinary, focused these relationships and made towns into urban places.

APPENDIX 1: *Mainstreet Maps*

Shaded streets indicate the town's business district.

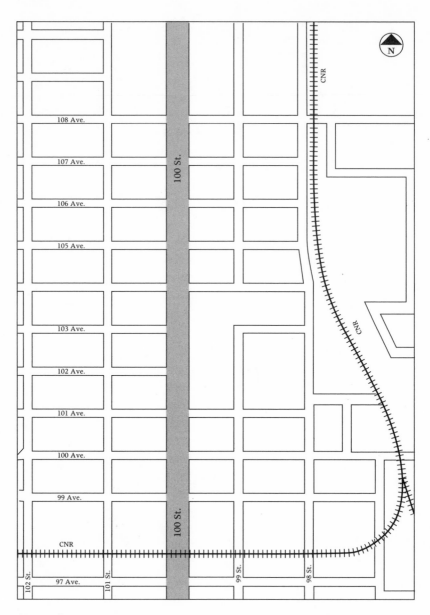

GRANDE PRAIRIE

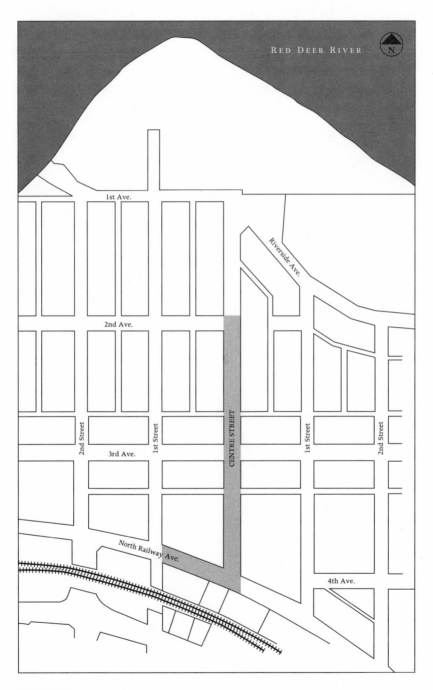

RED DEER RIVER

1st Ave.

2nd Ave.

Riverside Ave.

2nd Street

1st Street

CENTRE STREET

1st Street

2nd Street

3rd Ave.

North Railway Ave.

4th Ave.

DRUMHELLER

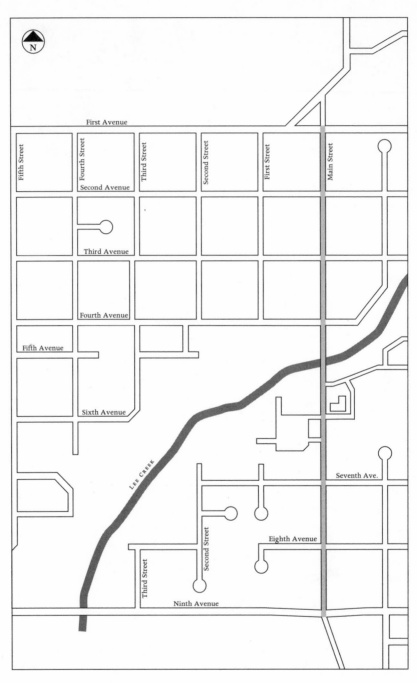

CARDSTON

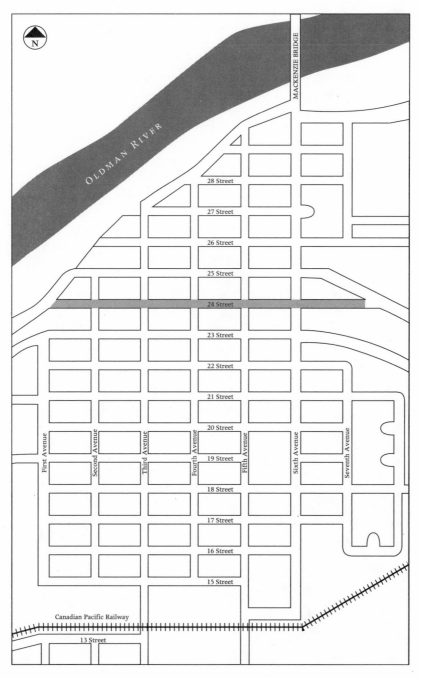

FORT MACLEOD

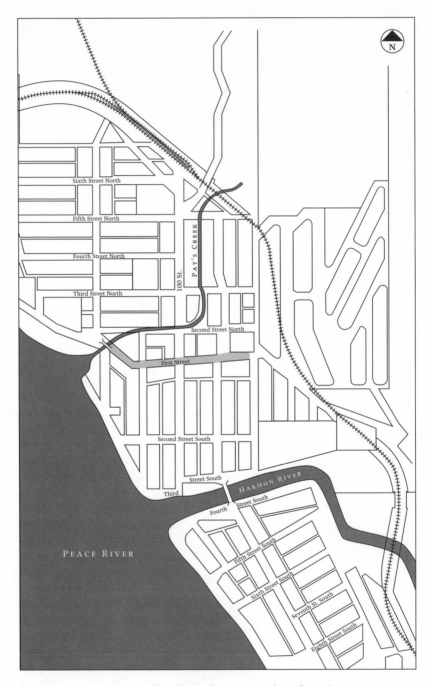

PEACE RIVER *(Streets are numbered according to original numbering).*

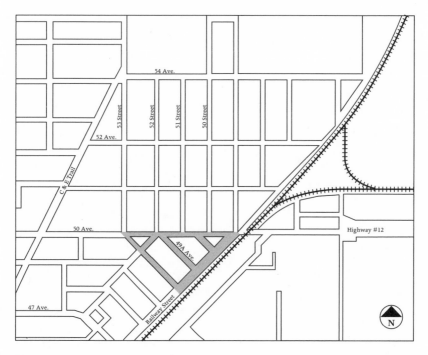

LACOMBE

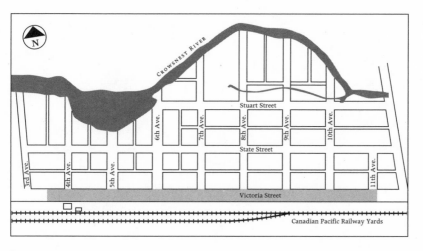

BLAIRMORE

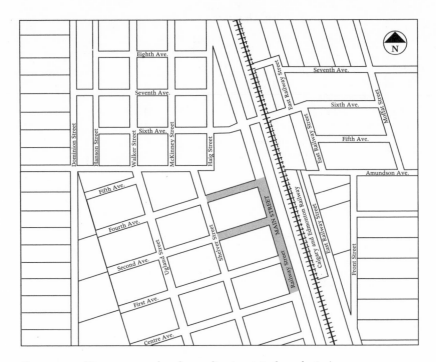

CLARESHOLM *(Streets are numbered according to original numbering)*

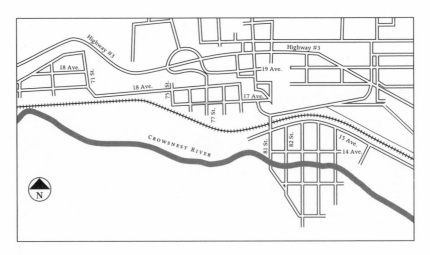

COLEMAN

Appendix ii:
Population
Tables

TABLE I

Number of Incorporated Urban Centres by Type, Aggregate Population and Percentage of Total Population, for Provinces and Territories, 1901–1941

Province and Census Year	Number at Each Census			Population Dwelling in			Percentage of Total Population Dwelling in		
	Cities	Towns	Villages	Cities	Towns	Villages	Cities	Towns	Villages
MANITOBA									
1901	2	12	8	47,960	14,782	7,694	18.79	5.79	3.02
1911	4	24	21	163,249	26,926	10,190	35.38	5.84	2.21
1921	4	30	18	214,071	38,241	9,304	35.09	6.27	1.52
1931	4	30	22	258,769	43,416	13,784	36.96	6.20	1.97
1941	4	30	23	264,687	43,362	13,824	36.27	5.94	1.90
SASKATCHEWAN									
1901	—	7	30		7,928	6,338		8.69	6.94
1911	4	50	195	62,294	36,844	32,257	12.65	7.48	6.55
1921	7	78	344	97,833	60,970	60,155	12.91	8.05	7.94
1931	8	80	378	149,015	64,817	77,073	16.17	7.03	8.36
1941	8	82	384	156,628	63,125	75,393	17.48	7.05	8.41
ALBERTA									
1901	1	6	21	4,091	9,164	5,278	5.60	12.55	7.23
1911	6	27	70	90,252	25,881	21,529	24.11	6.92	5.75
1921	6	55	114	147,246	50,145	25,513	25.02	8.52	4.34
1931	7	54	144	194,203	50,155	34,150	26.54	6.86	4.67
1941	7	52	142	215,894	53,623	37,069	27.12	6.73	4.66

Source: *Census of Canada*, 1941, Vol. II, Table 15, p. 369.

TABLE 2

Urban Populations, Towns in Study Sample and Alberta Cities, 1890–1946

	1891	1901	1911	1921	1931	1941	1946
TOWNS							
Blairmore	—	231	1137	1552	1629	1731	1767
Cardston	350*	639	1207	1612	1672	1864	2334
Claresholm	—	—	809	963	1156	1265	1306
Coleman	—	—	1557	1590	1704	1870	1809
Drumheller	—	—	—	2499	2987	2748	2659
Fort Macleod	507+	796	1844	1723	1447	1912	1649
Grande Prairie			457^	1061	1464	1724	2267
Lacombe	—	499	1029	1133	1259	1603	1808
Peace River	—	—	—	980	864	873	977
CITIES							
Calgary	3876	4392	43704	63305	83761	88904	100044
Edmonton		4176	31064	58821	79197	93817	113116
Lethbridge		2072	9035	11097	13489	14612	16522
Medicine Hat		1570	5608	9634	10300	10571	12859

*Approximate (*Macleod Gazette*, July 9, 1891)
+For 1895 (*Macleod Gazette*, May 10, 1895)
^For 1917

Compiled from *Census of Canada* except where noted.

TABLE 3
Population by Principal Origins, 1921, 1941

	Austrian/ German	Asian	British	Czeck/ Slovak/ Hungarian	French	Italian	Jewish	Low Countries	Polish	Russian/ Ukrainian	Scandi- navian/ Finnish	Other and Not Stated	TOTAL	British % of Total
BLAIRMORE														
1921	11	32	729	*	112	308	10	107	35	12	55	141	1552	47
1941	12	23	671	293	103	334	—	87	102	33	65	8	1731	39
CARDSTON														
1921	25	21	1356	*	27	11	—	6	—	—	138	28	1612	84
1941	85	19	1484	6	31	—	—	23	5	19	188	4	1864	80
CLARESHOLM														
1921	46	24	704	*	18	1	—	11	2	—	133	24	963	73
1941	56	11	868	14	57	—	2	24	13	14	203	3	1265	69
COLEMAN														
1921	19	18	832	*	46	216	—	42	143	36	43	195	1590	52
1941	33	38	925	278	41	233	—	39	126	112	26	19	1870	49
DRUMHELLER														
1921	155	33	1751	*	101	87	25	73	26	21	94	133	2499	70
1941	132	33	1950	33	75	95	29	108	86	51	94	62	2748	71

TABLE 3 *(cont.)*
Population by Principal Origins, 1921, 1941

	Austrian/ German	Asian	British	Czeck/ Slovak/ Hungarian	French	Italian	Jewish	Low Countries	Polish	Russian/ Ukrainian	Scandi- navian/ Finnish	Other and Not Stated	TOTAL	British % of Total
FORT MACLEOD														
1921	25	42	1487	*	81	12	—	13	3	3	33	24	1723	86
1941	36	27	1460	23	92	16	2	69	7	38	123	19	1912	76
GRANDE PRAIRIE														
1921	30	12	853	*	65	—	5	11	4	14	56	11	1061	80
1941	98	31	1166	9	112	—	5	123	23	42	88	27	1724	68
LACOMBE														
1921	46	9	940	*	11	—	—	12	7	9	91	8	1133	83
1941	71	27	1220	8	37	1	2	48	14	36	127	12	1603	76
PEACE RIVER														
1921	38	8	788	*	34	—	4	4	5	6	47	46	980	80
1941	59	5	640	—	63	—	—	25	13	8	57	3	873	73

* not reported
Source: *Census of Canada*, 1921, Table 27 (Vol.1) and 1941, Table 32.

NOTES

INTRODUCTION

1. *The Globe and Mail*, September 7, 1991.
2. On the town myth in the United States, see Lewis Atherton, "The Midwestern Country Town—Myth and Reality," *Agricultural History* 26 (1952): 73–80; Park Dixon Goist, *From Main Street to State Street: Town, City and Community in America* (Port Washington, New York: National University Publications, Kennikat Press, 1977), 3–55; Richard V. Francaviglia, "Main Street USA," *Landscape* 21 (1977): 18–22. On W.O. Mitchell's "Crocus," see Catherine McLay, "Crocus, Saskatchewan: A Country of the Mind," *Journal of Popular Culture* 14 (1980): 333–49.
3. When possible, we use the current name of towns, such as Grande Prairie (initially Grande Prairie City), Peace River (beginning life as Peace River Crossing) and Fort Macleod (variously known as Macleod and Fort Macleod since 1874).
4. Darrel A. Norris, "Preserving Main Street: Some Lessons of Leacock's Mariposa," *Journal of Canadian Studies* 17 (1982): 130.
5. L.D. McCann, "Urban Growth in Western Canada 1881–1961," *The Albertan Geographer* 5 (1969): 69.
6. C.A. Dawson and R.W. Murchie, *The Settlement of the Peace River Country. A Study of a Pioneer Area* (Toronto: Macmillan, 1934), 39.
7. In addition to many specific studies on social, economic and political history in the major cities, general histories on Alberta cities include Carl Betke, "The Development of Urban Community in Prairie Canada, Edmonton, 1898–1928" (Ph.D. diss. University of Alberta, 1981); John Gilpin, "The City of Strathcona, 1891–1912" (M.A. thesis, University of Alberta, 1978); Robert Dawe, "An Investigation into the Development of the Red Deer Community in Relation to the Development of Western Canada" (M.A. thesis, University of Alberta, 1954); Maxwell Foran, *Calgary: An Illustrated History* (Toronto: James Lorimer and Co. and the National Museum of Man, 1978); David C. Jones, L.J. Roy Wilson and Donny White, *The Weather Factory: A Pictorial History of Medicine Hat* (Saskatoon: Western Producer Prairie Books, 1988); Alex Johnston and Andy A. den Otter, *Lethbridge: A Centennial History*

(Lethbridge: City of Lethbridge and The Whoop-Up Country Chapter, Historical Society of Alberta, 1985).

8. D.G. Marshall, "Hamlets and Villages in the United States: Their Place in the American Way of Life," *American Sociological Review* 11 (1946): 165; J.T. Lemon, "Study of the Urban Past: Approaches by Geographers," Canadian Historical Association, *Historical Papers 1973*, 179–90. As an example of the range of current concern, see *People and Place: Studies in Small Town Life in the Maritimes,* ed. Larry McCann (Fredericton: Acadiensis Press and the [Mount Allison University] Committee for Studying Small Town Life in the Maritimes, 1987).

9. G. Stelter and A. Artibise, *Power and Place Canadian Urban Development in the North American Context* (Vancouver: University of British Columbia Press, 1986), 3.

10. Gilbert A. Stelter, "A Regional Framework for Urban History," *Urban History Review* 13 (1985): 196 (italics in original).

11. Fred Dahms, "The Process of Urbanization in the Countryside: A Case Study of Huron and Bruce Counties, 1891–1981," *Urban History Review* 12 (1984): 1–18; Stelter, "A Regional Framework," 201.

12. "Editorial," *Urban History Yearbook 1974*, 7.

13. Donald F. Davis, "The 'Metropolitan Thesis' and the Writing of Canadian Urban History," *Urban History Review* 14 (1985): 97.

14. David C. Jones, *Empire of Dust: Settling and Abandoning the Prairie Dry Belt* (Edmonton: The University of Alberta Press, 1987).

15. Dahms, "The Process of Urbanization in the Countryside," 3.

16. Peter Ennals, "The Main Streets of Maritime Canada," *SSAC Bulletin* 11 (1986): 11.

17. Stelter and Artibise, *Power and Place*, 3.

18. Paul Voisey, *Vulcan: The Making of a Prairie Community* (Toronto: University of Toronto Press, 1988).

19. Stelter, "A Regional Framework for Urban History," 197.

20. John Hudson, *Plains Country Towns* (Minneapolis: University of Minnesota Press, 1985), 6, 13.

21. Randy William Widdis, "Belleville and Environs: Continuity, Change and the Integration of Town and Country During the 19th Century," *Urban History Review* 19 (1991): 184-86.

22. Barbara Ruth Bailey, *Main Street Northeastern Oregon. The Founding and Development of Small Towns* (Portland: The Oregon Historical Society, 1982), xvii. See also Hal Kalman, "Canada's Main Streets," in *Reviving Main Street*, ed. Deryck Holdsworth (Toronto: University of Toronto Press and Heritage Canada Foundation, 1985), 3–29.

23. Michael Doucet and John Weaver found continuities also at work in Hamilton, Ontario, in the mid nineteenth century. Michael Doucet and John Weaver, "Town Fathers and Urban Continuity: The Roots of Community

Power and Physical Formation in Hamilton, Upper Canada in the 1830s," *Urban History Review* 13 (1984): 75–90. On continuity and transformation in social history, see Hugh Cunningham, *Leisure in the Industrial Revolution c. 1780 – c. 1880* (London: Croom Helm, 1980).

24. Elizabeth Bloomfield, "Community Ethos and Local Initiative in Urban Economic Growth: A Review of a Theme in Canadian Urban History," *Urban History Yearbook 1983*, 53–72.

I | THE ORIGIN AND DEVELOPMENT OF TOWNS IN ALBERTA

1. Voisey, *Vulcan*, 53–55; Bodil Jensen, "The County of Mountain View, Alberta: A Study in Community Development, 1890–1925" (M.A. thesis, University of Alberta, 1972), 34–36.
2. Hudson, *Plains Country Towns*, 15.
3. *Macleod Gazette*, August 14 and October 4, 1882.
4. *Macleod Gazette*, March 5, 1883, April 11 and November 3, 1885, October 13 and December 1, 1892.
5. Lowry Nelson, *The Mormon Village: A Pattern and Technique of Land Settlement* (Salt Lake City: University of Utah Press, 1952), 231.
6. A. James Hudson, *Charles Ora Card: Pioneer and Colonizer* (Cardston: The Author, 1963), 119.
7. John Lehr, "Mormon Settlements in Southern Alberta," (M.A. thesis, University of Alberta, 1971), 16–35; *Cardston Record*, August 6, 1898.
8. David W. Leonard and Victoria L. Lemieux, *A Fostered Dream* (Calgary: Detselig Enterprises Ltd, 1992), 41–45; Grande Prairie and District Old Timer's Association, *Pioneers of the Peace* (Calgary: D.W. Friesen and Sons Ltd., 1976), 67.
9. John A. Eagle, "J.D. McArthur and the Peace River Railway," *Alberta History* 29 (1981): 34–35.
10. Glenda Lamont, "Migrants and Migration in Part of the South Peace River Region, Alberta" (M.A. thesis, University of Alberta, 1970), 26–31.
11. *Peace River Record*, December 31, 1915.
12. Ann Holtz, "Small Town Alberta: A Geographical Study of the Development of Urban Form" (M.A. thesis, University of Alberta, 1987), iv.
13. Ibid., 49, 53–54.
14. Ibid., 50.
15. Deryck Holdsworth and John C. Everitt, "Bank Branches and Elevators: Expressions of Big Corporations in Small Prairie Towns," *Prairie Forum* 13 (1988): 175; Holtz, "Small Town Alberta," 50–52, 55;
16. Petition, March 28, 1903, Department of Municipal Affairs Papers, 74.174/1098, PAA. The C&E was an independent company leased by the CPR. In 1894, it was purchased by the CPR.

17. E.R. Patterson, "The Early History of Claresholm and District," in *Where the Wheatlands Meet the Range*, Claresholm History Book Club (Calgary: D.W. Friesen and Sons, 1974), 8.

18. Holtz, "Small Town Alberta," 63. Some land holders in effect paid the railway to locate a station on their land. In Red Deer, Leonard Gaetz persuaded the C&E to locate its station on his land in exchange for 600 acres at the site (Dawe, "The Development of the Red Deer Community," 49).

19. Dawson and Murchie, *Settlement of the Peace River Country*, 49–50.

20. McEachern to Department of Municipal Affairs, June 2, 1916, Village of Grande Prairie to Mitchell, June 22, 1917, and Order, Village of Grande Prairie, January 1, 1918, 74.174/100/1264, PAA.

21. For example, *Macleod Gazette*, January 24, 1889.

22. On this pattern elsewhere, see Paul Voisey, "The Urbanization of the Canadian Prairies 1871–1916," *Histoire sociale/Social History* 8 (1975): 77–101.

23. *Macleod Gazette*, September 1, 1892.

24. Ibid., August 11 and 18, 1892.

25. Ibid., November 3, August 25, July 28 and September 1, 1892.

26. File memo, June 4, 1915, 74.174/997a, PAA; *Macleod Gazette*, November 17 and December 1, 1892, January 19 and 26, 1893.

27. *Macleod Gazette*, December 5, 1889, June 16, 1899, December 3, 1893.

28. Ibid., June 16, 1899, March 8 and June 21, 1901.

29. *Drumheller Mail*, August 21, 1930, June 25, 1936.

30. T.D. Regehr, *The Canadian Northern Railway: Pioneer Road of the Northern Prairies, 1895–1918* (Toronto: Macmillan of Canada, 1976), 248–49; *Drumheller Mail*, September 28, 1988.

31. *Economic Survey, Town of Blairmore* (Edmonton: Alberta Industrial Development Board, 1950), 2; *Blairmore Enterprise*, August 22, 1911.

32. *Coleman Journal*, January 4, 1934.

33. W.L. Morton, "The Significance of Site in the Settlement of the American and Canadian Wests," *Agricultural History* 25 (1951): 97.

34. *Macleod Gazette*, September 15, 1892, July 7, 1893.

2 | Town Culture

1. Cecil Burgess, "The Town" (radio talk, June 4, 1928), 72–28–15, UAA.

2. David G. Bettison, John K. Kenward and Larrie Taylor, *Urban Affairs in Alberta* (Edmonton: University of Alberta Press, 1975), 10.

3. John H. Taylor, "Urban Autonomy in Canada: Its Evolution and Decline," in *Power and Place*, eds. Stelter and Artibise, 270.

4. For these arguments in Medicine Hat see *Medicine Hat Times*, September 21, 1888. The town was incorporated in late 1898.

5. Eric J. Hanson, *Local Government in Alberta* (Toronto: McClelland and Stewart Ltd., 1956), 25–26.

6. *Macleod Gazette*, February 14, 1889; Bettison, Kenward and Taylor, *Urban Affairs in Alberta*, 11.

7. *Macleod Gazette*, May 18, 1886, November 29, 1888. The Fort Macleod board of trade was possibly inspired by the one organized in Medicine Hat in 1887 (*Medicine Hat Times*, April 30, 1887).

8. *Macleod Gazette*, December 20, 1888.

9. Ibid., December 6, 1888.

10. Ibid., February 28, April 4 and December 5, 1889.

11. Ibid., January 26, 1893, August 17, 1894.

12. Petition, Lacombe, May 1, 1896, Claresholm correspondence, 1903–04, 74.174/1098, PAA; *Claresholm Review*, January 27, 1910.

13. *Cardston Alberta Star*, June 18, 1909.

14. *Grande Prairie Herald*, March 24 and May 26, 1914.

15. Hanson, *Local Government in Alberta*, 27. See for example, *Peace River Record*, March 14, 1915.

16. *Blairmore Enterprise*, February 2 and 16, and October 19, 1911.

17. Alan F.J. Artibise, "Continuity and Change: Elites and Prairie Urban Development 1914–1950," in *The Usable Urban Past: Planning and Politics in the Modern Canadian City*, eds. Alan F.J. Artibise and Gilbert A. Stelter (Toronto: Macmillan of Canada, 1977), 131.

18. *Cardston Globe*, July 15, 1913.

19. Sam Bass Warner, *The Private City: Philadelphia in Three Periods of its Growth* (Philadelphia: University of Philadelphia Press, 1968), 202–7; Alan F.J. Artibise, *Winnipeg: A Social History of Urban Growth 1874–1914* (Montreal: McGill-Queens University Press, 1975), 285–86.

20. *Claresholm Review*, July 3, 1908, November 17, 1911.

21. On the croaker as gossip, see *Claresholm Review*, June 7, 1907; *Cardston Alberta Star*, February 24, 1911; *Blairmore Enterprise*, September 5, 1913.

22. *Lacombe Western Globe*, April 20, 1909.

23. *Claresholm Review*, July 4, 1912; *Peace River Record*, February 14, 1919.

24. For example, *Lacombe Western Globe*, February 19, 1913.

25. *Blairmore Enterprise*, May 16, 1912, January 10, 1913; *Cardston Globe*, May 29, 1914.

26. *Claresholm Review*, June 7, 1907, July 31, 1908.

27. *Cardston Alberta Star*, September 30, 1910.

28. *Blairmore Enterprise*, March 20, 1914.

29. For example, *Blairmore Enterprise*, April 29, 1920.

30. *Cardston News*, May 1, 1930.

31. *Drumheller Mail*, August 16, 1928; *Cardston News*, February 24, 1927.

32. *Lacombe Western Globe*, November 12, 1931.

33. *Peace River Record*, July 29, 1926; *Drumheller Mail*, October 5, 1933. See also *Cardston News*, March 26, 1931.

34. For syndicated U.S. articles on these topics see, *Claresholm Review Advertiser*, February 23 and March 2, 1917.

35. Burgess, "Civic Pride" (radio talk, May 27, 1929), 72–28–19, UAA.
36. *Coleman Journal*, March 29, 1928, July 20, 1933, January 11, 1934; Horace L. Seymour, "The Problems of Small Communities," *The Press Bulletin*, November 20, 1931.
37. Quoted in *Coleman Journal*, July 30, 1942.
38. *Grande Prairie Herald*, October 25, 1926.
39. David C. Jones, "'There is Some Power About the Land'—The Western Agrarian Press and Country Life Ideology," *Journal of Canadian Studies* 17 (1982): 96–108. Also see for example, *Peace River Record*, July 8, 1934.
40. *Peace River Record*, March 27, 1924. The article was also printed in other papers, appearing as late as September 15, 1938 in the *Coleman Journal*.
41. *Claresholm Review Advertiser*, December 24, 1926.
42. *Cardston Globe*, September 14, 1916.
43. *Claresholm Review Advertiser*, November 29, 1918.
44. Voisey, *Vulcan*, 240. John Hudson draws the same conclusion about North Dakota (Hudson, *Plains Country Towns*, 130).
45. *Peace River Record*, August 18, 1916.
46. *Cardston News*, April 24, 1930; *Drumheller Mail*, June 7, 1928.

3 | TOWN GOVERNMENT

1. Taylor, "Urban Autonomy in Canada," 270.
2. Deputy Attorney General to Perrie, November 15, 1912, Department of the Attorney General Papers, 66.166/112c, PAA.
3. A.N. Reid, "Urban Municipalities in the North West Territories: Their Development and Machinery of Government," *Saskatchewan History* 7 (1954): 42–48; *Blairmore Enterprise*, November 30, 1917. Until 1907, village government used an elected overseer and three councillors. Thereafter a system of three councillors was used. Towns always had a mayor and councillors.
4. *Blairmore Enterprise*, April 14 and October 6, 1927.
5. *Macleod Gazette*, February 9, 1893.
6. See for example, *Claresholm Review*, August 26, 1909.
7. *Blairmore Enterprise*, March 26, 1915, March 10 and July 28, 1921; *Peace River Record*, October 25, 1929.
8. *Drumheller Review*, December 12, 1919, November 16, 1944; *Blairmore Enterprise*, February 10, 1927.
9. *Grande Prairie Northern Tribune*, June 21, 1934. On the events at Blairmore see *Blairmore Enterprise*, June 14, 1923, April 17 and May 15, 1924, January 29, 1925.
10. *Grande Prairie Northern Tribune*, June 21, 1934, April 18, 1935, March 12, 1936, April 22, 1937; *Drumheller Mail*, December 16, 1937; *Blairmore Enterprise*, March 28, 1935.

11. *Macleod Gazette*, May 4, 1894.

12. For example, *Medicine Hat News*, November 30, 1899.

13. *Macleod Spectator*, December 4, 1913; *Blairmore Enterprise*, February 5, 1925; *Claresholm Review*, November 20 and 27, 1913.

14. *Grande Prairie Herald Tribune*, December 4, 1947.

15. *Claresholm Review*, May 15, 1908, January 15 and 29, 1909.

16. *Drumheller Mail*, February 9, 1928.

17. *Blairmore Enterprise*, February 16, 1928, February 6, 1930.

18. Halliwell to Duncan, December 12, 1932, Department of the Attorney General Papers, 83.214/4b, PAA; *Coleman Journal*, January 24, 1940.

19. Memorandum, August 2, 1932, 83.214/4a, PAA.

20. RCMP Report 13, July 16, 1932, 83.214/4a, PAA.

21. *Blairmore Enterprise*, January 19, 1933, (letter to editor).

22. Duncan to Officer Commanding "K" Division, December 13 and 14, 1932, 83.214/4b, PAA.

23. *Blairmore Enterprise*, December 22, 1932.

24. Ibid., May 4, 1933.

25. Allen Seager, "Class Consciousness, Class Anarchy: Three Alberta Coal Towns During the Great Depression" (Paper Read to the Canadian Historical Association, Annual Meeting, Saskatoon, 1979, typescript), 33–36.

26. *Blairmore Enterprise*, March 2, 1933 (mayor's public notice).

27. Ibid., August 24, 1933, December 13, 1934, March 21, 1935.

28. Ibid., March 6, 1933.

29. Gray to Deputy Minister, May 9, 1933 (attachments), 74.174/973c, PAA; *Blairmore Enterprise*, June 8 and May 11, 1933.

30. *Blairmore Enterprise*, February 1 and 15, 1934.

31. Ibid., February 7, 1935.

32. Ibid., January 31, 1941, February 2 and 16, 1949.

33. Hanson, *Local Government in Alberta*, 32. The debt of cities in Alberta increased from $1 million to $41.9 million in the same period.

34. *Blairmore Enterprise*, December 28, 1911.

35. The project began with plans for a $50,000 building (the same amount spent by Medicine Hat, a city of 11,000 population), then increased to $165,000.

36. Kinnaird to Stedman, August 23, 1912 (Bylaw 267 attached), 74.174/997c, PAA; *Macleod Spectator*, August 7 and 12, 1913.

37. John Blue, *Alberta Past and Present: Historical and Biographical,* Vol. 1 (Chicago: Pioneer Historical Publishing Co, 1924), 162–69.

38. For example, Cardston in 1912 collected $12,500 in property and school taxes, leaving arrears of almost $5,000. In Fort Macleod these figures were about $32,000 and $19,000, while in Lacombe they were about $20,000 and about $12,000. Thus, arrears outstanding sometimes amounted to almost 75 percent of the year's property tax levy.

39. *Macleod Gazette*, October 9, 1896, November 25, 1898; *Blairmore Enterprise*, November 1, 1912.

40. Cardston earned $177 in 1909, the first year it collected a poll tax. In 1910, Claresholm earned $77 (*Cardston Alberta Star*, March 18, 1910; *Claresholm Review*, March 7, 1910).

41. *Blairmore Enterprise*, December 14, 1922, March 8, 1923.

42. In Claresholm in 1911 this translated into about $1,200 in revenue from licenses, while in Blairmore it was about $1,600.

43. Usually dog taxes brought in about $75 per year, although in Blairmore in 1912 where enforcement must have been strict, the town made $415. (*Blairmore Enterprise*, February 14, 1913).

44. Bettison, Kenward and Taylor, *Urban Affairs in Alberta*, 17.

45. Deputy Attorney General to Lawrence, February 13, 1914, 66.166/36b, PAA.

46. Brown to Deputy Minister, October 11, 1919, 74.174/1028d, PAA.

47. *Blairmore Enterprise*, February 13, 1914, August 27, 1915.

48. *Claresholm Review*, March 27, 1913.

49. Hodgson to Boyle, November 13, 1915, 74.174/997b, PAA; Coherty to Perrie, August 25, 1919 (attachments), 74.174/1267a, PAA; *Blairmore Enterprise*, June 9, 1916; "Annual Financial Statement," *Blairmore Enterprise*, April 1, 1920.

50. The *Alberta Tax Arrears Act* (1919) allowed defaulters to pay taxes in eight equal instalments with blended interest and principle. It required payment of current taxes before instalment payments on arrears could begin. This rendered it ineffective.

51. *Claresholm Review*, April 2, 1914. In 1936 Drumheller wanted its charter amended to allow for a rental tax (*Drumheller Mail*, March 12, 1936). This tax was charged in Medicine Hat.

52. *Blairmore Enterprise*, February 26, 1915.

53. Secretary Treasurer to Perrie, September 15, 1913, 74.174/972d, PAA; *Blairmore Enterprise*, January 17, 1913, April 28, 1916, January 19, 1917.

54. "Annual Report of the Department of Municipal Affairs," in *The Western Municipal News*, October 1922, 298–99.

55. *Claresholm Review Advertiser*, May 27, 1921.

56. *Drumheller Mail*, January 24, 1929.

57. Renshaw to Souter, July 24, 1940, Department of Municipal Affairs Papers, 78.133/118c, PAA; *Blairmore Enterprise*, January 19, 1917, January 11, 1918; *Drumheller Mail*, September 10, 1931.

58. *Drumheller Mail*, December 18, 1930; *Blairmore Enterprise*, March 5, 1925. Collecting these taxes was difficult. Town and school boundaries usually were not the same, forcing a town to collect school taxes outside its boundaries. Many of those living outside places like Drumheller with its poor and seasonal workforce were squatters. In 1928, there were 275 squatters in the school district, of whom only 120 had paid their current school taxes (*Drumheller Mail*, January 24, 1929).

59. *Drumheller Mail*, October 5, 1932.

60. Ibid., May 16, 1940, February 13, 1941.

61. Smith to Maynard, September 17, 1937, 74.174/978a, PAA.

62. *Drumheller Mail*, September 10, 1931, November 30, 1933, August 2, 1934.

63. Bettison, Kenward and Taylor, *Urban Affairs in Alberta*, 24. The connection between utility rates and local government was direct since most towns owned electrical plants, many owned local telephone companies, and all owned water and sewer systems.

64. Hanson, *Local Government in Alberta*, 20.

65. Recommendations Re: Town of Macleod and Macleod Public School District, February 16, 1925, 74.174/997a; Board of Public Utility Commissioners to Deputy Minister, August 17, 1932, 78.133/445c, PAA.

66. Bettison, Kenward and Taylor, *Urban Affairs in Alberta*, 24.

67. Ibid., 62.

68. Wolstfenholme to Deputy Minister, March 21, 1930, Department of Highways Papers, 67.303/1231/3093, PAA; Metcalf to Reid, July 9, 1932, 78.133/702c, PAA.

4 | SHAPING LOCAL PRIORITIES

1. Barry Potyondi, "In Quest of Limited Urban Status: The Town Building Process in Minnedosa, 1879–1906," in *Town and City: Aspects of Western Canadian Urban Development*, ed. Alan Artibise (Regina: Canadian Plains Research Centre, 1981).

2. Elizabeth Bloomfield, "Boards of Trade and Canadian Urban Development," *Urban History Review* 12 (1983): 77–83.

3. *Macleod Gazette*, April 11, 1888, May 9, 1889, May 8, 1890; *Coleman Journal*, July 5, 1928.

4. *Cardston Alberta Star*, September 30, 1910; *Cardston Globe*, January 9, 1913.

5. *Drumheller Review*, April 10, 1914; *Drumheller Mail*, February 27 and March 13, 1919; *Lacombe Western Globe*, February 2, 1909.

6. *Cardston Globe*, January 23, 1914; *Drumheller Mail*, November 11, 1943.

7. *Claresholm Review*, March 27, 1913.

8. *Claresholm Review*, December 5, 1912; *Macleod Spectator*, January 15, 1914; *Grande Prairie Herald*, February 13, 1917; *Macleod Gazette*, January 11, 1901.

9. *Lacombe Western Globe*, August 6, 1913; *Cardston Alberta Star*, September 30, 1910.

10. Auditor's Report, Cardston, September 30, 1913, 74.174/977C, PAA; *Cardston Globe*, January 9 and 23, 1914.

11. *Drumheller Review*, September 17, 1920. See also *Claresholm Review*, December 5, 1912.

12. Bloomfield, "Boards of Trade," 84.

13. *Lacombe Western Globe*, August 6, 1913; *Drumheller Mail*, January 22, 1931.

14. *Macleod Advertiser*, October 19, 1911, February 15, 1912; *Cardston Alberta Star*, January 6, 1911.

15. *Cardston Globe*, January 23, 1914; *Lacombe Western Globe*, February 19, 1913.

16. For example, Minutes, Macleod board of trade, February 15, 1906, Macleod Board of Trade Papers, M1430, GAI.

17. *Peace River Record*, May 11, 1922, January 18, 1923.

18. *Cardston News*, April 11, 1929, April 24, 1930, June 10, 1941; *Peace River Record*, April 5, 1940; *Drumheller Mail*, February 29, 1940.

19. Bloomfield, "Boards of Trade," 77–79.

20. *Lacombe Western Globe*, February 7, 1929; *Grande Prairie Herald*, May 11, 1928.

21. *Grande Prairie Herald*, February 21, 1922.

22. *Claresholm Local Press*, August 14, 1936, January 8, 1937, January 7 and September 8, 1938, April 16, 1942.

23. For example, *Macleod Times*, January 19, 1928.

24. *Lacombe Western Globe*, May 14, 1936.

25. *Macleod Gazette*, May 20 and June 3, 1904.

26. Constitution, Associate Boards of Trade of Southern Alberta, n.d. [1911], M1430, GAI; *Cardston Alberta Star*, December 14, 1911.

27. *Blairmore Enterprise*, November 9, 1922; *Cardston News*, February 4, 1926, March 8, 1938; *Claresholm Local Press*, October 30 and November 6, 1936, January 8, 1937.

28. *Grande Prairie Herald*, March 15, 1929; Address of Chairman W.D. Albright to First Annual Meeting of the General Council, Peace River Associated Boards of Trade, June 25, 1932, Information File, "Peace River" folder 1, PAA.

29. *Grande Prairie Northern Tribune*, September 21, 1933, November 29, 1934, May 21, 1936, May 15, 1947.

30. *Grande Prairie Herald*, October 12, 1920.

31. Address by W.D. Albright to Second Annual Meeting of the General Council, Peace River Associated Boards of Trade, June 8, 1933, Information File, "Peace River" folder 1, PAA; *Peace River Record Gazette*, May 1, 1947.

32. *Lacombe Globe*, June 9 and December 8, 1938.

33. For example, *Peace River Record*, April 5, 1940.

34. *Grande Prairie Herald Tribune*, March 20 and May 1, 1947.

35. Earl G. Drake, "Pioneer Journalism in Saskatchewan, 1878–1887," *Saskatchewan History* 5 (1952): 41–54.

36. *Grande Prairie Herald*, May 10, 1926.

37. *Drumheller Mail*, April 8, 1929; *Blairmore Enterprise*, May 17, 1946.

38. For example, *Claresholm Review*, February 12, 1909.

39. Minutes, Macleod board of trade, July 3, 1923, M1430, GAI.

40. *Claresholm Review*, August 28, 1913; *Cardston News*, September 9, 1926.

41. *Claresholm Review Advertiser*, August 11, 1916.

42. *Drumheller Mail*, April 22, 1936; *Claresholm Local Press*, October 1, 1942.

43. *Drumheller Mail*, May 17, 1928; *Claresholm Local Press*, November 6, 1947.

44. See for example, *Grande Prairie Herald*, September 19, 1930; *Drumheller Mail*, September 22, 1938.

45. Petersen to Spence, October 11, 1927, 78.133/102a, PAA.

46. *Cardston Globe*, December 5, 1912.

47. *Blairmore Enterprise*, January 18, 1912; *Claresholm Review*, July 8, 1915.

48. *Claresholm Review*, August 7, 1913; *Grande Prairie Herald Tribune*, January 31, 1946.

49. *Blairmore Enterprise*, May 17, 1946; *Cardston News*, September 9, 1926, October 2, 1930; *Grande Prairie Herald Tribune*, March 13, 1947; *Edmonton Journal*, June 11, 1956.

50. *Drumheller Mail*, July 12, 1928.

51. *Macleod Gazette*, July 1 and August 14, 1882; P.W.F. Rutherford, "The People's Press: The Emergence of the New Journalism in Canada, 1869–1899," *Canadian Historical Review* 56 (1975): 175–77.

52. *Macleod Gazette*, July 28, 1892, May 25, 1894.

53. *Drumheller Mail*, October 31, 1929, May 25, 1933.

54. On the Saskatchewan KKK, see Patrick Kyba, "Ballots and Burning Crosses, The Election of 1929," in *Politics in Saskatchewan*, eds. Doug Spafford and Norman Ward (Toronto: Longmans Canada, 1968), 105–33.

55. *Lacombe Western Globe*, December 5, 1929.

56. Ibid., May 29 and June 5, 1930.

57. *Macleod Gazette*, June 6, 1885; *Blairmore Enterprise*, September 10, 1915; *Lacombe Western Globe*, March 24, 1920.

58. *Lacombe Western Globe*, September 20, 1911; *Macleod Gazette*, July 3, 1903.

59. *Drumheller Mail*, September 17, 1936.

5 | TOWN ECONOMIC GROWTH

1. Harold A. Rendall, "The Trade Areas of Camrose, Wetaskiwin, and Ponoka," (M.A. thesis, University of Alberta, 1962), 95–96.

2. *Claresholm Review*, December 30, 1909.

3. Brian F. McLoughlin, *Canadian Pacific from Calgary to Edmonton* (Calgary: The British Railway Modellers of North America, n.d.), 4.

4. *Lacombe Western Globe*, October 23, 1912.

5. [Fred Schutz], *Pas ka poo. An Early History of Rimbey and the Upper Blindman Valley* (Rimbey: The Rimbey Advance, 1962), 131–35; McLoughlin, *Canadian Pacific From Calgary to Edmonton*, 18.

6. *Cardston Alberta Star*, July 26, 1907.

7. Card to Brownlee, January 5, 1925, Department of the Attorney General Papers, 75.126/16/628, PAA; *Cardston News*, March 18, 1926.

8. *Grande Prairie Herald*, January 13 and July 7, 1914, December 7, 1915, November 7, 1916.

9. *Dun & Bradstreet Commercial Ratings*, Grande Prairie and Lake Saskatoon, 1912–1930.

10. *Grande Prairie Herald*, March 23, 1928.

11. Ibid., March 26, 1918, February 21, 1922, May 11, 1925.

12. Address of Chairman W.D. Albright to Second Annual Meeting of the General Council, Associated Peace River Boards of Trade, June 8, 1933, Information File, "Peace River" folder 1, PAA; *Grande Prairie Northern Tribune*, February 8, 1937.

13. *Macleod Gazette*, May 5, 1893; Hanson, *Local Government in Alberta*, 12–15, 22.

14. For example, *Macleod Gazette*, May 3, 1895, February 24, 1899. The trip from Fort Macleod took four and a half hours to Pincher Creek and four hours to Lethbridge.

15. *Macleod Gazette*, February 24, 1899, July 13, 1905.

16. Bettison, Kenward and Taylor, *Urban Affairs in Alberta*, 45–46; Fred A. Dahms, "Regional Urban History: A Statistical and Cartographic Survey of Huron and Southern Bruce Counties 1864–1981," *Urban History Review* 15 (1987): 264.

17. *Blairmore Enterprise*, May 5, 1932 (reprinting *Hanna Herald*).

18. Ibid., May 23, 1913; *Cardston Globe*, Sept 14, 1916.

19. *Drumheller Mail*, February 14, 1929, September 15, 1938; *Claresholm Local Press*, July 13, 1939. City board of trade demands about roads were identical (Calgary Board of Trade to Fallow, February 28, 1936, PP, File 903A, PAA).

20. *Drumheller Mail*, February 12 and April 9, 1925; *Cardston News*, February 18, 1926.

21. *Drumheller Mail*, January 19, 1928.

22. *Blairmore Enterprise*, March 21, 1912, August 18, 1921, May 31, 1928.

23. *Drumheller Review*, December 24, 1920, July 26, 1928.

24. *Peace River Record*, December 31, 1915, May 7, 1925.

25. *Cardston News*, February 20, 1930, March 14, 1939; *Grande Prairie Herald Tribune*, February 15, 1945, March 20, 1947; *Peace River Record*, August 16, 1946.

26. *Cardston Record*, September 3, 1898; *Macleod Advertiser*, December 3, 1909; Minutes, Macleod board of trade, October 29, 1907, February 23, 1909, January 28, 1919, M1430, GAI.

27. *Lacombe Western Globe*, February 2, 1910; *Grande Prairie Herald*, March 23, 1928.

28. *Macleod Spectator*, January 15, 1914.

29. *Grande Prairie Herald*, March 23, 1928.

30. Voisey, "The Urbanization of the Canadian Prairies," 97.

31. *Macleod Advertiser*, April 6, 1911.

32. *Claresholm Review*, January 22, 1909.

33. David Breen, "The Canadian West and the Ranching Frontier 1875–1922," (Ph.D. dissertation, University of Alberta), 142.

34. *Macleod Gazette*, March 21, 1888; Breen, "The Canadian West and the Ranching Frontier," 128–87.

35. *Macleod Gazette*, December 13, 1887, January 4 and 25, 1888.

36. Breen, "The Canadian West and the Ranching Frontier," 351; *Macleod Spectator*, January 21, 1913.

37. For example, *Claresholm Local Press*, September 29, 1933.

38. *Claresholm Review*, September 30, 1909.

39. *Macleod Spectator*, January 21 and September 9, 1913; *Cardston Globe*, January 23, 1914.

40. *Macleod Spectator*, April 9, 1914.

41. Ibid., September 9, 1913, April 9, 1914.

42. Ibid., September 17 and 24, 1914.

43. Deputy Minister to Reid, October 28, 1913, 78.133/49/407, PAA; *Lacombe Western Globe*, April 10 and October 13, 1912.

44. *Peace River Record*, April 27, 1922; *Macleod Spectator*, January 21, 1913; *Grande Prairie Herald*, April 25, 1916.

45. *Blairmore Enterprise*, July 11 and March 21, 1912.

46. *Macleod Spectator*, January 15, 1914.

47. *Claresholm Review*, May 1, 1908, May 4, 1911.

48. *Lacombe Western Globe*, August 6, 1913; *Macleod Spectator*, January 21, 1913.

49. On the private approach in Saskatchewan see, C.O. White, "The Humboldt Municipal Electrical Utility: A Grassroots Feature of the Saskatchewan Power Corporation," *Saskatchewan History* 29 (1976): 103. On civic ownership in Winnipeg see Artibise, *Winnipeg: A Social History*, 88–101.

50. *Claresholm Review*, October 18, 1907; *Drumheller Review*, April 10, 1914.

51. Patterson, "The Early History of Claresholm," 38.

52. For example, *Blairmore Enterprise*, December 28, 1911; *Macleod Gazette*, October 19, 1900; John Weaver, "Edmonton's Perilous Course, 1904–1929," *Urban History Review* 2–77 (1977): 24–25.

53. For example, *Grande Prairie Herald Tribune*, January 21, 1937.

54. *Lacombe Western Globe*, October 13, 1912.

55. *Macleod Gazette*, June 14, 1887, January 4, July 25 and November 1, 1888.

56. *Macleod Advance*, June 4, 1907, August 28, 1908; *Lacombe Western Globe*, April 27, 1910.

57. *Macleod Spectator*, January 15, 1914; *Macleod Advertiser*, February 15, 1912.

58. *Macleod Gazette*, January 8, 1897 (financial statement).

59. *Macleod Gazette*, April 18, 1889, August 10, 1894, February 7 and July 24, 1896; *Dun & Bradstreet Commercial Ratings*, Macleod, Blairmore, 1910–1912; Taped and Written Interviews with Pioneers from Bellevue, Coleman and Blairmore, 72.355, Files 1–6, PAA.

60. Blue, *Alberta Past and Present*, Vol. 1, 165; Deputy Attorney General to Perrie, November 15, 1912, 66.166/112c, PAA; *Blairmore Enterprise*, October 24, 1913.

61. Thorold J. Tronrud, "Buying Prosperity: The Bonusing of Factories at the Lakehead 1885–1914," *Urban History Review* 19 (1990): 11.

62. *Macleod Advertiser*, July 11, 1912; *Peace River Record*, January 23, 1931.

63. *Drumheller Mail*, January 18, 1934.

64. *Peace River Record*, November 5, 1937; *Peace River Record Gazette*, April 20, 1945.

65. On this pattern in the Olds, Didsbury area, see Jensen, "The County of Mountain View," 90–93.

66. *Blairmore Enterprise*, July 31, 1924.

67. *Grande Prairie Herald*, March 10, 1914, July 18, 1916, July 6, 1928; *Grande Prairie Herald Tribune*, August 26, 1943, November 13, 1947.

68. *Cardston News*, March 14, 1939.

69. *Macleod Times*, May 11, 1922; Colwell to Mullen, October 6, 1944, Department of Agriculture Papers, 73.307/115, PAA.

70. *Cardston Globe*, February 18, 1926; *Cardston News*, February 10, 1927.

71. *Claresholm Local Press*, April 4, 1940. See also *Peace River Record Gazette*, May 5, 1944.

72. *Claresholm Local Press*, January 10, 1946; *Lacombe Western Globe*, April 9, 1936.

73. *Drumheller Mail*, March 22 and December 6, 1928, April 4, 1929, November 7, 1946; *Dun and Bradstreet Commercial Ratings*, Drumheller, 1932 and 1934.

74. Kirk Lambrecht, "Regional Development and Social Strife: Early Coal Mining in Alberta," *Prairie Forum* 4 (1979): 274–75. See also *Blairmore Enterprise*, October 8, 1937; *Drumheller Mail*, January 2, 1930, February 27, 1941, March 9, 1944.

75. *Macleod Times*, May 21, 1925; *Drumheller Mail*, December 14, 1933.

76. *Coleman Journal*, November 12, 1936, November 16, 1939; *Blairmore Enterprise*, October 8, 1937.

77. *Grande Prairie Herald*, April 8, 1913.

78. For example, Shield to Ross, April 30, 1924 and Ross to Shield, May 3, 1924, 67.303, PAA.

79. *Macleod Advertiser*, March 18, 1910.

80. Johnston to Attorney General, December 19, 1901, Resolution of Lethbridge board of trade, March 18, 1904, Campbell to Harvey, April 11, 1902, 66.166/188, PAA; *Grande Prairie Herald*, March 9, 1933.

81. Terry Chapman, "The Controversy Over Court Houses in Southern Alberta," *Alberta History* 37 (1989): 10; *Claresholm Review*, April 8, 1909.

82. Minutes, Board of Agricultural Education, August 20, 1913, Department of Agriculture Papers, 74.293, PAA; *Macleod Advertiser*, May 18, 1911; *Cardston Alberta Star*, February 24, 1911.

83. *Claresholm Review*, May 4 and 18, 1911.

84. *Claresholm Review Advertiser*, October 8, 1926; *Claresholm Local Press*, January 25, 1929, January 30, 1931, July 28, 1933.

85. *Claresholm Local Press*, January 9 and May 8, 1941, April 2, 1942, July 1, 1943, March 29, 1945.

86. *Claresholm Local Press*, October 15, 1942; *Drumheller Mail*, January 4, 1940, February 13, 1941, January 29, 1942.

87. Hanson, *Local Government in Alberta*, 36–39.

88. *Drumheller Review*, December 27, 1918.

89. Drumheller Valley Historical Association, *The Hills of Home*, second edition (Calgary: D.W. Friesen and Sons Ltd., 1974), 54.

90. *Grande Prairie Herald*, April 11, 1922; *Blairmore Enterprise*, February 2, 1945.

91. *Cardston News*, February 20, 1930.

92. Card to Minister, February 17, 1936, 67.303/3062/6, PAA.

93. *Grande Prairie Herald*, March 23, 1928; *Blairmore Enterprise*, May 2, 1929.

94. *Coleman Journal*, July 27, 1933.

95. *Drumheller Mail*, March 27, 1930, March 23, 1944.

96. *Cardston News*, February 20, 1930, February 18, 1932, July 7, 1936.

97. *Lacombe Western Globe*, June 19, 1930.

98. On phases of urban growth, see Spelt, *Urban Development in South Central Ontario* (Toronto: McClelland and Stewart, 1972), 186.

99. Quoted in Douglas McCalla, "An Introduction to the Nineteenth Century Business World," in *Essays in Canadian Business History*, ed. Tom Traves (Toronto: McClelland and Stewart, 1984), 16.

100. Edward K. Muller, "Regional Urbanization and the Selective Growth of Towns in North American Regions," *Journal of Historical Geography* 3 (1977): 22.

101. L.D. McCann, "Urban Growth in Western Canada 1881–1961," *The Albertan Geographer* 5 (1969): 65–66. On the significance of politics in Toronto's growth, see Spelt, *Urban Development in South-Central Ontario*.

102. *Cardston News*, October 23, 1930.

6 | DOING BUSINESS IN THE SMALL TOWN

1. *Dun and Bradstreet Commercial Ratings*, Macleod 1887, Macleod and Claresholm July 1910; *Macleod Gazette*, January 1, 1906.

2. Frits Pannekoek, "Wetaskiwin Business and Prince Edward Islanders," *Alberta History* 37 (1989): 10.

3. *Dun and Bradstreet Commercial Ratings*, September 1916 and 1917, Grande Prairie City and Edson; *Grande Prairie Herald*, July 6, 1915.

4. *Grande Prairie Northern Tribune*, March 18, 1937; *Dun and Bradstreet Commercial Ratings*, Grande Prairie, July 1939; *Cardston Alberta Star*, April 11, 1908.

5. Renshaw to Soutter, July 24, 1940, 78.133/118c, PAA; *Coleman Journal*, September 3, 1931.

6. This conclusion is based on obituaries and other references in town papers. See also Bettison, Kenward and Taylor, *Urban Affairs in Alberta*, 14; Pannekoek, "Wetaskiwin Business," 8.

7. *Macleod Gazette*, March 1, 1901; *Lacombe Western Globe*, April 14, 1938.

8. *Lacombe Western Globe*, April 4, 1929; *Dun and Bradstreet Commercial Ratings*, Lacombe, September 1929.

9. *Drumheller Mail*, May 14, 1931; *Coleman Journal*, October 4, 1928.

10 Ouimette to Deputy Minister, February 25, 1909, (letterhead) 74.174/77/1048, PAA.

11. *Cardston Record*, August 6, 1898; *Cardston Globe*, August 15, 1912; *Macleod Gazette*, September 9, 1904 (on Blairmore); *Dun and Bradstreet Commercial Ratings*, Cardston, 1898–1900.

12. Michael Winstanley, *The Shopkeeper's World 1830–1914* (Manchester: Manchester University Press, 1983), 16.

13. *Macleod Advertiser*, January 5, 1911; *Cardston Globe*, January 9, 1913.

14. *Peace River Record*, September 18, 1936; *Drumheller Mail*, May 29, 1947.

15. McCalla, "The Nineteenth Century Business World," 20.

16. For example, *Cardston Globe*, January 9, 1913.

17. *Cardston News*, August 21, 1930; Henry Klassen, "Cowdry Brothers: Private Bankers in Southwestern Alberta 1886–1905," *Alberta History* 37 (1989): 10–19.

18. *Macleod Gazette*, February 12, 1891.

19. *Dun and Bradstreet Commercial Ratings* for towns cited, 1902–45; *Macleod Advertiser*, July 9, 1909; *Coleman Journal*, May 24, 1918, November 12, 1925; *Coleman Miner*, December 9, 1910.

20. *Claresholm Review*, January 22 and December 30, 1909; *Claresholm Review Advertiser*, July 6, 1917; *Claresholm Local Press*, May 27, 1938; *Drumheller Mail*, August 23, 1918, July 21, 1932; *Cardston News*, November 19, 1931, May 4, 1933; *Grande Prairie Herald*, January 11, 1929.

21. Cross to Woods, March 8, 1909, 66.166/783a, PAA.

22. Donald G. Wetherell and Irene R.A. Kmet, *Homes in Alberta: Building, Trends, and Design* (Edmonton: University of Alberta Press, 1991), 139–40.

23. Bentley to Cross, September 8, 1908, 66.166/927, PAA.

24. *Drumheller Mail*, January 28, 1932.

25. Ibid.

26. *North West Territories Gazette*, March 15, 1899; *Blairmore Enterprise*, May 24, 1918; *Coleman Bulletin*, October 26, 1917.

27. Winstanley, *The Shopkeeper's World*, 83–88.

28. *Macleod Spectator*, September 9, 1913.

29. *Macleod Gazette*, July 24 and August 14, 1890; *Farm and Ranch Review*, April 20, 1910. See also *Claresholm Review Advertiser*, September 18, 1916 (letter to editor).

30. *Cardston News*, April 16, 1931; *Peace River Record*, December 11, 1931.

31. *Peace River Record*, October 16, 1931.

32. Brett Fairbairn, *Building a Dream: The Co-operative Retailing System in Western Canada 1928–1988* (Saskatoon: Western Producer Prairie Books, 1989), 15–16, 35–43. On wholesalers refusing to sell to co-ops, see 1915 correspondence, 66.166/1250, PAA.

33. John Benson, "Hawking and Peddling in Canada, 1867–1914," *Histoire sociale/Social History* 18 (1985): 75–83.

34. Memorandum, (n.d.) [1928], PP, File 242, PAA; Renshaw to Soutter, July 24, 1940, 78.133/118c, PAA.

35. *Blairmore Enterprise*, August 8, 1913.

36. *Farm and Ranch Review*, August 1905 (advertisement); *Macleod Gazette*, September 4, 1903.

37. *Farm and Ranch Review*, February 5, 1918. Showing the early importance of city stores in mail order, the terms "mail order house" and "department store" were often used synonymously in towns.

38. *Grande Prairie Herald*, February 10, 1914; *Red Deer Advocate*, February 13, 1914; *Blairmore Enterprise*, December 28, 1922.

39. Trowbridge to Brownlee, January 2, 1932, PP, File 358, PAA; ARMA, Memorandum to Aberhart, November 1935, PP, File 912A, PAA.

40. *Farm and Ranch Review*, June 20, 1910; Trowbridge to Brownlee, January 2, 1932, PP, File 358, PAA.

41. Stuart Ewen and Elizabeth Ewen, *Channels of Desire: Mass Images and the Shaping of American Consciousness* (New York: McGraw Hill Book Co., 1982), 63.

42. *Cardston News* (reprinting *Drumheller Mail*), February 25, 1926; *Grande Prairie Herald* (reprinting *Hanna Herald*), October 12, 1925; ARMA, Memorandum to Aberhart, November 1935, PP, File 912A, PAA.

43. *Macleod Advertiser*, November 24, 1910; *Drumheller Mail*, January 6, 1938.

44. *Coleman Journal*, March 12, 1936; *Lacombe Globe*, September 28, 1939, December 11, 1941; *Cardston News*, November 23, 1937, June 13, 1939.

45. Retail Merchants Association of Canada to Brownlee, June 4, 1926, PP, File 154B, PAA.

46. *Edmonton Journal*, March 13, 1920; *Grande Prairie Herald*, March 6, 1917.

47. Lt. Governor to Secretary of State, September 15, 1904, 192.4/80, SABR; *Macleod Gazette*, November 9, 1886; *Coleman Journal*, June 27, 1935.

48. Macdonald to Attorney General, April 15, 1911, 66.166/446, PAA; Western Canadian Fuel Association to Deputy Minister, July 28, 1925, 78.133/99b, PAA; *Drumheller Mail*, September 24, 1936.

49. *Macleod Spectator*, February 4, 1915; *Coleman Miner*, December 9, 1910.

50. Chief Inspector to Leslie, August 8, 1935, 78.133/115c, PAA.

51. For example, Saskatoon City Commissioner to Deputy Minister, August 5, 1935, 78.133/118c, PAA.

52. *Grande Prairie Herald*, September 21, 1920; Memorandum, ARMA Re: Transient Trading, Hawking and Peddling, n.d. [1927], PP, File 242, PAA.

53. Craig to Reid, October 23, 1930, 78.133/106a, PAA.

54. Soutter to Key, March 31, 1930, and Key to Soutter, April 11, 1930, 74.174/1032b, PAA.

55. LaFleche to Brownlee, March 3, 1928, PP, File 242, PAA; *Claresholm Review Advertiser*, June 17, 1921.

56. Taylor to Attorney General, December 31, 1913, 66.166/36b, PAA.

57. For example, *Grande Prairie Herald*, December 1, 1924.

58. *Peace River Record*, October 16, 1931.

59. Key to Deputy Minister, March 28, 1933, Lyne to Mayor, March 20, 1933, Key to Deputy Minister, January 4, 1938, 74.174/1032b, PAA; *Drumheller Mail*, November 24, 1932, January 31 and February 7, 1935, January 27, February 3 and March 10, 1938.

60. *Peace River Record*, October 2, 1931; *Macleod Gazette*, October 30, 1896.

61. *Claresholm Review Advertiser*, October 20, 1916 (re: Eaton's); *Claresholm Review*, July 6, 1917.

62. *Claresholm Review*, August 12, 1912; *Macleod Advertiser*, September 3, 1909; *Lacombe Western Globe*, June 14, 1934.

63. *Cardston Globe*, September 14, 1916; *Macleod Advertiser*, September 3 and 17, 1909.

64. *Cardston News*, March 7, 1935; *Cardston Globe*, September 14, 1916; *Claresholm Review*, September 18, 1913; *Cardston Alberta Star*, February 18, 1910.

65. Retail Merchants Association of Canada to Brownlee, June 4, 1926, PP, File 154B, PAA; Trowern to Brownlee, October 28, 1927, PP, File 242, PAA; ARMA Memorandum, November, 1935, PP, File 912A, PAA.

66. *Claresholm Review*, June 19, 1908.

67. *Cardston News*, July 2, 1931; *Drumheller Mail*, January 28, 1932; *Lacombe Western Globe*, December 6, 1934.

68. ARMA to Brownlee, (n.d) [1927], PP, File 242, PAA; Barons to Aberhart, November 21, 1936, PP, File 921A, PAA.

69. Godfrey M. Lebhar, *Chain Stores in America 1859–1959* (New York: Chain Store Publishing Co., 1959), 101–81.

70. Bettison, Kenward and Taylor, *Urban Affairs in Alberta*, 61.

71. *Cardston News*, April 12, 1934.

72. Ibid.; *Grande Prairie Northern Tribune*, March 26, 1936.

73. *Blairmore Enterprise*, October 25, 1934.

74. *Grande Prairie Northern Tribune*, March 26, 1936.

75. *Macleod Advertiser*, March 9 and May 4, 1911.

76. *Blairmore Enterprise*, September 19, 1912; *Macleod Spectator*, September 9 and October 2, 1913.

77. *Peace River Record*, October 2, 1931.

78. *Macleod Gazette*, February 21, 1889; Proceedings of the Alberta Coal Commission, September 24, 1935 (transcripts of hearings), Legislative Assembly Papers, 70.427/44, PAA; Claresholm Local History Book Club, *Where the Wheatlands Meet the Range*, 87.

79. *Claresholm Review*, June 28, 1907, January 8, 1914; *Cardston Alberta Star*, May 3 and 10, 1907; *Peace River Record*, May 24, 1929, October 2, 1931.

80. *Macleod Advance*, November 24 and December 8, 1908.

81. McKenzie to Agricultural Committee, March 17, 1933, PP, File 83C, PAA; *The Case for Alberta Part I: Alberta's Problems and Dominion Provincial Relations*

(Edmonton: King's Printer, 1938), 118; ARMA to Brownlee, January 23, 1931, PP, File 242, PAA.

82. Memorandum, January 23, 1931, PP, File 242, PAA; Hardwick to Brownlee, February 13, 1932, PP, File 83A, PAA.

83. *Claresholm Review Advertiser*, June 17, 1921; *Claresholm Local Press*, January 7, 1938.

84. *Claresholm Review*, September 25, 1913; *Cardston Globe*, November 12, 1914.

85. For example, *Cardston Globe*, November 12, 1914.

86. For example, *Cardston Alberta Star*, January 27, 1911; *Grande Prairie Herald*, June 1, 1925; *Coleman Journal*, May 13, 1926.

87. *Peace River Record*, May 22, 1931; *Drumheller Mail*, December 3, 1931; *Cardston News*, November 30, 1939.

88. *Blairmore Enterprise*, March 19, 1925.

89. William R. Leach, "Transformations in a Culture of Consumption: Women and Department Stores, 1890–1925," *The Journal of American History* 71 (1984): 322, 328.

90. *Drumheller Mail*, August 4, 1932; *Grande Prairie Herald*, May 25, 1925. On such events in other towns see: *Cardston News*, November 10 and 17, 1936; *Peace River Record*, November 6, 1924.

91. *Cardston News*, December 14, 1937, March 8, 1938; *Lacombe Globe*, December 8, 1938; *Peace River Record*, December 22, 1929, December 9, 1938.

92. *Lacombe Western Globe*, April 17, 1930, July 2, 1931.

93. *Claresholm Review*, June 13, 1912; *Blairmore Enterprise*, August 8, 1913; *Peace River Record*, December 5, 1914.

94. *Blairmore Enterprise*, April 19, 1928; *Drumheller Mail*, May 19, 1932.

95. McKee to English, July 10, 1931, 78.133/c, PAA; *Claresholm Review*, November 9, 1914, August 11, 1916.

96. *Cardston News*, May 23, 1929.

97. *Drumheller Mail*, November 24, 1932; *Peace River Record*, September 29, 1933; *Blairmore Enterprise*, August 24, 1933; *Grande Prairie Northern Tribune*, October 26, 1933.

98. "Alberta Made Goods Supper," (typescript) n.d. [November 1941], Taylor Papers, 70.219/140, PAA.

99. For example, *Claresholm Local Press*, October 16, 1936.

100. Smith to Denis, October 25, 1941, 70.219/140, PAA.

101. D'Arcy Hande, "Saskatchewan Merchants in the Great Depression: Regionalism and the Crusade Against Big Business," *Saskatchewan History* 43 (1991): 27–29.

102. *Grande Prairie Northern Tribune*, May 17, 1934; *Grande Prairie Herald*, November 2, 1925; ARMA to Brownlee, n.d [1927], PP, File 242, PAA.

103. *Grande Prairie Herald*, November 2, 1925.

104. *Peace River Record*, February 3, 1938; *Drumheller Mail*, February 21, 1935; C.B. Macpherson, *Democracy in Alberta* (Toronto: University of Toronto Press, 1953), 231.

105. *Cardston News*, September 9, 1926.

106. Winstanley, *The Shopkeeper's World*, 75–80; Michael Bliss, *A Living Profit. Studies in the Social History of Canadian Business, 1883–1911* (Toronto: McClelland and Stewart, 1974).

7 | TOWN PLANNING AND ITS IMPACT ON MAIN STREET

1. Holtz, "Small Town Alberta," 21; Howard Wright Marshall, "A Good Gridiron: The Vernacular Design of a Western Cow Town," in *Perspectives in Vernacular Architecture II*, ed. Camille Wells, pp. 81–88 (Columbia: University of Missouri Press, 1986). In prairie Canada, most town blocks were rectangular, unlike the United States where square blocks were common.

2. Holtz, "Small Town Alberta," 121.

3. *Macleod Gazette*, October 31, 1884.

4. Holtz, "Small Town Alberta," 123, 128; Stelter, "A Regional Framework for Urban History," 197; Regehr, *The Canadian Northern*, 190–91; *Macleod Gazette*, August 14, 1882.

5. Holtz, "Small Town Alberta," 92, 101–3.

6. Ibid., 92–100. For spatial distribution of these plans, see Holtz, Fig. 14, 125.

7. Ibid., 11, 114.

8. *Cardston Record*, April 28, 1899 (reprinting *Macleod Advance*).

9. Raymond Lifchez, "Inspired Planning: Mormon and Fourierist Communities in the Nineteenth Century," *Landscape* 20 (1976): 34.

10. Petition, April 17, 1899, Sessional Papers, Northwest Territories, R–283, Box 14, File xxi 3, SABR; *Cardston Record*, February 8, 1899; *Northwest Territories Gazette*, February 15, 1899, p. 4, and June 29, 1901, p. 3; Deputy Minister to Laurie, February 2, 1914, 74.174/977c, PAA; Jacobs to Department of Municipal Affairs, March 18, 1943, 78.133/419b, PAA. Cardston came under the *Town Act* in 1934.

11. Bettison, Kenward and Taylor, *Urban Affairs in Alberta*, 17–18.

12. Hanson, *Local Government in Alberta*, 27, 29; MacDonald and McBride to Pierre, May 12, 1913, and Pierre to Tett, March 20, 1913, 74.174/996d, PAA. In comparison, in 1956 the average density in Alberta towns was 1,000 per square mile, still a relatively low figure.

13. Western Canada Insurance Underwriters Association, *Supplementary Report*, Blairmore, April 30, 1932, Provincial Secretary Papers, 67.4/53, PAA; *Supplementary Report*, Coleman, October 20, 1936, 67.4/129, PAA; *Supplementary Report*, Drumheller, October 10, 1933, 67.4/153b, PAA; *Supplementary Report*, Peace River, June 11, 1930, 67.4/344, PAA; *Supplementary Report*, Cardston, April 28, 1932, 67.4/93, PAA; *Grande Prairie Herald*, August 23, 1926.

14. *Cardston Globe*, January 9, 1913; Beebe to Attorney General, May 14, 1903, 66.166/159, PAA.

15. In local opinion, this is said to be a response to the prevailing winds from the west. The landform of the business district, which drops sharply on the east side of main street, was probably more important (*Cardston News*, March 26, 1931).

16. *Macleod Gazette*, February 26, 1904; *Lacombe Western Globe*, August 24, 1909; *Peace River Record*, September 16, 1915; *Blairmore Enterprise*, May 8, 1924.

17. *Grande Prairie Northern Tribune*, November 12, 1936; Inspection Report, Lacombe, June 1, 1938, 67.4/279b, PAA; Inspection Report, Drumheller, January 31, 1939, 67.4/153b, PAA; Johnston to Moore, March 29, 1941, 67.4/129, PAA. As elsewhere in Canada, towns were too small to have residential areas divided solely by class. Yet there was always a residential area where the wealthiest tended to live. In mining towns, ethnicity and class significantly shaped residential segregation. At Coleman, two ethnic ghettoes, "Slav town" and "Bush town," emerged shortly after the town's formation. At Drumheller in 1929, there was shack housing throughout the town, but the north side of the river across from the town was largely shack housing of miners (*Coleman Miner*, June 19, 1908; *Drumheller Mail*, June 13 and July 11, 1929).

18. *Blairmore Enterprise*, March 14, April 25, May 30, July 11 and August 8, 1912, February 28, 1913, March 13, 1914. On growth of new or specialized commercial areas in response to corporate and economic developments, see Gunter Grad and Deryck Holdsworth, "Large Office Buildings and Their Changing Occupancy: King Street, Toronto, 1850–1880" *SSAC Bulletin* 10 (1985): 19–26.

19. Burgess, "The Town" (Radio Talk) June 4, 1928, 72–85–15, UAA; "What Our Towns Want" (Radio Talk, June 3, 1929), 72–28–20, UAA.

20. Conybeare to Cross, April 5, 1906, 66.166/460, PAA; *Cardston Globe*, July 18, 1912, May 22, 1920; *Cardston News*, February 18, 1926.

21. *Macleod Gazette*, February 22, August 4 and September 1, 1899, April 6, 1900.

22. For example, ibid., December 18, 1890; Chapman, "The Controversy Over Courts and Court Houses," 2–10.

23. *Cardston Record*, August 20, 1898; *Cardston Globe*, March 6, 1914; *Peace River Record*, January 8, 1932, July 5, 1938.

24. *Drumheller Mail*, December 26, 1918, February 27, 1930; *Cardston News*, July 11, 1939. A customs house was attached to the post office for examination of incoming parcels.

25. *Cardston News*, November 30, 1939.

26. Inspection Report, Lacombe, August 29, 1946, 67.4/280, PAA; *Blairmore Enterprise*, April 27, 1911; *Drumheller Mail*, March 7, 1919; *Cardston News*, May 7, 1940; *Coleman Journal*, May 4 and November 30, 1933, April 20, 1934.

27. Isabel Campbell, *Grande Prairie: Capital of the Peace* (Alberta: s.n. ca. 1968), 135.

28. *Grande Prairie Herald*, July 13 and August 3, 1920; *Grande Prairie Northern Tribune*, July 6, 1933, October 20, 1938, March 9 and 16, 1939; Inspection

Report, Grande Prairie, September 29, 1936, 67.4/218, PAA. The first library in Grande Prairie was in a church basement.

29. Bettison, Kenward and Taylor, *Urban Affairs in Alberta*, 18, 24, n.74, 58. "Town Planning Progress in Alberta," December 5, 1931, 78.133/406, PAA.

30. Horace Seymour, "The Problems of Small Communities," *The Press Bulletin*, November 20, 1931.

31. Burgess, "Civic Pride," 72–28–19, UAA.

32. *Blairmore Enterprise*, October 20, 1927; Burgess, "The Town," 72–28–15, UAA; Bettison, Kenward and Taylor, *Urban Affairs in Alberta*, 47; "Technical Observations on Town Planning Progress in Alberta," September 9, 1931, Department of Municipal Affairs Papers, 71.4, PAA.

33. *Drumheller Mail*, March 14 and 21, 1929.

34. *Peace River Record*, October 18, 1929.

35. *Drumheller Mail*, June 6, 1929; Burgess, "The Town," 72–28–15, UAA.

36. *Drumheller Mail*, June 6, 1929; *Cardston News*, September 18, 1930; *Grande Prairie Herald*, March 28, 1930.

37. "Town Planning Progress in Alberta," December 5, 1931, 78.133/406, PAA; *Lacombe Western Globe*, February 26, 1931.

38. *Grande Prairie Northern Tribune*, May 17, 1934; *Peace River Record*, May 2 and September 9, 1930, March 6, 1931, May 31, 1935. In 1931 the Drumheller town planning commission recommended the creation of a single municipal district for the valley. Later, a single government for the valley excluding the city of Drumheller was formed (*Drumheller Mail*, January 22, 1931).

39. Holtz, "Small Town Alberta," 49, 62–63.

40. *Blairmore Enterprise*, March 14 and May 16, 1912; *Cardston Alberta Star*, July 9, 1909; *Peace River Record*, October 24, 1930.

41. *Blairmore Enterprise*, June 14, 1923.

42. *Drumheller Mail*, February 27, 1930; *Coleman Journal*, September 17, 1936.

43. *Drumheller Mail*, July 25, 1929; Bettison, Kenward and Taylor, *Urban Affairs in Alberta*, 52–53, 55.

44. Burgess, "General Business Districts" (lecture notes, n.d. [ca. 1945]), 72–28–98, UAA.

45. *Drumheller Mail*, June 30, 1932.

46. *Drumheller Mail*, October 20, 1932; *Grande Prairie Herald Tribune*, June 8 and December 7, 1944, April 4 and 18, and June 27, 1946.

8 | BUILDING MAIN STREET

1. Herb Stovel, "Storefront Evolution," *Canadian Heritage*, May-June 1983, 17.

2. *Peace River Record*, November 29, 1929, April 23, 1937.

3. Ibid., December 31, 1915, April 12, 1929; *Grande Prairie Herald*, April 11, 1916.

4. *Cardston Globe*, May 3, 1919. For examples about the fear of higher assessment, see *Grande Prairie Herald*, April 26, 1926 and *Claresholm Local Press*, May 2, 1946.

5. *Claresholm Review Advertiser*, August 25, 1928; *Coleman Journal*, May 9 and June 27, 1929; *Grande Prairie Herald Tribune*, May 15, 1947.

6. For example, Western Canada Insurance Underwriters Association, *Supplementary Report*, Lacombe, October 23, 1938, 67.4/277b, PAA; *Supplementary Report*, Blairmore, April 30, 1932, 67.4/53, PAA; *Supplementary Report*, Coleman, October 20, 1936, 67.4/129, PAA; *Supplementary Report*, Drumheller, October 10, 1933, 67.4/153b, PAA; *Supplementary Report*, Peace River, June 11, 1930, 67.4/344, PAA; *Supplementary Report*, Cardston, April 28, 1932, 67.4/93, PAA; *Supplementary Report*, Claresholm, October 23, 1942, 67.4/116a, PAA; Inspection Report, Peace River, September 29, 1936, 67.4/218, PAA; Inspection Report, Peace River, September 10, 1936, 67.4/344, PAA; *Peace River Record*, March 25, June 24 and May 13, 1932.

7. *Macleod Gazette*, August 24, 1900, January 11, 1901. The construction of the Grier building was charted weekly in the paper, but its fate did not inspire confidence: shortly after completion, the roof, the chimney, and a portion of the roof joists were torn off during a wind storm.

8. Stovel, "Storefront Evolution," 18.

9. Fort Macleod Provincial Historical Area Society, *A Walking/Driving Tour of Fort Macleod's Historic Downtown and Residential Area*, (n.d, n.p.), 2–4.

10. *Macleod Gazette*, April 14, 1899; *Claresholm Review*, December 22, 1910; *Blairmore Enterprise*, October 13, 1910. On brick construction, see *Cardston Alberta Star*, June 17 and October 14, 1910 and *Lacombe Western Globe*, July 23, 1907.

11. Richardson to Mitchell, May 4, 1921, 74.174/98a, PAA.

12. *Cardston News*, November 2, 1939; *Claresholm Local Press*, April 11, 1946, May 22, 1947.

13. *Grande Prairie Herald Tribune*, May 2, 1940.

14. Greg Utas, "Calgary Architecture: 1875–1915," (M. Environmental Design thesis, University of Calgary, 1975), 16–18; Jennifer Attebery, *Building Idaho: An Architectural History* (Moscow, Idaho: University of Idaho Press, 1991), 51–53.

15. *Macleod Gazette*, June 23, 1885.

16. Henry-Russel Hitchcock, *Architecture: Nineteenth and Twentieth Centuries* (New York: Penguin Books, 4th Integrated Edition, 1977), 626 n.531.1.

17. One effort to transcend the complexity of stylistic analysis is to use "compositional" types. Richard Longsteth found seven types in U.S. commercial buildings (Richard Longstreth, "Compositional Types in American Commercial Architecture," in *Perspectives in Vernacular Architecture II*, ed. Camille Wells, pp. 12–24 (Columbia: University of Missouri Press, 1986).

18. *Macleod Spectator*, December 14, 1913.

19. Utas, "Calgary Architecture, 1875–1915," 42; *Cardston News*, April 30, 1909.

20. Lyle Dick, "The Architecture of Image and Domination: Winnipeg's Confederation Life Building," *SSAC Bulletin* 12 (1987): 3–6.

21. Robert L. Alexander, "A Shopkeeper's Renaissance: Academic Design and Popular Architecture in Late Nineteenth Century Iowa City," in *Perspectives in Vernacular Architecture II*, ed. Camille Wells (Columbia: University of Missouri Press, 1986), 200, 207.

22. David Spector, "Edmonton Bank Architecture: The Neo Classical Age, 1904–1914," *Alberta History* 34 (1986): 11–16; Holdsworth and Everrit, "Bank Branches and Elevators," 50–55.

23. *Historical Walking and Driving Tour: Lacombe* (Edmonton: Alberta Culture and Multiculturalism, n.d.), item 19.

24. Dorothy Field, "The Moderne Style," *Alberta Past* 6 (1990): 1, 12.

25. Ibid., 1.

26. *Drumheller Mail*, June 20, 1929.

27. Field, "The Moderne Style," 1.

28. *Drumheller Mail*, July 28, 1932.

29. *Coleman Journal*, August 17, 1933.

30. Ibid., August 16, 1934.

31. *Peace River Record*, August 12 and September 2, 1932. See also *Cardston News*, July 20, 1937.

32. *Claresholm Local Press*, July 15 and September 23, 1938.

33. *Coleman Journal*, May 17, 1934.

34. *Macleod Gazette*, April 5, 1906.

35. Ibid., May 10, 1901.

36. *Cardston News*, September 23, 1926. See also *Lacombe Western Globe*, March 19, 1920.

37. *Coleman Journal*, May 3 and August 30, 1945.

38. *Drumheller Mail*, October 25, 1934. See also *Lacombe Globe*, August 24, 1939.

39. *Claresholm Local Press*, July 15 and September 23, 1938.

40. *Peace River Record Gazette*, April 20, 1945; *Coleman Journal*, March 13, 1941; *Drumheller Mail*, September 17, 1942.

41. Inspection Report, Grande Prairie, September 29, 1936, 67.4/218, PAA; Keith Walden, "Speaking Modern: Language, Culture and Hegemony in Grocery Window Displays 1887–1920," *Canadian Historical Review* 70 (1989): 287–90; *Macleod Spectator*, March 30, 1916.

42. Kelly Crossman, *Architecture in Transition: From Art to Practice 1885–1906* (Kingston and Montreal: McGill-Queen's University Press, 1987), 68.

43. Leach, "Transformations in a Culture of Consumption," 323.

44. *Macleod Advertiser*, April 6, 1911. See also *Blairmore Enterprise*, July 11, 1912.

45. *Peace River Record*, March 18, 1932.

46. *Blairmore Enterprise*, June 16, 1921; *Coleman Journal*, October 29, 1925.

47. *Grande Prairie Herald*, May 9, 1930.

48. *Claresholm Review*, October 20, 1910, August 10, 1911; *Blairmore Enterprise*, December 27, 1912; *Macleod Gazette*, December 19, 1902; *Macleod Advance*, May 5, 1908.

49. *Grande Prairie Herald*, July 21, 1921; *Coleman Journal*, October 20, 1927; *Peace River Record*, January 4, 1935.

50. *Blairmore Enterprise*, December 24, 1915, April 22, 1926; *Peace River Record*, February 9, 1945; *Grande Prairie Herald Tribune*, August 12, 1943.

51. *Macleod Gazette*, December 21, 1886; *Cardston News*, December 14, 1937; *Grande Prairie Northern Tribune*, December 12, 1935.

52. *Grande Prairie Herald*, April 11, 1916, July 24, 1923. For other bylaws see *Coleman Miner*, February 3, 1911 and Deputy Attorney General to Gregson, August 28, 1907 [Lacombe], 66.166/781, PAA.

53. *Drumheller Mail*, August 22, 1940.

54. *Coleman Journal*, January 21, 1932.

55. Ibid., January 21 and September 22, 1932.

56. *Drumheller Mail*, February 28, 1929; *Blairmore Enterprise*, June 13, 1935; *Grande Prairie Northern Tribune*, June 3, 1937; *Grande Prairie Herald Tribune*, March 28, 1946; *Cardston News*, March 26, 1931, September 6, 1938.

57. *Coleman Journal*, July 18, 1935 (reprinting *Blairmore Enterprise*).

58. *Blairmore Enterprise*, January 31, 1935, September 3, 1937, May 6, 1938; *Drumheller Mail*, February 7, 1935, April 30 and June 6, 1936, August 26, 1937.

59. *Claresholm Review*, September 30, 1909; *Drumheller Mail*, October 25, 1934.

60. Burgess, "Civic Pride," 72–28–19, UAA; "What Our Towns Want," (Radio Talk, June 3, 1929), 72–28–20, UAA.

61. Burgess, "The Town," 72–28–15, UAA.

62. Burgess, "Speech to Barrhead Chamber of Commerce," June 4, 1947 (italics in original), 72–28–63, UAA.

63. Burgess, "Improvement of Business Street Fronts," March 15, 1946, 72–28–60, UAA.

64. *Cardston News*, November 30, 1933.

65. Pierce Lewis, "Small Town in Pennsylvania," *Annals of the Association of American Geographers* 62 (1972): 348–51.

66. *Claresholm Review*, December 22, 1910.

9 | "Sources of Comfort and Convenience":
The Improvement of Main Street

1. *Blairmore Enterprise*, May 16 and February 22, 1912.

2. *Claresholm Review*, August 17, 1908.

3. *Macleod Gazette*, December 12, 1884, July 10, 1896.

4. *Coleman Journal*, December 19, 1935. On the same conditions in North Battleford, Saskatchewan, see Joseph Drummond Shepley, "Reminiscences of a Pioneer Land Surveyor," *Saskatchewan History* 41 (1988): 69.

5. For example, *Macleod Gazette*, November 2, 1900.

6. *Blairmore Enterprise*, September 26, 1913; Cameron to Deputy Attorney General, May 11, 1908, 74.174/1048, PAA; Deputy Minister to Beebe, May 13, 1908, 74.174/1040, PAA.

7. Correspondence, bylaws and clippings, Lacombe sidewalks, March 17 and July 28, 1913, May 11, 1915, 74.174/996c and 996d, PAA; *Lacombe Western Globe*, May 4 and 18, 1910, June 12, 1912; *Macleod Advertiser*, June 24, 1910. Fort Macleod's sidewalk building was so ambitious that in 1910 it overspent its sidewalk budget by $20,000 (ibid., September 15, 1910). On sidewalk construction elsewhere see *Cardston Alberta Star*, November 12, 1909 and *Grande Prairie Herald*, April 11, 1916.

8. *Drumheller Mail*, September 7 and 21, and August 10, 1933; *Grande Prairie Herald*, August 7, 1923. Tar sands were used in Vegreville and other towns for roads and sidewalks. Barry Ferguson, *Athabasca Oil Sands, Northern Resource Exploration 1875–1951* (Regina: Canadian Plains Research Centre, 1985), 63–64. See also *Good Roads*, September 1925, 20.

9. *Cardston News*, July 18, 1939; *Drumheller Mail*, June 4, 1936.

10. *Lacombe Western Globe*, September 28 and October 27, 1938; *Claresholm Review*, July 15, 1909; *Blairmore Enterprise*, February 22, 1912; *Drumheller Mail*, January 5, 1928; *Lacombe Globe*, July 11, 1940.

11. Wolfgang Schivelbusch, *Disenchanted Night: The Industrialization of Light in the Nineteenth Century*, trans. Angela Davis (Berkeley: University of California Press, 1988), 81–134. As Schivelbusch notes, however, continuous light also became a symbol of surveillance and tyranny.

12. *Coleman Journal*, January 27, 1938.

13. *Grande Prairie Herald Tribune*, October 17 and November 7, 1930, January 16, 1931, September 27, 1945, October 24, 1946; *Western Business and Industry*, May 1947, 51.

14. *Macleod Gazette*, May 11, 1886; *Claresholm Review*, December 9, 1909, August 10, 1911; *Claresholm Local Press*, May 3, 1935, May 6, 1938, March 13, 1947.

15. *Cardston Globe*, July 6, 1916; *Cardston News*, June 9, 1927, December 5, 1929, January 8, 1931; *Drumheller Mail*, August 23, 1928; *Grande Prairie Herald*, May 10, 1929; *Grande Prairie Herald Tribune*, April 18, 1940.

16. *Macleod Gazette*, July 10, 1896; *Claresholm Review*, June 5, 1913, March 12, 1920; *Lacombe Western Globe*, April 17, 1930.

17. *Claresholm Review*, November 10, 1910; *Coleman Journal*, August 16, 1934; *Cardston News*, August 11, 1936; *Drumheller Mail*, May 6, 1937.

18. *Drumheller Mail*, September 22, 1938, November 30, 1939, September 4, 1941, June 26, 1947.

19. *Grande Prairie Herald*, July 22, 1927.

20. For examples see Lacombe, A Bylaw Regulating Streets, March 5, 1907, 66.166/781, PAA and *Coleman Miner*, February 3, 1911.

21. *Claresholm Review*, June 1, 1911; *Drumheller Mail*, September 1, 1928, October 20, 1932, June 14, 1934. Motor vehicle registrations in 1928 included: Claresholm, 672; Drumheller, 479; Lacombe, 502; Medicine Hat, 1012; Calgary, 9,961 (*Claresholm Review Advertiser*, June 1, 1928).

22. *Cardston News*, October 27, 1927.

23. *Drumheller Mail*, July 23 and September 24, 1936, May 20, 1937; *Cardston News*, June 13, 1939.

24. *Drumheller Mail*, October 7, 1937; *Cardston News*, September 21, 1937, June 25, 1940; *Blairmore Enterprise*, December 17, 1937.

25. *Grande Prairie Herald*, July 22, 1927; *Drumheller Mail*, September 19, 1940; *Drumheller Mail*, May 24, 1928; *Lacombe Globe*, June 9, 1938.

26. *Drumheller Mail*, October 14, 1937, May 24, 1938.

27. Ibid., October 21, 1937; *Lacombe Globe*, September 22, 1938.

28. *Grande Prairie Herald Tribune*, August 14, 1947; Horace Seymour, "The Problems of Small Communities," *The Press Bulletin*, November 20, 1931; *Lacombe Globe*, May 5, 1938.

29. *Cardston News*, September 21, 1937; Gerald T. Bloomfield, "No Parking Here to Corner: London Reshaped by the Automobile," *Urban History Review* 18 (1989): 139–58.

30. Legal mechanism for health enforcement and definitions of sanitation for unincorporated settlements were created by the *Unincorporated Towns Ordinance*. Enforcement rested on voluntary reporting of unsanitary conditions.

31. *Macleod Gazette*, September 18, 1890.

32. Ibid., November 26, 1897, August 7, 1896.

33. Peter Waite, *Arduous Destiny: Canada 1867–1896* (Toronto: McClelland and Stewart, 1971), 3.

34. *Annual Report, Department of Agriculture, Northwest Territories 1903*, "Public Health," 126. See also *Annual Reports*, 1899–1904.

35. Beebe to Attorney General, May 14, 1903, 66.166/159, PAA (italics in original); Minutes, Macleod Board of Trade, March 26, 1909, M1430, GAI; *Blairmore Enterprise*, February 22, 1912; *Grande Prairie Herald*, May 28, 1918.

36. Wetherell and Kmet, *Homes in Alberta*, 50–52.

37. *Macleod Advertiser*, May 6, 1910.

38. *Claresholm Review Advertiser*, January 2, 1920, April 11 and May 16, 1919.

39. *Blairmore Enterprise*, March 23, 1917; *Drumheller Mail*, November 21, 1918. On conditions on the eve of the epidemic, see *Drumheller Review*, March 8, 1918, *Lacombe Western Globe*, January 22, 1919, *Blairmore Enterprise*, November 1, 1918.

40. *Coleman Journal*, November 2, 1944, April 5, 1945, September 19, 1946.

41. Ross to Hogge, February 23, 1959, PP, File 2070B, PAA; *Grande Prairie Herald*, December 27, 1920; *Prairie Northern Tribune*, September 16, 1937.

42. *Drumheller Mail*, December 5, 1929.

43. *Blairmore Enterprise*, September 13, 1919; Bylaw No. 10 Grande Prairie, June 5, 1916 (and attachments), 66.166/36a, PAA; *Claresholm Review Advertiser*, May 4, 1917; *Coleman Journal*, August 30, 1934, January 13, 1944; *Peace River Record*, August 10, 1928.

44. Minkler to Renshaw, July 30, 1936, 78.133/443c, PAA; Draft Bylaw, Macleod, December 14, 1923 and Carruthers to Spence, June 10, 1929, 74.174/996a, PAA; Pattinson to Souter, June 15, 1937 and Souter to Pattinson, June 22, 1937, 78.133/423c, PAA.

45. *Drumheller Mail*, June 7 and 14, and October 4, 1928, September 4, 1930, July 23, 1931, December 1, 1932; *Annual Report Department of Public Health*, Sanitary Engineering Division, 1943.

46. For example, *Macleod Advance*, September 23, 1907.

47. *Blairmore Enterprise*, May 30, 1913; *Grande Prairie Herald*, May 1, 1931; *Claresholm Review Advertiser*, May 4, 1928.

48. *Grande Prairie Herald*, April 24, 1931.

49. *Coleman Journal*, July 12, 1934.

50. *Conservation of Life*, 2 (1916): 96; *Claresholm Review*, March 11, 1909; *The Municipal World*, November 1937, 219–20.

51. *Conservation of Life*, 2 (1916): 96; *Macleod Gazette*, October 20, 1885, June 8 and November 16, 1886, July 7, 1892, September 10, 1897.

52. *Peace River Record*, March 11, 1932; *Blairmore Enterprise*, April 18 and September 12, 1912; *Lacombe Western Globe*, January 11, 1911.

53. *Peace River Record*, September 16, 1915; *Coleman Bulletin*, August 4, 1916. For a representative example of a fire investigation, see Report Re: Lacombe, October 1 and 23, 1907, 66.166/805, PAA.

54. Burgess, "Town Beautiful," 72–28–63, UAA; *Claresholm Review*, January 13, 1910.

55. *Cardston Globe*, May 9, 1912. For the same sentiments, see *Claresholm Review*, March 11, 1909 and *Lacombe Western Globe*, January 11, 1911.

56. Drumheller Bylaw No. 152, December 12, 1921, 74.174/1028b, PAA; *Grande Prairie Herald*, July 12, 1921; *The Western Municipal News*, November 1922, 323.

57. For two examples of this pattern, see Edward Krahn, "Portage La Prairie: A Profile of a Western City," *SSAC Bulletin* 9 (1984): 13, and Utas, "Calgary Architecture: 1875–1915," 21.

58. *Claresholm Review*, July 7, 1910.

59. For example, Sage to Fire Commissioner, July 7, 1936, 67.4/279b, PAA; Wetherell and Kmet, *Homes in Alberta*, 120–21, 161. Blairmore was an exception, having a fire and building bylaw for residential areas in 1922 (*Blairmore Enterprise*, July 27, 1922).

60. *Macleod Gazette*, February 21, 1902; *Macleod Advertiser*, May 30, 1912; *Grande Prairie Herald*, April 19, 1921; *Peace River Record*, April 18, 1919; *Blairmore Enterprise*, August 3, 1911, April 25, 1912.

61. Western Canada Insurance Underwriters' Association, *Supplementary Report*, Coleman, October 20, 1936, 67.4/129, PAA; *Supplementary Report*, Blairmore, April 30, 1932, 67.4/53, PAA; *Supplementary Report*, Peace River, June 11, 1930, 67.4/344 PAA; *Supplementary Report*, Claresholm, October 23, 1942, 67.4/116a, PAA; *Supplementary Report*, Drumheller, October 10, 1933, 67.4/153b, PAA; *Supplementary Report*, Cardston, April 28, 1932, 67.4/93, PAA. There was confusion about the terms "fire resistant" and "fire retardant." The former meant a construction material that would not hold back the fire but that the wall would still be standing after a fire, while a "fire retardant" material would hold back a fire. In 1909 it was recommended that these terms be used instead of the less precise "fire proof" (*Construction*, December 1909, 118–20).

62. Inspection Report, Peace River, September 10, 1936, 67.4/344, PAA.

63. *Lacombe Western Globe*, September 24, 1907, November 17, 1909; *Macleod Advertiser*, August 27, 1909, May 30, 1912; *Peace River Record*, January 30 and March 12, 1920.

64. *Grande Prairie Herald*, August 23, 1926, January 17, 1930; Inspection Report, Grande Prairie, September 29 and October 8, 1936, 67.4/218, PAA; Inspection Report, Grande Prairie, June 10, 1947, 67.4/219, PAA.

65. *Peace River Record*, November 14, 1941; Inspection Report, Claresholm, August 30, 1946, 67.4/116b, PAA.

66. *Coleman Journal*, March 25, 1926.

10 | STREET LIFE

1. *Grande Prairie Herald*, February 8, 1916.

2. Retail Merchants Association, Report of Delegates, n.d. [ca. 1918], 75.126/2/118, PAA; G. Flintoff Recollection, Notebook No. 2, Alberta Folk Archive, BPSC. Central place theory viewed such trips as being single purpose and regular (Darrel A. Norris, "Theory and Observation: A Perspective on Consumer Trip Behaviour and the Decline of the Ontario Hamlet," *Urban History Review* 10 (1981) 1–11).

3. *Claresholm Review Advertiser*, February 23, 1917. See also *Municipal Review of Canada*, December 1928.

4. Hudson, *Plains Country Towns*, 119; *Cardston News*, February 18, 1941.

5. *Cardston Alberta Star*, October 23, 1908; *Blairmore Enterprise*, January 5 and August 10, 1911.

6. *Macleod Advertiser*, April 20 and May 4, 1911; *Claresholm Review*, November 14, 1912; *Claresholm Review Advertiser*, July 5, 1918.

7. *Grande Prairie Herald*, December 3, 1913.

8. *Cardston Globe*, February 20, 1913; *Macleod Advertiser*, April 20, 1911; *Lacombe Western Globe*, July 20, 1910; *Grande Prairie Herald*, July 31, 1917.

9. Donald G. Wetherell and Irene R.A. Kmet, *Useful Pleasures: The Shaping of Leisure in Alberta 1896–1945* (Regina: Alberta Culture and Canadian Plains Research Centre, 1990), 247–78.

10. *Grande Prairie Herald*, December 13, 1917.

11. *Blairmore Enterprise*, August 11, 1921.

12. *Peace River Record*, November 21, 1930; *Grande Prairie Herald*, October 17, June 6 and 13, 1930.

13. *Peace River Record*, July 25, 1930; *Coleman Journal*, October 13, 1938.

14. *Peace River Record*, May 6, 1932, April 5, 1940. On renovation of Drumheller cinemas, see *Drumheller Mail*, November 4, 1929, July 21, 1932, September 19, 1935.

15. *Claresholm Review*, February 17, 1916; *Macleod Advertiser*, May 4, 1911.

16. For example, *Grande Prairie Herald*, May 1, 1931.

17. *Coleman Journal*, August 21, 1941.

18. *Cardston News*, May 19, 1927; *Peace River Record*, July 18, 1930; *Coleman Journal*, August 21, 1941.

19. *Blairmore Enterprise*, December 28, 1922.

20. For example, *Grande Prairie Northern Tribune*, April 22, 1937.

21. *Grande Prairie Herald*, June 8, 1920; *Coleman Journal*, September 10, 1935.

22. *Claresholm Local Press*, May 6, 1938.

23. Ibid., May 6, 1938.

24. Ibid., April 11, 1946.

25. Spencer to Hoadley, February 8, 1927, 74.174/978c, PAA; *Cardston News*, February 24, 1927.

26. For examples see *Claresholm Review*, July 13, 1917 and *Macleod Times*, September 5, 1929.

27. *Grande Prairie Northern Tribune*, October 5, 1933; *Claresholm Review Advertiser*, August 31, 1917; *Coleman Journal*, October 14 and December 16, 1943.

28. *Macleod Gazette*, March 17, 1892; *Macleod Spectator*, February 11, 1913.

29. *Grande Prairie Herald*, January 1, 1915; *Peace River Record*, February 25, 1915; *Cardston Alberta Star*, November 27, 1908.

30. *Macleod Gazette*, November 23, 1894, September 30, 1898.

31. *Claresholm Review Advertiser*, July 14, 1916.

32. Gold to Browning, August 17 and July 26, 1917, Department of the Attorney General Papers, 83.192/408, PAA; *Peace River Record*, September 15, 1921; Superintendent to Browning, March 22, 1920, 83.192/407, PAA; Browning to Hanna, September 14, 1917, 66.166/1240b, PAA.

33. APP Report, May 19, 1926, 75.126/2571, PAA.

34. *Grande Prairie Herald*, May 6, 1924; *Cardston News*, January 17 and June 17, 1926.

35. *Drumheller Mail*, July 12, 1928, March 7, 1940; *Claresholm Local Press*, September 11, 1931; *Grande Prairie Herald Tribune*, April 11, 1946.

36. *Peace River Record*, October 24, 1914; *Drumheller Mail*, September 18, 1919; *Macleod Advertiser*, March 9, 1911; *Macleod Spectator*, March 26, 1914.

37. *Cardston Globe*, February 15, 1912.

38. For example, Report of Pool Room Inspector, March 12, 1918, May 19, 1919, 75.126, Files 67b and 70, PAA; Billiard Room Licenses Issued, September 7, 1926, 75.126/76, PAA.

39. *Cardston Globe*, September 11, 1913.

40. *Cardston Alberta Star*, January 15 and March 26, 1909; *Blairmore Enterprise*, September 1, 1910, December 1 and 7, 1911.

41. *An Act to Regulate Pool Rooms* [1914], 66.166/1192b, PAA.

42. *Coleman Bulletin*, June 15, 1918. See also, Miller to Attorney General May 1, 1918, 75.126/67a, PAA; Wetherell and Kmet, *Useful Pleasures*, 354.

43. *Cardston Alberta Star*, November 18, 1910.

44. Pool Room Act Reports, 75.126/72–76, PAA.

45. *Cardston News*, November 30, 1939; *Grande Prairie Northern Tribune*, March 8, 1945.

46. *Claresholm Review*, May 6, 1909; A Bylaw Regulating Streets (Lacombe), March 5, 1907, 66.166/781, PAA; By-Law 418 (Edmonton), June 21, 1912, 66.166/600, PAA; *Coleman Miner*, February 3, 1911.

47. *Claresholm Review*, May 1, 1913; *Blairmore Enterprise*, May 16, 1913, August 26, 1920; *Claresholm Review*, December 22, 1910. On ethnicity, see also McKellar to Deputy Minister, May 1, 1909, 66.166/132b, PAA.

48. *Drumheller Review*, September 3, 1920; Crime Report No. 180, Grande Prairie Detachment, April 4, 1917, and APP Report, Peace River, July 27, 1917, 66.166/127a, PAA; *Grande Prairie Herald*, October 17, 1930.

49. *Drumheller Mail*, April 7, 1932; *Cardston Globe*, July 26, 1919; *Cardston News*, May 31, 1934, August 3, 1933.

50. *Cardston News*, September 10, 1935, September 10, 1940.

51. *Macleod Gazette*, April 11, 1888, August 7, 1896; *Coleman Journal*, July 11, 1935; *Blairmore Enterprise*, March 13, 1914; *Claresholm Local Press*, January 10, 1946.

52. *Macleod Gazette*, September 16, 1898.

53. A Bylaw Regulating Streets (Lacombe), March 1907, 66.166/781, PAA; *Coleman Miner*, February 3, 1911; *Drumheller Mail*, April 4, 1929; *Macleod Gazette*, September 28, 1900; *Blairmore Enterprise*, September 22, 1910.

54. *Grande Prairie Herald Tribune*, August 14, 1947.

55. *Macleod Times*, June 16, 1920; *Claresholm Review*, September 30, 1909.

56. Donna Norell, "'The Most Humane Institution in the Village': The Women's Rest Room in Rural Manitoba," *Manitoba History* 11 (1986): 38–40.

57. *Annual Report of the Department of Agriculture of the Province of Alberta [for] 1920*, 69; *Macleod News*, May 2, 1918.

58. *Peace River Record*, November 17, 1939, November 22, 1946.

59. *Macleod Gazette*, September 25, 1903; *Claresholm Review*, August 25, 1910.

60. *Macleod Gazette*, August 25, 1893.

61. *Grande Prairie Herald*, January 1, 1924; *Drumheller Mail*, January 30, 1936, January 30, 1941.

62. *Claresholm Review*, November 24 and December 1, 1910; *Drumheller Mail*, January 19, 1933; *Cardston News*, July 27, 1939.

63. *Drumheller Mail*, November 30, 1939; *Cardston News*, March 21, 1929; *Grande Prairie Herald Tribune*, July 11, 1940.

64. *Macleod Gazette*, November 2, 1900; *Blairmore Enterprise*, November 4, 1938; *Lacombe Western Globe*, November 10, 1920; *Grande Prairie Herald*, October 30, 1923; *Coleman Journal*, October 29, 1942.

65. *Macleod Gazette*, June 15 and 22, 1886, November 10, 1885.

66. Sarah Carter, *Lost Harvests: Prairie Indian Reserve Farmers and Government Policy* (Kingston and Montreal: McGill-Queen's University Press, 1990), 149–58. On local agreement with these policies, see *Macleod Gazette*, October 2, 1890, March 24, 1893.

67. *Macleod Advertiser*, July 22, 1910; *Claresholm Review*, July 14, 1910; *Lacombe Western Globe*, March 9, 1933.

68. *Claresholm Review Advertiser*, October 12, 1917; Hugh Dempsey, *The Gentle Persuader: A Biography of James Gladstone* (Saskatoon: Western Producer Prairie Books, 1986), 29.

69. *Macleod Gazette*, February 23, 1886; Vagrancy Bylaw, Blairmore Bylaw No. 15, April 25, 1918, Justice of the Peace Papers, 69.210/2485, PAA.

70. Gerald Friesen, *The Canadian Prairies: A History* (Toronto: University of Toronto Press, 1984), 170; James Pitsula, "The Treatment of Tramps in Late Nineteenth Century Toronto," *Historical Papers 1980* (Toronto: Canadian Historical Association, 1980): 116–32.

71. *Claresholm Review*, July 15, 1909, February 10, 1910, August 21, 1913.

72. *Drumheller Mail*, January 5, 1928.

73. *Claresholm Local Press*, April 20, August 6 and September 4, 1937.

74. *Drumheller Mail*, October 12, 1933.

75. *Claresholm Local Press*, April 12, 1929, November 17, 1933; *Coleman Journal*, May 17, 1934; *Lacombe Globe*, August 24, 1939.

76. RCMP Report Re: Blairmore, October 30, 1931, 83.214/11, PAA; *Drumheller Mail*, September 24, 1942.

77. Norris, "Preserving Main Street," 134.

11 | BUILDING COMMUNITY THROUGH LEISURE

1. *Blairmore Enterprise*, June 28, 1940; *Drumheller Mail*, September 28, 1988.

2. Dawson and Murchie, *The Settlement of the Peace River Country*, 175–76.

3. *Macleod Times*, December 8, 1921; Wetherell and Kmet, *Useful Pleasures*, 74–76.

4. *Claresholm Review*, September 16, 1909, January 20 and 27, 1910; *Claresholm Review Advertiser*, November 3, 1916.

5. Dawson and Murchie, *The Settlement of the Peace River Country*, 181; Voisey, *Vulcan*, 194–95.

6. Grande Prairie W.A. Minutes, May 18, 1932, January 17, 1929, Anglican Papers, A17/9 Box A.F., PAA.

7. Dawson and Murchie, *The Settlement of the Peace River Country*, 248; *Coleman Journal*, January 9, 1936.

8. *Claresholm Review Advertiser*, November 29, 1918; *Coleman Bulletin*, July 14, 1916; *Drumheller Mail*, September 28, 1988; *Lacombe Globe*, April 16, 1942; Dawson and Murchie, *The Settlement of the Peace River Country*, 177, 184.

9. Nelson, *The Mormon Village*, 231; *Cardston Record*, September 17, 1898; *Cardston Globe*, November 16, 1911, January 2, 1914.

10. "Identification of Block 21, Lots 1–4, Plan 1793E, Cardston," n.d. [ca. 1946], Alberta General Insurance Company Papers, 82.147/31, PAA; *Cardston News*, January 7, 1936, June 4, 1940, June 17, 1941.

11. *Coleman Journal*, August 28, 1908.

12. *Blairmore Enterprise*, May 30, 1913.

13. For example, *Lacombe Western Globe*, October 25, 1911.

14. *Grande Prairie Herald*, May 16, 1930.

15. *Coleman Journal*, May 4, 1933.

16. *Claresholm Review Advertiser*, November 13, 1925.

17. Seager, "Class Consciousness, Class Anarchy," 16.

18. *Lacombe Western Globe*, December 20, 1928.

19. *Drumheller Mail*, May 4, 1933; *Cardston News*, June 9 and 16, 1936; *Claresholm Local Press*, November 6, 1936;

20. *Coleman Journal*, January 27, 1938; *Blairmore Enterprise*, November 20, 1924, February 12, 1925. The carnival queen idea was heavily promoted by service clubs. They adopted it from their parent organizations in the United States and helped implant it in Canada.

21. Deputy Attorney General to Kennedy, October 8, 1926, 83.192/119, PAA.

22. *Grande Prairie Herald Tribune*, July 10, 1931, August 14, 1947.

23. *Drumheller Mail*, May 2, 1946.

24. For example, *Lacombe Globe*, October 15, 1942.

25. *Blairmore Enterprise*, July 25, 1913.

26. For example, *Claresholm Review Advertiser*, November 26, 1926, February 6, 1931.

27. *Grande Prairie Herald*, July 19, 1929.

28. *Claresholm Local Press*, January 31, 1930; *Drumheller Mail*, July 19, 1934.

29. *Drumheller Mail*, April 11, 1919.

30. For example, *Macleod News*, July 24, 1919 and *Blairmore Enterprise*, July 24, 1919.

31. Seager, "Class Consciousness, Class Anarchy," 3; *Drumheller Mail*, January 22, 1925.

32. *Claresholm Local Press*, October 17, 1946.

33. *Claresholm Review Advertiser*, November 29, 1918; *Grande Prairie Herald*, February 8, 1916.

34. *Claresholm Review Advertiser*, November 3, 1916.

35. *Grande Prairie Northern Tribune*, March 8, 1945, April 11, 1946, March 20, 1947.

36. For example, *Drumheller Mail*, May 4, 1944, April 4, 1946.

37. *Macleod Gazette*, June 4, 1883.

38. *Claresholm Review*, August 2, 1907, May 22, 1908; *Claresholm Review Advertiser*, June 8, 1917.

39. *Cardston Alberta Star*, July 8, 1910; *Cardston Globe*, July 18, 1913; *Cardston News*, March 26, 1931.

40. *Grande Prairie Herald*, July 6, 1915, July 8, 1924; *Macleod Gazette*, July 6, 1905.

41. *Macleod Gazette*, October 19, 1886; *Grande Prairie Herald*, April 25, and June 6, 1916; *Claresholm Review Advertiser*, July 12, 1918, July 23, 1926.

42. *Grande Prairie Herald*, August 5, 1927; *Cardston News*, July 6, 1933, November 23, 1937, July 26, 1938, July 27, 1939; *Coleman Journal*, August 8, 1946.

43. *Macleod Advertiser*, September 5, 1912; *Claresholm Local Press*, July 7, 1933, July 13, 1939.

44. *Coleman Journal*, July 7, 1927; *Macleod Gazette*, June 24, 1897; *Blairmore Enterprise*, June 29, 1911; *Claresholm Review*, June 5, 1911.

45. *Peace River Record*, May 10, 1935.

46. For example, *Lacombe Western Globe*, May 13, 1937.

47. *Peace River Record*, May 10, 1935; *Cardston News*, May 9, 1935; *Drumheller Mail*, May 8, 1939.

48. *Coleman Journal*, May 5, 1932; *Drumheller Mail*, May 8, 1939.

49. *Coleman Journal*, July 11, 1932, May 18, 1933; *Blairmore Enterprise*, May 26, 1932.

50. *Blairmore Enterprise*, April 24, 1924 (report on Fort Macleod); *Macleod Times*, July 10, 1924.

51. *Cardston News*, July 6, 1937.

52. Peter G. Goheen, "Symbols in the Streets: Parades in Victorian Urban Canada," *Urban History Review* 18 (1990): 237.

53. *Cardston News*, July 13 and June 29, 1937.

54. *Grande Prairie Northern Tribune*, May 13, 1937; *Macleod Times*, July 10, 1924. On window decorations in other towns see *Drumheller Review*, September 6, 1918 and *Coleman Journal*, August 1, 1946.

55. *Cardston News*, March 18, 1926; *Coleman Journal*, August 1, 1946; *Macleod Times*, July 10, 1924.

56. *Peace River Record*, November 30, 1922, May 4, 1932; *Claresholm Review*, May 26, 1910; *Cardston Globe*, May 20, 1915.

57. *Peace River Record*, February 3, 1928, February 15, 1935; *Claresholm Local Press*, February 22, 1929, February 26, 1932; *Grande Prairie Herald*, February 16, 1925.

58. *Peace River Record*, April 27, 1922; *Claresholm Local Press*, July 15, 1932.

59. Wetherell and Kmet, *Useful Pleasures*, 125–29.

60. *Peace River Record*, June 12, 1936; *Grande Prairie Herald*, October 19, 1928; *Lacombe Globe*, November 5, 1942.

61. *Drumheller Mail*, June 5, 1941; *Blairmore Enterprise*, April 7, 1910; *Drumheller Review*, April 24, 1914; *Drumheller Mail*, January 30, 1919, June 19, 1925; *Cardston News*, January 7, 1936.

62. For example, *Cardston News*, February 18, 1926.

63. *Claresholm Local Press*, July 15, 1932.

64. *Claresholm Review*, March 24, 1910; *Coleman Journal*, February 9, 1934.

65. For example, *Drumheller Mail*, June 18, 1925.

66. *Cardston Globe*, April 24, 1913.

67. *Claresholm Review Advertiser*, December 17, 1926.

68. *Claresholm Local Press*, April 15, 1938 (reprinting *Drumheller Mail*); *Coleman Journal*, November 5, 1925.

69. *Claresholm Review*, March 23, 1911; *Peace River Record*, October 27, 1939.

70. *Blairmore Enterprise*, July 18, 1929; *Cardston News*, November 12, 1925, February 27 and November 20, 1930.

71. *Drumheller Review*, March 8, 1918; Tooley to Deputy Minister, March 23, 1925, 74.174/1032c, PAA; Gray to Spence, August 16, 1934, 74.174/973g, PAA; *Drumheller Mail*, December 12 and 26, 1940. The only other commercial sport facilities in the towns studied were miniature golf courses. While always finding great initial enthusiasm, they were fads and even more marginal businesses than ice arenas. See for example, *Macleod Times*, September 11, 1930.

72. *Drumheller Mail*, May 22, 1933; *Coleman Journal*, September 8, 1926; *Claresholm Local Press*, August 20, 1942.

73. For example, *Drumheller Mail*, December 19, 1919, October 1, 1920.

74. Ibid., December 12, 1919.

75. Sovereign to Souter, July 25, 1938, 78.133/515c, PAA; *Claresholm Review*, November 26, 1914.

76. Bylaw No 10–F, Town of Lacombe, November 30, 1912, 74.174/996d, PAA; *Lacombe Western Globe*, September 4, 1912.

77. Wilson to Potts, April 24, 1930, 74.174/1033a, PAA; *Claresholm Review Advertiser*, December 16, 1927; *Macleod Times*, September 4, 1930.

78. *Drumheller Mail*, October 16, 1947; *Claresholm Local Press*, March 20, 1947.

12 | ENHANCING THE COMMUNITY: PARKS AND HORTICULTURE

1. Burgess, "The Town," 72–28–15, UAA.
2. Edwinna von Baeyer, *Rhetoric and Roses: A History of Canadian Gardening* (Markham: Fitzhenry and Whiteside, 1984), 66–97; *Lacombe Western Globe*, April 23, 1913.
3. Holtz, "Small Town Alberta," 130; *Drumheller Mail*, June 13, 1918.
4. *Lacombe: The First Century* (Lacombe Chamber of Commerce, 1982), 280.
5. *Claresholm Review*, April 30, 1914, July 20, 1917, May 10, 1918; *Claresholm Review Advertiser*, May 2, 1919; *Claresholm Local Press*, August 24, 1931, May 26, 1932, May 6 and August 19, 1938, August 17, 1939.
6. *Coleman Miner*, July 30, August 27 and September 17, 1909; *Coleman Bulletin*, October 11, 1918; *Coleman Journal*, May 10, 1928, January 16, 1947.
7. *Grande Prairie Herald*, May 29, 1931; *Drumheller Mail*, October 25, 1934.
8. *Blairmore Enterprise*, August 25, 1921, August 5, 1926.
9. *Lacombe Western Globe*, April 23, 1913; *Cardston Globe*, April 10, 1914.
10. Ronald Rees, *New and Naked Land: Making the Prairies Home* (Saskatoon: Western Producer Prairie Books, 1988), 86–94; Greg Thomas and Ian Clarke, "The Garrison Mentality and the Canadian West," *Prairie Forum* 4 (1970): 85.
11. *Grande Prairie Herald Tribune*, May 15, 1947; *Peace River Record*, April 12, 1935.
12. *Coleman Journal*, January 27, 1938; *Drumheller Mail*, April 18, 1929.
13. *Coleman Journal*, August 16, 1935; Report, Canadian Labour Defence League, Crowsnest Pass, August 17, 1934, 83.214/1, PAA; Clippings, 1937, Information File, "Blairmore," PAA.
14. *Lacombe Western Globe*, April 23, 1913; *Peace River Record*, April 5 and 12, 1935.
15. *Lacombe Western Globe*, April 23, 1913; *Cardston Globe*, April 10, 1914.
16. *Lacombe Western Globe*, June 13, 1935; *Claresholm Local Press*, February 11 and May 4, 1938; *Cardston News*, August 7, 1930.
17. *Claresholm Review*, March 16, 1911.
18. von Baeyer, *Rhetoric and Roses*, 23, 33; *Macleod Gazette*, April 27, 1900.
19. For example, *Lacombe Western Globe*, September 4, 1912.
20. *Macleod Gazette*, May 12, 1893; *Lacombe Western Globe*, April 23, 1913; *Claresholm Review*, August 26, 1909.
21. For example, *Macleod Gazette*, May 16, 1888; *Grande Prairie Herald*, March 20, 1923.
22. *Macleod Gazette*, May 12, 1893, April 10, 1896, June 23, 1899.
23. *Medicine Hat Times*, April 8, 1886.
24. *Macleod Gazette*, May 16, 1888.
25. *Grande Prairie Herald*, June 1, 1928, May 24, 1929. See also *Claresholm Review Advertiser*, March 23, 1928 and *Cardston News*, February 18, 1926.

26. *Claresholm Review*, August 26, 1909; *Claresholm Review Advertiser*, March 9 and 16, 1928; *Cardston Globe*, July 24, 1920; *Blairmore Enterprise*, June 24, 1938; *Drumheller Mail*, October 22, 1942.

27. *Blairmore Enterprise*, May 12, 1921, April 22, 1926; *Drumheller Mail*, June 25, 1925, March 21, 1929, October 5, 1933, June 8, 1939.

28. *Grande Prairie Herald*, November 11, 1927; *Cardston News*, August 7, 1930; *Drumheller Mail*, May 17, 1934. On noxious weeds, see *Drumheller Mail*, July 19, 1928 and *Peace River Record*, May 29, 1947.

29. *Claresholm Local Press*, April 6, 1934.

30. *Cardston News*, June 14, 1934.

31. *Lacombe Western Globe*, August 29, 1940.

13 | TOWN LIFE

1. David M. Rayside, "Small Town Fragmentation and the Politics of Community," *Journal of Canadian Studies* 24 (1989): 104–5, 118.

2. Hudson, *Plains Country Towns*, 8; Thomas Harvey, "Railroad Towns: Urban Form on the Prairie," *Landscape* 27 (1983): 34.

3. Bettison, Kenward and Taylor, *Urban Affairs in Alberta*, 13.

COMMENT
on PRIMARY
SOURCES

A variety of sources were drawn upon in studying Alberta small towns. The most valuable manuscript information was found in the voluminous records of the Alberta Department of Municipal Affairs and the Department of the Attorney General at the Provincial Archives of Alberta, Edmonton. Both contributed material on incorporation and the day-to-day working of local government in Alberta. Since the Department of the Attorney General provided legal opinion on matters referred to it by town officials and by the Department of Municipal Affairs, its records were also important in understanding the concerns as well as the legal parameters of town government. These collections provided information on the specific towns in our study, as well as more general material that revealed the nature of town concerns and life. The papers of both departments provided much direct information on installation of utilities, health, bylaws, taxation, debt, town finance, and, among other topics, elections. They also provided much insight and information about town layout, buildings, local business and economy, and transportation.

Additional material at the Provincial Archives on these topics, as well as others, was found in the records of the Department of Agriculture, the Department of Highways, the papers of the Legislative Assembly and the Justice of the Peace records. A particularly good guide to the physical condition and construction of main street buildings in the interwar years were the papers of the Department of the Provincial Secretary, which was responsible for fire prevention. The records of the Alberta General Insurance Company contributed similar information for the 1940s. The Premiers' Papers also contained valuable but scattered information on most aspects of town life, especially with respect to retail trade from the 1920s to the 1940s. Although the Provincial Archives has extensive holdings of tax rolls and land records, the scale of this study prohibited their use—methods of valuation and assessment over the years were too varied to justify the creation of a standardized statistical reference for all the towns before 1947. Similar variations in categorization, as well as the scale of our inquiry, also posed the same problems in the development of comprehensive statistics about town business using the *Dun and Bradstreet Commercial Ratings*, which are held on microfilm at the Provincial Archives of Alberta. These records nonetheless provided valuable specific information on the number and pecuniary strength of most businesses operating in the towns. They also were used for determining the longevity of businesses and the existence of branch operations.

Manuscript records outside the Provincial Archives were found to be less plentiful for the towns in question. A number of collections at the Glenbow Alberta Institute Archives in Calgary contained information about towns in southern Alberta. One especially useful collection was that of Fort Macleod's board of trade. Local museums in some towns also contained some records, especially photographs. These were an essential source for uncovering many elements in the physical evolution of main street and for appreciating the intangible, but essential, feel of small town life. Since all the towns studied are part of the Alberta Main Street programme, the Main Street co-ordinators in each town and the records they have collected as part of the rehabilitation of main street buildings contributed much guidance on the history and evolution of the towns. Unfortunately, few towns have given much attention to preserving local records, and those that exist consist largely of town council minutes. Overall, we found town council minutes a disappointing source; in some cases the minute taking was so brief as to be cryptic. In many cases, newspaper reports of town council and town affairs provided better context and more detailed description.

This example indicates the value of newspapers in studying small towns. Because manuscript sources generally tended to be official records, most often generated by, or in response to, the provincial government in Edmonton, town newspapers were a useful source for gauging local opinion and for reports of events. We researched completely all existing copies of newspapers for each town in the study sample, from their beginning up to 1947. Although even their holdings are broken in a few cases, the Legislative Library in Edmonton has the most complete holdings of historical newspapers in Alberta.

Newspapers proved to be a surprisingly valuable and essential source. Sufficient manuscript sources were available for general verification of newspaper reports and opinion, and we found the criticism expressed by some historians of newspapers as historical sources to be overstated. While most newspapers were indeed merciless in their boosterism, their reporting, advertisements, and editorials were valuable for analyzing town life, opinion, and evolution. Circulation figures are not available as the Audit Bureau of Circulations did not collect statistics on Alberta town newspapers before 1947. Nevertheless, when papers from a large number of towns were studied, both for specific information as well as with a critical eye to the use of language, discourse, and attitude, broad patterns of town life were revealed.

BIBLIOGRAPHY
of CITED
SECONDARY
WORKS

Alexander, Robert L. "A Shopkeeper's Renaissance: Academic Design and Popular Architecture in Late Nineteenth Century Iowa City." In *Perspectives in Vernacular Architecture II*, edited by Camille Wells. Columbia: University of Missouri Press, 1986.

Artibise, Alan F.J. *Winnipeg: A Social History of Urban Growth 1874–1914*. Montreal: McGill-Queen's University Press, 1975.

———. "Continuity and Change: Elites and Prairie Urban Development 1914–1950." In *The Usable Urban Past: Planning and Politics in the Modern Canadian City*, edited by Alan F.J. Artibise and Gilbert A. Stelter. Toronto: Macmillan of Canada, 1977.

Atherton, Lewis. "The Midwestern Country Town—Myth and Reality." *Agricultural History* 26 (1952).

Attebery, Jennifer. *Building Idaho: An Architectural History*. Moscow, Idaho: University of Idaho Press, 1991.

Bailey, Barbara Ruth. *Main Street Northeastern Oregon. The Founding and Development of Small Towns*. Portland: The Oregon Historical Society, 1982.

Benson, John. "Hawking and Peddling in Canada, 1867–1914." *Histoire sociale/Social History* 18 (1985).

Betke, Carl. "The Development of Urban Community in Prairie Canada, Edmonton, 1898–1928." Ph.D. dissertation, University of Alberta, 1981.

Bettison, David G., Kenward, John K. and Taylor, Larrie. *Urban Affairs in Alberta*. Edmonton: University of Alberta Press, 1975.

Bliss, Michael. *A Living Profit. Studies in the Social History of Canadian Business, 1883–1911*. Toronto: McClelland and Stewart, 1974.

Bloomfield, Elizabeth. "Boards of Trade and Canadian Urban Development." *Urban History Review* 12 (1983).

————. "Community Ethos and Local Initiative in Urban Economic Growth: A Review of a Theme in Canadian Urban History." *Urban History Yearbook 1983*.

Bloomfield, Gerald T. "No Parking Here to Corner: London Reshaped by the Automobile." *Urban History Review*, 18 (1989).

Blue, John. *Alberta Past and Present: Historical and Biographical*. Vol. 1. Chicago: Pioneer Historical Publishing Co, 1924.

Breen, David "The Canadian West and the Ranching Frontier 1875–1922." Ph.D. dissertation, University of Alberta, 1972.

Carter, Sarah. *Lost Harvests: Prairie Indian Reserve Farmers and Government Policy*. Kingston and Montreal: McGill-Queen's University Press, 1990.

Chapman, Terry. "The Controversy Over Court Houses in Southern Alberta." *Alberta History* 37 (1989).

Crossman, Kelly. *Architecture in Transition: From Art to Practice 1885–1906*. Kingston and Montreal: McGill-Queen's University Press, 1987.

Cunningham, Hugh. *Leisure in the Industrial Revolution c. 1780 – c. 1880*. London: Croom Helm, 1980.

Dahms, Fred A. "The Process of Urbanization in the Countryside: A Case Study of Huron and Bruce Counties, 1891–1981." *Urban History Review* 12 (1984).

————. "Regional Urban History: A Statistical and Cartographic Survey of Huron and Southern Bruce Counties 1864–1981." *Urban History Review* 15 (1987).

Davis, Donald F. "The 'Metropolitan Thesis' and the Writing of Canadian Urban History." *Urban History Review* 14 (1985).

Dawe, Robert. "An Investigation into the Development of the Red Deer Community in Relation to the Development of Western Canada." M.A. thesis, University of Alberta, 1954.

Dawson, C.A. and Murchie, R.W. *The Settlement of the Peace River Country. A Study of a Pioneer Area*. Toronto: Macmillan, 1934.

Dempsey, Hugh. *The Gentle Persuader: A Biography of James Gladstone*. Saskatoon: Western Producer Prairie Books, 1986.

Dick, Lyle. "The Architecture of Image and Domination: Winnipeg's Confederation Life Building." *SSAC Bulletin* 12 (1987).

Doucet, Michael and Weaver, John. "Town Fathers and Urban Continuity: The Roots of Community Power and Physical Formation in Hamilton, Upper Canada in the 1830s." *Urban History Review* 13 (1984).

Drake, Earl G. "Pioneer Journalism in Saskatchewan, 1878–1887." *Saskatchewan History* 5 (1952).

Drumheller Valley Historical Association. *The Hills of Home*, 2nd edition. Calgary: D.W. Friesen and Sons Ltd., 1974.

Eagle, John A. "J.D. McArthur and the Peace River Railway." *Alberta History* 29 (1981).

"Editorial." *Urban History Yearbook 1974*.

Ennals, Peter. "The Main Streets of Maritime Canada." *SSAC Bulletin* 11 (1986).

Ewen, Stuart and Ewen, Elizabeth. *Channels of Desire: Mass Images and the Shaping of American Consciousness*. New York: McGraw Hill Book Co., 1982.

Fairbairn, Brett. *Building a Dream: The Co-operative Retailing System in Western Canada 1928–1988*. Saskatoon: Western Producer Prairie Books, 1989.

Ferguson, Barry. *Athabasca Oil Sands, Northern Resource Exploration 1875–1951*. Regina: Canadian Plains Research Centre, 1985.

Field, Dorothy. "The Moderne Style." *Alberta Past* 6 (1990).

Finkel, Alvin. "Social Credit and the Unemployed." *Alberta History* 31 (1983).

Foran, Maxwell. *Calgary: An Illustrated History*. Toronto: James Lorimer and Co. and the National Museum of Man, 1978.

Fort Macleod Provincial Historical Area Society. *A Walking/Driving Tour of Fort Macleod's Historic Downtown and Residential Area*. n.d, n.p.

Francaviglia, Richard V. "Main Street USA." *Landscape* 21 (1977).

Friesen, Gerald. *The Canadian Prairies: A History*. Toronto: University of Toronto Press, 1984.

Gilpin, John. "The City of Strathcona, 1891–1912." M.A. thesis, University of Alberta, 1978.

Goheen, Peter G. "Symbols in the Streets: Parades in Victorian Urban Canada." *Urban History Review* 18 (1990).

Goist, Park Dixon. *From Main Street to State Street: Town, City and Community in America*. Port Washington, New York: National University Publications, Kennikat Press, 1977.

Grad, Gunter and Holdsworth, Deryck. "Large Office Buildings and Their Changing Occupancy: King Street, Toronto, 1850–1880." *SSAC Bulletin* 10 (1985).

Grande Prairie and District Old Timer's Association. *Pioneers of the Peace*. Calgary: D.W. Friesen and Sons Ltd., 1976.

Hande, D'Arcy. "Saskatchewan Merchants in the Great Depression: Regionalism and the Crusade Against Big Business." *Saskatchewan History* 43 (1991).

Hanson, Eric J. *Local Government in Alberta*. Toronto: McClelland and Stewart Ltd., 1956.

Harvey, Thomas. "Railroad Towns: Urban Form on the Prairie." *Landscape* 27 (1983).

Historical Walking and Driving Tour: Lacombe. Edmonton: Alberta Culture and Multiculturalism, n.d.

Hitchcock, Henry-Russel. *Architecture: Nineteenth and Twentieth Centuries*, 4th Integrated Edition. New York: Penguin Books, 1977.

Holdsworth, Deryck and Everitt, John C. "Bank Branches and Elevators: Expressions of Big Corporations in Small Prairie Towns." *Prairie Forum* 13 (1988).

Holtz, Ann. "Small Town Alberta: A Geographical Study of the Development of Urban Form." M.A. thesis, University of Alberta, 1987.

Hudson, A. James. *Charles Ora Card: Pioneer and Colonizer*. Cardston: The Author, 1963.

Hudson, John. *Plains Country Towns*. Minneapolis: University of Minnesota Press, 1985.

Jensen, Bodil. "The County of Mountain View, Alberta: A Study in Community Development, 1890–1925." M.A. thesis, University of Alberta, 1972.

Johnston, Alex, and den Otter, Andy A. *Lethbridge: A Centennial History*.
Lethbridge: City of Lethbridge and The Whoop-Up Country Chapter, Historical
Society of Alberta, 1985.

Jones, David C. "'There is Some Power About the Land'—The Western Agrarian
Press and Country Life Ideology." *Journal of Canadian Studies* 17 (1982).

———. *Empire of Dust: Settling and Abandoning the Prairie Dry Belt*. Edmonton: The
University of Alberta Press, 1987.

Jones, David C., Wilson, L.J. Roy, and White, Donny. *The Weather Factory: A
Pictorial History of Medicine Hat*. Saskatoon: Western Producer Prairie Books,
1988.

Kalman, Hal. "Canada's Main Streets." In *Reviving Main Street*, edited by Deryck
Holdsworth. Toronto: University of Toronto Press and Heritage Canada
Foundation, 1985.

Klassen, Henry. "Cowdry Brothers: Private Bankers in Southwestern Alberta
1886–1905." *Alberta History* 37 (1989).

Krahn, Edward. "Portage La Prairie: A Profile of a Western City." *SSAC Bulletin* 9
(1984).

Kyba, Patrick. "Ballots and Burning Crosses, The Election of 1929." In *Politics in
Saskatchewan*. Edited by Doug Spafford and Norman Ward. Toronto: Longmans
Canada, 1968.

Lacombe: The First Century. Lacombe Chamber of Commerce, 1982.

Lambrecht, Kirk. "Regional Development and Social Strife: Early Coal Mining in
Alberta." *Prairie Forum* 4 (1979).

Lamont, Glenda. "Migrants and Migration in Part of the South Peace River Region,
Alberta." M.A. thesis, University of Alberta, 1970.

Leach, William R. "Transformations in a Culture of Consumption: Women and
Department Stores, 1890–1925." *The Journal of American History* 71 (1984).

Lebhar, Godfrey M. *Chain Stores in America 1859–1959*. New York: Chain Store
Publishing Co., 1959.

Lehr, John. "Mormon Settlements in Southern Alberta." M.A. thesis, University of
Alberta, 1971.

Lemon, J.T. "Study of the Urban Past: Approaches by Geographers." *Historical
Papers 1973*. Toronto: Canadian Historical Association, 1973.

Leonard, David W. and Lemieux, Victoria L. *A Fostered Dream*. Calgary: Detselig
Enterprises Ltd, 1992.

Lewis, Pierce. "Small Town in Pennsylvania." *Annals of the Association of American
Geographers* 62 (1972).

Lifchez, Raymond. "Inspired Planning: Mormon and Fourierist Communities in the
Nineteenth Century." *Landscape* 20 (1976).

Longstreth, Richard. "Compositional Types in American Commercial Architecture."
In *Perspectives in Vernacular Architecture II*, edited by Camille Wells. Columbia:
University of Missouri Press, 1986.

Macpherson, C.B. *Democracy in Alberta*. Toronto: University of Toronto Press, 1953.

Marshall, D.G. "Hamlets and Villages in the United States: Their Place in the American Way of Life." *American Sociological Review* 11 (1946).

Marshall, Howard Wright. "A Good Gridiron: The Vernacular Design of a Western Cow Town." In *Perspectives in Vernacular Architecture II*, edited by Camille Wells. Columbia: University of Missouri Press, 1986.

McCalla, Douglas. "An Introduction to the Nineteenth Century Business World." In *Essays in Canadian Business History*, edited by Tom Traves. Toronto: McClelland and Stewart, 1984.

McCann, L.D. "Urban Growth in Western Canada 1881–1961." *The Albertan Geographer* 5 (1969).

McCann, Larry, ed. *People and Place: Studies in Small Town Life in the Maritimes.* Fredericton: Acadiensis Press and the [Mount Allison University] Committee for Studying Small Town Life in the Maritimes, 1987.

McLay, Catherine. "Crocus, Saskatchewan: A Country of the Mind." *Journal of Popular Culture* 14 (1980).

McLoughlin, Brian F. *Canadian Pacific from Calgary to Edmonton.* Calgary: The British Railway Modellers of North America, n.d.

Morton, W.L. "The Significance of Site in the Settlement of the American and Canadian Wests." *Agricultural History* 25 (1951).

Muller, Edward K. "Regional Urbanization and the Selective Growth of Towns in North American Regions." *Journal of Historical Geography* 3 (1977).

Nelson, Lowry. *The Mormon Village: A Pattern and Technique of Land Settlement.* Salt Lake City: University of Utah Press, 1952.

Norell, Donna. "'The Most Humane Institution in the Village': The Women's Rest Room in Rural Manitoba." *Manitoba History* 11 (1986).

Norris, Darrel A. "Theory and Observation: A Perspective on Consumer Trip Behaviour and the Decline of the Ontario Hamlet." *Urban History Review* 10 (1981).

———. "Preserving Main Street: Some Lessons of Leacock's Mariposa." *Journal of Canadian Studies* 17 (1982).

Pannekoek, Frits. "Wetaskiwin Business and Prince Edward Islanders." *Alberta History* 37 (1989).

Patterson, E.R. "The Early History of Claresholm and District." In Claresholm History Book Club, *Where the Wheatlands Meet the Range.* Calgary: D.W. Friesen and Sons, 1974.

Pitsula, James. "The Treatment of Tramps in Late Nineteenth Century Toronto." *Historical Papers 1980.* Toronto: Canadian Historical Association, 1980.

Potyondi, Barry. "In Quest of Limited Urban Status: The Town Building Process in Minnedosa, 1879–1906." In *Town and City: Aspects of Western Canadian Urban Development*, edited by Alan Artibise. Regina: Canadian Plains Research Centre, 1981.

Rayside, David M. "Small Town Fragmentation and the Politics of Community." *Journal of Canadian Studies* 24 (1989).

Rees, Ronald. *New and Naked Land: Making the Prairies Home*. Saskatoon: Western Producer Prairie Books, 1988.

Regehr, T.D. *The Canadian Northern Railway: Pioneer Road of the Northern Prairies, 1895–1918*. Toronto: Macmillan of Canada, 1976.

Reid, A.N. "Urban Municipalities in the North West Territories: Their Development and Machinery of Government." *Saskatchewan History* 7 (1954).

Rendall, Harold A. "The Trade Areas of Camrose, Wetaskiwin, and Ponoka." M.A. thesis, University of Alberta, 1962.

Rutherford, P.W.F. "The People's Press: The Emergence of the New Journalism in Canada, 1869–1899." *Canadian Historical Review* 56 (1975).

Schivelbusch, Wolfgang. *Disenchanted Night: The Industrialization of Light in the Nineteenth Century*. Translated by Angela Davis. Berkeley: University of California Press, 1988.

[Schutz, Fred]. *Pas ka poo. An Early History of Rimbey and the Upper Blindman Valley*. Rimbey: The Rimbey Advance, 1962.

Seager, Allen. "Class Consciousness, Class Anarchy: Three Alberta Coal Towns During the Great Depression." Paper Read to the Canadian Historical Association, Annual Meeting, Saskatoon, 1979 (typescript).

Shepley, Joseph Drummond. "Reminiscences of a Pioneer Land Surveyor." *Saskatchewan History* 41 (1988).

Spector, David. "Edmonton Bank Architecture: The Neo Classical Age, 1904–1914." *Alberta History* 34 (1986).

Spelt, Jacob. *Urban Development in South-Central Ontario*. Toronto: McClelland and Stewart, 1972.

Stelter, Gilbert and Artibise, Alan F.J. *Power and Place: Canadian Urban Development in the North American Context*. Vancouver: University of British Columbia Press, 1986.

Stelter, Gilbert A. "A Regional Framework for Urban History." *Urban History Review* 13 (1985).

Stovel, Herb. "Storefront Evolution." *Canadian Heritage*, May-June 1983.

Taylor, John H. "Urban Autonomy in Canada: Its Evolution and Decline." In *Power and Place: Canadian Urban Development in the North American Context*, edited by Gilbert Stelter and Alan Artibise. Vancouver: University of British Columbia Press, 1986.

Thomas Greg, and Clarke, Ian. "The Garrison Mentality and the Canadian West." *Prairie Forum* 4 (1970).

Tronrud, Thorold J. "Buying Prosperity: The Bonusing of Factories at the Lakehead 1885–1914." *Urban History Review* 19 (1990).

Utas, Greg. "Calgary Architecture: 1875–1915." M. Environmental Design thesis, University of Calgary, 1975.

Voisey, Paul. "The Urbanization of the Canadian Prairies 1871–1916." *Histoire sociale/Social History* 8 (1975).

———. *Vulcan: The Making of a Prairie Community*. Toronto: University of Toronto Press, 1988.

von Baeyer, Edwinna. *Rhetoric and Roses: A History of Canadian Gardening.* Markham: Fitzhenry and Whiteside, 1984.

Waite, Peter. *Arduous Destiny: Canada 1867–1896.* Toronto: McClelland and Stewart, 1971.

Walden, Keith. "Speaking Modern: Language, Culture and Hegemony in Grocery Window Displays 1887–1920." *Canadian Historical Review* 70 (1989).

Warner, Sam Bass. *The Private City: Philadelphia in Three Periods of its Growth.* Philadelphia: University of Philadelphia Press, 1968..

Weaver, John. "Edmonton's Perilous Course, 1904–1929." *Urban History Review* 2–77 (1977).

Wetherell, Donald G. and Kmet, Irene R.A. *Useful Pleasures: The Shaping of Leisure In Alberta 1896–1945.* Regina: Canadian Plains Research Centre, 1990.

————. *Homes in Alberta: Building, Trends, and Design.* Edmonton: University of Alberta Press, 1991.

White, C.O. "The Humboldt Municipal Electrical Utility: A Grassroots Feature of the Saskatchewan Power Corporation." *Saskatchewan History* 29 (1976).

Widdis, Randy William. "Belleville and Environs: Continuity, Change and the Integration of Town and Country During the 19th Century." *Urban History Review* 19 (1991).

Winstanley, Michael. *The Shopkeeper's World 1830–1914.* Manchester: Manchester University Press, 1983.

INDEX

ABOUT
the AUTHORS

Donald Wetherell and Irene Kmet are historical consultants from Edmonton, Alberta. Dr. Wetherell received his B.A. and M.A. in history from the University of Saskatchewan and his Ph.D. in history from Queen's University. Ms. Kmet received her B.A. from the University of Saskatchewan and her LL.B. from Queen's University.

Donald Wetherell has taught at the University of Alberta, and Irene Kmet practised law for almost a decade before they began to work together in historical consulting in 1983. They have completed a wide range of museum and historic sites planning projects as well as major research studies in Western Canadian history. In 1994 they were appointed as Adjunct Researchers to the Canadian Circumpolar Institute, University of Alberta.

Wetherell and Kmet's first book, *Useful Pleasures: The Shaping of Leisure in Alberta, 1896-1945* (Canadian Plains Research Centre and Alberta Culture and Multiculturalism, 1990) examines leisure and recreational activities in Alberta and their connection to and impact on the province's culture. Their second book, *Homes in Alberta. Building, Trends and Design 1870-1967* (University of Alberta Press, 1991) explores the evolution of domestic architecture in Alberta, including factors such as housing styles and design, building techniques, the housing market and government policy.

Dr. Wetherell is also the author, with Elise Corbet, of *Breaking New Ground. A Century of Farm Equipment Manufacturing on the Canadian Prairies* (Fifth House Publishers, 1993). Currently, Wetherell and Kmet are working on a history of Northern Alberta.